ROBERT GREENE

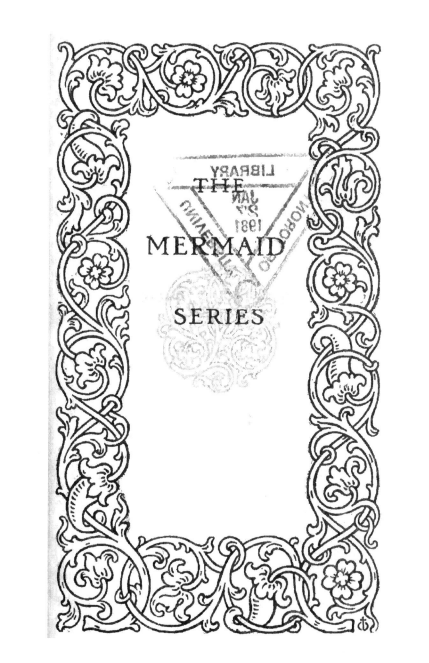

THE

MERMAID

SERIES

THE MERMAID SERIES

Literal Reproductions of the Old Text, with etched
Frontispieces

Other Volumes in Preparation

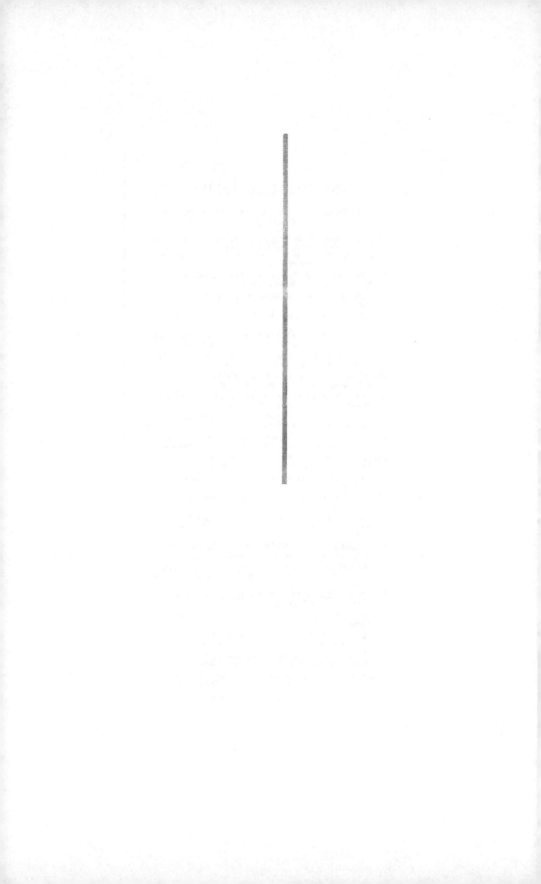

ROBERT GREENE.

From John Dickenson's "Greene in Conceipt" (1598).

CONTENTS

CONTENTS

INTRODUCTION

HY should art answer for the infirmities of manners?" asks Thomas Nash in defending the memory of his dead comrade, Robert Greene, against the attacks of Gabriel Harvey. Some such consideration as this has been needed to rescue Greene's fame from the uncritical hostility of later times. It has been the misfortune of the man to be remembered by posterity chiefly through adverse personal documents. The assaults of a frustrate and dying man on a successful rival like curses soon turned home to roost. Gabriel Harvey, the Kenrick of his day, crowned the dead poet with bays more pathetic than the sordid wreath placed by Isam's hand. And to complete the tale of disfavour Greene himself tells his own story with a morbid self-consciousness only exceeding Bunyan's, and a thrifty purpose to turn even his sins to pence. Though during Greene's life and after his death circumstances were unmeet to dispassionate biography, it may promote the calmer mood of a later age to inquire into the conditions of his disordered career and the sources of his unique genius. "Debt and deadly sin, who is not subject to?" cries Nash. "With any notorious crime I never knew him tainted." Nash refers Greene back to human nature. With Nash, at the best but lukewarm, and with Symonds, no partisan of Greene's, one believes that circumstances as well as natural frailty made Greene what he came

presented by way of recreation by men with other means
of subsistence, was manifestly an avoidance of the implications of the situation at hand.

It was not until after the plague of 1586, and the return
of the companies from the provinces, that the university
playwrights rose to a commanding place in the life of the
time. And then, though their plays were still performed
at court, it was to the people that the dramatists made
their appeal. Marlowe, and Greene, and Peele and
Lodge now constituted the group of the university wits.
The support that the court had before either withheld, or
but fitfully given, was now vouchsafed liberally at the
Theatre and the Curtain. The university dramatists
knew well what was demanded of them. Dismissing
the topics treated by Lyly, and by Peele in his early play,
The Arraignment of Paris (1584), and discarding by
degrees the allegorical and didactic as found in
the popular drama of the preceding time, they began
to dramatise the spirit of contemporary life in the
form of stories built from legend and romance, and
instinct with the leonine spirit of awakening England.
Marlowe's *Tamburlaine* is as true to Elizabethan
England as is Dekker's more realistic *Shoemaker's
Holiday ;* and Peele's *Old Wives' Tale* and Greene's
Friar Bacon and Friar Bungay are both native in
England's soil. In the years between 1584 and 1593
the number of companies greatly increased. Fleay
mentions nine companies as performing at court between
these dates. Besides the Queen's players, who com-
prised, perhaps, two or more companies, there were
companies of my Lord Admiral, Pembroke, Sussex and
other lords. Normally the playwrights wrote only for
the company to which they were attached. It is believed
that at one time Lodge, Peele, Marlowe and Greene were
together as playwrights for the Queen's men playing at
the Theatre. Later the first three went over to the support of the Admiral's men, and thereafter often changed
their allegiance, but Greene probably wrote only for the

Queen's players until his death. Soon other dramatists aligned themselves with the movements of the new drama, and out of the jealous rivalry aroused by the entrance into the field of dramatic authorship of such non-university playwrights as Kyd and Shakespeare there developed the maze of controversy and vituperation that has made the Elizabethan age famous as an era of personal pamphleteering.

But though the drama was occupying an increasingly prominent place in the life of the time the professional actors and playwrights were in decided ill-repute. With the managers and with the actors the returns from the stage were sufficient to salve the hurt of the odium under which their profession rested. Richard Burbage died a rich man, and Alleyn, who played in at least one of Greene's plays, became so wealthy that he could found a college. So also, as we learn from the slighting references to them by the dramatists, the actors were well able to line their pockets with the returns of their calling. But the pamphlet literature of the time reveals the extraordinary hostility with which all connected with the theatre were viewed. Gosson's *School of Abuse* (1579), *A Second and Third Blast of Retrait from Plays and Theatres* (1580), Stubb's *Anatomy of Abuses* (1583), and Babington's *Exposition of the Commandments* (1583) contain vigorous attacks on the stage as an institution and on all who follow its fortunes. Distrust and jealousy were common within the ranks of the actors and playwrights. So Chettle does not know Marlowe and does not wish to know him; Nash, though he defends Greene against Harvey, expressly disclaims any intimacy; and we shall learn that Greene was jealous of Marlowe during a large portion of his period of dramatic authorship. But the playwrights abominated the actors even more than they distrusted each other. Frequently they refer to actors as puppets and apes dressed up in another's feathers. Greene, in *Never too Late*, calls the actor "Esop's crow," and in *A Groatsworth of Wit*, in the famous passage refer-

ring to Shakespeare, he calls the actors "burrs,"
"puppets that speak from our mouths," and "antics
garnished in our colours." The author of *The Return
from Parnassus* (1602) calls them "mimic apes," and
Florio, in his preface to *Montaigne's Essays* (translated
1603) refers to actors as "base rascals, vagabond abjects,
and porterly hirelings." Though proud of their calling
as literary men the dramatists looked with shame on their
writing for the stage. Lodge, who in 1580 had defended
poetry and plays against Gosson, in *Scilla's Metamorphosis* of 1589 declared his determination "to write no
more of that whence shame doth grow." If Greene
refers to plays at all he calls them "vanities"; connects
their composition with the basest efforts of life, and
arraigns dependence on "so mean a stay." Even
Shakespeare "in disgrace with fortune and men's eyes"
beweeps alone his "outcast state" (Sonnet XXIX), and
exclaims "For I am shamed by that which I bring
forth" (Sonnet LXXII). Conditions like these are not
likely to bring the better social adjustments into play, or
to call into a profession those who value name and fame
supremely. Schelling[1] calls attention to the fact that
playwriting took a higher position at the beginning of the
seventeenth century than it had taken at the end of the
previous century, and compares Marlowe, Shakespeare,
Greene and Jonson, the sons of low life, with Beaumont,
Fletcher, Chapman, Middleton and Marston, the sons of
gentlemen. By the time the sons of gentlemen were
ready to take to playwriting the path had been made ready
for them by their predecessors. Society of the times in
which Greene lived was not ready to treat either a playwright or an actor as a good citizen. And a son of a nobleman, entering the ranks of the pioneers, would have given
his life as a sacrifice just as did Marlowe and Greene.
Lodge was the son of a Lord Mayor, Peele's father was
a man of some education, and Lyly had influential con-
nections at court; yet the only man of the entire school

[1] In his *Elizabethan Drama*, ii. 376.

of "university wits" who escaped a life of misery and a
death of want was Lodge, and he in 1596 deserted literature for medicine. We cannot consider Greene's
"memory a blot" [1] on a time that is truly represented
as well by the tragical as the heroic outlines of his
character and history.

The sources of our knowledge and deduction concerning Greene's life are of four classes—records, autobiographical pamphlets and allusions, contemporary references, legends. To the indubitable records belong the
university registers, the stationers' registers, and the title
pages to his printed books. From the first we learn that
Greene was entered as a sizar at St John's College,
Cambridge, 26th November 1575, that he was admitted to
the degree of B.A. some time in 1578, that he proceeded
to the degree of M.A., after residence at Clare Hall, Cambridge, in 1583; from the second we learn that his first
book was the first part of *Mamillia*, entered for publication 3rd October 1580, though not published until 1583,
and other facts concerning the time of publication of his
successive books and plays; from the signature to the
Maiden's Dream, "R. Greene, *Nordericensis*," and to the
address to Lodge's *Euphues Shadow*, "Robert Greene
Norfolciensis," we learn that Greene was born in Norfolk.
Of a lower order of certainty as to their application to
Greene, yet still satisfying the closest scrutiny, is the
record in the parish register of St Leonard's, Shoreditch,
of the burial of Greene's illegitimate child, Fortunatus
Greene, 12th August 1593; and the record in the
register of St George, Tombland, uncovered and inter-
preted by Collins, indicating that the dramatist himself
was the second child of Robert Greene, a saddler, and
Jane his wife, and was baptised the 11th of July 1558.

To the second class of biographical materials belong
Greene's own prose works, the *Mourning Garment, Never*

[1] As does Ingram in his *Christopher Marlowe and his Associates.*

too Late, with the second part, *Francesco's Fortunes*,
the *Groatsworth of Wit*, all partly autobiographical;
and *The Repentance of Robert Greene*, confessedly autobiographical, but, until lately, of questioned authenticity.
The biographical material in these works is ample,
but its value is discounted by certain considerations
involved in the motives of Greene's pamphlet composition.   When Greene began to write, art was not yet
strong enough to command a popular hearing without
the assistance of a didactive motive.   Adapting himself
to the conditions with a tact that made him the most
broadly read writer of his time, Greene made edification
the end of his writing from the first.   His second work
to be entered on the Stationers' Register, March 1581,
had a distinct moral purpose: " Youth, seeing all his ways
so troublesome, abandoning virtue and leaning to vice,
recalleth his former follies with an inward repentance."
In choosing topics for popular pamphlets Greene tells
such a story as that derived from Aelian in *Planetomachia*
(1585), or he tells over the story of the prodigal son as in
the *Mourning Garment*.   And throughout his life moral
purpose remained a factor in his prose and drama.   He
turned from romances to the composition of the conny-
catching pamphlets, in the trust " that those discourses
will do great good, and be very beneficial to the commonwealth of England."   *A Looking-Glass for London and
England* is a pure moral interlude.   Often he moralises
when it is unnecessary to do so, or when he has to change
his original to introduce a didactic motive.   Even the
Palmer who tells the tale of *Never too Late* is himself
penitent for his past sins.   In *Friar Bacon and Friar
Bungay* the jolly friar of Brazen-nose is made at the end to
surrender his calling through motives of remorse as far as
possible from the spirit of his life, and *James IV.* ends
with a penitent sovereign begging forgiveness for his sins.
These facts show, if they show anything, that the motive
of repentance was a conventional thing with Greene, and
that however faithful it may have been to his own ex-

perience not the least advantage in its use lay in its popularity. That it was a popular motive is shown by the vogue of such books as Tarlton's *News out of Purgatory* (1590), and by the fact that T. Newman, in a dedication to *Greene's Vision* (1592), asserts that "many have published repentances in his name." That much of Greene's autobiographical material is veracious we have corroborative evidence to prove; we should, however, not be justified in accepting it all without question. There is a bland shamelessness in the confession of sins that is itself one of the best signs of health. When Greene says, "I saw and practised such villainy as is abominable to declare," he is expressing in phrase strikingly similar to Hamlet's words to Ophelia, "I am myself indifferent honest; but yet I could accuse me of such things that it were better my mother had not borne me," a characteristic moral attitude of the times.

What do we learn from the romances concerning Greene's life? The *Mourning Garment* is a modernised version of the prodigal son story, and its relation to Greene's own history may be slight or even factitious. The story of *Never too Late* touches Greene more closely. In this there is recounted the fortunes of "a gentleman of an ancient house, called Francesco; a man whose parentage though it were worshipful, yet it was not indued with much wealth; insomuch that his learning was better than his revenues, and his wit more beneficial than his substance." This Francesco, "casting his eye on a gentleman's daughter that dwelt not far from Caerbranck," named Isabel, fell in love with her, and married her against the opposition of Fregoso, her father. For five years "they laboured to maintain their loves, being as busy as bees, and as true as turtles, as desirous to satisfy the world with their desert as to feed the humours of their own desires." At the end of this time they were reconciled with Fregoso, and "they counted this smile of fortune able to countervail all the contrary storms that the adverse planets had inflicted upon them."

Now after two years " it so chanced that Francesco had
necessary business to dispatch certain his urgent affairs
at the chief city of that island, called Troynovant :
thither, with leave of his father, and farewell to his wife,
he departed after they were married seven years." In
the city he surrendered to the lures of a courtesan,
Infida, and " seated in her beauty, he lived a long while,
forgetting his return to Caerbranck." For three years
the two lovers " securely slumbered in the sweetness of
their pleasures," ignoring the womanly complaints of
Isabel and neglectful of the passage of time. Then finding
that " all his corn was on the floor, that his sheep were
clipt, and the wool sold," Infida turned him out of doors.
Francesco laments his hard fortune in an invective
against courtesans that stings with the passion of the
author's personal feeling. In his " perplexity he passed
over three or four days till his purse was clean empty "
and he was compelled " to carry his apparel to the brokers,
and with great loss to make money to pay for his diet."
" In this humour he fell in amongst a company of players,
who persuaded him to try his wit in writing of comedies,
tragedies, or pastorals, and if he could perform anything
worth the stage, then they would largely reward him for
his pains. Francesco, glad of this motion, seeing a means
to mitigate the extremity of his want, thought it no dishonour to make gain of his wit or to get profit by his
pen : and therefore, getting him home to his chamber,
writ a comedy; which so generally pleased all the audience
that happy were those actors in short time that could
get any of his works, he grew so exquisite in that faculty."
The remainder of the story relates Isabel's repulse of the
seductions of an admirer, Infida's unsuccessful efforts
at reconciliation with the now prosperous Francesco, and
the latter's penitent return to his faithful wife.

The story told in *A Groatsworth of Wit* quite closely
resembles that of *Never too Late* and is clearly autobiographical. To this fact Greene bears witness when,
near the end of the story, he writes: " Here, gentlemen,

break I off Roberto's speech, whose life in most part
agreeing with mine, found one self punishment as I have
done. Hereafter suppose me the said Roberto, and I
will go on with that he promised." In this story, "an
old new-made gentleman" named Gorinius, living in
an island city " made rich by merchandise, and populous
by long space," had two sons, the one a scholar, named
Roberto, married and but little regarded, the other named
Lucanio, the heir-apparent of his father's ill-gathered
goods. On his death-bed Gorinius bequeathed his entire
property to Lucanio: " only I reserve for Roberto, thy
well-read brother, an old groat (being the stock I first
began with), wherewith I wish him to buy a groatsworth of wit." Upon the death of Gorinius, and the
distribution of the property according to will, Roberto
" grew into an inward contempt of his father's unequal
legacy, and determinate resolution to work Lucanio all
possible injury." As Lucanio " was of a condition
simple, shamefast, and flexible to any counsel," Roberto
seemed on a fair way to success, until Lamilia, a courtesan
with whom he had plotted for Lucanio's undoing, re-
pudiated the understanding and informed the heir of the
plot against his gold. Forbidden the house, " Roberto,
in an extreme ecstasy, rent his hair, curst his destiny,
blamed his treachery, but most of all exclaimed against
Lamilia, and in her against all enticing courtesans." . . .
" With this he laid his head on his hand, and leant his
elbow on the ground, sighing out sadly, ' Heu patior telis
vulnera facta meis! ' " Roberto's lamentations were over-
heard by one sitting on the other side of the hedge, who,
getting over, offered such comfort as his ability would
yield, doing so " the rather," as he said, " for that I
suppose you are a scholar, and pity it is men of learning
should live in lack." Greatly wondering Roberto asked
how he might be employed. " ' Why, easily,' quoth he,
' and greatly to your benefit; for men of my profession
get by scholars their whole living.' ' What is your
profession?' said Roberto. ' Truly, sir,' said he, ' I

am a player.' 'A player!' quoth Roberto; 'I took you
rather for a gentleman of great living; for if by outward
habit men should be censured, I tell you, you would be
taken for a substantial man.' 'So am I where I dwell,'
quoth the player, 'reputed able at my proper cost to
build a windmill.' " Roberto now again asked how he
was to be used. " ' Why, sir, in making plays,' said the
other; 'for which you shall be well paid, if you will take
the pains.' Roberto, perceiving no remedy, thought
it best to respect his present necessity, (and), to try his
wit, went with him willingly." As Roberto's fortunes
improved Lucanio's drooped, until finally " Roberto
hearing of his brother s beggary, albeit he had little
remorse of his miserable state, yet did he seek him out,
to use him as a property; whereby Lucanio was somewhat
provided for." The character and miserable end of
Roberto as a result of the profession he had assumed
may be given in Greene's own words: " For now when the
number of deceits caused Roberto to be hateful almost
to all men, his immeasurable drinking had made him the
perfect image of the dropsy, and the loathsome scourge
of lust tyrannised in his bones. Living in extreme
poverty, and having nothing to pay but chalk, which
now his host accepted not for current, this miserable
man lay comfortlessly languishing, having but one groat
left (the just proportion of his father's legacy), which
looking on, he cried, 'O, now it is too late, too late to
buy wit with thee; and therefore will I see if I can sell
to careless youth what I negligently forgot to buy.' "

To a somewhat different class of testimony belongs
The Repentance of Robert Greene, probably an authen-
tic exemplar of that very popular class of deathbed
repentance that was multiplied by other hands after
Greene's death. Little can be found in this work but
admonitions to a higher life and caveats against lust.
Such details as are given are presented with no chronology.
Of his early life Greene tells us that " being at the

University of Cambridge, I light amongst wags as lewd
as myself, with whom I consumed the flower of my
youth; who drew me to travel into Italy and Spain,
in which places I saw and practised such villainy as is
abominable to declare. . . .   At my return into England,
I ruffled out in my silks, in the habit of malcontent,
and seemed so discontent that no place would please
me to abide in, nor no vocation cause me to stay myself
in: but after I had by degrees proceeded Master of Arts,
I left the university and away to London; where (after
I had continued some short time, and driven myself out
of credit with sundry of my friends) I became an author
of plays, and a penner of love-pamphlets, so that I soon
grew famous in that quality, that who for that trade
grown so ordinary about London as Robin Greene?"
Once, Greene tells us, he felt a terror of God's judgment.
This followed a lecture by a "godly learned man" in
St Andrew's Church in the city of Norwich. But when
his companions fell upon him, in a jesting manner
calling him Puritan and precisian, and wished he might
have a pulpit, what he had learned went quite out of his
remembrance. "Soon after I married a gentleman's
daughter of good account, with whom I lived for a
while; but . . . after I had a child by her, I cast her
off, having spent up the marriage money which I had
obtained by her.

"Then left I her at six or seven, who went into Lincolnshire, and I to London; where in short space I fell
into favour with such as were of honourable and good
calling." But though he knew how to get a friend he
"had not the gift or reason how to keep a friend."
Further he tells us that he had wholly betaken himself
to the planning of plays, that "these vanities and other
trifling pamphlets I penned of love and vain fantasies
was my chiefest stay of living," and that he had refrained
his wife's company for six years.

What may be the value of the third class of biographical material, that derived from contemporary

references, is, perhaps, best revealed by reviewing the
history of the controversy with Gabriel Harvey. In 1590
Richard Harvey, the second of three brothers, attacked
all poets and writers, and Lyly and Nash particularly,
in a pamphlet entitled *The Lamb of God*, terming them
"piperly make-plays and make-bates," and comparing
them with Martin. Though not himself attacked,
Greene, because "he writ more than four others,"
retorted in defence of his brother dramatists in *A Quip
for an Upstart Courtier* (1592), making a satirical thrust
at the Harveys as the sons of a rope-maker. At the
request of Greene's physician the most offensive lines
were expunged from all except possibly the first edition.
But the harm had been done. Greene died before the
Harveys could or would make answer. Then, in Gabriel
Harvey's *Four Letters* (1592), the memory of Greene was
attacked in one of the most venomous pamphlets known
to the literature of vilification. Harvey's four epistles
were followed by Nash's *Strange News*, and other
controversial pamphlets, in which Nash attempts,
rather light-heartedly, to defend Greene's memory.
Other writers who take occasion to speak a good word
for Greene, after his death, are Chettle in *A Kind
Hart's Dream* (1593), a certain R. B., author of *Greene's
Funerals* (1594), and Meres in *Palladis Tamia* (1598).
Strange as it may seem it is impossible to decide that
Harvey seriously wronged Greene in his accounts of fact.
Like Greene, Harvey has been too much abused on
account of his unfortunate quarrels with men whom
history was to discover were his superiors. His pedantry,
his egotism, and the very virulence of his hatred seem to
nullify the effect of his assault, without greatly militating
against the truth of the account he gives. Nash, who is
vigorous in his expressions of respect for his friend, is
notably weak in his rebuttals of fact. With the exception of some manifest exaggerations, Harvey's account of
Greene's death-bed, of his association with Cutting Ball
and his sister, and of his son Fortunatus, must be

accepted as substantially a true one. Harvey's account
will not be given here but it is epitomised when " we come
to finish up his life."

There remain for consideration, and in most part for
dismissal, a few traditions that have grown up about the
name of Greene. Early biographers, among whom was
Dyce, attempted to show that Greene had at one time
been a minister. This opinion was partly based upon
the two manuscript notes on a copy of *George-a-Greene :*
" Written by . . . a minister who acted the piner's pt in it
himselfe. Teste W. Shakespeare," and " Ed. Juby saith
that yᵉ play was made by Ro. Greene." Aside from the fact
that these notes are not shown to have any authority, and
may, in fact, contradict each other, the probabilities are
all against the hypothesis that Greene was ever a minister.
Nowhere in his singularly open personal revelations does
he suggest that he ever acted as such. Indeed, his expressions are inconsistent with such an idea. " In all
my life I never did any good," he writes in his *Repentance*,
and in the same tract he tells of that incipient con-
version that was nipped in the bud by the ridicule of his
fellows. Surely this account does not sound like the
confession of an ex-minister, and these same copesmates
would certainly not have maintained silence had they
known that Greene had held a living. Considerations of
time make it impossible that Greene should have been
the Robert Greene who, in 1576, was one of the Queen's
chaplains, for at this time he could not have been more
than eighteen years old; nor is it at all likely that he is
the Greene who, in 1584-5, was vicar of Tollesbury in
Essex, for in these years he was engaged in the unclerical
exercise of preparing for printing *The Mirror of Modesty,
Morando The Tritameron of Love, The Card of Fancy*, and
Planetomachia. The theory that Greene was an actor
is traced back to the manuscript notes already quoted,
and to some ambiguous remarks by Harvey in his *Four
Letters*. Fleay's ingenious conjecture that Greene is
identical with that Rupert Persten who accompanied

Leicester's company to Saxony and Denmark in 1585-87, and that this name is equivalent to "Robert the Parson," is discredited on philological grounds as well as for its general lack of weight. That Greene may have now and then assumed a part upon the stage is quite possible; but that he never associated himself with the actor's calling is made quite clear from his contemptuous treatment of actors in the passages already quoted. It is perhaps not entirely necessary to dismiss the theory, based on the entry on the title-page of *Planetomachia*, "By Robert Greene, Master of Arts and student in physic," that Greene had intended to study medicine, and was hindered from pursuing his purpose by his success in literature. It is likely, however, that Greene here uses the term "physic" in the sense of "natural philosophy," as it was used by Chaucer and Gower, and that he had particular desire to defend his ability to treat an astronomical topic such as that of *Planetomachia*.

We have, in a disjointed manner, no doubt, presented Greene's life under the heads of the sources from which our information is gained, rather than in regular chronological sequence, in order that due discrimination may be used in constructing the finished scheme of his life's activities. To the imaginative reader there is material enough and to spare, but to the exact scientist there is a bare modicum. Without rash assumptions it seems safe to imagine that Greene's father, like Rabbi Bilessi and Gorinius, was well-to-do; that with the exception of the duration of his domestic life, Greene's married life is substantially represented by the story of Isabel and Francesco; that as a playwright Greene experienced the vicissitudes suggested in *Never too Late* and *A Groatsworth of Wit ;* and that his death is substantially represented by Harvey in *Four Letters.* Attempting a bare outline of Greene's life one would feel safe in assuming that he was born not earlier than 1558; that he took his bachelor's degree at St John's College, Cambridge, in

1578; thereafter toured the continent, probably after the 3rd of October 1580, at which date the first part of *Mamillia* was registered; that returning he took his M.A. at Clare Hall in 1583, and immediately began the composition of love pamphlets and comedies, the latter being now lost; that he married not later than 1585, lived with his wife until after the birth of a child, in 1586 deserted her, and went to London never to return.   There undertaking the composition of serious plays, the first extant play is produced in 1587 or 1588, he is incorporated Master of Arts at Oxford in July 1588, and continues "that high and loose course of living which poets generally follow" (Anthony Wood), writing love pamphlets until about 1590, and then, in obedience to a promise repeatedly made by himself, pressing forward the exposure of the devices used by cozeners and conny‑catchers, until his untimely death on 3rd September 1592.

During the last twelve years of a short but varied and active life Greene was more or less prominently before the public eye.   For much of this time he was easily the most widely read of English writers.   His literary activities were scattered over a broad range of topics and styles.   In his work there are represented the wit, the romance, the bombast, the Euphuism, the Arcadianism, and no less the new naturalism of his time.   He expressed himself in novellas, in pamphlets, in controversial broadsides, in comedies, in serious plays, and in Italianate verse. . He was in fact the first *litterateur* [1] of England,

----

[1] Nash repeatedly bears witness to Greene's popularity. "In a night and a day would he have yarkt up a pamphlet as well as in seven year, and glad was that printer that might be so blest to pay him dear for the very dregs of his wit" (*Strange News*). Harvey condemns him for "putting forth new, newer, and newest books of the maker" (*Four Letters*).   Greene remained popular long after his death.   In Sir Thomas Overbury's "Character" of *A Chambermaid*, he tells us "She reads Greene's works over and over"; and Anthony Wood informs us that since Greene's time his works "have been mostly sold on ballad-mongers' stalls." In the introduction to Rowland's *'Tis Merrie when Gossips meete* (1602), (*Hunterian Club Publications*, vol. i.) there is a dialogue

c

and his prose fiction represents what Herford has called
" for English-speaking contemporaries the most consider-
able body of English narrative which the language yet
contained." Twenty-seven romances and prose tracts
were published during Greene's lifetime, excluding *The
Defence of Conny-catching*, which cannot with certainty be
ascribed to him; and nine tracts and plays, including the
doubtful *George-a-Greene*, were published after his death.

Aside from Greene's remarkable versatility and rapidity
of workmanship,[1] his most striking characteristic as an
author is his ability immediately to adapt himself to the
changing literary demands of the hour. This will be seen
to have particular significance in connection with the
question of the chronology of his plays, yet it is pertinent
here as pointing the dividing line between his earlier and
later interests in composition. At the end of *Never too
Late* (1590) Greene says, " And therefore as soon as may
be, gentlemen, look for Francesco's further fortunes,
and after that my *Farewell to Folly*, and then adieu to all
amorous pamphlets." And in the dedication of *Francesco's Fortunes* (Part II. of *Never too Late*) he advised
his gentlemen readers to look for " more deeper matters."
So also at the end of his *Mourning Garment* (1590)
Greene announces that he will write no more love
pamphlets. This work must serve as the first-fruits of
his new labours and the last farewell to his fond desires.

indicating that Greene's works are still in demand. Ben Jonson
in *Every Man out of his Humour* (1599) alludes to Greene's works,
whence one " may steal with more security," referring undoubtedly,
as does Rowland, to the great mass of Greene's published work.

[1] Upon which Nash comments : " Let other men (as they please)
praise the mountain that in seven years brings forth a mouse, or the
Italianate pen, that of a packet of pilfries, affordeth the press a
pamphlet or two in an age, and then in dignified array, vaunts
Ovid's and Plutarch's plumes as their own ; but give me the man,
whose extemporal vein in any humour, will excel our greatest art
master's deliberate thoughts ; whose invention quicker than his
eye, will challenge the proudest rhetorician, to the contention of
like perfection, with like expedition."—(Prefatory Address to
Greene's *Menaphon*.)

Again, in the dedicatory epistle to *Farewell to Folly*,
licensed in 1587 but not published until 1591, about which
time it is reasonable to suppose the epistle was written,
he says this is "the last I mean ever to publish of such
superficial labours." That he is sincere in this promise is
clear from the fact that, while he published *Philomela* in
1592, he is careful in doing so to explain that it had been
hatched long ago and was now given his name at the
solicitation of his printer. We have here fixed a point
about the year 1590 for the beginning of new and more
serious work. Two theories have been advanced to
explain the nature of this work. The one theory, which
has among its adherents Collins; the latest editor of
Greene's complete plays, supposes that Greene must refer
to the beginning of his play-writing. Against this
theory there are the strong objections that Greene must
have written plays before he made any promise to engage
in more serious writing, the strong circumstantial and
internal evidence that several of the extant plays ante-
date such a promise, and the no less significant fact that
Greene had no pride in his work as a playwright and no
respect for the calling as a serious occupation. The second
theory is that Greene had long contemplated the exposure
of the arts and devices of the under-world of prey, and that
the year 1590 represents approximately the time at which
he ceased the composition of romantic and mytholo-
gising pamphlets, which associated him with Lyly and
Sidney and the more affected of the university writers,
and began the composition of realistic studies in the rogue
society of his own time. There is no reason to suppose
that Greene was not sincere in his desire to present
an edifying picture of the dangers surrounding London
youth and the weaknesses and vanities in English society.[1]

[1] "But I thank God that he put it in my head, to lay open the
most horrible cosenages of the common Conny-catchers, Coseners,
and Cross-biters, which I have indifferently handled in those my
several discourses already imprinted. And my trust is that these
discourses will do great good, and be very beneficial to the commonwealth of England."—*The Repentance of Robert Greene.*

The first pamphlet, *A Notable Discovery of Cosenage*, was printed in 1591, and was "written for the general benefit of all gentlemen, citizens, apprentices, country farmers and yeomen." Thereafter followed *The Second Part of Conny-catching, The Third and Last Part of Conny-catching, A Disputation Between a He Conny-catcher and a She Conny-catcher*, and others of the same type, of equal or less authenticity. All of these are very far from the old romance in content, in method and in language; Greene is now bold, slashing and fearless, and wields something of the scorpion whip of Nash in his taunting cruelty of assault. Changing his attitude he now stands very near his subject; he writes from among the society he castigates. There is some unusual significance in this new attitude of Greene's, particularly for drama. We shall find, it is believed, the same distinction between Greene's earlier and later plays, not as clearly marked as the change in prose, but definite enough to establish within the dramatic work of Greene a line of cleavage separating the mythology-loaded language and unnatural incident of the *Tamburlaine* and *Spanish Tragedy* type of play from the plays of simple poetry and homely rural atmosphere that were to prepare the way for the domestic drama of Heywood and Dekker and Munday and Chettle, and to have a real influence on the dramaturgy of Shakespeare.

Upon the question of the chronology of Greene's plays no editor can afford to be dogmatic. Yet so carefully have the varied spiritual forces of Greene's life been studied in connection with the manifest literary influences of his time, and so painstaking have been the deductions from those facts with which we are provided, that one feels safe in laying down, upon the researches of such scholars as Dyce, Fleay, Storojenko, Gayley and Collins,[1] an almost certain scheme of succession and

---

[1] It is regretfully that one recognises that Collins does not belong at the head of this list. The surprising defects of the long-awaited definitive edition of Greene must now speak for themselves; its manifest excellences are well able to do so.

chronology of Greene's extant dramas. A point of departure is provided by the theory of Collins, often vigorously insisted upon, that Greene did not begin to write plays until about 1590. In this belief Collins is joined by C. H. Hart,[1] who adduces the passage from Greene's *Farewell to Folly*, quoted two pages above, as a reason for thinking Greene took up playwriting near the end of his life. Against any such theory there are strong specific as well as important general objections. It would require that all of Greene's plays, in addition to half a dozen pamphlets, should have been written between the opening of 1591 and the time of Greene's death in 1592. In *A Groatsworth of Wit* Greene all but certainly refers to himself as an "arch play-making poet," and in *The Repentance of Robert Greene* he says, "I became an author of plays and a penner of love pamphlets." Certainly that total dissolution that follows the practices of his calling could not have taken place in two years, nor would one who thus joins the composition of plays and poems have waited until ten years after the licensing of his first tract in 1580 to write his first play. If *Never too Late* and *A Groatsworth of Wit* have any autobiographical value whatever those portions that treat of playwriting experience are worthy the most credence, and the theory that Greene should have taken up playwriting late is quite inconsistent with the purport of both of them.

But aside from any such considerations as these, there are certain general principles having to do with the customs of literary composition of the time, and particularly of the group in which Greene moved, that make it quite improbable that Greene should have waited until 1590 before beginning to write plays. Nothing is clearer than that the movements of these pre-Shakespearean groups were not movements of the individual but of the mass. There is in the work of this era the utmost possible play and interplay of influence. Marlowe was

[1] Writing in *Notes and Queries*, 1905.

the only strikingly originative writer of the times, yet the facets of his contact with the literary life of England and the Continent have by no means as yet been numbered. Any new style of composition immediately assumed the dignity of a school. Lyly's style became so popular that Euphuism became a convention. So the appearance of the *Arcadia*, of *Tamburlaine*, of a romance by Greene, was followed by a flood of imitative works. Greene's *Tully's Love* is used in *Every Woman in Her Humour*, a comedy of humours after the model of Jonson; the author of *Sir John Oldcastle* borrows from *The Pinner of Wakefield* the swallowing of the seals; Harvey accuses Nash of being "the ape of Greene," and Greene of being the "ape of Euphues"; *Tamburlaine* is imitated again and again, sometimes in whole, as in *Alphonsus of Arragon, Selimus*, and *The Battle of Alcazar*, but more often through the unconscious influence of its affected language and dramatic types. As much can be said of the imitation of Kyd's *Spanish Tragedy*. Traces of the same source-book appear in Greene's *Friar Bacon and Friar Bungay* and Marlowe's *Dr Faustus*, and identical lines appear in Greene's *Orlando Furioso* and Peele's *Old Wives' Tale*. The same comedy appears in *A Looking-Glass for London and England, Locrine* and *Selimus*, and *The Taming of a Shrew* contains lines from *Tamburlaine* and *Dr Faustus*. Shakespeare borrows from Greene, Oberon for *A Midsummer Night's Dream*; features of the story of *Euphues, his Censure to Philautus* for *Troilus and Cressida*; features of *Farewell to Folly* for *Much Ado About Nothing;* characters from the *Mourning Garment* for Polonius and Laertes, and innumerable reminiscent lines. Sometimes the influence is more complicate still. Greene in *Pandosto* borrows from Lyly's *Campaspe*, and Shakespeare, borrowing from Greene for his *Winter's Tale*, approximates Lyly's form; and Greene, ridiculing Marlowe's *Tamburlaine*, makes some allusions that indicate that he as well as Marlowe must have been

acquainted with Primaudaye. Cases of this kind are
so frequent that they seem to have no individual bearing,
but to refer to the general conditions of art composition
of the day. In such a system of community of ideas
Greene was entirely at home. Of this we have abundant
evidence in his often displayed ability to feel the popular
pulse, and to make himself a part of every growing
movement. His first works were written under the
influence of the Italian school. In these early works
there is a strong strain of Euphuism, which is made explicit in his *Euphues, his Censure to Philautus* (1587).
Two years later a new style had arisen through the
composition of Sidney's *Arcadia* (published in 1590),
and Greene aligns himself with the new pastoral movement in his *Menaphon*. Not content with the tacit
desertion of the conceits of Lyly he gives his new work
the sub-title *Camilla's Alarum to Slumbering Euphues*,
and attacks his old models for artificiality. So also
Greene is quick to utilise contemporary events to add to
the popular appeal of his writings. From the publication of the *Spanish Masquerado* (1589), celebrating the
victory over the *Spanish Armada*, there is every reason
to believe Greene received his warmest recognition at
court; and sincere as were his conny-catching pamphlets
we may be sure that their value was not lessened in
Greene's eyes by their popular appeal. Greene was
neither more nor less of an imitator than his fellows; his
ideals and methods of composition were, no doubt, those
of his time, and if we cannot claim for him that he
consistently broke ground in new domains of expression, we may at any rate be certain that he did not
fall far behind in the progressive motion of the art of
his era.

The significance of these things in the study of the
chronology of Greene's plays should be manifest. There
were during Greene's literary life three extraordinary
dramatic successes on the London stage—*Tamburlaine,
Dr Faustus* and *The Spanish Tragedy*. It is reasonable

to suppose that the man who, in prose composition, always struck when the iron was hot, would, as a playwright, use the same expedition to take advantage of a popular wave of enthusiasm. That Greene's *Alphonsus of Arragon* was written under the inspiration of Marlowe's *Tamburlaine*, and that *Friar Bacon and Friar Bungay* was written as a reflex from *Dr Faustus* is so certain as to require no demonstration. And it is only less certain that we have in *Orlando Furioso* a reminiscence of *Tamburlaine* and of *The Spanish Tragedy*, and that *James IV.* was inspired as a pseudo-historical play by the growing popularity of the chronicle type. According to the best authority obtainable *Tamburlaine* appeared in 1587, *The Spanish Tragedy* before 1587, and *Dr Faustus* in 1588. With these conditions before us, and in the light of Greene's known character and the habits of the times, it is scarcely possible to think that Greene should have waited until *Dr Faustus* had somewhat dimmed the lustre of *Tamburlaine* before imitating the latter; or that he should have ignored the undoubted vigour of the magician motive to imitate a form that had enjoyed prior popularity, only to take up for treatment a drama in the occult spirit, when this type in its turn had been laid on the shelf in favour of the newer form of chronicle play. Ignoring then for the present *A Looking-Glass for London and England*, which is not entirely Greene's own composition, and *George-a-Greene*, concerning which doubts must exist, we are provided with the order of succession of the four remaining plays in the order of publication of their prototypes: *Alphonsus of Arragon, Orlando Furioso, Friar Bacon and Friar Bungay, James IV.* Further investigation provides more explicit chronological data.

Alphonsus of Arragon* is the earliest of Greene's extant plays. Its date has been set at 1587 or 1588 by Gayley, who has carefully worked over the conclusions of Fleay, Storojenko and others. That Greene had been interested in Alphonsus as early as 1584 is clear from his mention

of the name in the dedication to *The Card of Fancy.*
The play was not written before *Tamburlaine,* for that
hero is mentioned in it; on the other hand there are
several considerations that seem to show that it was
written soon after *Tamburlaine* in an effort to share
some of that play's popularity. Greene's words in the
prologue:

> "Will now begin to treat of bloody Mars,
>   Of doughty deeds and valiant victories,"

seem to announce a purpose to begin a new warlike vein.
The play resembles *Tamburlaine* in bombast, in rant,
in comparing a victorious warrior with the gods, in the
motive of Asiatic and Mohammedan conquest, and in
its double original design. Unlike *Tamburlaine* only one
of the parts was completed. There is a possibility that
the two plays are mentioned in conjunction by Peele
in his well-known "Farewell" verses to Sir John Norris
and his companions (1589):

> "Bid theatres and proud tragedians,
>   Bid Mahomet's Poo and mighty Tamburlaine,
>   King Charlemayne, Tom Stukeley and the rest,
>   Adieu."

By the ingenuity of Mr Fleay we are able to conjecture
that "Mahomet's Poo" probably refers to the brazen
head, or poll, through which the Prophet speaks in the
fourth act of the play.

That Alphonsus was not successful on the stage seems
likely when one compares the play with the successful
productions of the day. Its failure is indicated by the
fact that, though a second part was promised in the
epilogue, no such part is known to have been written.
More interesting still, for the light it throws on the
fortunes of this play, and on Greene's relationship with
his contemporaries, is the study of the antagonism that
suddenly appears in all of Greene's allusions to Marlowe.
This feeling apparently dates from the beginning of 1588,
or about the time of the probable first performance of
Alphonsus of Arragon. It is first marked in the very

satirical allusion to *Tamburlaine* contained in the address
to the gentleman readers prefixed to *Perimedes* (1588).
In this the author expresses a purpose to "keep my
old course to palter up something in prose using mine
old poesie still *Omne tulit punctum*, although lately two
Gentlemen Poets made two madmen of Rome beat it
out of their paper bucklers, and had it in derision for
that I could not make my verses jet upon the stage in
tragical buskins, every word filling the mouth like the
faburden of Bo-Bell, daring God out of heaven with that
Atheist Tamburlaine or blaspheming with the mad
priest of the sun." He ends this passage as follows:
"If I speak darkly, gentlemen, and offend with this
digression, I crave pardon, in that I but answer in print
what they have offered on the stage." Just who the
two poets and two madmen of Rome may have been it is
now impossible to say. What stands out clear is that
Greene has been attacked on the stage for failing to make
his "verses jet upon the stage in tragical buskins,"
after the manner of Marlowe's *Tamburlaine;* and as
Marlowe was the atheist, and not Tamburlaine, it is
also clear that Greene has a feeling of resentment against
his brother poet. The explanation that seems most
sensible is that Greene has attempted to write a play
in Marlowe's vein, has failed, and being publicly taunted
for his failure, either by Marlowe himself or by his parti-
sans, expresses his determination to continue writing
in prose, the form of composition that has already
brought him fame. Greene's animosity toward Marlowe
continued for several years. In Nash's address prefixed to Greene's *Menaphon* (1589)[1] the same feeling is
manifested, possibly at the instigation of Greene. Here
Nash, perhaps to throw contempt on Marlowe as a
writer of plays, vaunts Greene as a writer of romance.
Menaphon, he holds, excels the achievements of men who,
unable to write romance, "think to outbrave better

---

[1] *Menaphon* was probably written a year or so earlier, but
Nash's address was probably dated from the year of publication.

pens with the swelling bombast of a bragging blank
verse." The same attack is persistently pushed in the
poem, also prefixed to *Menaphon*, by Thomas Barnaby
(signing himself by anagram Brabine), in the words " the
pomp of speech that strives to thunder from a stage man's
throat." Again and again Greene and his friends return
to the attack on Marlowe, now in *Francesco's Fortunes*,
in a slighting reference to the trade of Marlowe's father,[1]
now in *Greene's Vision*, and finally in *A Groatsworth of
Wit*, in which, though in more friendly guise, Greene
reproves Marlowe for his atheism.[2] There can be little
doubt that thus was displayed the rancour of the unsuccessful as against the successful dramatist. The
play of *Alphonsus of Arragon* is in fact quite unworthy
to be placed beside Marlowe's *Tamburlaine* in any comparison for literary excellence. Whether Greene recog-
nised this or not he was undoubtedly influenced in his
later play composition by the failure of his first effort.
Without immediately striking out in any new vein he
now proceeds to burlesque and to parody where first
he had imitated.

About 1585 there was produced Thomas Kyd's *The
Spanish Tragedy*, a tragedy of blood, of madness, and
revenge, with many ingredients of the Senecan plays.
This play and Marlowe's *Tamburlaine* were the chief

---

[1] If we are to believe that *Edward III.* is Marlowe's play the
reference of this passage to Marlowe is made certain, for Greene
ridicules the words 'Ave Cæsar' that occur in the play. The
only other play in which the words are known to occur is *Orlando
Furioso* by Greene himself. It would be too much to say that
their use there is in ridicule of Marlowe, though even that is
possible.

[2] It may be, though it is not certain, that Greene was attacking
Marlowe in the epistle prefixed to his *Farewell to Folly* (1591), in
which he tells the gentleman students that his *Mourning Garment*
had been so popular that the pedlar found the books "too dear for
his pack, that he was fain to bargain for the life of Tomliuclin to
wrap up his sweet powders in those unsavoury papers." If
"Tomliuclin" is a misprint for Tamburlaine this is Greene's most
direct and spiteful attack on Marlowe.

sensations of the English stage of the sixteenth century.
No single play of Shakespeare's can be said to have had
the instantaneous popular success and the immediate
and widespread imitation given to both of these plays.
In the next play that Greene wrote unaided after the
failure of his *Alphonsus of Arragon* there is discernible
an entire change in the author's attitude. He is no more
originative than he was before, but he does not again
attempt to treat an imitative drama in the spirit of its
original. Certain of the scenes of *Alphonsus of Arragon*
were ridiculous enough, but they were undertaken in no
apparent spirit of burlesque. In *Orlando Furioso* Greene
proceeds to parody the two most popular types holding
the boards in his day. The real hero of *Orlando Furioso*
is not the mad French knight, Orlando, but Sacripant.
And Sacripant is a foiled Tamburlaine, a high aspiring
king whose ambition comes to nothingness. In the spirit
of Macbeth, who himself had something of Tamburlaine's
lust of conquest, are the words of Sacripant: " I hold
these salutations as ominous; for saluting me by that
which I am not, he presageth what I shall be." And in
the musings of Sacripant there operates the spirit of
Tamburlaine. " Sweet are the thoughts that smother from
conceit," he reflects; his chair presents " a throne of
majesty "; his thoughts " dream on a diadem "; he
becomes " co-equal with the gods." The lines beginning
" Fair queen of love," spoken by Orlando (p. 187 of this
edition) remind us of the lofty yearning love of Tamburlaine for Zenocrate. As a play *Orlando Furioso* is
Tamburlaine by perversions, and purposely so. Its chief
martial spirit strives for high ends by ignoble means.
He fails to win his mistress, and he fails to win his throne;
done out of both by a madman. If this play is a per-
version of the *Tamburlaine* motive, it is also a burlesque
on the tragedy of blood. There are indications
that Greene would have been quite willing to ridicule
Kyd. Nash, in the same preface to *Menaphon* in which
he had ridiculed Marlowe, satirises Kyd in the famous

lines, "blood is a beggar," and "whole Hamlets, I should say handfuls of tragical speeches." Kyd, as a non-university man, represented that rising coterie, of which Shakespeare was the master, against whom the jealous shafts of the university wits were directed. The signs of the influence of the tragedy of blood type are many. In the balanced and parallel lines of Senecan character, and found little elsewhere in Greene:

> " Only by me was lov'd Angelica,
>   Only for me must live Angelica,"

and

> " ' Angelica doth none but Medor love,'
>   Angelica doth none but Medor love !" ;

in the allusions to Orestes, " Orestes was never so mad in his life as you were "; in the symbols of a classic Hades, Pluto and Averne; in the interspersed quotations from Latin and Italian; in the vague continental setting; in the use of a chorus; in the unheroic revenge motive; in the burlesque death, and the tearing of limb from limb; in "Orlando's sudden insanity and the ridiculously inadequate occasion of it, the headlong *dénouement*, the farcical technique, the mock heroic atmosphere, the paradoxical absence of pathos, the absurdly felicitous conclusion,—all seemingly unwitting," [1] we have either imitated or burlesqued the characteristics of the popular revenge and blood play.

That *Orlando Furioso* was not written after 1591 is clear from a passage in *A Defence of Conny-catching* (1592) in which Greene is charged with selling the play twice, once to the Queen's players for twenty nobles, and, when these had gone to the provinces, to the Admiral's men for as many more. As the Queen's players left the court 26th December 1591, the play must have existed before that date. A reference to the Spanish Armada provides 30th July 1588 as a posterior limit. No valid conclusions can be drawn from certain resemblances between

[1] Gayley, *Representative English Comedies*, p. 410.

lines in this play and lines in Peele's *Old Wives' Tale*,[1]
on account of uncertainty as to the date of the latter
play. There seems no reason to doubt that Gayley is
right in pointing out 26th December 1588 as the date
of the first performance of the play before the Queen at
court.

About the time that Greene's *Orlando Furioso* appeared
there was presented, perhaps at the same play-house, the
Theatre, Marlowe's play, *Dr Faustus*. In this play
Marlowe treated with characteristic intensity the tragical
story of a magician who aspired for wisdom as *Tam-
burlaine* had aspired for power. Magic and witchcraft
were popular in English literature. The story of *Dr
Faustus* was issued in German in 1587, and an English
translation was probably made about the same time.
The prose narrative of *The Famous History of Friar
Bacon* must also have been well known. Magic and
incantation had already been used by Greene in the
Brazen Head of *Alphonsus of Arragon*, in Melissa of
Orlando Furioso, and in the priests of Rasni in *A
Looking-Glass for London and England*. But that
Marlowe was the first to see a large dramatic motive in
the conventional magic is certain. Here again we must
accept it that Marlowe was the leader and Greene the
adapter. We must agree with Collins that "the presumption in favour of *Faustus* having preceded Greene's
play is so overwhelmingly strong that we cannot suppose
that Marlowe borrowed from Greene." But Greene's
Friar Bacon and Friar Bungay is by no means an imitation
of *Dr Faustus*, nor is it a mere parody. Through his
new mastery of technique Greene was deriving a method
of his own that was to make him an effective and independent story-teller. Also there was developing in his art
a refinement and sanity that revolted from the broadly-
drawn conceits and exaggerated passion of Marlowe's
early style. There is something suggestively ironical in
the opposition of the titles of the two plays, the *honourable*

[1] *Orlando Furioso*, ii. 76-79; *Old Wives' Tale*, ii. 808-811.

history of *Friar Bacon and Friar Bungay*, as compared
with the *tragical* history of *Dr Faustus*. So also there
must be some delicate satire in the comic summoning of
Burden and the Hostess as opposed to the impressive
evocation of Alexander and Helen. And one of the
chief episodes in the play may have a jocose oblique reference to *Dr Faustus*. "It is hardly too great an assumption," says Ward, "to regard Bacon's victory over
Vandermast as a cheery outdoing by genuine English
magic of the pretentious German article," represented in
the play of *Dr Faustus*. In *Friar Bacon and Friar
Bungay* we have the first extant expression of Greene's
independent genius working along characteristic lines.
Though Marlowe provides him his starting-point, the
treatment is Greene's alone. While lacking in originative-
ness this play reveals that clearly - marked individual
attitude toward art and the people of his brain that was
to give Greene's plays a pronounced influence in the development of domestic comedy. And, according to
Henslowe's records, the play was as great a success as
Dr Faustus had been.

It seems likely that *Friar Bacon and Friar Bungay* appeared the year following the production of *Dr Faustus*
in 1588. The year 1589 is also indicated by other evidence. In theme the play resembles Greene's *Tully's Love*
of that year. In verse it is not unlike *Orlando Furioso*,
which had appeared in 1588. A striking piece of col-
lateral evidence is adduced by Fleay, who, noting
Edward's remark in Act I., "Lacy, thou know'st next
Friday is Saint James'," is able to show that 1589 is the
only year between 1578 and 1595 in which St James's day
falls on Friday. Further confirmation of this date arises
from a satirical thrust by Greene at the now unknown
author of *Fair Em, the Miller's Daughter of Manchester*, in
his letter prefixed to *Farewell to Folly*. *Fair Em* bears
about the same relationship to *Friar Bacon and Friar
Bungay* that this play bears to *Dr Faustus*. In other words,
while it is not exactly an imitation, it is in many respects

a reflection and a parody of the earlier play. The chief points in which *Fair Em* parodies Greene's play are in the title, in which the author, "somewhat affecting the letter," plays upon Greene's "Fair Maid of Fressingfield"; in the relationship of a king with his courtier in the courtship of a mistress, in Lubeck's fidelity to William the Conqueror in the matter of his love for Mariana contrasted with Lacy's treachery to Edward in courting Margaret; in Em's scornful refusal to return to Mandeville after he has discarded her contrasted with Margaret's hasty forgiveness of Lacy after his unkind desertion; and in the fact that, while in *Friar Bacon* Lacy is put into disguise to pursue his love suits, in *Fair Em* it is the king who masquerades to gain a mistress. Greene no more relished the imitation of his work in 1591 than he did the following year, when he wrote *A Groatsworth of Wit*. His allusion to this play in his *Farewell to Folly* epistle is identified by his quoting two lines that occur toward the end of the play, "A man's conscience is a thousand witnesses," and "Love covereth the multitude of sins." Upon such sentiments in the drama Greene throws ridicule in the following words: "O, 'tis a jolly matter when a man hath a familiar style and can indite a whole year and never be beholding to art? But to bring Scripture to prove anything he says, and kill it dead with the text in a trifling subject of love, I tell you is no small piece of cunning." The most important point in these lines is the indication that a year had been spent in the composition of the play Greene was ridiculing. If we are to accept it that *Fair Em* is in any respect an imitation of *Friar Bacon and Friar Bungay* we must count at least a year before the production of *Fair Em* to find the date of Greene's play. Accepting early 1591 as the point after which *Fair Em* could not have been written,[1] *Friar Bacon* must have been produced at least a year before that time, in 1589, or early in 1590.

---

[1] See Storojenko, Huth Library, vol. I., p. 235, and Gayley, *Representative English Comedies*, p. 412.

Supposing, on account of the beautiful eulogy to Elizabeth at the close of the play, that it must have been intended for presentation at court, Gayley suggests St Stephen's day, 26th December 1589, as the probable date of the play's production.

There is an element in the play of *Friar Bacon and Friar Bungay* which, viewed in the light of the dramatic influences of the times, reveals again Greene's quickness of apprehension of a significant new strain in the drama. It is the introduction of Prince Edward, the King of England, and the Emperor of Germany, into the fabric of his plot. This play must precede Marlowe's *Edward II.* by several months, and at this point we are able finally to dissociate Greene's genius from the direct influence of his great contemporary. In order to develop this point it may be well to glance hastily at the history of the chronicle type of play in England to the time of Greene's *James IV*. Plays on subjects drawn from English history had been more or less common since the production of *Gorboduc* in 1562. Three Latin plays, *Byrsa Basilica*, and the two college plays by Thomas Legge, *Richardus Tertius*, had come somewhat near to the true chronicle type. But it was not until the latter years of the ninth decade of the century that dramatists began on any large scale to utilise the history and mythology of England's kings and wars for the celebrating of her contemporary glories. Even before the Spanish Armada England had become conscious of her own power and eager for the display of her prowess. It was under the stimulus of this growing consciousness of might that the first true chronicle play, *The Famous Victories of Henry the Fifth*, was written. In this play a dramatist for the first time displays an adequate sense of the objective value of the materials derived from history, combined with that insight into human nature and largeness of imaginative power that are necessary to make of the dry records of Holinshed and Stow a moving dramatic story. *The Life and Death of Jack Straw*, which also probably

d

preceded the Armada in its first production, is, while not so good as *The Famous Victories*, a play of vigorous characterisation and native English colouring of historical events. But we are probably not far from the truth in supposing that it was the year 1588 that brought the complete development of the chronicle type. From this year dates the production of the two parts of *The Troublesome Reign of King John of England*, the date being indicated by the allusion to *Tamburlaine* in the prologue. *The First Part of the Contention betwixt two Famous Houses of York and Lancaster*, etc., and *The True Tragedy of Richard, Duke of York*, etc., upon which are based the second and third parts of Shakespeare's *Henry VI.* trilogy, must be dated little, if any, later. *The Troublesome Reign* is known to have been performed by the Queen's men after the other university men had left Greene alone as representative of this company. The theory that connects Greene's name with the composition is, however, so much a matter of conjecture that nothing can be gained from its consideration. Following these two works, almost certainly not preceding them, as some have thought, comes Marlowe's *Edward II.*, the faultless masterpiece of his dramatic composition, produced probably in 1590. And within a few years, in quick succession, there came *Edward III.*, *Richard II.*, and *Richard III.*, the *Henry VI.* trilogy, and the culminating trilogy of the two parts of *Henry IV.* and *Henry V.*

Greene's *Friar Bacon and Friar Bungay*, which appeared in the midst of a movement toward the chronicle type of play, so far adopted its formulas as to introduce historic English characters into the fabric of a story based on prose romance. No feature whatever of the chronicle element as introduced into the play is found in the source-book, nor is there any historical warrant for any of the action presented under the names of the kings. Greene's later attitude toward the rapidly-growing chronicle type of play reveals the motives and characteristics of his art at its maturity. He is still

willing to borrow from the dominant types of art holding
the stage at the time such expedients as shall serve to
adjust his work to the popular demand. But he no
longer transcends his own powers in an attempt at
imitation, or does violence to his own principles of
beauty in a parody of the work of a rival. His note is
now a clear and individual one, and to the day of
his death it sounds upon a definite key. Greene's
powers were no more equal to the blowing into pulsing
life of the dead bones of the chronicles of Stow and
Holinshed than they were efficient to answer in verse
to the lure of "impossible things" after the manner of
Marlowe. Greene may have expressed himself in a
chronicle play as did Marlowe in *Edward II.*, and as did
others of his time, but the simple fact is that no chronicle
play of unmixed type can with certainty be assigned
to him, and until a light is thrown that modifies somewhat the view here outlined we must regard his part in
the composition of *The Troublesome Reign* and *The True
Tragedy* as distinctly a subordinate one. These considerations are of some importance in considering *James
IV.* and *George-a-Greene.* Assuming that *George-a-
Greene* is Greene's work, it is clear that here he but
modified the chronicle play type to his own purposes,
and that he based his story, not on historical narrative,
but on the legends of the people as retained in ballad and
prose romance. Nor is *James IV.* based on historical
records. Going back to the source from which he drew
his early stories, he rests his plot on the first novel of the
third decade of Giraldi Cinthio's *Hecatommithi.* The
play's sole claim to be counted in the chronicle
group is based on the fact that certain of the imaginary
characters of Cinthio's fiction are provided with
the names of members of the English ruling family.
The events of the story have no connection with history,
and Greene's title, *The Scottish History of James the
Fourth, slain at Flodden,* is but an ingenious device
to reach with a romantic and misleading title the

interest of an audience now newly turned toward historical topics.

No evidence whatever can be adduced to show that Greene was in any respect indebted to Marlowe's *Edward II.* for his pseudo-chronicle on *James IV.* Present information makes it seem probable that the plays were performed about the same time, Marlowe's play being, perhaps, a few months the earlier. The plays are quite different. Each dramatist had attained to the maturity of his powers through the purification of his artistic ideals, but whereas Marlowe's last play is held to the outlines of a rigorous art with an almost poignant reticence, Greene's *James IV.* manifests the sweetening and mellowing touch of a dignified and manly philosophy. Nor can we see any indebtedness in Greene's play to Peele's *Edward I.*, though the cruel abuse of the memory of Queen Elinor contained in that play can get its only justification on the theory that the play was written immediately after the Spanish Armada, and therefore two years before *James IV.* But there is one chronicle play that Greene may have seen and that may have influenced him slightly. It is not possible here to go into the question of the authorship of *Edward III.* So excellent is the play in its choicest passages that one would not be loath to assign portions of it to Marlowe, or to Shakespeare, or to impute the entire play to the collaboration of these poets. One would even welcome evidence that the hand of Greene is to be seen in the play. Fleay assigns the play to Marlowe and sets its date of production at 1590 or earlier, basing these suppositions upon a citation from this play in a presumably satirical allusion to Marlowe in Greene's *Never too Late;* perhaps a strained double hypothesis, but one that has the possibility of truth.[1] One would tend to the theory that

---

[1] Greene's satirical use in *Never too Late* of the words "Ave Cæsar," which occur in *Edward III.*, Act i. Sc. 1, and his connecting of them with a cobbler, seem to constitute Fleay's case. The matter has already been mentioned in connection with Greene's

the play was written by Marlowe, on account of the total
absence of comedy and a dulcet sweetness in the blank
verse. If so it was an early study and must be placed
before *Edward II*. *Edward III*. is like *James IV*. in
the fact that it is not a pure chronicle play, but is based
for its most effective scenes upon a romantic episode
from Painter's *Palace of Pleasure*. As *James IV*. goes
back to a novella of Cinthio, the ultimate source of the
romantic by-plot of *Edward III*. is a novel by Bandello.
The historical portions of the play are based on Holinshed.
These romantic scenes, which comprise scene 2 of the
first act and the entirety of the second act, are strikingly
similar to the large theme of *James IV*. The love of
King Edward for the beautiful Countess of Salisbury,
whose castle he has rescued, is similar in its passion and
its ill-success to the love of James for Ida. Both stories
deal with Scottish wars, though in *Edward III*. the
romantic element arises as a result of the English king's
protection of his subject, the Countess of Salisbury,
against the Scots, whereas in *James IV*. the wars result
from the unfortunate love of the Scottish king for his
subject, Ida, and his consequent attempt to kill his
English wife, Dorothea. Like James, Edward is willing
to kill his queen in order to gain his love. The Countess
of Salisbury's lines,

> "As easy may my intellectual soul
> Be lent away, and yet my body live,
> As lend my body, palace to my soul,
> Away from her, and yet retain my soul,"

have something of Ida's incorruptible purity of principle
when she asks Ateukin "can his warrant keep my soul
from hell?" Ida's scorn of the man who would

> "be a king of men and worldly pelf
> Yet hath no power to rule and guide himself,"

---

jealousy of Marlowe. The latest editor of *Edward III.*, C. F.
Tucker Brooke, in *The Shakespeare Apocrypha*, ignores the sup-
position that the play may be by Marlowe and dismisses the theory
that it was by two hands. He puts forward the claims of Peele,
not, however, with great weight.

is like King Edward's—

> "Shall the large limit of fair Britanny
> By me be overthrown, and shall I not
> Master this little mansion of myself?
> Give me an armour of eternal steel!
> I go to conquer kings; and shall I not then
> Subdue myself?"[1]

In no pre-Shakespearean drama outside of Greene's own work is the simple beauty of chaste womanhood presented with the passion and sympathy that are to be found in *Edward III.* Certainly Ida of *James IV.*, the Countess of Salisbury of *Edward III.*, and Imogen of Shakespeare's *Cymbeline* are a trio of womanly beauty and purity. In respect of poetry, the Countess of Salisbury scenes of *Edward III.*, in spite of their somewhat cloying sweetness, transcend any sustained passages in Greene's works. Yet the poetry of *James IV.* is of the same order. If Greene could but have prolonged his vagrant notes of beauty he would have equalled the best in this play. In respect of dramaturgy and human psychology *James IV.* is far in advance of *Edward III.* The simple and undeveloped story of love is in the hands of the more skilled plotter of plays complicated to a fit representation of the social implications of an act, and the passion of Edward is in James developed to the awful inward struggle of a sinning soul. In the absence of facts as to the authorship of *Edward III.*, and as to the date of its composition, it is impossible to draw any conclusions as to influence or inter-relationship. It is clear, however, that Greene's play is written in the spirit of *Edward III.*, in that it is an adaptation of the romantic motive that Greene knew so well how to compass to the purposes of the popular chronicle play.

James IV., which is the last undoubted play of Greene's composition, is also the best. Dramatically it is far in advance of any other of his plays, and there is almost no trace of the affected classical and mythological allusion

---

[1] And for another expression of the same idea see *Friar Bacon and Friar Bungay*, p. 264.

that had marked his earlier writing. Considerations of style and structure indicate that it was written soon after *Friar Bacon and Friar Bungay*. Allusions to contemporary events, such as Dorothea's mention of the Irish uprisings, the idea of a union of England and Scotland, that run through the play, and the brave words spoken by Dorothea, who is not herself a maid, as a delicate compliment to Elizabeth in her French wars,

> " Shall never Frenchman say an English maid
>   Of threats of foreign force will be afraid," .

indicate that the play was produced about 1590. Gayley suggests that it was presented by Greene's company at court on 26th December 1590, or as one of their five performances in 1591. A pretty point is also made by the same scholar based upon a resemblance between lines in this play and certain lines of Peele's. Though the matter is too confused to serve well as chronological data it seems worthy of review if only for the reason that slightly different results may be reached than those indicated by Gayley. In the first scene of the first act of *James IV*. Ida has the following lines:

> " And weel I wot, I heard a shepherd sing,
>   That, like a bee, love hath a little sting."

Comparing this with lines in the fragment of Peele's *The Hunting of Cupid*, preserved in a manuscript volume of extracts by Drummond of Hawthornden, the conclusion is reached that it is Peele, the writer of pastoral, to whom Greene refers as " shepherd," and that Greene's lines are a direct transcription from Peele. Referring to the Stationers' Registers we learn that Peele's *The Hunting of Cupid* was listed for 26th July 1591, certainly later than we should be willing to place the beginning of composition on Greene's *James IV*. The formal proviso, " That if it be hurtful to any other copy before licensed . . . this to be void," may or may not indicate the existence of an earlier copy. That the general motive was in the air and had caught the ear of Greene

is clear from the snatches and fragments of it we find
in his late work. In the *Mourning Garment*, registered
1590, are lines moving upon the same rhyme and answer-
ing the same interrogation as Peele's verses:

> " Ah, what is love ? It is a pretty thing.
>   As sweet unto a shepherd as a king " [1]

One who gets this haunting strain in mind cannot fail
to notice how frequently Greene uses the rhyme of *thing,
bring, king,* and *sting* in *James IV.* Once it is:

> " Although a bee be but a little thing,
>   You know, fair queen, it hath a bitter sting."

And in the first scene of the second act Greene plays
upon the repetition of this rhyme. Peele himself again
uses the refrain in *Decensus Astræ,* licensed October
1591. The argument from the fact that " weel I wot "
in Ida's line seems to reflect the same clause in *The
Hunting of Cupid* would be stronger were it not that
" weel I wot " occurs only in the Drummond manuscript
and is not found in the fragment quoted by Dyce [2] from
the Rawlinson manuscript. Here instead of " weel I
wot " is found " for sure." As Greene himself has used
the refrain in a song sung by a shepherd's wife it leaves
room to doubt that either the swains of *The Hunting* or
Peele himself was the shepherd. It is clear that the first
general use of the motive had occurred in Greene's
Mourning Garment. The positive objections to placing
James IV. subsequent to July 1591 lead one to one of
three conclusions: (1) Peele's lyric had long been written
before it was entered in the *Stationers' Registers,* and in
manuscript form inspired the strains in the *Mourning
Garment* and *James IV.* ; (2) Greene himself provides the
prototype of Peele's lyric in his *Mourning Garment* verse
and its cognate form in *James IV.* ; (3) or, as seems most

---

[1] The refrain, "O, what is love ! it is some mighty power," occurs
with almost a lyric note in *George-a-Greene.*
[2] *The Old Dramatists—Greene and Peele,* p. 603.

probable, fragmentary strains that have been found are reminiscences of a popular song that has not yet been traced.

We have, a little arbitrarily perhaps, grouped the four indubitable plays of Greene's unassisted composition in order to formulate the developing characteristics of his dramatic genius. Yet there are other plays that raise problems no less interesting than those we have considered, and that might, were we able unquestioningly to assign them to Greene, go far to clarify the obscure places in his biography and his art. That Greene had a part in *A Looking-Glass for London and England* there is, of course, no doubt, but we are not yet able to say how much of the play is his composition, and the question of its date provides some difficulties. We incline to the view that it was an early play. Lodge was absent from England in 1588 on a voyage with Captain Clark to the Islands of Terceras and the Canaries. In August 1591 he sailed from Plymouth with Cavendish and did not return until 1593, after Greene's death. *A Looking-Glass* was then either written before 1588 or between 1589 and 1591. Collins, arguing from passages in the play remotely paralleled by biblical allusions in *Greene's Vision* and the *Mourning Garment*, decides that it was produced in 1590. This conclusion cannot be accepted because, as Collins himself admits, references to Nineveh and Jonas are frequent in the literature of the time. Of the three reasons given by Collins for supposing that the play was not written before 1588 one is based on the slender hypothesis that as it is not proved that Greene wrote plays before 1590 this one could not have been earlier; and another is based on a gratuitous assumption that this play is that comedy "lastly writ" with "Young Juvenal" and mentioned in *A Groatsworth of Wit*.[1] The argument that the realistic passage beginning "The fair Triones with their glimmering light" could only have been written after Lodge's first maritime experience carries more

[1] For comment on this *see* p. lviii.

weight, but cannot stand long as against counter evidence of any force whatever. Nor do we see any strength in the theory that this play is a product of Greene's era of repentance. As has been shown, Greene uses repentance as a didactic motive from the first. Considering this as a moralising play one may with better force place it in the earlier years of less complex dramatic inspiration. It is difficult to conceive that in 1589, when Greene was almost certainly engaged in writing *Friar Bacon and Friar Bungay*, he should have been willing to go back to the motive of the interludes. As the spirit of the play is earlier than Greene's mature work, so its associations are with the earlier rather than with the later work of Lodge. *An Alarum against Usurers*, the influence of which is often apparent, was published in 1584. In the years from 1589 to 1591 inclusive Lodge was engaged on another type of work, represented by *Scilla's Metamorphosis, Rosalynde, The History of Robert, second Duke of Normandy*, and *Catharos*, certainly as far removed as possible from the moralising vein of *A Looking-Glass*. Two published expressions by Lodge lean rather to the earlier than the later date. In *Scilla's Metamorphosis* (1589) Lodge vows,

> " To write no more of that whence shame doth grow,
>   [Nor] tie my pen to penny-knaves delight."

Certainly we cannot believe that Lodge was abjuring playwriting at the very moment that he was preparing *A Looking-Glass*. The other passage occurs in Lodge's *Wits Misery* (1596), in which Lodge says it is odious " in stage plays to make use of historical scripture." This passage should be viewed in connection with a passage in the epistle prefixed to Greene's *Farewell to Folly* (1591), taunting the author of *Fair Em* for " blasphemous rhetoric," and for borrowing from the scripture. Whatever may be the claims of consistency we must suppose that the argument from good policy would tend to the conclusion that the scriptural drama of Greene and Lodge

was written as long as possible before these uncompromis-
ing words. Setting narrow limits, we should say that
A Looking-Glass was produced between the date of the
production of *Tamburlaine* and of the destruction of the
Spanish Armada. In the deification of Rasni, " god on
earth, and none but he," there are traces of an aspiring
kingliness, and the lament of Rasni over Remilia, his
queen, has the yearning note sounded in Tamburlaine's
grief over the dying Zenocrate. That the play was not
written during the intense excitement incident to the
Armada would seem probable on general principles, for
there is no hint either of imminent national danger or of
the intoxication of success. The undoubted reflections of
The Spanish Tragedy in this play can serve only to place
it in near conjunction with *Orlando Furioso* as an early
play. Whether it preceded or followed that play it is
impossible now to decide.[1] As to Greene's share in the
work it is impossible to speak with even the semblance of
authority. The comic portions sound like Greene's work,[2]
and if Greene wrote Act v. scene 4 of *James IV.* he
was quite capable of writing the moralising part. In
simplicity of construction the play is quite unlike Greene's
other dramatic works, just as it is much better than
Lodge's *The Wounds of Civil War.* Arguing from the
position of their names on the title-page, one is tempted
to believe that the play was planned and drafted by

[1] Though we accept the theory of the early composition of *A
Looking-Glass* we fail to follow the arguments of Fleay and Gayley,
derived from the introduction of *Perimedes* (licensed 29th March
1588), that in " the mad priest of the sun," mentioned in connection
with Atheist Tamburlaine, Greene can have any reference to the
priests of Rasni in Act iv. Scene 3. Certainly Greene could not have
held up such tame heroics for comparison with Marlowe's vigorous
declamation. Careful scrutiny fails to show that Greene was
mentioning a work of his own. The mad priests of the sun would
seem rather to be other products of the pen of Marlowe, or to be
the work of some other dramatist, possibly Kyd, whom, with
Marlowe, Greene was attacking. (*See* Koeppel in Herrig's *Archiv*,
102, p. 357.)
[2] Particularly the parts of Adam, Smith, and Alcon. It is hard
to suppose that Spenser in his line, " pleasing Alcon," in the *Tears
of the Muses* (1591), could have been referring to Lodge.

Lodge, and put forth by Greene somewhat after the
manner used in his edition of his friend's *Euphues Shadow*
(1592).

The anonymous authorship of *George-a-Greene*, *Locrine*
and *Selimus* provides problems that must continue to
vex critics for some time to come. None of them is
assigned to Greene on absolute evidence of any weight,
yet strong support has been given to the theory of
Greene's authorship of each of them. In the case of the
first so respectable has been the following that no editor
would care definitely to exclude the play from his list.
Yet the best evidence is questionable, and much of the
evidence is quite adverse to the theory of Greene's
authorship. The manuscript notes on a copy of the
Quarto of 1599, assigning the play to a minister who had
played the pinner's part himself, and in another hand to
Robert Greene (quoted on p. xxiii.), cannot to-day be considered good evidence. Judged by the well-known tests
of textual and structural criticism the play almost
absolutely fails to connect itself either with Greene or
his contemporary university writers. Few plays of the
late eighties are so isolated from the clearly-marked characteristics of the drama of the time. Of *Euphues*, of
Tamburlaine, of *The Spanish Tragedy*, of Seneca, of the
religious play, there are few, if any, traces. The rhetorical
structure shows none of the artificial balances and climaxes
so common at the time; there is neither ghost, chorus,
dumb show nor messenger; there is no high aspiring
figure, no madness, no revenge; and the bloodshed is
decent. The lyrics are English and not Italian. Indeed
so far is it from the classical style that it seems difficult
to believe that a university man wrote the play. The
rich mythology of the university wits is entirely wanting.
Such classical allusions as are to be found are the stock
figures of a layman's vocabulary, Leda, Helena, Venus
and Hercules, the rudimentary mythology of the age. The
play lies nearer to the ground in an absolute realism of
the soil than any known in this group. The milk cans

of *Friar Bacon and Friar Bungay* may be pure pastoral;
the country setting of *George-a-Greene* is pure rustic,
and is not helped at all by literature. So also the play
lacks many of Greene's characteristic notes. It was
performed at the Rose by Sussex' men, while so far as is
known Greene remained faithful to the Queen's company
throughout his life. It lacks that satirical under-current,
that ironic veiled counter cuff at his rivals, that personal
innuendo in the midst of a good story that is so characteristic of Greene.

But in spite of the facts that are brought to his judgment the beauties of the play are such as to compel every
editor to soften judgment by inclination and include the
play among Greene's dramas. Certainly Greene is the
only university man of his day who, knowing the
affectations of literature, at the same time knew real life
in the concrete well enough to write *George-a-Greene*.
If truth were told it was through plays of the type
of *George-a-Greene*, rather than through the more ambi-
tious university men's plays, that the current of pure
English comedy was to flow. And it is because *George-
a-Greene* integrates itself so perfectly with the development of Greene's dramatic genius, and represents so well
that realism reached by a settling down of art from
above, rather than arising from the vulgar fact, that we
are willing to say that if Greene did not write this play
he could have written one much like it. *George-a-Greene*
seems to bring to consummation the developing principles
of Greene's art. As in the case of *Friar Bacon and Friar
Bungay* there is in this play a quite unhistorical chronicle
element concerning English kings. But unlike *James IV.*,
which is derived from an Italian original, this play tells
an English story based on the native Robin Hood
strain. Again, like *Friar Bacon*, the original story,
which contains no romantic element, is augmented by a
love story. If the play is Greene's it may represent the
last and purest expression of his charming doctrine of
beauty and his simple philosophy of content. To Greene

beauty lay in fresh and joyous colours and in uncomplex forms. And his philosophy of repose is evolved out of the sublimation of the emotional riot of his early life. Again and again these notes are struck in *George-a-Greene*. Now it is the well-known strain:

> " The sweet content of men that live in love
> Breeds fretting humours in a restless mind."

Again it is contentment put into better precept:

> " a poor man that is true
> Is better than an earl, if he be false ; "

and

> " 'tis more credit to men of base degree,
> To do great deeds, than men of dignity."

George's words, " Tell me, sweet love, how is thy mind content," " Happy am I to have so sweet a love," and " I have a lovely leman, as bright of blee as is the silver moon," sound like Greene's style matured and softened by experience. Yet that the play is Greene's one would not dare to say. Its present form displays either hasty composition or garbled version, or both, for it is neither consistent nor well integrated. In one breath Cuddy has never seen George, and in the next delivers to King Edward a message which " at their parting George did say to me." The episodes of Jane-a-Barley, Cuddy and Musgrove, George-a-Greene and the horses in the corn, the shoemakers and the " Vail Staff " custom, Robin Hood and his followers, are but fragments thinly and crudely knit together. Perhaps this play is a unique exemplar of a class of hurriedly-sketched popular plays written by Greene for the provinces and printed from a mutilated stage copy.[1]

---

[1] As to date of the play we can say only that if Greene's it must be the last one of his extant workmanship. It would not be safe to draw conclusions from the mention of *George-a-Greene* in Tarlton's *News out of Purgatory*, as Tarlton was probably alluding to the source of the narrative used by Greene. Nor does the mention of " martial Tamburlaine " in the first scene help further than to indicate that the play was written after 1587.

The Lamentable Tragedy of Locrine has been ascribed to Shakespeare, Marlowe, Peele and Greene. The two former ascriptions are clearly uncritical, and the two latter present many difficulties. According to Symonds, "The best passages of the play . . . are very much in the manner of Greene." In this opinion joins Brooke, the editor of *The Shakespeare Apocrypha*. With certain portions of the argument associating *Locrine* with Greene we are in harmony. The play was issued by that Thomas Creede who had published Greene's *Alphonsus of Arragon*, *A Looking-Glass*, and *James IV*. In flashes of poetry, in classical allusion, in high-sounding phrases, the play is sometimes astoundingly in the temper of *Orlando Furioso* and *Alphonsus of Arragon*. We care little for the evidence that is deduced from literal parallels. More often than not these were purposed copyings or imitations, or involuntary reminiscences of lingering refrains. But there is such a thing as an author's peculiar verbal coin, which is stamped with his sign, and can be paid out by him alone. One who knows his author well cannot but be struck with the frequent occurrence of Greene's own turn of phrase, a style that is clearly to be distinguished from the style of any other poet of his time. Brutus' salutation to his followers at the beginning of the play is much after the manner of Marsilius' welcome to the princes who were come to woo Angelica. Trumpart's imprecations by "sticks and stones," "brickbats and bones," "briars and brambles," "cook shops and shambles," remind one of Orlando's equally ludicrous "Woods, trees, leaves; leaves, trees, woods." The lyrical clownery of Strumbo is often strikingly like that of Miles in *Friar Bacon*. The senile revenge motive of Corineus resembles that of Carinus in *Orlando Furioso*. The use of the capital founded by Brutus, Troynovant, is repeated in *Never too Late*.[1] So also Guendoline's

---

[1] This name was, however, quite common in this sense, Peele himself using it in his *Farewell* and in *Polyhmnia*.

pleas for the life of her faithless husband—" his death
will more augment my woes "—are quite in the spirit of
Dorothea's pity for her sinning husband in *James IV*.
Strumbo's use of his plackets to hide food in while
Humber is starving resembles in comic intent Adam's
same expedient in starving Nineveh. Certain verse
propositions seem to ring with Greene's own timbre :

" The poorest state is farthest from annoy " (ii. 2, 37).[1]

" After we passed the groves of Caledone,
  Where murmuring rivers slide with silent streams,
  We did behold the straggling Scythians camp," etc. (ii. 3, 23).

" Why this, my lord, experience teaches us :
  That resolution is a sole help at need " (iii. 2, 61).

"Oh, that sweet face painted with nature's dye,
  Those roseall cheeks mixt with a snowy white,
  That decent neck surpassing ivory " (iv. 1, 91).

" *Loc.* Better to live, than not to live at all.
  Estrild. Better to die renowned for chastity
  Than live with shame and endless infamy " (iv. 1, 133).[2]

Other minor phrases that are even more characteristic
of Greene's note are, " daughters of proud Lebanon,"
" Aurora, handmaid of the sun," " party coloured
flowers," " shady groves " (often repeated), " girt with a
corselet of bright shining steel," " rascal runnagates,"
" overlook with haughty front," " injurious fortune,"
and " injurious traitor," " watery " (frequently repeated
even where unnecessary), " silver streams " (often repeated), " sweet savours," " regiment," " argent
streams," " university of bridewell " (to be compared
with Miles' jests), " uncouth rock," " Puryflegiton "
(often used ; Greene uses Phlegethon), " Anthropophagie,"
" countercheck," " triple world," " beauty's paragon,"
" those her so pleasing looks," " straggling " (as an
adjective expressing contempt ; often used, and quite
characteristic of Greene).

[1] The reference is to the edition in *The Shakespeare Apocrypha*.
[2] Compare this with a line in *James IV*. (Act ii. Sc. 1), " Better,
than live unchaste, to lie in grave."

The considerations outlined are sufficient to incline one favourably toward the theory of Greene's authorship of *Locrine*. Yet the difficulties are such as for the present to deny the play a place among Greene's works. The date is in great doubt. The first edition of 1595 "newly set forth, overseen and corrected by W. S.," is evidently a revamped version. We cannot agree with Brooke that the play appeared before *Tamburlaine*, for, among many strains of the dramas of *The Misfortunes of Arthur* type there are mingled undoubted influences from the revenge plays and *Tamburlaine*. It is difficult to adjust the play to any scheme of activities that has been worked out for Greene. Certainly it did not ante-date *Alphonsus of Arragon*, for there is every reason to take the prologue of that play at its word. Upon the hypothesis that it is Greene's work we should place it just before *Orlando Furioso*, the play which it resembles above all others, and about the same time as *A Looking-Glass for London and England*, which in respect of comedy it greatly resembles.

It is impossible to view with any favour the theory of Greene's authorship of *Selimus*. In every respect the play is divergent from Greene's characteristic tone and method. Grosart's theory that this play may be supposed to take the place of the promised second part of *Alphonsus of Arragon* has no weight. Like the latter play *Selimus* is the first part of a work that had been planned in series, and in no respect does it supplement Greene's first play. Like *Alphonsus of Arragon* the play is constructed with such slavish fidelity to the *Tamburlaine* principles that it is difficult to think Greene could have written *Selimus* after the failure of *Alphonsus*. Constructively the play is unlike Greene's work. The declamation is more sustained and the action is less crowded than in Greene's other plays. The many parallel passages quoted by Grosart prove nothing more than that borrowing was the order of the age. Nor is anything proved by the fact that the same clown comedy is introduced into *Locrine*,

e

Selimus and *A Looking-Glass for London and England.*
If *Locrine* is Greene's work it was probably written about
the time that he was collaborating with Lodge, and he
may have introduced the same comedy into both plays.
It is no more of an assumption that the author of *Selimus*
borrowed his comedy from *Locrine* than that Greene
would use the same tricks three times within two years.
The blank verse of *Selimus*, built largely on a system
of rhymed stanzas, is very far from that of *Locrine* and
of Greene's undoubted plays. To illustrate this no
better passages could be chosen than those produced by
Collins to evidence the similarity of the verse of the two
plays. The vexed problem of the part taken by Greene
in the *Henry VI.* plays can be treated now only as a
subject for interesting but comparatively fruitless speculation. So also must be considered the ingenious and
almost convincing circumstantial argument that *A Knack
to Know a Knave* is the comedy "lastly writ" by
Greene and "Young Juvenal," and mentioned in *A
Groatsworth of Wit.*[1]

We said in beginning that Greene is clearly typical
of his time. And indeed his plays are complexes of
the dominant dramatic types of the years just before
Shakespeare. In his work are focused the strains
leading from the three most clearly marked dramatic
movements of the age. The English morality com-
bines with rustic low life to produce the interlude,
which continues its course of didacticism and horse-play
until the end of the century. The Senecan drama
scatters ghosts and horrors through English plays until
it is etherealised in the poetry of *Tamburlaine,* and
laughed to death in the parodies of *The Spanish Tragedy*

[1] *See* Gayley, *Representative English Comedies*, p. 422. Opinion
to-day seems strongly to favour the theory that it was Nash to
whom Greene referred in the famous passage in *A Groatsworth of
Wit*, and not Lodge. Considerations of age, of personal association
of the comparative gifts of satire of Nash and Lodge strengthen
this view. Nash helped Marlowe in the composition of a tragedy
why not Greene in the composition of a comedy?

The English chronicle play gives life to the dry bones of history, and celebrates the solidarity of an England united over the face of the globe, and through all the eras of her splendid history. Of all these elements the one that remains in Greene's work from beginning to end is the didactic strain. *A Looking-Glass for London and England* is the last full flowering of English religious drama. Yet didactic elements appear in Friar Bacon's strangely unmotivated repentance, and in the interpolated scene of a lawyer, a merchant and a divine in *James IV.* In Greene's dramas many of the types and figures from a bygone stage are mingled with the newer creations of his invention. The vices of the interludes spring up incongruously in the midst of the characters of a later drama. In *Friar Bacon* the Vice is again carried off to hell on the back of the Devil, just as had been done years before in simpler plays; and in the same play, by the use of the expedient of perspective glasses, two actions are represented as taking place in widely separate localities, after the manner of the early masques. And aside from these persisting formulas from an older drama there are influences and obligations in relation with Lyly and Marlowe and Kyd that are literally too numerous for enumeration. As significant as any service Greene performed for English drama is the assimilation to a single dramatic end of the adverse expedients of a heterogeneous dramaturgy.

Technically Greene's contribution to the stage was most significant. Nash called him master above all others in " plotting of plays." Part of this mastery comes from his recognition of the technical requirement of continuous action on the stage. Better than any of his contemporaries, not excluding Kyd, he knew that action is of equal importance with speech in the exposition of a dramatic story. Wherever possible he visualises before his audience the successive stages in the progress of his plot, not by the use of ghosts and chorus, who serve merely a narrative purpose, but by bringing before his readers palpable expedients illustrative of the theme of the action. The use of the Brazen Head in *Alphonsus of Arragon;* the incantations of Melissa in *Orlando Furioso;* the raising of the arbor, and the death of Remilia under the incantations of the Magi in *A Looking-Glass for London and England ;* the use of a visible magic to transport Burden and Helen, to raise Hercules and the tree, and to present the downfall of the Brazen Head in *Friar Bacon,* all reveal an ability to adapt the properties and expedients of the stage of the time to the purposes of the plot. This is further exemplified in the facility with which from the beginning Greene utilises such spectacular expedients as the letting down of the throne of Venus from above in *Alphonsus of Arragon,* and the descent of the throne of Oseas the prophet in *A Looking-Glass.* Not only does he use the palpable tricks of stagecraft, but he adapts these to the purposes of his dramatic exposition. The perspective glass in *Friar Bacon* which serves to present two scenes at the same time serves also to connect two strains of the plot and to further the action by arousing Prince Edward's suspicion of the fidelity of Lacy. So magic, which in *Dr Faustus* serves only to raise a spectacle, in this play is used as a plot expedient to delay the marriage of Margaret and Lacy. The stage directions are more full and circumstantial in Greene's plays than in those of either Marlowe or Peele, and reveal the same tendency to heighten the effect of plot by action and display.

Greene's dramas present a steady development in effectiveness of plot involution. The first plays are marked by a large amount of action and a great number of narrative fragments very crudely and inorganically clustered around the central character. *Alphonsus of Arragon* is Greene's poorest work in this as in every other respect. Its first act is marked by hesitation and indirection; accident, coincidence and inconsistency are the rule throughout. The play is practically divided into two parts, in the first of which Alphonsus is the central figure, while

Amurack serves as protagonist in the second.. *Orlando Furioso* is structurally an improvement on its predecessor, and in *A Looking-Glass for London and England* an excellent unity of action has been attained. It is in *Friar Bacon and Friar Bungay* that Greene effected the most substantial advance in play technique made before Shakespeare. This is nothing less than the weaving of two distinct plots into the unity of a single dramatic narrative. On account of the crowding of the action and the sensations, the play is unbalanced and unorganised. *Friar Bacon's* activities are divided into two distinct parts; his victory over Vandermast and his loss of the Brazen Head, and they are scattered through a half-dozen episodes. For perfect balance Prince Edward surrenders Margaret too early in the play and thus makes necessary the introduction of further retarding action based upon an unexplainable whim of Lacy. Yet granting the inchoate character of the play we must admit that in effecting the combination of the story of Friar Bacon with the story of Prince Edward, Lacy and the Fair Maid of Fressingfield, Greene accomplished an unusually significant innovation. In *James IV.* Greene's technique is at its best. Even in the faulty version that comes down to us we see traces of Greene's experimenting temper. In dumb shows he is reinstating a popular feature of older plays. His induction serves as a model for Shakespeare's *Taming of the Shrew ;* and one of its characters, Oberon, is a rough draft for the fairy of that name in *A Midsummer Night's Dream*, as Bohan is a prototype of Jaques in *As You Like It.* But Greene's induction is better integrated with his play than is Shakespeare's induction of Sly, the Lords and the Servants, for the two characters, Slipper and Nano, who appear first in the induction, are sent out into the play to serve as connecting links for all of its action. *James IV.* is the only one of Greene's plays that has unity of action. The plot is introduced with a masterly directness and economy. The fatal situation breaks on the reader at the beginning, and throughout the play the crux of the action remains the love of the King of Scots for another than his queen. Ateukin springs up at the psychological moment and at the dramatic crisis. The first act of the play, dramatically quite the best first act written outside of Shakespeare up to his time, provides the king's marriage to Dorothea, the revelation of his love for Ida, the enlistment of Ateukin in the cause of the king's love, and a lover for Ida to make her inaccessible. Aside from the development of the tragedy of this situation there enters into the play only one minor episode, the love of Lady Anderson for the young knight (in reality Queen Dorothea) whom she is succouring in her castle. That Greene chose to end the play after the manner of comedy, and not, as the situation would seem to require, and the taste of the age must have demanded, with the death of the erring king, is an effective indication of his later freedom from restraint and of his personal philosophy of art.

As Marlowe moved from the sublime passion of his *Tamburlaine* theme to the cold reserve of his *Edward II.*, Greene also, casting off the turgid eloquence of his early style, attained at the end to an art of contemplative repose and genial humanity. The critic likes to feel that in stripping away the excrescences from his art he was discovering his own soul. In treating Greene as a representative Elizabethan, one should not ignore the individuality of the man that stamps all his work with a new impress. Without being original in structure or style Greene was individual in outlook and temper. He had a keener eye for the little things than any dramatist of his time, and he had also a better sympathy for the quick flashing moods and manifestations of human character. His knowledge of the concrete realities of character is an attribute of the man himself. In depicting fairies he lacks, as did Lyly, the imagination to vitalise an unreal world in the spirit of a Shakespeare. He chooses his characters from the world around him and studies them

in their native habitat. His clowns, though belonging
to an ancient family, are racy of the soil of England, and
are fellows with Shadow, and Launce, and Speed and
Grumio. Warren and Ermsby are Englishmen of a
sturdy type, and Sir Cuthbert Anderson and Lady
Anderson, are studied as if in their Scotch castle. But
Greene did something more than present the exteriors of
men as types. He studied their psychology, and knew
the warring forces within the individual soul, the power of
circumstance, and ambition, and love to direct the forces
of character into untoward paths. He knew that logic
of human nature that counts consistency untrue, and
constructs motives out of the syllogisms of perversity.
So he divides the part of the Capitano, in the original story
upon which *James IV.* was based, into two parts, one the
working intelligence, Ateukin, and the other the execu-
tioner, Jaques. So also the King of Scots is no puppet.
He struggles as he falls, and his fall is reflected in his
distraught mind. And in the depiction of women Greene
lavishes the finest forces of his genius. Nash called him
" the Homer of women," and that phrase is worth the
entirety of *Strange News* in defending Greene's fame.
Sometimes he goes to his own baser experience for his
comment, and then there is, as in *Orlando Furioso* (p. 191),
a touch of the awful invective delivered against prosti-
tutes in his *Never too Late.* But Greene's later art was
better than this. Scottish Ida, who wins the heart of
the King of Scots from English Doll, is no courtesan.
Something of the respect and love that breathes through
Greene's allusions to Doll his wife is seen in his treatment
of all womankind. Even Angelica in *Orlando Furioso,*
unformed as are her outlines, represents that fidelity of a
patient Grizzel so well exemplified in Margaret in *Friar
Bacon* and Dorothea in *James IV.* Nothing in Marlowe's
Queen Isabella of *Edward II.*, Zenocrate of *Tamburlaine,*
Abigail of *The Jew of Malta*, can equal the sweet and
simple womanliness of Greene's gallery, comprising Isabel
in *Never too Late*, Bellaria and Fawnia in *Pandosto,*

Sephestia in *Menaphon*, Philomela and the shepherd's wife in the *Mourning Garment*, Margaret in *Friar Bacon and Friar Bungay*, and Ida and Dorothea in *James IV*.

Greene's skill in the treatment of character grew out of his knowledge of life, and is involved in his most significant and enduring contribution to the stage. This is the introduction of realism onto a stage that was essentially romantic, and it arises from the application of dramatic art to the experiences of everyday life. Greene's low life is not artificial pastoral, nor is it the boorish clownage of the interludes. It is the characteristic life of England that we see in Harrison's *Description*, refined and beautified by a mature and chastened art. Only in such art can come the homely ideal of " beauty tempered with . . . huswifery." By the time of *Friar Bacon and Friar Bungay* Greene's art has come home. Now in a series of domestic thumb sketches he shows us Margaret:

" And there amongst the cream bowls she did shine
As Pallas 'mongst her princely huswifery,"

and the hostess in the kitchen,

" Spitting the meat 'gainst supper for my guess,"

and the hay, and butter, and cheese displays of Harleston fair. " He was of singular pleasaunce, the very supporter, and, to no man's disgrace be this intended, the only comedian, of a vulgar writer, in this country," writes Chettle in *A Kind Hart's Dream*, summing up in striking phrase the true contemporary judgment of Greene's greatest distinction. But there is another aspect of his genius. He loved the active life of out-of-doors, and he indulged a vigorous spirit of participation in the life around him. But he saw behind things into the spirit, and his treatment of events is dignified with a rich philosophy drawn from his manifold contact with the most lavish era in England's history. To him a drama is more than an isolated and a meaningless show. In *Francesco's Fortunes* he outlines the kind of play that he himself wrote: " Therein they painted out in the persons the course of the world, how either it was graced with honour, or discredited with vices." He leaves the hollow-sounding verbiage of his early plays to comment with the lawyer on "the manners and the fashions of this age." His *James IV.* is a play of contemplation. Bohan is an early "malcontent," and Andrew, noting the downfall of his prince, exclaims, "Was never such a world, I think, before." With the heart of a democrat Greene understands alike the problems of kings and yeomen. The counsel of the King of England to Dorothea on the obligations and dangers of sovereignty is sage and rational, and Ida's comments on the "greatest good "— that it lies not "in delights, or pomp, or majesty "— are rich with the best philosophy. In *A Quip for an Upstart Courtier* Clothbreeches asks, "Doth true virtue consist in riches, or humanity in wealth? is ancient honour tied to outward bravery? or not rather true nobility, a mind excellently qualified with rare virtues? ' So often is this note struck in Greene's plays that we might call it a personal one were it not that it is beginning to appear commonly in the literature of the time.

Summing up Greene's contribution to the drama of his age we should say that it lies in the essential comedy of his outlook on life, his inherent *vis comica ;* in his loving insight into human nature in its familiar aspects; in his distrust of exaggeration and his tendency to turn this to burlesque; and in his beautiful philosophy of the eternal verities. Out of the drama of Greene there developed the new romantic comedy of Shakespeare and the realism of joy of domestic drama. After *George-a-Greene* there came the Huntingdon plays of Munday and Chettle, in which the woodland knight, Robin Hood, appears again. After *Friar Bacon and Friar Bungay* there came *Fair Em, A Knack to Know a Knave, John-a-Kent and John-a-Cumber,* and Dekker's *Shoemaker's Holiday.* Heywood and Samuel Rowley and Munday and Dekker and the author of *The Merry Devil of Edmonton* share with Shakespeare indisputable strains of his individual note.

Professor Herford calls attention to the conflict, in Greene's life, between "the fresh, unworn sense of beauty and poetry," and "the bitter, disillusioned cynicism of premature old age." That conflict was a necessary one. It was present also in the discrepancy between the lyric note of Marlowe's yearning fancy and the hard reserve laid upon his later pen by bitter suffering. Both of these were true Elizabethans. They were true to their times in the vastness of their conceptions and in the narrowness of their lives, in their poetic triumphs no less than in their personal defeats. The marvellous thing is that in the midst of riotous life they should have learned repose in art, that though writing in a tavern their muse should have remained chaste. Marlowe remained to the end the poet of "air and fire." From Greene we get in the drama the first clear note of the English woodland joy that had echoed fitfully in English non-dramatic verse from the days of Chaucer and the unknown author of *Alysoun.*

A Groatsworth of Wit has been so often cited as a record in the history of English drama that its value as a human document has been forgotten. Of Greene's attack therein on Shakespeare there is no need to say anything here. To those who have any concern with Greene himself it is interesting chiefly for its revelation of the awful melancholy of his last days and his pathetic sense of the wrongs suffered by the little school of dramatists of which he was a member. The sense of pity produced by reading this book is intensified by a study of Greene's last days as suggested in his own succeeding book, *The Repentance of Robert Greene,* and in the pamphlets of Harvey and Nash. Greene died on the 3rd of September 1592, of a malady following a surfeit of Rhenish wine and pickled herring. Before his death he received commendations from his wife, and his last written words were addressed to her in a request to pay the debt incurred by his sickness. We are told that after his death the keeper of his garret crowned his head with bays. Fourteen years later, when, with the exception of Lodge, the last of the university wits had passed away, and Shakespeare, whom they had all feared, had taken his abiding place, Dekker in his tract, *A Knight's Conjuring*, shows Marlowe, Greene and Peele, together once more in Elysium, under the "shades of a large vine, laughing to see Nash, that was but newly come to their college, still haunted with the sharp and satirical spirit that had followed him here upon earth."

THE text of this edition is based on Dyce's modernised text of 1861 compared with the later collations of Grosart and Collins, and editions of single plays by Ward, Manly and Gayley. The editor has been conservative in accepting modifications of Dyce's text. The act and scene divisions as found in Collins have been adopted, and the location of scenes has been indicated throughout.

A

ALPHONSUS, KING
OF ARRAGON

THE first extant edition of *Alphonsus, King of Arragon*, was printed in quarto by Thomas Creede in 1599. Lowndes mentions a quarto of 1597 of which no trace can be found. Of the two copies of the quarto of 1599 now known, one is in the library of the Duke of Devonshire, and the other is in the Dyce Library at South Kensington. *Alphonsus* is not mentioned by Henslowe in his *Diary*, nor is there any record of the play in the Stationers' Registers. Nothing certain can be said concerning the circumstances and dates of composition and first performance of Greene's plays. But there can be no doubt that this is one of Greene's earliest plays, for in the Prologue Greene says through the mouth of Venus :

> " And this my hand, which usèd for to pen
> The praise of love and Cupid's peerless power,
> Will now begin to treat of bloody Mars."

Nor can there be any doubt that the play was written in imitation of Marlowe's *Tamburlaine*, mention of which occurs in IV. 3. A second part, " when I come to finish up his life," is promised in the Epilogue. That the second part was not written is probably an indication of the failure of the piece. In the Preface to Greene's *Perimedes* of 29th March 1588, we learn that two " gentlemen poets " had caused two actors to mock Greene's motto, *Omne tulit punctum*, because his verse fell short of the bombast and blasphemy of Marlowe's early style. It has been suggested that it may have been the verse of *Alphonsus* that was ridiculed. Certainly it must have been this play, or a lost early play, for it was in drama that the " mighty line " appeared. There is in Peele's *Farewell*, April 1589, a reference to a piece of mechanism occurring in this play which closely connects it with Marlowe's first play, " Mahomet's Poo and mighty Tamburlaine." This has been discussed in the General Introduction. Greene's play is based distantly on the history of Alphonso I. of Naples and V. of Arragon (1385-1454), though with no pretence to historical accuracy.

DRAMATIS PERSONÆ

CARINUS, the rightful heir to the crown of Arragon.
ALPHONSUS, his son.
FLAMINIUS, King of Arragon.
BELINUS, King of Naples.
DUKE OF MILAN.
ALBINIUS.
FABIUS.
LÆLIUS.
MILES.
AMURACK, the Great Turk.
ARCASTUS, King of the Moors.
CLARAMONT, King of Barbary.
CROCON, King of Arabia.
FAUSTUS, King of Babylon.
BAJAZET.
Two Priests of MAHOMET.
Provost, Soldiers, Janissaries, etc.
FAUSTA, wife to Amurack.
IPHIGINA, her daughter.
MEDEA, an enchantress.
MAHOMET (speaking from the Brazen Head)
VENUS.
The NINE MUSES.

THE COMICAL HISTORY OF ALPHONSUS, KING OF ARRAGON

ACT THE FIRST

PROLOGUE

After you have sounded thrice, let VENUS *be let down from the top of the stage.*

VENUS.   Poets   are   scarce,   when
        goddesses themselves
    Are forc'd to leave their high and
        stately seats,
    Plac'd on the top of high Olympus'
        Mount,
    To seek them out, to pen their
champions' praise.
The time hath been when Homer's sugar'd Muse
Did make each echo to repeat his verse,
That every coward that durst crack a spear,
And tilt and tourney for his lady's sake,
Was painted out in colours of such price
As might become the proudest potentate.
But now-a-days so irksome idless' slights,

7

And cursèd charms have witch'd each student's mind,
That death it is to any of them all,
If that their hands to penning you do call.
O Virgil, Virgil, wert thou now alive,
Whose painful pen, in stout Augustus' days,
Did dain [1] to let the base and silly fly
To scape away without thy praise of her,
I do not doubt but long or ere this time,
Alphonsus' fame unto the heavens should climb ;
Alphonsus' fame, that man of Jove his seed,
Sprung from the loins of the immortal gods,
Whose sire, although he habit on the earth,
May claim a portion in the fiery pole,
As well as any one whate'er he be.
But, setting by Alphonsus' power divine,
What man alive, or now amongst the ghosts,
Could countervail his courage and his strength?
But thou art dead, yea, Virgil, thou art gone,
And all his acts drown'd in oblivion.
And all his acts drown'd in oblivion? [2]
No, Venus, no, though poets prove unkind,
And loth to stand in penning of his deeds,
Yet rather than they shall be clean forgot,
I, which was wont to follow Cupid's games
Will put in ure [3] Minerva's sacred art;
And this my hand, which usèd for to pen
The praise of love and Cupid's peerless power,
Will now begin to treat of bloody Mars,
Of doughty deeds and valiant victories.

> *Enter* MELPOMENE, CLIO, ERATO, *with their* Sisters,
> *playing all upon sundry instruments,* CALLIOPE
> *only excepted, who coming last, hangeth down*
> *the head, and plays not of her instrument.*

[1] disdain: often used.   [2] Such repetition is common, see
pp. 37, 188, 190.   [3] Use.

But see whereas[1] the stately Muses come,
Whose harmony doth very far surpass
The heavenly music of Apollo's pipe !
But what means this ?   Melpomene herself
With all her sisters sound their instruments,
Only excepted fair Calliope,
Who, coming last and hanging down her head,
Doth plainly show by outward actions
What secret sorrow doth torment her heart.

[*Stands aside.*

Mel. Calliope, thou which so oft didst crake[2]
How that such clients cluster'd to thy court,
By thick and threefold, as not any one
Of all thy sisters might compare with thee,
Where be thy scholars now become, I trow?
Where are they vanish'd in such sudden sort,
That, while as we do play upon our strings,
You stand still lazing, and have naught to do ?
  Clio. Melpomene, make you a why of that?
I know full oft you have [in] authors read,
The higher tree, the sooner is his fall,
And they which first do flourish and bear sway,
Upon the sudden vanish clean away.
  Cal. Mock on apace ; my back is broad enough
To bear your flouts as many as they be.
That year is rare that ne'er feels winter's storms ;
That tree is fertile which ne'er wanteth fruit ;
And that same Muse hath heapèd well in store
Which never wanteth clients at her door.
But yet, my sisters, when the surgent seas
Have ebb'd their fill, their waves do rise again,
And fill their banks up to the very brims ;
And when my pipe hath eas'd herself a while,

---

[1] Often used for " where," as " whenas " is used for " when."
[2] Boast.

Such store of suitors shall my seat frequent,
That you shall see my scholars be not spent.

 Erato. Spent, quoth you, sister? then we were to
  blame,
If we should say your scholars all were spent:
But pray now tell me when your painful pen
Will rest enough?

 Mel. When husbandmen shear hogs.

 Ven. [*coming forward*]. Melpomene, Erato,[1] and the
  rest,
From thickest shrubs Dame Venus did espy
The mortal hatred which you jointly bear
Unto your sister high Calliope.
What, do you think if that the tree do bend,
It follows therefore that it needs must break?
And since her pipe a little while doth rest,
It never shall be able for to sound?
Yes, Muses, yes, if that she will vouchsafe
To entertain Dame Venus in her school,
And further me with her instructions,
She shall have scholars which will dain to be
In any other Muse's company.

 Cal. Most sacred Venus, do you doubt of that?
Calliope would think her three times blest
For to receive a goddess in her school,
Especially so high an one as you,
Which rules the earth, and guides the heavens too.

 Ven. Then sound your pipes, and let us bend our
  steps
Unto the top of high Parnassus Hill,
And there together do our best devoir
For to describe Alphonsus' warlike fame,
And, in the manner of a comedy,
Set down his noble valour presently.

   [1] A false quantity.

Cal. As Venus wills, so bids Calliope.
Mel. And as you bid, your sisters do agree.

            [Exeunt.

SCENE I.—*Near Naples.*

Enter CARINUS *and* ALPHONSUS.

Cari. My noble son, since first I did recount
The noble acts your predecessors did
In Arragon against their warlike foes,
I never yet could see thee joy at all,
But hanging down thy head as malcontent,
Thy youthful days in mourning have been spent.
Tell me, Alphonsus, what might be the cause
That makes thee thus to pine away with care?
Hath old Carinus done thee any offence
In reckoning up these stories unto thee?
What ne'er a word but mum?   Alphonsus, speak,
Unless your father's fatal day you seek.
 Alphon. Although, dear father, I have often vow'd
Ne'er to unfold the secrets of my heart
To any man or woman, whosome'er
Dwells underneath the circle of the sky;
Yet do your words so cónjure me, dear sire,
That needs I must fulfil that you require.
Then so it is.   Amongst the famous tales
Which you rehears'd done by our sires in war,
Whenas you came unto your father's days,
With sobbing notes, with sighs and blubbering tears,
And much ado, at length you thus began:
"Next to Alphonsus should my father come
For to possess the diadem by right

Of Arragon, but that the wicked wretch
His younger brother, with aspiring mind,
By secret treason robb'd him of his life,
And me his son of that which was my due."
These words, my sire, did so torment my mind,
As had I been with Ixion [1] in hell,
The ravening bird could never plague me worse;
For ever since my mind hath troubled been
Which way I might revenge this traitorous fact,
And that recover which is ours by right.

 Cari. Ah, my Alphonsus, never think on that!
In vain it is to strive against the stream:
The crown is lost, and now in hucksters' hands,
And all our hope is cast into the dust.
Bridle these thoughts, and learn the same of me,—
A quiet life doth pass an empery.

 Alphon. Yet, noble father, ere Carinus' brood
Shall brook his foe for to usurp his seat,
He'll die the death with honour in the field,
And so his life and sorrows briefly end.
But did I know my froward fate were such
As I should fail in this my just attempt,
This sword, dear father, should the author be
To make an end of this my tragedy.
Therefore, sweet sire, remain you here a while,
And let me walk my Fortune for to try.
I do not doubt but, ere the time be long,
I'll quite his cost, or else myself will die.

 Cari. My noble son, since that thy mind is such
For to revenge thy father's foul abuse,
As that my words may not a whit prevail
To stay thy journey, go with happy fate,
And soon return unto thy father's cell,
With such a train as Julius Cæsar came

   [1] Another false quantity.

To noble Rome, whenas he had achiev'd [1]
The mighty monarch of the triple world.
Meantime Carinus in this silly [2] grove
Will spend his days with prayers and orisons,
To mighty Jove to further thine intent:
Farewell, dear son, Alphonsus, fare you well.   [*Exit.*

   Alphon. And is he gone? then hie, Alphonsus, hie,
To try thy fortune where thy fates do call.
A noble mind disdains to hide his head,
And let his foes triumph in his overthrow.
                       [*Makes as though to go out.*

Enter ALBINIUS.

   Albi. What loitering fellow have we spièd here?
Presume not, villain, further for to go,
Unless [3] you do at length the same repent.
   Alphon. [*coming towards* ALBINIUS]. "Villain," say'st
     thou? nay, "villain" in thy throat!
What, know'st thou, skipjack, whom thou villain call'st?
   Albi. A common vassal I do villain call.
   Alphon. That shalt thou soon approve, persuade thyself,
Or else I'll die, or thou shalt die for me.
   Albi. What, do I dream, or do my dazzling eyes
Deceive me? Is't Alphonsus that I see?
Doth now Medea use her wonted charms
For to delude Albinius' fantasy?
Or doth black Pluto, king of dark Avern,
Seek to flout me with his counterfeit?
His body like to Alphonsus' framèd is;
His face resembles much Alphonsus' hue;
His noble mind declares him for no less;
'Tis he indeed. Woe worth Albinius,
Whose babbling tongue hath caus'd his own annoy!
Why doth not Jove send from the glittering skies

---

   [1] Attained the position of.   [2] Simple, rude.
          [3] Lest; often so used.

His thunderbolts to chástise this offence?
Why doth Dame Terra cease [1] with greedy jaws
To swallow up Albinius presently?
What, shall I fly and hide my traitorous head,
From stout Alphonsus whom I so misus'd?
Or shall I yield?   Tush, yielding is in vain:
Nor can I fly, but he will follow me.
Then cast thyself down at his grace's feet,
Confess thy fault, and ready make thy breast
To entertain thy well-deservèd death.   [*Kneels.*

   Alphon. What news, my friend? why are you so blank,
That erst before did vaunt it to the skies?

   Albi. Pardon, dear lord! Albinius pardon craves
For this offence, which, by the heavens I vow,
Unwittingly I did unto your grace;
For had I known Alphonsus had been here,
Ere that my tongue had spoke so traitorously,
This hand should make my very soul to die.

   Alphon. Rise up, my friend, thy pardon soon is got:
                              [ALBINIUS *rises up.*
But, prithee, tell me what the cause might be,
That in such sort thou erst upbraided'st me?

   Albi. Most mighty prince, since first your father's sire
Did yield his ghost unto the Sisters Three,
And old Carinus forcèd was to fly
His native soil and royal diadem,
I, for because I seemèd to complain
Against their treason, shortly was forewarn'd
Ne'er more to haunt the bounds of Arragon,
On pain of death.   Then like a man forlorn,
I sought about to find some resting-place,
And at the length did hap upon this shore,
Where showing forth my cruel banishment,
By King Belinus I am succourèd.

[1] Here and on p. 59 used in the sense of "neglect" or "refrain from."

But now, my lord, to answer your demand :
It happens so, that the usurping king
Of Arragon makes war upon this land
For certain tribute which he claimeth here ;
Wherefore Belinus sent me round about
His country for to gather up [his] men
For to withstand this most injurious foe ;
Which being done, returning with the king,
Despitefully I did so taunt your grace,
Imagining you had some soldier been,
The which, for fear, had sneakèd from the camp.

Alphon. Enough, Albinius, I do know thy mind :
But may it be that these thy happy news
Should be of truth, or have you forgèd them ?

Albi. The gods forbid that e'er Albinius' tongue
Should once be found to forge a feignèd tale,
Especially unto his sovereign lord :
But if Alphonsus think that I do feign,
Stay here a while, and you shall plainly see
My words be true, whenas you do perceive
Our royal army march before your face ;
The which, if't please my noble lord to stay,
I'll hasten on with all the speed I may.

Alphon. Make haste, Albinius, if you love my life ;
But yet beware, whenas your army comes,
You do not make as though you do me know,
For I a while a soldier base will be,
Until I find time more convenient
To show, Albinius, what is mine intent.

Albi. Whate'er Alphonsus fittest doth esteem,
Albinius for his profit best will deem.   [*Exit.*

Alphon. Now do I see both gods and fortune too
Do join their powers to raise Alphonsus' fame ;
For in this broil I do not greatly doubt
But that I shall my cousin's courage tame.

But see whereas Belinus' army comes,
And he himself, unless I guess awry:
Whoe'er it be, I do not pass [1] a pin;
Alphonsus means his soldier for to be.

[*He stands aside.* [2]

SCENE II.—*The Camp of* BELINUS.

Enter BELINUS, ALBINIUS, FABIUS, *marching with their*
    Soldiers; *they make a stand.* ALPHONSUS *discovered*
    at one side.

Beli. Thus far, my lords, we trainèd have our camp
For to encounter haughty Arragon,
Who with a mighty power of straggling mates
Hath traitorously assailèd this our land,
And burning towns, and sacking cities fair,
Doth play the devil wheresome'er he comes.
Now, as we are informèd of our scouts,
He marcheth on unto our chiefest seat,
Naples, I mean, that city of renown,
For to begirt it with his bands about,
And so at length, the which high Jove forbid,
To sack the same, as erst he other did.
If which should hap, Belinus were undone,
His country spoil'd, and all his subjects slain:
Wherefore your sovereign thinketh it most meet
For to prevent the fury of the foe,
And Naples succour, that distressèd town,
By entering in, ere Arragon doth come,
With all our men, which will sufficient be
For to withstand their cruel battery.

[1] Care.   [2] It should be remembered that the scene divisions
are not made by Greene.

Albi. The silly serpent, found by country swain,
And cut in pieces by his furious blows,
Yet if her head do 'scape away untouch'd,
As many write, it very strangely goes
To fetch an herb, with which in little time
Her batter'd corpse again she doth conjoin:
But if by chance the ploughman's sturdy staff
Do hap to hit upon the serpent's head,
And bruise the same, though all the rest be sound
Yet doth the silly serpent lie for dead,
Nor can the rest of all her body serve
To find a salve which may her life preserve.
Even so, my lord, if Naples once be lost,
Which is the head of all your grace's land,
Easy it were for the malicious foe
To get the other cities in their hand:
But if from them that Naples town be free,
I do not doubt but safe the rest shall be;
And therefore, mighty king, I think it best,
To succour Naples rather than the rest.

Beli. 'Tis bravely spoken; by my crown I swear,
I like thy counsel, and will follow it.
But hark, Albinius, dost thou know the man,
That doth so closely overthwart us stand?

                              [*Pointing towards* ALPHONSUS.

Albi. Not I, my lord, nor never saw him yet.

Beli. Then, prithee, go and ask him presently,
What countryman he is, and why he comes
Into this place? perhaps he is some one,
That is sent hither as a secret spy
To hear and see in secret what we do.

                [ALBINIUS *and* FABIUS *go toward* ALPHONSUS.

Albi. My friend, what art thou, that so like a spy
Dost sneak about Belinus' royal camp?

Alphon. I am a man.

B

Fabi. A man! we know the same:
But prithee, tell me, and set scoffing by,
What countryman thou art, and why you come,
That we may soon resolve the king thereof?

Alphon. Why, say I am a soldier.

Fabi. Of whose band?

Alphon. Of his that will most wages to me give.

Fabi. But will you be
Content to serve Belinus in his wars?

Alphon. Ay, if he'll reward me as I do deserve,
And grant whate'er I win, it shall be mine
Incontinent.

Albi. Believe me, sir, your service costly is:
But stay a while, and I will bring you word
What King Belinus says unto the same.

                    [*Goes towards* BELINUS.

Beli. What news, Albinius? who is that we see?

Albi. It is, my lord, a soldier that you see,
Who fain would serve your grace in these your wars,
But that, I fear, his service is too dear.

Beli. Too dear, why so? what doth the soldier crave?

Albi. He craves, my lord, all things that with his sword
He doth obtain, whatever that they be.

Beli. [*To* ALPHONSUS]. Content, my friend; if thou
        wilt succour me,
Whate'er you get, that challenge as thine own;
Belinus gives it frankly unto thee,
Although it be the crown of Arragon.
Come on, therefore, and let us hie apace
To Naples town, whereas by this, I know,
Our foes have pitch'd their tents against our walls.

Alphon. March on, my lord, for I will follow you;
And do not doubt but, ere the time be long,
I shall obtain the crown of Arragon.

                            [*Exeunt.*

ACT THE SECOND

PRÓLOGUE

Enter BELINUS, ALBINIUS, FABIUS *and* ALPHONSUS
with Soldiers; *alarum, and then enter* VENUS.

ENUS. Thus from the pit of pilgrim's
      poverty
    Alphonsus 'gins by step and step to
      climb
    Unto the top of friendly Fortune's
      wheel:
    From banish'd state, as you have
      plainly seen,
He is transform'd into a soldier's life,
And marcheth in the ensign of the king
Of worthy Naples, which Belinus hight;
Not for because that he doth love him so,
But that he may revenge him on his foe.
Now on the top of lusty barbèd steed
He mounted is, in glittering armour clad,

Seeking about the troops of Arragon,
For to encounter with his traitorous niece.[1]
How he doth speed, and what doth him befall,
Mark this our act, for it doth show it all.

                                [*Exeunt.*

SCENE I.—*A Battle-field.*

Alarum. Enter FLAMINIUS *on one side,* ALPHONSUS *on the other. They fight;* ALPHONSUS *kills* FLAMINIUS.

Alphon. Go pack thou hence unto the Stygian lake,
And make report unto thy traitorous sire
How well thou hast enjoy'd the diadem
Which he by treason set upon thy head ;
And if he ask thee who did send thee down,
Alphonsus say, who now must wear thy crown.

Alarum. Enter LÆLIUS.

Læli. Traitor, how dar'st thou look me in the face,
Whose mighty king thou traitorously hast slain ?
What, dost thou think Flaminius hath no friends
For to revenge his death on thee again?
Yes, be you sure that, ere you 'scape from hence,
Thy gasping ghost shall bear him company,
Or else myself, fighting for his defence,
Will be content by those thy hands to die.
   Alphon. Lælius, few words would better thee become,
Especially as now the case doth stand ;
And didst thou know whom thou dost threaten thus,

---

[1] In Elizabethan writers this term is used in both genders to express general relationship. Here it means cousin.

We should you have more calmer out of hand :
For, Lælius, know that I Alphonsus am,
The son and heir to old Carinus, whom
The traitorous father of Flaminius
Did secretly bereave his diadem.
But see the just revenge of mighty Jove !
The father dead, the son is likewise slain
By that man's hand who they did count as dead,
Yet doth survive to wear the diadem,
When they themselves accompany the ghosts
Which wander round about the Stygian fields.
                              [LÆLIUS *gazes upon* ALPHONSUS.
Muse not hereat, for it is true I say ;
I am Alphonsus, whom thou hast misus'd.
   Læli. The man whose death I did so oft lament ?
                                             [*Kneels.*
Then pardon me for these uncourteous words,
The which I in my rage did utter forth,
Prick'd by the duty of a loyal mind ;
Pardon, Alphonsus, this my first offence,
And let me die if e'er I flight [1] again.
   Alphon. Lælius, I fain would pardon this offence,
And eke accept thee to my grace again,
But that I fear that, when I stand in need
And want your help, you will your lord betray :
How say you, Lælius, may I trust to thee ?
   Læli. Ay, noble lord, by all the gods I vow ;
For first shall heavens want stars, and foaming seas
Want watery drops, before I'll traitor be
Unto Alphonsus, whom I honour so.
   Alphon. Well then, arise ; and for because I'll try
                              [LÆLIUS *arises.*
If that thy words and deeds be both alike,
Go haste and fetch the youths of Arragon,

            [1] Strive, contend.

Which now I hear have turn'd their heels and fled:
Tell them your chance, and bring them back again
Into this wood; where in ambushment lie,
Until I send or come for you myself.

   Læli. I will, my lord.
                             [*Exit.*

   Alphon. Full little think Belinus and his peers
What thoughts Alphonsus casteth in his mind;
For if they did, they would not greatly haste
To pay the same the which they promis'd me.

Enter BELINUS, ALBINIUS, FABIUS, *with their* Soldiers,
             marching.

   Beli. Like simple sheep, when shepherd absent is
Far from his flock, assail'd by greedy wolves,
Do scattering fly about, some here, some there,
To keep their bodies from their ravening jaws,
So do the fearful youths of Arragon
Run round about the green and pleasant plains,
And hide their heads from Neapolitans;
Such terror have their strong and sturdy blows
Struck to their hearts, as for a world of gold,
I warrant you, they will not come again.
But, noble lords, where is the knight become
Which made the blood be-sprinkle all the place
Whereas he did encounter with his foe?
My friend, Albinius, know you where he is?

   Albi. Not I, my lord, for since in thickest ranks
I saw him chase Flaminius at the heels,
I never yet could set mine eyes on him.
But see, my lord, whereas the warrior stands,
Or else my sight doth fail me at this time.
      [*Spies out* ALPHONSUS, *and shows him to* BELINUS.

Beli. 'Tis he indeed, who, as I do suppose,
Hath slain the king, or else some other lord,
For well I wot, a carcass I do see
Hard at his feet lie struggling on the ground.
Come on, Albinius, we will try the truth.

　　　　[BELINUS *and* ALBINIUS *go towards* ALPHONSUS.
Hail to the noble victor of our foes !

Alphon. Thanks, mighty prince; but yet I seek not
　　this :
It is not words must recompense my pain,
But deeds.   When first I took up arms for you,
Your promise was, whate'er my sword did win
In fight, as his Alphonsus should it crave.
See, then, where lies thy foe Flaminius,
Whose crown my sword hath conquer'd in the field ;
Therefore, Belinus, make no long delay,
But that discharge you promis'd for to pay.

Beli. Will nothing else satisfy thy conquering mind
Besides the crown ? Well, since thou hast it won,
Thou shalt it have, though far against my will.

　　[ALPHONSUS *sits in the chair;* BELINUS *takes the*
　　　　crown off FLAMINIUS' *head, and puts it on that*
　　　　of ALPHONSUS.
Here doth Belinus crown thee with his hand
The King of Arragon.
　　　　　　　　　　[*Trumpets and drums sound within.*
　　　　　　　　What, are you pleas'd?

Alphon. Not so, Belinus, till you promise me
All things belonging to the royal crown
Of Arragon, and make your lordings swear
For to defend me to their utmost power
Against all men that shall gainsay the same.

Beli. Mark, what belongèd erst unto the crown
Of Arragon, that challenge as thine own ;
Belinus gives it frankly unto thee.

And swears by all the powers of glittering skies
To do my best for to maintain the same,
So that it be not prejudicial
Unto mine honour, or my country-soil.

Albi. And by the sacred seat of mighty Jove
Albinius swears that first he'll die the death,
Before he'll see Alphonsus suffer wrong.

Fabi. What erst Albinius vow'd we jointly vow

Alphon. Thanks, mighty lords ; but yet I greatly fear
That very few will keep the oaths they swear.
But, what, Belinus, why stand you so long,
And cease from offering homage unto me?
What, know you not that I thy sovereign am,
Crownèd by thee and all thy other lords,
And now confirmèd by your solemn oaths?
Feed not thyself with fond persuasions,
But presently come yield thy crown to me,
And do me homage, or by heavens I swear
I'll force thee to it maugre all thy train.

Beli. How now, base brat! what, are thy wits thine
   own,
That thou dar'st thus abraid ¹ me in my land?
'Tis best for thee these speeches to recall,
Or else, by Jove, I'll make thee to repent
That ere thou sett'st thy foot in Naples' soil.

Alphon. "Base brat," say'st thou? as good a man as
   thou
But say I came but of a base descent,
My deeds shall make my glory for to shine
As clear as Luna in a winter's night.
But for because thou bragg'st so of thy birth,
I'll see how it shall profit thee anon.

Fabi. Alphonsus, cease from these thy threatening
   words,

¹ Upbraid.

And lay aside this thy presumptuous mind,
Or else be sure thou shalt the same repent.

   Alphon. How now, sir boy! will you be prattling
     too?
'Tis best for thee to hold thy tattling tongue,
Unless I send some one to scourge thy breech.
Why, then, I see 'tis time to look about
When every boy Alphonsus dares control:
But be they sure, ere Phoebus' golden beams
Have compassèd the circle of the sky,
I'll clog their tongues, since nothing else will serve
To keep those vilde [1] and threatening speeches in.
Farewell, Belinus, look thou to thyself:
Alphonsus means to have thy crown ere night.

                                [Exit.

   Beli. What, is he gone? the devil break his neck,
The fiends of hell torment his traitorous corpse!
Is this the quittance of Belinus' grace,
Which he did show unto that thankless wretch,
That runagate, that rakehell, yea, that thief?
For, well I wot, he hath robb'd me of a crown.
If ever he had sprung from gentle blood,
He would not thus misuse his favourer.

   Albi. "That runagate, that rakehell, yea, that thief"!
Stay there, sir king, your mouth runs over-much;
It ill becomes the subject for to use
Such traitorous terms against his sovereign.
Know thou, Belinus, that Carinus' son
Is neither rakehell, [no], nor runagate.
But be thou sure that, ere the darksome night
Do drive god Phœbus to his Thetis' lap,
Both thou, and all the rest of this thy train,
Shall well repent the words which you have sain.

   Beli. What, traitorous villain, dost thou threaten me?—

                [1] Same as "vile."

Lay hold on him, and see he do not 'scape :
I'll teach the slave to know to whom he speaks.

   Albi. To thee I speak, and to thy fellows all ;
And though as now you have me in your power,
Yet doubt I not but that in little space
These eyes shall see thy treason recompens'd,
And then I mean to vaunt our victory.

   Beli. Nay, proud Albinius, never build on that ;
For though the gods do chance for to appoint
Alphonsus victor of Belinus' land,
Yet shalt thou never live to see that day ;—
And therefore, Fabius, stand not lingering,
But presently slash off his traitorous head.

   Albi. Slash of his head ! as though Albinius' head
Were then so easy to be slashèd off :
In faith, sir, no ; when you are gone and dead,
I hope to flourish like the pleasant spring.

   Beli. Why, how now, Fabius ! what, do you stand in
      doubt
To do the deed ? what fear you ? who dares seek
For to revenge his death on thee again,
Since that Belinus did command it so ?
Or are you wax'd so dainty, that you dare
Not use your sword for staining of your hands ?
If it be so, then let me see thy sword,
And I will be his butcher for this time.

           [FABIUS *gives* BELINUS *his sword drawn*
Now, Sir Albinius, are you of the mind
That erst you were ? what, do you look to see,
And triumph in, Belinus' overthrow ?
I hope the very sight of this my blade
Hath chang'd your mind into another tune.

   Albi. Not so, Belinus, I am constant still ;
My mind is like to the asbeston-stone,
Which, if it once be heat in flames of fire,

Denieth to becomen cold again :

Even so am I, and shall be till I die.

And though I should see Atropos appear,

With knife in hand, to slit my thread in twain,

Yet ne'er Albinius should persuaded be

But that Belinus he should vanquish'd see.

　Beli. Nay, then, Albinius, since that words are vain

For to persuade you from this heresy,

This sword shall sure put you out of doubt.

　　[BELINUS *offers to strike off* ALBINIUS' *head : alarum ;*
　　　　enter ALPHONSUS *and his* Men ; BELINUS *and*
　　　　FABIUS *fly, followed by* ALPHONSUS *and*
　　　　ALBINIUS.

SCENE II.—*Another Part of the Field.*

Enter LÆLIUS, MILES, *and* Servants.

　Læli. My noble lords of Arragon, I know

You wonder much what might the occasion be

That Lælius, which erst did fly the field,

Doth egg you forwards now unto the wars ;

But when you hear my reason, out of doubt

You'll be content with this my rash attempt.

When first our king, Flaminius I do mean,

Did set upon the Neapolitans,

The worst of you did know and plainly see

How far they were unable to withstand

The mighty forces of our royal camp,

Until such time as froward fates we thought,—

Although the fates ordain'd it for our gain,—

Did send a stranger stout, whose sturdy blows

And force alone did cause our overthrow.
But to our purpose : this same martial knight
Did hap to hit upon Flaminius,
And lent our king then such a friendly blow
As that his gasping ghost to Limbo went.
Which when I saw, and seeking to revenge,
My noble lords, did hap on such a prize
As never king nor keisar got the like.

Miles. Lælius, of force we must confess to thee,
We wonder'd all whenas you did persuade
Us to return unto the wars again ;
But since our marvel is increasèd much
By these your words, which sound of happiness :
Therefore, good Lælius, make no tarrying,
But soon unfold thy happy chance to us.

Læli. Then, friends and fellow soldiers, hark to me ;
When Lælius thought for to revenge his king
On that same knight, instead of mortal foe,
I found him for to be our chiefest friend.

Miles. Our chiefest friend ! I hardly can believe
That he, which made such bloody massacres
Of stout Italians, can in any point
Bear friendship to the country or the king.

Læli. As for your king, Miles, I hold with you,
He bare no friendship to Flaminius,
But hated him as bloody Atropos ;
But for your country, Lælius doth avow
He loves as well as any other land,
Yea, sure, he loves it best of all the world.
And, for because you shall not think that I
Do say the same without a reason why,
Know that the knight Alphonsus hath to name,
Both son and heir to old Carinus, whom
Flaminius' sire bereavèd of his crown ;
Who did not seek the ruin of our host

For any envy he did bear to us,
But to revenge him on his mortal foe ;
Which by the help of high celestial Jove
He hath achiev'd with honour in the field.
   Miles. Alphonsus, man ! I'll ne'er persuaded be
That e'er Alphonsus may survive again,
Who with Carinus, many years ago,
Was said to wander in the Stygian fields.
   Læli. Truth, noble Miles : these mine ears have heard,
For certainty reported unto me,
That old Carinus, with his peerless son,
Had felt the sharpness of the Sisters' shears ;
And had I not of late Alphonsus seen
In good estate, though all the world should say
He is alive, I would not credit them.
But, fellow soldiers, wend you back with me,
And let us lurk within the secret shade
Which he himself appointed unto us ;
And if you find my words to be untroth,
Then let me die to recompense the wrong.

   Alarum : re-enter ALBINIUS *with his sword drawn.*

   Albi. Lælius, make haste : soldiers of Arragon,
Set lingering by, and come and help your king,
I mean Alphonsus, who, whilst that he did
Pursue Belinus at the very heels,
Was suddenly environèd about
With all the troops of mighty Milan-land.
   Miles. What news is this ! and is it very so ?
Is our Alphonsus yet in human state,
Whom all the world did judge for to be dead ?
Yet can I scarce give credit to the same :
Give credit ! yes, and since the Milan Duke
Hath broke his league of friendship, be he sure,

Ere Cynthia, the shining lamp of night,
Doth scale the heavens with her hornèd head,
Both he and his shall very plainly see
The league is burst that causèd long the glee.

  Læli. And could the traitor harbour in his breast
Such mortal treason 'gainst his sovereign,
As when he should with fire and sword defend
Him from his foes, he seeks his overthrow?
March on, my friends: I ne'er shall joy at all,
Until I see that bloody traitor's fall.

                                    [*Exeunt.*

    Alarum: BELINUS *flies, followed by* LÆLIUS;
        FABIUS *flies, followed by* ALBINIUS; *the* DUKE
        OF MILAN *flies, followed by* MILES.

ACT THE THIRD

PROLOGUE

Alarum. Enter VENUS.

VENUS. No sooner did Alphonsus with
    his troop
    Set on the soldiers of Belinus' band,
    But that the fury of his sturdy blows
    Did strike such terror to their daunted
      minds
    That glad was he which could escape
    away,
With life and limb, forth of that bloody fray.
Belinus flies unto the Turkish soil,
To crave the aid of Amurack their king;
Unto the which he willingly did consent,
And sends Belinus, with two other kings,
To know God Mahomet's pleasure in the same.
Meantime the empress by Medea's help
Did use such charms that Amurack did see,
In soundest sleep, what afterward should hap.
How Amurack did recompense her pain,
With mickle more, this act shall show you plain.
                          [Exit.

SCENE I.—*Camp of* ALPHONSUS, *near Naples.*

Enter one, carrying two crowns upon a crest; ALPHONSUS,
ALBINIUS, LÆLIUS, *and* MILES, *with their* Soldiers.

Alphon. Welcome, brave youths of Arragon, to me,
Yea, welcome, Miles, Lælius, and the rest,
Whose prowess alone hath been the only cause
That we, like victors, have subdu'd our foes.
Lord, what a pleasure was it to my mind,
To see Belinus, which not long before
Did with his threatenings terrify the gods,
Now scud apace from warlike Lælius' blows.
The Duke of Milan, he increas'd our sport,
Who doubting that his force was over-weak
For to withstand, Miles, thy sturdy arm,
Did give more credence to his frisking skips
Than to the sharpness of his cutting blade.
What Fabius did to pleasure us withal,
Albinius knows as well as I myself;
For, well I wot, if that thy tirèd steed
Had been as fresh and swift in foot as his,
He should have felt, yea, known for certainty,
To check Alphonsus did deserve to die.
Briefly, my friends and fellow-peers in arms,
The worst of you deserve such mickle praise,
As that my tongue denies for to set forth
The demi-parcel of your valiant deeds;
So that, perforce, I must by duty be
Bound to you all for this your courtesy.
    Miles. Not so, my lord; for if our willing arms
Have pleasur'd you so much as you do say,
We have done naught but that becometh us,
For to defend our mighty sovereign.

As for my part, I count my labour small,
Yea, though it had been twice as much again,
Since that Alphonsus doth accept thereof.
  Alphon. Thanks, worthy Miles : lest all the world
Should count Alphonsus thankless for to be,
Lælius, sit down, and, Miles, sit by him,
And that receive the which your swords have won.
                          [LÆLIUS *and* MILES *sit down.*
First, for because thou, Lælius, in these broils,
By martial might, didst proud Belinus chase
From troop to troop, from side to side about,
And never ceas'd from this thy swift pursuit
Until thou hadst obtain'd his royal crown,
Therefore, I say, I'll do thee naught but right,
And give thee that which thou well hast won.
                          [*Sets the crown on his head.*
Here doth Alphonsus crown thee, Lælius, King
Of Naples' town, with all dominions
That erst belongèd to our traitorous foe,
That proud Belinus, in his regiment.
                          [*Trumpets and drums sounded.*
Miles, thy share the Milan Dukedom is,
For, well I wot, thy sword deserv'd no less ;
                          [*Sets the crown on his head.*
The which Alphonsus frankly giveth thee,
In presence of his warlike men-at-arms ;
And if that any stomach [1] this my deed,
Alphonsus can revenge thy wrong with speed.
                          [*Trumpets and drums sounded.*
Now to Albinius, which in all my toils
I have both faithful, yea, and friendly, found :
Since that the gods and friendly fates assign
This present time to me to recompense

                          [1] Resent.

C

The sundry pleasures thou hast done to me,
Sit down by them, and on thy faithful head
        [Takes the crown from his own head.
Receive the crown of peerless Arragon.

   Albi. Pardon, dear lord, Albinius at this time,
It ill becomes me for to wear a crown
Whenas my lord is destitute himself.
Why, high Alphonsus, if I should receive
This crown of you, the which high Jove forbid,
Where would yourself obtain a diadem?
Naples is gone, Milan possessèd is,
And naught is left for you but Arragon.

   Alphon. And naught is left for me but Arragon!
Yes, surely, yes, my fates have so decreed,
That Arragon should be too base a thing
For to obtain Alphonsus for her king.
What, hear you not how that our scatter'd foes,
Belinus, Fabius, and the Milan duke,
Are fled for succour to the Turkish court?
And think you not that Amurack their king,
Will, with the mightiest power of all his land,
Seek to revenge Belinus' overthrow?
Then doubt I not but, ere these broils do end,
Alphonsus shall possess the diadem
That Amurack now wears upon his head.
Sit down therefóre, and that receive of me
The which the fates appointed unto thee.

   Albi. Thou King of Heaven, which by Thy power
      divine
Dost see the secrets of each liver's heart,
Bear record now with what unwilling mind
I do receive the crown of Arragon.

   [ALBINIUS *sits down by* LÆLIUS *and* MILES;
     ALPHONSUS *sets the crown on his head.*
   Alphon. Arise, Albinius, King of Arragon,

Crownèd by me, who, till my gasping ghost
Do part asunder from my breathless corpse,
Will be thy shield against all men alive
That for thy kingdom any way do strive.

       [*Trumpets and drums sounded.*

Now since we have, in such an happy hour,
Confirm'd three kings, come, let us march with speed
Into the city, for to celebrate
With mirth and joy this blissful festival.

           [*Exeunt.*

SCENE II.—*Palace of* AMURACK *at Constantinople.*

Enter AMURACK, BELINUS, FABIUS, ARCASTUS,
 CLARAMONT *and* BAJAZET, *with their train.*

 Amu. Welcome, Belinus, to thy cousin's court,
Whose late arrival in such posting pace
Doth bring both joy and sorrow to us all;
Sorrow, because the fates have been so false
To let Alphonsus drive thee from thy land,
And joy, since that now mighty Mahomet
Hath given me cause to recompense at full
The sundry pleasures I receiv'd of thee.
Therefore, Belinus, do but ask and have,
For Amurack doth grant whate'er you crave.
 Beli. Thou second sun, which with thy glimpsing beams
Dost clarify each corner of the earth,
Belinus comes not, as erst Midas did
To mighty Bacchus, to desire of him
That whatsoe'er at any time he touch'd
Might turnèd be to gold incontinent.

Nor do I come as Jupiter did erst
Unto the palace of Amphitryon,
For any fond or foul concupiscence
Which I do bear to Alcumena's hue.
But as poor Saturn, forc'd by mighty Jove
To fly his country, banish'd and forlorn,
Did crave the aid of Troos, King of Troy,
So comes Belinus to high Amurack;
And if he can but once your aid obtain,
He turns with speed to Naples back again.

   Amu. My aid, Belinus! do you doubt of that?
If all the men-at-arms of Africa,
Of Asia likewise, will sufficient be
To press the pomp of that usurping mate,
Assure thyself, thy kingdom shall be thine,
If Mahomet say ay unto the same;
For were I sure to vanquish all our foes,
And find such spoils in ransacking their tents
As never any keisar did obtain,
Yet would I not set foot forth of this land,
If Mahomet our journey did withstand.

   Beli. Nor would Belinus, for King Crœsus' trash,
Wish Amurack to displease the gods,
In pleasuring me in such a trifling toy.
Then, mighty monarch, if it be thy will,
Get their consents, and then the act fulfil.

   Amu. You counsel well; therefore, Belinus, haste,
And, Claramont, go bear him company,
With King Arcastus, to the city walls:
Then bend with speed unto the darksome grove,
Where Mahomet, this many a hundred year,
Hath prophesied unto our ancestors.
Tell to his priests that Amurack, your king,
Is now selecting all his men-at-arms
To set upon that proud Alphonsus' troop:

(The cause you know, and can inform them well,
That makes me take these bloody broils in hand?)
And say that I desire their sacred god,
That Mahomet which ruleth all the skies,
To send me word, and that most speedily,
Which of us shall obtain the victory.

                          [*Exeunt all except* BAJAZET *and* AMURACK.

You, Bajazet, go post away apace
To Syria, Scythia, and Albania,
To Babylon, with Mesopotamia,
Asia, Armenia, and all other lands
Which owe their homage to high Amurack:
Charge all their kings with expedition
To gather up the chiefest men-at-arms
Which now remain in their dominions,
And on the twentieth day of the same month
To come and wait on Amurack their king,
At his chief city Constantinople.
Tell them, moreover, that, whoso doth fail,
Naught else but death from prison shall him bail.

                          [*Exit* BAJAZET. *Music within.*

What heavenly music soundeth in my ear?
Peace, Amurack, and hearken to the same.

           [*Hearkening to the music* AMURACK *falls asleep.*

        Enter MEDEA, FAUSTA *and* IPHIGENA.

Medea. Now have our charms fulfill'd our minds full
    well;
High Amurack is lullèd fast asleep,
And doubt I not but, ere he wakes again,
You shall perceive Medea did not gibe
Whenas she put this practice in your mind.
Sit, worthy Fausta, at thy spouse his feet.
Iphigena, sit thou on the other side:

       [FAUSTA *and* IPHIGENA *sit down at* AMURACK'S *feet.*

Whate'er you see, be not aghast thereat,
But bear in mind what Amurack doth chat.
　　　　　　[*Does ceremonies belonging to conjuring.*
Thou, which wert wont, in Agamemnon's days,
To utter forth Apollo's oracles
At sacred Delphos, Calchas I do mean,
I charge thee come ; all lingering set aside,
Unless the penance you thereof abide :
I cónjure thee by Pluto's loathsome lake,
By all the hags which harbour in the same,
By stinking Styx, and filthy Phlegethon,
To come with speed, and truly to fulfil
That which Medea to thee straight shall will !
　　　　　[CALCHAS *rises up,*[1] *in a white surplice*
　　　　　　　and a cardinal's mitre.
　　Calc. Thou wretched witch, when wilt thou make an
　　　　end
Of troubling us with these thy cursèd charms ?
What mean'st thou thus to call me from my grave ?
Shall ne'er my ghost obtain his quiet rest ?
　　Medea, Yes, Calchas, yes, your rest doth now
　　　　approach ;
Medea means to trouble thee no more,
Whenas thou hast fulfill'd her mind this once.
Go, get thee hence to Pluto back again,
And there inquire of the Destinies
How Amurack shall speed in these his wars :
Peruse their books, and mark what is decreed
By Jove himself, and all his fellow-gods ;
And when thou know'st the certainty thereof,
By fleshless visions show it presently
To Amurack, in pain of penalty.

　　[1] In the use of the descending throne, trap-door, property tomb,
balcony and curtain, as well as in plastic use of scenes (pp. 42 and
248) Greene illustrates the best practice of his time.

Calc. Forc'd by thy charm, though with unwilling
    mind,
I haste to hell, the certainty to find.
                        [*Sinks down where he came up.*
Medea. Now, peerless princess, I must needs be
    gone;
My hasty business calls me from this place.
There resteth naught, but that you bear in mind
What Amurack, in this his fit, doth say;
For mark, what dreaming, madam, he doth prate,
Assure yourself that that shall be his fate.
Fausta. Though very loth to let thee so depart,
Farewell, Medea, easer of my heart.   [*Exit* MEDEA.
                        [*Instruments sound within.*
Amu. [*speaking in a dream*]. What, Amurack, dost
    thou begin to nod?
Is this the care that thou hast of thy wars?
As when thou shouldst be prancing of thy steed,
To egg thy soldiers forward in thy wars,
Thou sittest moping by the fire-side?
See where thy viceroys grovel on the ground;
Look where Belinus breatheth forth his ghost;
Behold by millions how thy men do fall
Before Alphonsus, like to silly sheep;
And canst thou stand still lazing in this sort?
No, proud Alphonsus, Amurack doth fly
To quail thy courage, and that speedily.
                        [*Instruments sound within.*
And dost thou think, thou proud injurious god,
Mahound I mean, since thy vain prophecies
Led Amurack into this doleful case,
To have his princely feet in irons clapt,
Which erst the proudest kings were forc'd to kiss,
That thou shalt 'scape unpunish'd for the same?
No, no, as soon as by the help of Jove

I 'scape this bondage, down go all thy groves,
Thy altars tumble round about the streets,
And whereas erst we sacrific'd to thee,
Now all the Turks thy mortal foes shall be.

       [*Instruments sound within.*

Behold the gem and jewel of mine age,
See where she comes, whose heavenly majesty
Doth far surpass the brave and gorgeous pace
Which Cytherea, daughter unto Jove,
Did put in ure whenas she had obtain'd
The golden apple at the shepherd's hands.
See, worthy Fausta, where Alphonsus stands,
Whose valiant courage could not daunted be
With all the men-at-arms of Africa ;
See now he stands as one that lately saw
Medusa's head, or Gorgon's hoary hue.

       [*Instruments sound within.*

And can it be that it may happen so ?
Can fortune prove so friendly unto me
As that Alphonsus loves Iphigena ?
The match is made, the wedding is decreed :
Sound trumpets, ho ! strike drums for mirth and
  glee !
And three times welcome son-in-law to me !

  Fausta [*rising up in a fury and waking* AMURACK].

  Fie, Amurack, what wicked words be these ?
How canst thou look thy Fausta in her face,
Whom thou hast wrongèd in this shameful sort ?
And are the vows so solemnly you sware
Unto Belinus, my most friendly niece,
Now wash'd so clearly from thy traitorous heart ?
Is all the rancour which you erst did bear
Unto Alphonsus worn so out of mind
As, where thou shouldst pursue him to death,
You seek to give our daughter to his hands ?

The gods forbid that such a heinous deed
With my consent should ever be decreed :
And rather than thou shouldst it bring to pass,
If all the army of Amazones
Will be sufficient to withhold the same,
Assure thyself that Fausta means to fight
'Gainst Amurack for to maintain the right.

 Iphi. Yea, mother, say,—which Mahomet forbid,—
That in this conflict you should have the foil,
Ere that Alphonsus should be call'd my spouse,
This heart, this hand, yea, and this blade, should be
A readier means to finish that decree.

 Amu. [*rising in a rage*]. What threatening words
  thus thunder in mine ears ?
Or who are they, amongst the mortal troops,
That dare presume to use such threats to me ?
The proudest kings and keisars of the land
Are glad to feed me in my fantasy ;
And shall I suffer, then, each prattling dame
For to upbraid me in this spiteful sort ?
No, by the heavens, first will I lose my crown,
My wife, my children, yea, my life and all.
And therefore, Fausta, thou which Amurack
Did tender erst, as the apple of mine eye,
Avoid my court, and, if thou lov'st thy life,
Approach not nigh unto my regiment.
As for this carping girl, Iphigena,
Take her with thee to bear thee company,
And in my land I rede[1] be seen no more,
For if you do, you both shall die therefóre. [*Exit.*

 Fausta. Nay, then, I see 'tis time to look about,
Delay is dangerous, and procureth harm :
The wanton colt is tamèd in his youth ;
Wounds must be cur'd when they be fresh and green ;

    [1] Advise.

And pleurisies, when they begin to breed,
With little care are driven away with speed.
Had Fausta then, when Amurack begun
With spiteful speeches to control and check,
Sought to prevent it by her martial force,
This banishment had never hapt to me.
But the echinus, fearing to be gor'd,
Doth keep her younglings in her paunch so long,
Till, when their pricks be waxen long and sharp,
They put their dam at length to double pain:
And I, because I loath'd the broils of Mars,
Bridled my thoughts, and pressèd down my rage;
In recompense of which my good intent
I have receiv'd this woful banishment.
Woful, said I? nay, happy I did mean,
If that be happy which doth set one free;
For by this means I do not doubt ere long
But Fausta shall with ease revenge her wrong.
Come, daughter, come: my mind foretelleth me
That Amurack shall soon requited be.

SCENE III.—*A Grove.*

Fausta *and* Iphigena *discovered; enter* Medea,
meeting them.[1]

Medea. Fausta, what means this sudden flight of yours?
Why do you leave your husband's princely court,
And all alone pass through these thickest groves,

---

[1] Here clearly a change of scene is supposed. Between the two scenes the Quarto has only this stage direction to Fausta: "Make as though you were a-going out, *Medea* meet her and say." As some time is supposed to elapse between the two scenes they are here differentiated. Such is not the case in *George-a-Greene* (p. 439) in which the action goes right on in two settings.

More fit to harbour brutish savage beasts
Than to receive so high a queen as you?
Although your credit would not stay your steps
From bending them into these darkish dens,
Yet should the danger, which is imminent
To every one which passeth by these paths,
Keep you at home with fair Iphigena.
What foolish toy hath tickled you to this?
I greatly fear some hap hath hit amiss.

 Fausta. No toy, Medea, tickled Fausta's head,
Nor foolish fancy led me to these groves,
But earnest business eggs my trembling steps
To pass all dangers, whatsoe'er they be.
I banish'd am, Medea, I, which erst
Was empress over all the triple world,
Am banish'd now from palace and from pomp.
But if the gods be favourers to me,
Ere twenty days I will revengèd be.

 Medea. I thought as much, when first from thickest
  leaves
I saw you trudging in such posting pace.
But to the purpose: what may be the cause
Of this strange and sudden banishment?

 Fausta. The cause, ask you? A simple cause, God
  wot;
'Twas neither treason, nor yet felony,
But for because I blam'd his foolishness.

 Medea. I hear you say so, but I greatly fear,
Ere that your tale be brought unto an end,
You'll prove yourself the author of the same.
But pray, be brief; what folly did your spouse?
And how will you revenge your wrong on him?

 Fausta. What folly, quoth you? Such as never yet
Was heard or seen, since Phœbus first 'gan shine.
You know how he was gathering in all haste
His men-at-arms, to set upon the troop

Of proud Alphonsus; yea, you well do know
How you and I did do the best we could
To make him show us in his drowsy dream
What afterward should happen in his wars.
Much talk he had, which now I have forgot;
But at the length this surely was decreed,
How that Alphonsus and Iphigena
Should be conjoin'd in Juno's sacred rites.
Which when I heard, as one that did despise
That such a traitor should be son to me,
I did rebuke my husband Amurack:
And since my words could take no better place,
My sword with help of all Amazones
Shall make him soon repent his foolishness.

Medea. This is the cause, then, of your banishment?
And now you go unto Amazone
To gather all your maidens in array,
To set upon the mighty Amurack?
O foolish queen, what meant you by this talk?
Those prattling speeches have undone you all.
Do you disdain to have that mighty prince,
I mean Alphonsus, counted for your son?
I tell you, Fausta, he is born to be
The ruler of a mighty monarchy.
I must confess the powers of Amurack
Be great; his confines stretch both far and near;
Yet are they not the third part of the lands
Which shall be rulèd by Alphonsus' hands:
And yet you dain to call him son-in-law.
But when you see his sharp and cutting sword
Piercing the heart of this your gallant girl,
You'll curse the hour wherein you did denay
To join Alphonsus with Iphigena.

Fausta. The gods forbid that e'er it happen so!
Medea. Nay, never pray, for it must happen so.

Fausta. And is there, then, no remedy for it?

Medea. No, none but one, and that you have for-
    sworn.

Fausta. As though an oath can bridle so my mind
As that I dare not break a thousand oaths
For to eschew the danger imminent!
Speak, good Medea, tell that way to me,
And I will do it, whatsoe'er it be.

Medea. Then, as already you have well decreed,
Pack to your country, and in readiness
Select the army of Amazones:
When you have done, march with your female troop
To Naples' town, to succour Amurack:
And so, by marriage of Iphigena,
You soon shall drive the danger clean away.

Iphi. So shall we soon eschew Charybdis' lake,
And headlong fall to Scylla's greedy gulf.
I vow'd before, and now do vow again,
Before I wed Alphonsus, I'll be slain.

Medea. In vain it is to strive against the stream ;
Fates must be follow'd, and the gods' decree
Must needs take place in every kind of cause.
Therefore, fair maid, bridle these brutish thoughts,
And learn to follow what the fates assign.
When Saturn heard that Jupiter his son
Should drive him headlong from his heavenly seat
Down to the bottom of the dark Avern,
He did command his mother presently
To do to death the young and guiltless child :
But what of that? the mother loath'd in heart
For to commit so vile a massacre ;
Yea, Jove did live, and, as the fates did say,
From heavenly seat drave Saturn clean away.
What did avail the castle all of steel,
The which Acrisius caused to be made

To keep his daughter Danaë clogg'd in?
She was with child for all her castle's force;
And by that child Acrisius, her sire,
Was after slain, so did the fates require.
A thousand examples I could bring hereof;
But marble stones need no colouring,
And that which every one doth know for truth
Needs no examples to confirm the same.
That which the fates appoint must happen so,
Though heavenly Jove and all the gods say no.

    Fausta. Iphigena, she sayeth naught but truth;
Fates must be follow'd in their just decrees;
And therefore, setting all delays aside,
Come, let us wend unto Amazone,
And gather up our forces out of hand.

    Iphi. Since Fausta wills and fates do so command,
Iphigena will never it withstand.

                   [Exeunt.

ACT THE FOURTH

PROLOGUE

Enter VENUS.

HUS have you seen how Amurack
  himself,
  Fausta his wife, and every other king
  Which hold their sceptres at the Turk
   his hands,
  Are now in arms, intending to destroy,
  And bring to naught, the Prince of
Arragon.
Charms have been us'd by wise Medea's art,
To know before what afterward shall hap;
And King Belinus, with high Claramont,
Join'd to Arcastus, which with princely pomp
Doth rule and govern all the warlike Moors,
Are sent as legates to God Mahomet,
To know his counsel in these high affairs.
Mahound, provok'd by Amurack's discourse,
Which, as you heard, he in his dream did use,
Denies to play the prophet any more;
But, by the long entreaty of his priests,

47

He prophesies in such a crafty sort
As that the hearers needs must laugh for sport.
Yet poor Belinus, with his fellow kings,
Did give such credence to that forgèd tale
As that they lost their dearest lives thereby,
And Amurack became a prisoner
Unto Alphonsus, as straight shall appear.

                                         [Exit.

SCENE I.—*The Temple of* MAHOMET.

*Let there be a Brazen Head set in the middle of the place
    behind the stage, out of the which cast flames of fire ;
    drums rumble within.   Enter two* Priests.

  First Pr. My fellow priest of Mahound's holy house,
What can you judge of these strange miracles
Which daily happen in this sacred seat?
                         [Drums rumble within.
Hark, what a rumbling rattleth in our ears !
   [Flames of fire are cast forth of the Brazen Head.
See flakes of fire proceeding from the mouth
Of Mahomet, that god of peerless power !
Nor can I tell, with all the wit I have,
What Mahomet, by these his signs, doth crave.
  Sec. Fr. Thrice ten times Phœbus with his golden
    beams
Hath compassèd the circle of the sky,
Thrice ten times Ceres hath her workmen hir'd,
And fill'd her barns with fruitful crops of corn,
Since first in priesthood I did lead my life ;
Yet in this time I never heard before
Such fearful sounds, nor saw such wondrous sights ;

Nor can I tell, with all the wit I have,
What Mahomet, by these his signs, doth crave.

   Mahomet [*speaking out of the Brazen Head*]. You
      cannot tell, nor will you seek to know:
O perverse priests, how careless are you wax'd,
As when my foes approach unto my gates,
You stand still talking of " I cannot tell ! "
Go pack you hence, and meet the Turkish kings
Which now are drawing to my temple ward ;
Tell them from me, God Mahomet is dispos'd
To prophesy no more to Amurack,
Since that his tongue is waxen now so free,
As that it needs must chat and rail at me.

                        [*The* Priests *kneel.*

   First Pr. O Mahomet, if all the solemn prayers
Which from our childhood we have offer'd thee,
Can make thee call this sentence back again,
Bring not thy priests into this dangerous state !
For when the Turk doth hear of this repulse,
We shall be sure to die the death therefóre.

   Mahomet [*speaking out of the Brazen Head*]. Thou
      sayest truth ; go call the princes in :
I'll prophesy unto them for this once ;
But in such wise as they shall neither boast,
Nor you be hurt in any kind of wise.

   Enter BELINUS, CLARAMONT, ARCASTUS *and* FABIUS,
      conducted by the Priests.

   First Pr. You kings of Turkey, Mahomet our god,
By sacred science having notice that
You were sent legates from high Amurack
Unto this place, commanded us, his priests,
That we should cause you make as mickle speed
As well you might, to hear for certainty
Of that shall happen to your king and ye.

   D

Beli. For that intent we came into this place ;
And sithens that the mighty Mahomet
Is now at leisure for to tell the same,
Let us make haste and take time while we may,
For mickle danger happeneth through delay.

 Sec. Pr. Truth, worthy king, and therefore you
   yourself,
With your companions, kneel before this place,
And listen well what Mahomet doth say.

 Beli. As you do will, we jointly will obey.
     [*All kneel down before the Brazen Head.*

Mahomet [*speaking out of the Brazen Head*]. Princes
  of Turkey, and ambassadors
Of Amurack to mighty Mahomet,
I needs must muse that you, which erst have been
The readiest soldiers of the triple world,
Are now become so slack in your affairs
As, when you should with bloody blade in hand
Be hacking helms in thickest of your foes,
You stand still loitering in the Turkish soil.
What, know you not how that it is decreed
By all the gods, and chiefly by myself,
That you with triumph should all crownèd be ?
Make haste, kings, lest when the fates do see
How carelessly you do neglect their words,
They call a council, and force Mahomet
Against his will some other things to set.
Send Fabius back to Amurack again,
To haste him forwards in his enterprise ;
And march you on, with all the troops you have,
To Naples ward, to conquer Arragon,
For if you stay, both you and all your men
Must needs be sent down straight to Limbo-den.

 Sec. Pr. Muse not, brave kings, at Mahomet's discourse,

For mark what he forth of that mouth doth say,
Assure yourselves it needs must happen so.
Therefore make haste, go mount you on your steeds,
And set upon Alphonsus presently :
So shall you reap great honour for your pain,
And 'scape the scourge which else the fates ordain.

                                        [All rise up.

   Beli. Then, proud Alphonsus, look thou to thy
     crown :
Belinus comes, in glittering armour clad,
All ready prest [1] for to revenge the wrong
Which, not long since, you offer'd unto him ;
And since we have God Mahound on our side,
The victory must needs to us betide.
   Cla. Worthy Belinus, set such threats away,
And let us haste as fast as horse can trot
To set upon presumptuous Arragon.—
You, Fabius, haste, as Mahound did command,
To Amurack with all the speed you may.
   Fabi. With willing mind I hasten on my way.

                                          [Exit.

   Beli. And thinking long till that we be in fight,
Belinus hastes to quail Alphonsus' might.   *[Exeunt.*

SCENE II.—*Near Naples.*

        Alarum awhile. Enter CARINUS.

   Cari. No sooner had God Phœbus' brightsome beams
Begun to dive within the western seas,
And darksome Nox had spread about the earth
Her blackish mantle, but a drowsy sleep
Did take possession of Carinus' sense,

                [1] Prepared.

And Morpheus show'd me strange disguisèd shapes.
Methought I saw Alphonsus, my dear son,
Plac'd in a throne all glittering clear with gold,
Bedeck'd with diamonds, pearls, and precious stones,
Which shin'd so clear, and glitter'd all so bright,
Hyperion's coach that well be term'd it might.
Above his head a canopy was set,
Not deck'd with plumes, as other princes use,
But all beset with heads of conquer'd kings,
Enstall'd with crowns, which made a gallant show,
And struck a terror to the viewers' hearts.
Under his feet lay grovelling on the ground
Thousands of princes, which he in his wars
By martial might did conquer and bring low:
Some lay as dead as either stock or stone,
Some other tumbled, wounded to the death;
But most of them, as to their sovereign king,
Did offer duly homage unto him.
As thus I stood beholding of this pomp,
Methought Alphonsus did espy me out,
And, at a trice, he leaving throne alone,
Came to embrace me in his blessèd arms.
Then noise of drums and sound of trumpets shrill
Did wake Carinus from this pleasant dream.
Something, I know, is now foreshown by this:
The gods forfend that aught should hap amiss!
                                [CARINUS *walks up and down.*

            Enter the DUKE OF MILAN *in pilgrim's apparel.*

Duke of M. This is the chance of fickle Fortune's
            wheel;
A prince at morn, a pilgrim ere't be night:
I, which erewhile did dain for to possess

The proudest palace of the western world,
Would now be glad a cottage for to find,
To hide my head ; so Fortune hath assign'd.
Thrice Hesperus with pomp and peerless pride
Hath heav'd his head forth of the eastern seas,
Thrice Cynthia, with Phœbus' borrow'd beams,
Hath shown her beauty through the darkish clouds,
Since that I, wretched duke, have tasted aught,
Or drunk a drop of any kind of drink.
Instead of beds set forth with ebony,
The greenish grass hath been my resting-place,
And for my pillow stuff'd with down,
The hardish hillocks have suffic'd my turn.
Thus I, which erst had all things at my will,
A life more hard then death do follow still.
   Cari. [*aside*].   Methinks I hear, not very far from
      hence,
Some woful wight lamenting his mischance :
I'll go and see if that I can espy
Him where he sits, or overhear his talk.
   Duke of M. O Milan, Milan, little dost thou think,
How that thy duke is now in such distress !
For if thou didst, I soon should be releas'd
Forth of this greedy gulf of misery.
   Cari. [*aside*]. The Milan Duke ! I thought as much
      before,
When first I glanc'd mine eyes upon his face.
This is the man which was the only cause
That I was forc'd to fly from Arragon.
High Jove be prais'd which hath allotted me
So fit a time to quite that injury.—
Pilgrim, God speed.
   Duke of M. Welcome, grave sir, to me.
   Cari. Methought as now I heard you for to speak
Of Milan-land : pray, do you know the same ?

Duke of M. Ay, aged father, I have cause to know
Both Milan-land and all the parts thereof.

Cari. Why, then, I doubt not but you can resolve
Me of a question that I shall demand.

Duke of M. Ay, that I can, whatever that it be.

Cari. Then, to be brief: not twenty winters past,
When these my limbs, which wither'd are with age,
Were in the prime and spring of all their youth,
I, still desirous, as young gallants be,
To see the fashions of Arabia,
My native soil, and in this pilgrim's weed,
Began to travel through unkennèd lands.
Much ground I pass'd, and many soils I saw;
But when my feet in Milan-land I set,
Such sumptuous triumphs daily there I saw
As never in my life I found the like.
I pray, good sir, what might the occasion be,
That made the Milans make such mirth and glee?

    Duke of M. This solemn joy whereof you now do
        speak,
Was not solémnisèd, my friend, in vain;
For at that time there came into the land
The happiest tidings that they e'er did hear;
For news was brought upon that solemn day
Unto our court, that Ferdinandus proud
Was slain himself, Carinus and his son
Was banish'd both for e'er from Arragon;
And for these happy news that joy was made.

    Cari. But what, I pray, did afterward become
Of old Carinus with his banish'd son?
What, hear you nothing of them all this while?

    Duke of M. Yes, too-too much, the Milan Duke may
        say.
Alphonsus first by secret means did get
To be a soldier in Belinus' wars,

Wherein he did behave himself so well
As that he got the crown of Arragon ;
Which being got, he dispossess'd also
The King Belinus which had foster'd him.
As for Carinus he is dead and gone :
I would his son were his companion.

   Cari. A blister build upon that traitor's tongue !
But, for thy friendship which thou showed'st me,
Take that of me, I frankly give it thee.
               [Stabs the DUKE OF MILAN, *who dies.*
Now will I haste to Naples with all speed,
To see if Fortune will so favour me
To view Alphonsus in his happy state.   *[Exit.*

SCENE III.—*Camp of* AMURACK, *near Naples.*

Enter AMURACK, CROCON, FAUSTUS *and* FABIUS,
   with the Provost *and* Turkish Janissaries.

   Amu. Fabius, come hither : what is that thou sayest ?
What did God Mahound prophesy to us ?
Why do our viceroys wend unto the wars
Before their king had notice of the same ?
What, do they think to play bob-fool with me ?
Or are they wax'd so frolic now of late,
Since that they had the leading of our bands,
As that they think that mighty Amurack
Dares do no other than to soothe them up ?
Why speak'st thou not ? what fond or frantic fit
Did make those careless kings to venture it ?
   Fabi. Pardon, dear lord ; no frantic fit at all,
No frolic vein, nor no presumptuous mind,
Did make your viceroys take these wars in hand :

But forc'd they were by Mahound's prophecy
To do the same, or else resolve to die.

    Amu. So, sir, I hear you, but can scarce believe
That Mahomet would charge them go before,
Against Alphonsus with so small a troop,
Whose number far exceeds King Xerxes' troop.

    Fabi. Yes, noble lord, and more than that, he said
That, ere that you, with these your warlike men,
Should come to bring your succour to the field,
Belinus, Claramont, and Arcastus too
Should all be crown'd with crowns of beaten gold,
And borne with triumph round about their tents.

    Amu. With triumph, man! did Mahound tell them so?—
Provost, go carry Fabius presently
Unto the Marshalsea; [1] there let him rest,
Clapt sure and safe in fetters all of steel,
Till Amurack discharge him from the same;
For be he sure, unless it happen so
As he did say Mahound did prophesy,
By this my hand forthwith the slave shall die.

    [*They lay hold of* FABIUS, *and make as though to
carry him out.*

                     Enter a Messenger.

    Mess. Stay, Provost, stay, let Fabius alone:
More fitteth now that every lusty lad
Be buckling on his helmet, than to stand
In carrying soldiers to the Marshalsea.

    Amu. Why, what art thou, that darest once presume
For to gainsay that Amurack did bid?

    Mess. I am, my lord, the wretched'st man alive,
Born underneath the planet of mishap;

---

  [1] Among Elizabethan playwrights the use of the names of
English institutions, prisons, cathedrals and inns, in foreign scene-
settings, is quite common.

Erewhile, a soldier of Belinus' band,
But now—
  Amu.   What now?
  Mess.   The mirror of mishap;
Whose captain's slain, and all his army dead,
Only excepted me, unhappy wretch.
  Amu. What news is this! and is Belinus slain?
Is this the crown which Mahomet did say
He should with triumph wear upon his head?
Is this the honour which that cursèd god
Did prophesy should happen to them all?
O Dædalus, an wert thou now alive,
To fasten wings upon high Amurack,
Mahound should know, and that for certainty,
That Turkish kings can brook no injury!
  Fabi. Tush, tush, my lord; I wonder what you mean,
Thus to exclaim against high Mahomet:
I'll lay my life that, ere this day be past,
You shall perceive his tidings all be waste.
  Amu. We shall perceive, accursèd Fabius!
Suffice it not that thou hast been the man
That first didst beat those baubles in my brain,
But that, to help me forward in my grief,
Thou seekest to confirm so foul a lie?
Go, get thee hence, and tell thy traitorous king
What gift you had, which did such tidings bring.—
                  [Stabs FABIUS, *who dies.*
And now, my lords, since nothing else will serve,
Buckle your helms, clap on your steelèd coats,
Mount on your steeds, take lances in your hands;
For Amurack doth mean this very day
Proud Mahomet with weapons to assay.
  Mess. Mercy, high monarch! it is no time now
To spend the day in such vain threatenings
Against our god, the mighty Mahomet:

More fitteth thee to place thy men-at-arms
In battle 'ray, for to withstand your foes,
Which now are drawing towards you with speed.
                    [*Drums sounded within.*
Hark, how their drums with dub-a-dub do come!
To arms, high lord, and set these trifles by,
That you may set upon them valiantly.
    Amu. And do they come? you kings of Turkey-[land],
Now is the time in which your warlike arms
Must raise your names above the starry skies.
Call to your mind your predecessors' acts,
Whose martial might, this many a hundred year,
Did keep those fearful dogs in dread and awe,
And let your weapons show Alphonsus plain,
That though that they be clappèd up in clay,
Yet there be branches sprung up from those trees,
In Turkish land, which brook no injuries.
Besides the same, remember with yourselves
What foes we have; not mighty Tamburlaine,
Nor soldiers trainèd up amongst the wars,
But fearful boors, pick'd from their rural flock,
Which, till this time, were wholly ignorant
What weapons meant, or bloody Mars doth crave.
More would I say, but horses that be free
Do need no spurs, and soldiers which themselves
Long and desire to buckle with the foe,
Do need no words to egg them to the same.

Enter ALPHONSUS, *with a canopy carried over him by*
    three Lords, *having over each corner a king's head*
    crowned; with him ALBINIUS, LÆLIUS *and* MILES
    with crowns on their heads, and their Soldiers.

Besides the same, behold whereas our foes
Are marching towards us most speedily.

Courage, my lords, ours is the victory.

Alphon. Thou pagan dog, how dar'st thou be so bold
To set thy foot within Alphonsus' land?
What, art thou come to view thy wretched kings,
Whose traitorous heads bedeck my tent so well?
Or else, thou hearing that on top thereof
There is a place left vacant, art thou come
To have thy head possess the highest seat?
If it be so, lie down, and this my sword
Shall presently that honour thee afford.
If not, pack hence, or by the heavens I vow,
Both thou and thine shall very soon perceive
That he that seeks to move my patience
Must yield his life to me for recompense.

Amu. Why, proud Alphonsus, think'st thou Amurack,
Whose mighty force doth terrify the gods,
Can e'er be found to turn his heels, and fly
Away for fear from such a boy as thou?
No, no, although that Mars this mickle while
Hath fortified thy weak and feeble arm,
And Fortune oft hath view'd with friendly face
Thy armies marching victors from the field,
Yet at the presence of high Amurack
Fortune shall change, and Mars, that god of might,
Shall succour me, and leave Alphonsus quite.

Alphon. Pagan, I say thou greatly art deceiv'd:
I clap up Fortune in a cage of gold,
To make her turn her wheel as I think best;
And as for Mars whom you do say will change,
He moping sits behind the kitchen-door,
Prest at command of every scullion's mouth,
Who dares not stir, nor once to move a whit,
For fear Alphonsus then should stomach it.

Amu. Blasp-hém-ous dog, I wonder that the earth
Doth cease from renting underneath thy feet,

To swallow up that canker'd corpse of thine.
I muse that Jove can bridle so his ire
As, when he hears his brother so misus'd,
He can refrain from sending thunderbolts
By thick and threefold, to revenge his wrong.
Mars fight for me, and fortune be my guide!
And I'll be victor, whatsome'er betide.

Albi. Pray loud enough,[1] lest that you pray in vain:
Perhaps God Mars and Fortune are asleep.

Amu. An Mars lies slumbering on his downy bed,
Yet do not think but that the power we have,
Without the help of those celestial gods,
Will be sufficient, yea, with small ado,
Alphonsus' straggling army to subdue.

Læli. You had need as then to call for Mahomet,
With hellish hags to perform the same.

Faustus. High Amurack, I wonder what you mean,
That, when you may, with little toil or none,
Compel these dogs to keep their tongues in peace,
You let them stand still barking in this sort:
Believe me, sovereign, I do blush to see
These beggar's brats to chat so frolicly.

Alphon. How now, sir boy! Let Amurack himself,
Or any he, the proudest of you all,
But offer once for to unsheath his sword,
If that he dares, for all the power you have.

Amu. What, dar'st thou us? myself will venture it.—
To arms, my mate!

> [AMURACK *draws his sword;* ALPHONSUS *and all
> the other* Kings *draw theirs. Alarum;*
> AMURACK *and his company fly, followed by*
> ALPHONSUS *and his company.*

---

[1] Evidently a reminiscence of 1 Kings xviii. 27.

ACT THE FIFTH

PROLOGUE

Alarum.   Enter VENUS.

VENUS. Fierce is the fight, and bloody
　　　is the broil.
　　　No sooner had the roaring cannon shot
　　　Spit forth the venom of their firèd
　　　　paunch,
　　　And with their pellets sent such troops
　　　　of souls
Down to the bottom of the dark Avern,
As that it cover'd all the Stygian fields;
But, on a sudden, all the men-at-arms,
Which mounted were on lusty coursers' backs,
Did rush together with so great a noise
As that I thought the giants one time more
Did scale the heavens, as erst they did before.
Long time dame Fortune temper'd so her wheel
As that there was no vantage to be seen
On any side, but equal was the gain;
But at the length, so God and Fates decreed,
Alphonsus was the victor of the field,
And Amurack became his prisoner;
Who so remain'd, until his daughter came,
And by her marrying did his pardon frame.　　*[Exit.*

SCENE I.—*A Battle-field near Naples.*

Alarum: AMURACK *flies, followed by* ALPHONSUS, *who takes him prisoner and carries him in. Alarum: as* CROCON *and* FAUSTUS *are flying, enter* FAUSTA *and* IPHIGENA, *with their army, meeting them.*

Fausta. You Turkish kings, what sudden flight is
    this?
What mean the men, which for their valiant prowess
Were dreaded erst clean through the triple world,
Thus cowardly to turn their backs and fly?
What froward fortune happen'd on your side?
I hope your king in safety doth abide?
    Cro. Ay, noble madam, Amurack doth live,
And long I hope he shall enjoy his life;
But yet I fear, unless more succour come,
We shall both lose our king and sovereign.
    Fausta. How so, King Crocon? dost thou speak in
    jest,
To prove if Fausta would lament his death?
Or else hath anything hapt him amiss?
Speak quickly, Crocon, what the cause might be,
That thou dost utter forth these words to me.
    Cro. Then, worthy Fausta, know that Amurack
Our mighty king, and your approvèd spouse,
Prick'd with desire of everlasting fame,
As he was pressing in the thickest ranks
Of Arragonians, was, with much ado,
At length took prisoner by Alphonsus' hands.
So that, unless you succour soon do bring,
You lose your spouse, and we shall want our king.
    Iphi. O hapless hap, O dire and cruel fate!
What injury hath Amurack, my sire,
Done to the gods, which now I know are wroth,

Although unjustly and without a cause?
For well I wot, not any other king,
Which now doth live, or since the world begun
Did sway a sceptre, had a greater care
To please the gods than mighty Amurack:
And for to quite our father's great good-will,
Seek they thus basely all his fame to spill?
 Fausta. Iphigena, leave off these woful tunes:
It is not words can cure and ease this wound,
But warlike swords; not tears, but sturdy spears.
High Amurack is prisoner to our foes:
What then? Think you that our Amazones,
Join'd with the forces of the Turkish troop,
Are not sufficient for to set him free?
Yes, daughter, yes, I mean not for to sleep
Until he is free, or we him company keep.—
March on, my mates.   [*Exeunt.*

SCENE II.—*Another Part of the Field.*

Alarum : enter ALPHONSUS *in flight, followed by*
IPHIGENA.

 Iphi. How now, Alphonsus! you which never yet
Could meet your equal in the feats of arms,
How haps it now that in such sudden sort
You fly the presence of a silly maid?
What, have you found mine arm of such a force
As that you think your body over-weak
For to withstand the fury of my blows?
Or do you else disdain to fight with me,
For staining of your high nobility?

Alphon. No, dainty dame, I would not have thee
  think
That ever thou or any other wight
Shall live to see Alphonsus fly the field
From any king or keisar whosome'er :
First will I die in thickest of my foe,
Before I will disbase mine honour so.
Nor do I scorn, thou goddess, for to stain
My prowess with thee, although it be a shame
For knights to combat with the female sect :[1]
But love, sweet mouse, hath so benumbed my wit,
That, though I would, I must refrain.from it.

 Iphi. I thought as much when first I came to
  wars ;
Your noble acts were fitter to be writ
Within the tables of Dame Venus' son,
Than in God Mars his warlike registers :
Whenas your lords are hacking helms abroad,
And make their spears to shiver in the air,
Your mind is busied in fond Cupid's toys.
Come on, i' faith, I'll teach you for to know
We came to fight, and not to love, I trow.

 Alphon. Nay, virgin, stay. An if thou wilt vouch-
  safe
To entertain Alphonsus' simple suit,
Thou shalt ere long be monarch of the world :
All christen'd kings, with all your pagan dogs,
Shall bend their knees unto Iphigena ;
The Indian soil shall be thine at command,
Where every step thou settest on the ground
Shall be received on the golden mines ;
Rich Pactolus,[2] that river of account,
Which doth descend from top of Tmolus Mount,

<hr>

   [1] Sex.   [2] A false quantity.

Shall be thine own, and all the world beside,
If you will grant to be Alphonsus' bride.

   Iphi. Alphonsus' bride! nay, villain, do not think
That fame or riches can so rule my thoughts.
As for to make me love and fancy him
Whom I do hate, and in such sort despise,
As, if my death could bring to pass his bane,
I would not long from Pluto's port remain.

   Alphon. Nay, then, proud peacock, since thou art
     so stout
As that entreaty will not move thy mind,
For to consent to be my wedded spouse,
Thou shalt, in spite of gods and fortune too,
Serve high Alphonsus as a concubine.

   Iphi. I'll rather die than ever that shall hap.

   Alphon. And thou shalt die unless it come to pass.
   [ALPHONSUS *and* IPHIGENA *fight.* IPHIGENA *flies*
        followed by ALPHONSUS.

SCENE III.—*The Camp of* ALPHONSUS.

Alarum. Enter ALPHONSUS *with his rapier,* ALBINIUS,
   LÆLIUS, MILES, *with their* Soldiers; AMURACK,
   FAUSTA, IPHIGENA, CROCON, *and* FAUSTUS, *all
   bound, with their hands behind them.* AMURACK
   looks angrily on FAUSTA.

Enter MEDEA.

   Medea. Nay, Amurack, this is no time to jar:
Although thy wife did, in her frantic mood,
Use speeches which might better have been spar'd,
Yet do thou not judge this same time to be
A season to requite that injury.

E

More fitteth thee, with all the wit thou hast,
To call to mind which way thou mayst release
Thyself, thy wife, and fair Iphigena,
Forth of the power of stout Alphonsus' hands;
For, well I wot, since first you breathèd breath,
You never were so nigh the snares of death.
Now, Amurack, your high and kingly seat,
Your royal sceptre, and your stately crown,
Your mighty country, and your men-at-arms,
Be conquer'd all, and can no succour bring.
Put, then, no trust in these same paltry toys,
But call to mind that thou a prisoner art,
Clapt up in chains, whose life and death depend
Upon the hands of thy most mortal foe.
Then take thou heed, that whatsome'er he say,
Thou dost not once presume for to gainsay.

Amu. Away, you fool! think you your cursèd charms
Can bridle so the mind of Amurack
As that he will stand crouching to his foe?
No, no, be sure that, if that beggar's brat
Do dare but once to contrary my will,
I'll make him soon in heart for to repent
That e'er such words 'gainst Amurack he spent.

Medea. Then, since thou dost disdain my good advice,
Look to thyself, and if you fare amiss,
Remember that Medea counsel gave,
Which might you safe from all those perils save.
But, Fausta, you, as well you have begun,
Beware you follow still your friend's advice:
If that Alphonsus do desire of thee
To have your daughter for his wedded spouse,
Beware you do not once the same gainsay,
Unless with death he do your rashness pay.

Fausta. No, worthy wight; first Fausta means to die
Before Alphonsus she will contrary.

Medea. Why, then, farewell.—But you, Iphigena,
Beware you do not over-squeamish wax,
Whenas your mother giveth her consent.
   Iphi. The gods forbid that e'er I should gainsay
That which Medea bids me to obey.   · [*Exit* MEDEA.

ALPHONSUS, *who all this while has been talking to*
   ALBINIUS, *rises up out of his chair.*

   Alphon. Now, Amurack, the proud blasphémous
      dogs,
For so you term'd us, which did brawl and rail
Against God Mars, and fickle Fortune's wheel,
Have got the goal for all your solemn prayers.
Yourself are prisoner, which as then did think
That all the forces of the triple world
Were insufficient to fulfil the same.
How like you this?   Is Fortune of such might,
Or hath God Mars such force or power divine,
As that he can, with all the power he hath,
Set thee and thine forth of Alphonsus' hands?
I do not think but that your hope's so small
As that you would with very willing mind
Yield for my spouse the fair Iphigena,
On that condition, that without delay
Fausta and you may scot-free 'scape away.
   Amu. What, think'st thou, villain, that high Amurack
Bears such a mind as, for the fear of death,
He'll yield his daughter, yea, his only joy,
Into the hands of such a dunghill-knight?
No, traitor, no ; for [though] as now I lie
Clapt up in irons and with bolts of steel,
Yet do there lurk within the Turkish soil
Such troops of soldiers that, with small ado,
They'll set me scot-free from your men and you.

Alphon. "Villain," say'st thou? "traitor" and "dung-
 hill-knight"?
Now, by the heavens, since that thou dost deny
For to fulfil that which in gentle wise
Alphonsus craves, both thou and all thy train
Shall with your lives requite that injury.——
Albinius, lay hold of Amurack,
And carry him to prison presently,
There to remain until I do return
Into my tent; for by high Jove I vow,
Unless he wax more calmer out of hand,
His head amongst his fellow-kings shall stand.

Amu. No, villain, think not that the fear of death
Shall make me calmer while I draw my breath.
      [Exit in custody of ALBINIUS.

Alphon. Now, Lælius, take you Iphigena,
Her mother Fausta, with these other kings,
And put them into prisons severally;
For Amurack's stout stomach shall undo
Both he himself and all his other crew.

Fausta [*kneeling*]. O sacred prince, if that the salt
 brine tears,
Distilling down poor Fausta's wither'd cheeks,
Can mollify the hardness of your heart,
Lessen this judgment, which thou in thy rage
Hast given on thy luckless prisoners.

Alphon. Woman, away! my word is gone and past;
Now, if I would, I cannot call it back.
You might have yielded at my first demand,
And then you needed not to fear this hap.——
        [FAUSTA *rises.*
Lælius make haste, and go thou presently
For to fulfil that I commanded thee.

Iphi. [*kneeling*]. Mighty Alphonsus, since my mother's
 suit

Is so rejected that in any case
You will not grant us pardon for her sake,
I now will try if that my woful prayers
May plead for pity at your grace's feet.
When first you did, amongst the thickest ranks,
All clad in glittering arms encounter me,
You know yourself what love you did protest
You then did bear unto Iphigena:
Then for that love, if any love you had,
Revoke this sentence, which is too-too bad.

 Alphon. No, damsel; he that will not when he may,
When he desires, shall surely purchase nay:
If that you had, when first I proffer made,
Yielded to me, mark, what I promis'd you
I would have done; but since you did deny,
Look for denial at Alphonsus' hands.

  [IPHIGENA *rises, and stands aside.* ALPHONSUS *talks*
   with ALBINIUS.

   Enter CARINUS *in pilgrim's apparel.*

 Cari. [*aside*]. O friendly Fortune, now thou show'st
  thy power
In raising up my son from banish'd state
Unto the top of thy most mighty wheel!
But, what be these which at his sacred feet
Do seem to plead for mercy at his hands?
I'll go and sift this matter to the full.

   [*Goes toward* ALPHONSUS, *and speaks to*
    one of his soldiers.

Sir knight, an may a pilgrim be so bold
To put your person to such mickle pain
For to inform me what great king is this,
And what these be, which, in such woful sort,
Do seem to seek for mercy at his hands?

Sol. Pilgrim, the king that sits on stately throne
Is call'd Alphonsus; and this matron hight
Fausta, the wife to Amurack the Turk;
That is their daughter, fair Iphigena;
Both which, together with the Turk himself,
He did take prisoners in a battle fought.

 Alphon. [*spying out* CARINUS]. And can the gods be
   found so kind to me
As that Carinus now I do espy?
'Tis he indeed.——Come on, Albinius:
The mighty conquest which I have achiev'd,
And victories the which I oft have won,
Bring not such pleasure to Alphonsus' heart
As now my father's presence doth impart.

  [ALPHONSUS *and* ALBINIUS *go toward* CARINUS:
   ALPHONSUS *stands looking on him.*

 Cari. What, ne'er a word, Alphonsus? art thou dumb?
Or doth my presence so perturb thy mind
That, for because I come in pilgrim's weed,
You think each word which you do spend to me
A great disgrace unto your name to be?
Why speak'st thou not? if that my place you crave,
I will be gone, and you my place shall have.

 Alphon. Nay, father, stay; the gods of heaven forbid
That e'er Alphonsus should desire or wish
To have his absence whom he doth account
To be the loadstar [1] of his life!
What, though the Fates and Fortune, both in one,
Have been content to call your loving son
From beggar's state unto this princely seat,
Should I therefore disdain my agèd sire?
No, first both crown and life I will detest,
Before such venom breed within my breast.

---

 [1] Dyce's query "loadstar" is adopted instead of "load-stone" of
the quarto.

What erst I did, the sudden joy I took
To see Carinus in such happy state,
Did make me do, and nothing else at all,
High Jove himself do I to witness call.

    Cari. These words are vain; I knew as much before.
But yet, Alphonsus, I must wonder needs
That you, whose years are prone to Cupid's snares,
Can suffer such a goddess as this dame
Thus for to shed such store of crystal tears.
Believe me, son, although my years be spent,
Her sighs and sobs in twain my heart do rent.

    Alphon. Like power, dear father, had she over me,
Until for love I looking to receive
Love back again, not only was denied,
But also taunted in most spiteful sort:
Which made me loathe that which I erst did love,
As she herself, with all her friends, shall prove.

    Cari. How now, Alphonsus! you which have so
        long
Been trainèd up in bloody broils of Mars,
What, know you not that castles are not won
At first assault, and women are not woo'd
When first their suitors proffer love to them?
As for my part, I should account that maid
A wanton wench, unconstant, lewd, and light,
That yields the field before she venture fight;
Especially unto her mortal foe,
As you were then unto Iphigena.
But, for because I see you fitter are
To enter lists and combat with your foes
Than court fair ladies in God Cupid's tents,
Carinus means your spokesman for to be,
And if that she consent, you shall agree.

    Alphon. What you command Alphonsus must not fly,
Though otherwise perhaps he would deny.

Cari. Then, dainty damsel, stint these trickling tears,
Cease sighs and sobs, yea, make a merry cheer:
Your pardon is already purchasèd,
So that you be not over-curious [1]
In granting to Alphonsus' just demand.

Iphi. Thanks, mighty prince; no curioser I'll be
Than doth become a maid of my degree.

Cari. The gods forbid that e'er Carinus' tongue
Should go about to make a maid consent
Unto the thing which modesty denies:
That which I ask is neither hurt to thee,
Danger to parents, nor disgrace to friends,
But good and honest, and will profit bring
To thee and those which lean unto that thing.
And that is this:—since first Alphonsus' eyes
Did hap to glance upon your heavenly hue,
And saw the rare perfection of the same,
He hath desirèd to become your spouse:
Now, if you will unto the same agree,
I dare assure you that you shall be free.

Iphi. Pardon, dear lord; the world goes very hard
When womenkind are forcèd for to woo.
If that your son had lovèd me so well,
Why did he not inform me of the same?

Cari. Why did he not! what, have you clean forgot
What ample proffers he did make to you,
When, hand to hand, he did encounter you?

Iphi. No, worthy sir, I have not it forgot;
But Cupid cannot enter in the breast
Where Mars before had took possession:
That was no time to talk of Venus' games
When all our fellows were press'd in the wars.

Cari. Well, let that pass: now canst thou be content
To love Alphonsus and become his spouse?

---

[1] Over-scrupulous.

Iphi. Ay, if the high Alphonsus could vouchsafe
To entertain me as his wedded spouse.

Alphon. If that he could ! what, dost thou doubt of
   that ?
Jason did jet [1] whenas he had obtain'd
The golden fleece by wise Medea's art ;
The Greeks rejoicèd when they had subdu'd
The famous bulwarks of most stately Troy ;
But all their mirth was nothing in respect
Of this my joy, since that I now have got
That which I long desirèd in my heart.

Cari. But what says Fausta to her daughter's
   choice ?

Fausta. Fausta doth say, the gods have been her
   friends,
To let her live to see Iphigena
Bestowèd so unto her heart's content.

Alphon. Thanks, mighty empress, for your gentleness ;
And, if Alphonsus can at any time
With all his power requite this courtesy,
You shall perceive how kindly he doth take
Your forwardness in this his happy chance.

Cari. Albinius, go call forth Amurack :
We'll see what he doth say unto this match.
                    [ALBINIUS *brings forth* AMURACK.
Most mighty Turk, I, with my warlike son
Alphonsus, loathing that so great a prince
As you should live in such unseemly sort,
Have sent for you to proffer life or death ;
Life, if you do consent to our demand,
And death, if that you dare gainsay the same.
Your wife, high Fausta, with Iphigena,
Have given consent that this my warlike son
Should have your daughter for his bedfellow :

                    [1] Exult, strut.

Now resteth naught but that you do agree,
And so to purchase sure tranquillity.

   Amu. [*aside*]. Now, Amurack, advise thee what thou
     say'st;
Bethink thee well what answer thou wilt make:
Thy life and death dependeth on thy words.
If thou deny to be Alphonsus' sire,
Death is thy share; but if that thou consent,
Thy life is sav'd.   Consent! nay, rather die:
Should I consent to give Iphigena
Into the hands of such a beggar's brat?
What, Amurack, thou dost deceive thyself;
Alphonsus is the son unto a king:
What then? then worthy of thy daughter's love.
She is agreed, and Fausta is content;
Then Amurack will not be discontent.

         [*Takes* Iphigena *by the hand, and gives*
               her to Alphonsus.

Here, brave Alphonsus, take thou at my hand
Iphigena, I give her unto thee;
And for her dowry, when her father dies,
Thou shalt possess the Turkish empery.
Take her, I say, and live King Nestor's years:
So would the Turk and all his noble peers.

   Alphon. Immortal thanks I give unto your grace.

   Cari. Now, worthy princes, since, by help of Jove,
On either side the wedding is decreed,
Come, let us wend to Naples speedily
For to solémnise it with mirth and glee.

   Amu. As you do will, we jointly do agree.

                  [*Exeunt omnes.*

EPILOGUE

Enter VENUS *with the* Muses.

VENUS. Now, worthy Muses, with un-
    willing mind
    Venus is forc'd to trudge to heaven
      again,
    For Jupiter, that god of peerless
      power,
    Proclaimèd hath a solemn festival
In honour of Dame Danaë's luckless death;
Unto the which, in pain of his displeasure,
He hath invited all the immortal gods
And goddesses, so that I must be there,
Unless I will his high displeasure bear.
You see Alphonsus hath, with much ado,
At length obtainèd fair Iphigena,
Of Amurack her father, for his wife;
Who now are going to the temple wards,
For to perform Dame Juno's sacred rites;
Where we will leave them, till the feast be done,
Which, in the heavens, by this time is begun.
Meantime, dear Muses, wander you not far
Forth of the path of high Parnassus' hill,

75

That, when I come to finish up his life,[1]
You may be ready for to succour me :
Adieu, dear dames ; farewell, Calliope.
   Cal. Adieu, you sacred goddess of the sky.
      [*Exit* VENUS ; *or, if you can conveniently, let a
        chair come down from the top of the stage, and
        draw her up.*
Well, loving sisters, since that she is gone,
Come, let us haste unto Parnassus' hill,
As Cytherea did lately will.
   Melpom. Then make you haste her mind for to fulfil.
      [*Exeunt omnes, playing on their instruments.*

[1] From this line we are made to conclude that Greene intended
to write a second part of *Alphonsus of Arragon.*

A LOOKING-GLASS
FOR LONDON AND
ENGLAND

A Looking-Glass for London and England is first mentioned in Henslowe's *Diary* as performed by Lord Strange's servants, 8th March 1592. At this time it was not a new play, and it is probable that it had first belonged to the Queen's players, to whom Greene was attached, and that it was by them turned over to Strange's company along with several other plays when the Queen's company went to the provinces in 1591. Henslowe records four performances of the play between 8th March and 7th June 1592. It was printed by Thomas Creede and entered on the *Stationers' Registers*, 5th March 1594, as written by Thomas Lodge and Robert Greene, gent. There is every indication that the play was successful. For two decades after its appearance Jonah and the Whale were popular in puppet-shows, and allusions in Beaumont and Fletcher, Ben Jonson and Cowley indicate the vogue of Nineveh on the puppet-stage. Five early quartos are mentioned by Collins: 1594, in the library of the Duke of Devonshire; 1598, in the Bodleian and the British Museum; 1602, in the British Museum; 1617, in the Bodleian and the British Museum; and apparently an actor's edition with many variants, formerly in Heber's Library, now in that of Mr Godfrey Locker Lampson, of the conjectural date 1598. The assignment of authorship of different portions of the play is difficult and not entirely profitable. Fleay assigns "most and best" of the play to Lodge. From their resemblance to the *Alarum Against Usurers* Collins assigns the following scenes to Lodge: I. 3; II. 3; V. 2. He also assigns the speeches of Oseas and Jonas, and the scenes displaying marine technology, to Lodge, viz.: III. 2; IV. 1. (*See* also Gayley, *Representative English Comedies*, p. 405, n.) This play was one of the earliest in which Greene had a hand and has been rightly called "a modernised morality."

DRAMATIS PERSONÆ

RASNI, King of Nineveh.
KING OF CILICIA.
KING OF CRETE.
KING OF PAPHLAGONIA.
THRASYBULUS, a young gentleman, reduced to poverty.
ALCON, a poor man.
RADAGON, } his sons.
CLESIPHON, }
Usurer.
Judge.
Lawyer.
Smith.
ADAM, his man.
First Ruffian.
Second Ruffian.
Governor of Joppa.
Master of a Ship.
First Searcher.
Second Searcher.
A Man in devil's attire.
Magi, Merchants, Sailors, Lords, Attendants, etc.
REMILIA, sister to RASNI.
ALVIDA, wife to the KING OF PAPHLAGONIA.
SAMIA, wife to ALCON.
Smith's Wife.
Ladies.
An Angel.
An Evil Angel.
OSEAS.
JONAS.

A LOOKING-GLASS FOR LONDON
AND ENGLAND

ACT THE FIRST

SCENE I.—*The Palace of* RASNI *in Nineveh.*

Enter RASNI, *with the* KINGS OF CILICIA, CRETE *and* PAPHLAGONIA, *from the overthrow of* JEROBOAM, *King of Jerusalem.*

RASNI. So pace ye on, triumphant warriors;
    Make Venus' leman,[1] arm'd in all his pomp,
    Bash at the brightness of your hardy looks;
    For you, the viceroys and the cavaliers,
That wait on Rasni's royal mightiness:—
Boast, petty kings, and glory in your fates,
That stars have made your fortunes climb so high,
To give attend on Rasni's excellence.
Am I not he that rules great Nineveh,

---

[1] Lover.

Rounded with Lycus' silver-flowing streams?
Whose city-large diametri contains,
Even three days' journey's length from wall to wall;
Two hundred gates carv'd out of burnish'd brass,
As glorious as the portal of the sun;
And, for to deck heaven's battlements with pride,
Six hundred towers that topless touch the clouds.
This city is the footstool of your king;
A hundred lords do honour at my feet;
My sceptre straineth both the parallels:
And now t' enlarge the highness of my power
I have made Judea's monarch flee the field,
And beat proud Jeroboam from his holds,
Winning from Cadiz to Samaria.
Great Jewry's God, that foil'd stout Benhadad,
Could not rebate [1] the strength that Rasni brought;
For be he God in heaven, yet, viceroys, know,
Rasni is god on earth, and none but he.
　　K. of Cil. If lovely shape, feature by nature's skill
Passing in beauty fair Endymion's,
That Luna wrapt within her snowy breasts,
Or that sweet boy that wrought bright Venus' bane,
Transform'd unto a purple hyacinth;
If beauty nonpareil in excellence,
May make a king match with the gods in gree, [2]
Rasni is god on earth, and none but he.
　　K. of Crete. If martial looks, wrapt in a cloud of
　　　　wars,
More fierce than Mavors lighteneth from his eyes,
Sparkling revenge and dire disparagement;
If doughty deeds more haught than any done,
Seal'd with the smile of fortune and of fate,
Matchless to manage lance and curtle-axe;
If such high actions, grac'd with victories,

　　　　[1] Beat back.　　　　　　[2] Degree.

May make a king match with the gods in gree,
Rasni is god on earth, and none but he.
  K. of Paph. If Pallas' wealth—
  Rasni. Viceroys, enough ; peace, Paphlagon, no more.
See where's my sister, fair Remilia,
Fairer than was the virgin Danaë
That waits on Venus with a golden show ;
She that hath stol'n the wealth of Rasni's looks,
And tied his thoughts within her lovely locks,
She that is lov'd, and love unto your king,
See where she comes to gratulate my fame.

  Enter RADAGON, *with* REMILIA, ALVIDA, *and* Ladies,
      bringing a globe seated on a ship.

  Remil. Victorious monarch, second unto Jove
Mars upon earth, and Neptune on the seas,
Whose frown strows all the ocean with a calm,
Whose smile draws Flora to display her pride,
Whose eye holds wanton Venus at a gaze,
Rasni, the regent of great Nineveh ;
For thou hast foil'd proud Jeroboam's force,
And, like the mustering breath of Æolus,
That overturns the pines of Lebanon,
Hast scatter'd Jewry and her upstart grooms,
Winning from Cadiz to Samaria ;—
Remilia greets thee with a kind salute,
And, for a present to thy mightiness,
Gives thee a globe folded within a ship,
As king on earth and lord of all the seas,
With such a welcome unto Nineveh
As may thy sister's humble love afford.
  Rasni. Sister ! the title fits not thy degree ;
A higher state of honour shall be thine.
The lovely trull that Mercury entrapp'd

Within the curious pleasure of his tongue,
And she that bash'd the sun-god with her eyes,
Fair Semele, the choice of Venus' maids,
Were not so beauteous as Remilia.
Then, sweeting, sister shall not serve the turn,
But Rasni's wife, his leman and his love:
Thou shalt, like Juno, wed thyself to Jove,
And fold me in the riches of thy fair;[1]
Remilia shall be Rasni's paramour.
For why,[2] if I be Mars for warlike deeds,
And thou bright Venus for thy clear aspect,
Why should not from our loins issue a son
That might be lord of royal sovereignty,
Of twenty worlds, if twenty worlds might be?
What say'st, Remilia, art thou Rasni's wife?

 Remil. My heart doth swell with favour of thy
   thoughts;
The love of Rasni maketh me as proud
As Juno when she wore heaven's diadem.
Thy sister born was for thy wife, my love:
Had I the riches nature locketh up
To deck her darling beauty when she smiles,
Rasni should prank him in the pride of all.

 Rasni. Remilia's love is far more richer[3] priz'd
Than Jeroboam's or the world's subdue.
Lordings, I'll have my wedding sumptuous,
Made glorious with the treasures of the world:
I'll fetch from Albia shelves of margarites,[4]
And strip the Indies of their diamonds,
And Tyre shall yield me tribute of her gold,
To make Remilia's wedding glorious.
I'll send for all the damosel queens that live
Within the reach of Rasni's government,

---

[1] Beauty [2] Because. [3] Dyce's suggestion is accepted instead of "either" of the quartos. [4] Pearls.

To wait as hand-maids on Remilia,
That her attendant train may pass the troop
That gloried Venus at her wedding-day.

K. of Crete. O my Lord, not sister to thy love!
'Tis incest and too foul a fact for kings;
Nature allows no limits to such lust.

Radag. Presumptuous viceroy, dar'st thou check thy
    lord,
Or twit him with the laws that nature loves?
Is not great Rasni above nature's reach,
God upon earth, and all his will is law?

K. of Crete. O, flatter not, for hateful is his choice,
And sister's love will blemish all his worth.

Radag. Doth not the brightness of his majesty
Shadow his deeds from being counted faults?

Rasni. Well hast thou answer'd with him, Radagon;
I like thee for thy learnèd sophistry.—
But thou of Crete, that countercheck'st thy king,
Pack hence in exile;—Radagon the crown!—
Be thou vicegerent of his royalty,
And fail me not in what my thoughts may please,
For from a beggar have I brought thee up,
And grac'd thee with the honour of a crown.—
Ye quondam king, what, feed ye on delays?

K. of Crete. Better no king than viceroy under him,
That hath no virtue to maintain his crown.   [*Exit.*

Rasni. Remilia, what fair dames be those that wait
Attendant on thy matchless royalty?

Remil. 'Tis Alvida, the fair wife to the King of
    Paphlagonia.

Rasni. Trust me, she is a fair:—thou'st, Paphlagon, a
    jewel,
To fold thee in so bright a sweeting's arms.

Radag. Like you her, my lord?

Rasni. What if I do, Radagon?

Radag. Why, then she is yours, my lord; for marriage
Makes no exception, where Rasni doth command.

K. of Paph. Ill dost thou counsel him to fancy wives.

Radag. Wife or not wife, whatso he likes is his.

Rasni. Well answer'd, Radagon; thou art for me:
Feed thou mine humour, and be still a king:——
Lords, go in triumph of my happy loves,
And, for to feast us after all our broils,
Frolic and revel it in Nineveh.
Whatso'er befitteth your conceited thoughts,
Or good or ill, love or not love, my boys,
In love, or what may satisfy your lust,
Act it, my lords, for no man dare say no.
Divisum imperium cum Jove nunc teneo.

[*Exeunt.*

SCENE II.—*A Public Place in Nineveh.*

Enter, brought in by an Angel, OSEAS, *the Prophet,
and let down over the stage in a throne.*

Angel. Amaze not, man of God, if in the spirit
Thou'rt brought from Jewry unto Nineveh;
So was Elias wrapt within a storm,
And set upon Mount Carmel by the Lord:
For thou hast preach'd long to the stubborn Jews,
Whose flinty hearts have felt no sweet remorse,
But lightly valuing all the threats of God,
Have still perséver'd in their wickedness.
Lo, I have brought thee unto Nineveh,
The rich and royal city of the world,
Pamper'd in wealth, and overgrown with pride,
As Sodom and Gomorrah full of sin.
The Lord looks down, and cannot see one good,

Not one that covets to obey His will;
But wicked all, from cradle to the crutch.
Note, then, Oseas, all their grievous sins,
And see the wrath of God that pays revenge;
And when the ripeness of their sin is full,
And thou hast written all their wicked thoughts,
I'll carry thee to Jewry back again,
And seat thee in the great Jerusalem;
There shalt thou publish in her open streets
That God sends down His hateful wrath for sin
On such as never heard His prophets speak:
Much more will He inflict a world of plagues
On such as hear the sweetness of His voice,
And yet obey not what His prophets speak.
Sit thee, Oseas, pondering in the spirit
The mightiness of these fond people's [1] sins.

Oseas. The will of the Lord be done!

           [*Exit* Angel.

Enter ADAM [2] *and his crew of* Ruffians, *to go to drink.*

Ruffian. Come on, smith, thou shalt be one of the crew, because thou knowest where the best ale in the town is.

Adam. Come on, in faith, my colts; I have left my master striking of a heat, and stole away because I would keep you company.

First Ruf. Why, what, shall we have this paltry smith with us?

Adam. "Paltry smith"! why, you incarnative knave,

[1] Foolish.

[2] In rearranging a corrupt text Dyce made "Clown" and "Adam" two distinct persons. It is clear from the first sentence in Act iv., Scene 4, that they are identical. Clown's first three speeches are given in the first four quartos to Smith, meaning Adam, the Smith's man. It should be noticed that First Ruffian calls Adam "smith," and "this paltry smith."

what are you that you speak petty treason against the smith's trade?

First Ruf. Why, slave, I am a gentleman of Nineveh.

Adam. A gentleman! good sir, I remember you well, and all your progenitors: your father bare office in our town; an honest man he was, and in great discredit in the parish, for they bestowed two squires' livings on him, the one was on working-days, and then he kept the town stage, and on holidays they made him the sexton's man, for he whipped dogs out of the church. Alas, sir, your father,—why, sir, methinks I see the gentleman still: a proper youth he was, faith, aged some forty and ten; his beard rat's colour, half black, half white; his nose was in the highest degree of noses, it was nose *autem glorificam*,[1] so set with rubies that after his death it should have been nailed up in Copper-smiths-hall for a monument. Well, sir, I was beholding to your good father, for he was the first man that ever instructed me in the mystery of a pot of ale.

Second Ruf. Well said, smith; that crossed him over the thumbs.

First Ruf. Villain, were it not that we go to be merry, my rapier should presently quit[2] thy opproprious terms.

Adam. O Peter, Peter, put up thy sword, I prithee heartily, into thy scabbard; hold in your rapier; for though I have not a long reacher, I have a short hitter. —Nay then, gentlemen, stay me, for my choler begins to rise against him; for mark the words, "a paltry smith"! O horrible sentence! thou hast in these words, I will stand to it, libelled against all the sound horses, whole

---

[1] The same pun occurs in *Friar Bacon and Friar Bungay*, Act IV., Scene 1.   [2] Requite.

horses, sore horses, coursers, curtals, jades, cuts, hackneys and mares: whereupon, my friend, in their defence, I give thee this curse,—thou shalt not be worth a horse of thine own this seven year.

First Ruf. I prithee, smith, is your occupation so excellent?

Adam. "A paltry smith"! Why, I'll stand to it, a smith is lord of the four elements; for our iron is made of the earth, our bellows blow out air, our floor holds fire, and our forge water. Nay, sir, we read in the Chronicles that there was a god of our occupation.

First Ruf. Ay, but he was a cuckold.

Adam. That was the reason, sir, he call'd your father cousin. "Paltry smith"! Why, in this one word thou hast defaced their worshipful occupation.

First Ruf. As how?

Adam. Marry, sir, I will stand to it, that a smith in his kind is a physician, a surgeon and a barber. For let a horse take a cold, or be troubled with the bots, and we straight give him a potion or a purgation, in such physical manner that he mends straight: if he have outward diseases, as the spavin, splent, ringbone, windgall or fashion,[1] or, sir, a galled back, we let him blood and clap a plaster to him with a pestilence, that mends him with a very vengeance: now, if his mane grow out of order, and he have any rebellious hairs, we straight to our shears and trim him with what cut it please us, pick his ears and make him neat. Marry, ay, indeed, sir, we are slovens for one thing; we never use muskballs to wash him with, and the reason is, sir, because he can woo without kissing.

First Ruf. Well, sirrah, leave off these praises of a smith, and bring us to the best ale in the town.

Adam. Now, sir, I have a feat above all the smiths

[1] Farcy.

in Nineveh; for, sir, I am a philosopher that can
dispute of the nature of ale; for mark you, sir, a pot of
ale consists of four parts,—imprimus the ale, the toast,
the ginger, and the nutmeg.

First Ruf. Excellent!

Adam. The ale is a restorative, bread is a binder:
mark you, sir, two excellent points in phsyic; the
ginger, O, ware of that! the philosophers have written of
the nature of ginger, 'tis expulsitive in two degrees;
you shall hear the sentence of Galen,

"It will make a man belch, cough, and fart,
     And is a great comfort to the heart,"—

a proper posy, I promise you; but now to the noble
virtue of the nutmeg; it is, saith one ballad (I think an
English Roman was the author), an underlayer to the
brains, for when the ale gives a buffet to the head, O
the nutmeg! that keeps him for a while in temper.
Thus you see the description of the virtue of a pot of
ale; now, sir, to put my physical precepts in practice,
follow me: but afore I step any further—

First Ruf. What's the matter now?

Adam. Why, seeing I have provided the ale, who is
the purveyor for the wenches? for, masters, take this
of me, a cup of ale without a wench, why, alas, 'tis like
an egg without salt, or a red-herring without mustard!

First Ruf. Lead us to the ale; we'll have wenches
enough, I warrant thee.

[*Exeunt.*

Oseas. Iniquity seeks out companions still,
And mortal men are armèd to do ill.
London, look on, this matter nips thee near:
Leave off thy riot, pride, and sumptuous cheer;
Spend less at board, and spare not at the door,

But aid the infant, and relieve the poor;
Else seeking mercy, being merciless,
Thou be adjudg'd to endless heaviness.

SCENE III.—*At the* Usurer's.

Enter the Usurer, THRASYBULUS, *and* ALCON.[1]

Usurer. Come on, I am every day troubled with
these needy companions: what news with you? what
wind brings you hither?

Thras. Sir, I hope, how far soever you make it off,
you remember, too well for me, that this is the day
wherein I should pay you money that I took up of you
a late in a commodity.[2]

Alc. And, sir, sir-reverence of your manhood and
gentry, I have brought home such money as you lent
me.

Usurer. You, young gentleman, is my money ready?

Thras. Truly, sir, this time was so short, the commodity so bad, and the promise of friends so broken,
that I could not provide it against the day; wherefore
I am come to entreat you to stand my friend, and to
favour me with a longer time, and I will make you
sufficient consideration.

Usurer. Is the wind in that door? If thou hast my
money, so it is: I will not defer a day, an hour, a
minute, but take the forfeit of the bond.

---

[1] The Quartos designate the two latter as "*A young Gentleman
and a poor Man.*"

[2] Merchandise which the borrower took in lieu of part of the sum
to be secured from the usurer.

Thras. I pray you, sir, consider that my loss was great by the commodity I took up: you know, sir, I borrowed of you forty pounds, whereof I had ten pounds in money, and thirty pounds in lute-strings, which when I came to sell again, I could get but five pounds for them, so had I, sir, but fifteen pounds for my forty. In consideration of this ill bargain, I pray you, sir, give me a month longer.

Usurer. I answered thee afore, not a minute; what have I to do how thy bargain proved? I have thy hand set to my book that thou receivedst forty pounds of me in money.

Thras. Ay, sir, it was your device that, to colour the statute, but your conscience knows what I had.

Alc. Friend, thou speakest Hebrew to him when thou talkest to him of conscience; for he hath as much conscience about the forfeit of an obligation, as my blind mare, God bless her, hath over a manger of oats.

Thras. Then there is no favour, sir?

Usurer. Come to-morrow to me, and see how I will use thee.

Thras. No, covetous caterpillar, know that I have made extreme shift rather than I would fall into the hands of such a ravening panther; and therefore here is thy money, and deliver me the recognisance of my lands.

Usurer [*aside*]. What a spite is this!—hath sped of his crowns! If he had missed but one half hour, what a goodly farm had I gotten for forty pounds! Well, 'tis my cursed fortune. O, have I no shift to make him forfeit his recognisance?

Thras. Come, sir, will you despatch and tell your money?

[*It strikes four o'clock.*

Usurer [*aside*]. Stay, what is this o'clock? four :—let

me see—"to be paid between the hours of three and
four in the afternoon": this goes right for me.—You,
sir, hear you not the clock, and have you not a counter-
pane [1] of your obligation? The hour is past, it was to
be paid between three and four; and now the clock
hath strucken four: I will receive none, I'll stand to
the forfeit of the recognisance.

Thras. Why, sir, I hope you do but jest; why, 'tis
but four, and will you for a minute take forfeit of my
bond? If it were so, sir, I was here before four.

Usurer. Why didst thou not tender thy money then?
if I offer thee injury, take the law of me, complain to
the judge: I will receive no money.

Alc. Well, sir, I hope you will stand my good master
for my cow. I borrowed thirty shillings on her, and
for that I have paid you eighteen-pence a week, and
for her meat you have had her milk, and I tell you, sir,
she gives a pretty sup: now, sir, here is your money.

Usurer. Hang, beggarly knave! comest to me for
a cow? did I not bind her bought and sold for a
penny, and was not thy day to have paid yesterday?
Thou gettest no cow at my hand.

Alc. No cow, sir! alas, that word "no cow" goes as
cold to my heart as a draught of small drink in a frosty
morning! "No cow," sir! Why, alas, alas, Master Usurer,
what shall become of me, my wife, and my poor child?

Usurer. Thou gettest no cow of me, knave! I cannot
stand prating with you; I must be gone.

Alc. Nay, but hear you, Master Usurer: "no cow!"
Why, sir, here's your thirty shillings: I have paid you
eighteen-pence a week, and therefore there is reason
I should have my cow.

Usurer. What pratest thou? have I not answered
thee, thy day is broken?

[1] Counterpart, duplicate.

Alc. Why, sir, alas, my cow is a commonwealth to me! for first, sir, she allows me, my wife, and son, for to banquet ourselves withal, butter, cheese, whey, curds, cream, sod-milk, raw-milk, sour-milk, sweet-milk, and butter-milk : besides, sir, she saved me every year a penny in almanacs, for she was as good to me as a prognostication ; if she had but set up her tail, and have gallop'd about the mead, my little boy was able to say, " O, father, there will be a storm "; her very tail was a calendar to me : and now to loose my cow ! alas, Master Usurer, take pity upon me !

Usurer. I have other matters to talk on ; farewell, fellows.

Thras. Why, but, thou covetous churl, wilt thou not receive thy money, and deliver me my recognisance?

Usurer. I'll deliver thee none ; if I have wronged thee, seek thy mends at the law.   [*Exit.*

Thras. And so I will, insatiable peasant.

Alc. And, sir, rather than I will put up this word "no cow," I will lay my wife's best gown to pawn. I tell you, sir, when the slave uttered this word "no cow," it struck to my heart, for my wife shall never have one so fit for her turn again ; for, indeed, sir, she is a woman that hath her twiddling-strings broke.

Thras. What meanest thou by that, fellow?

Alc. Marry, sir, sir-reverence of your manhood, she breaks wind behind ; and indeed, sir, when she sat milking of her cow and let a fart, my other cows would start at the noise, and kick down the milk and away ; but this cow, sir, the gentlest cow ! my wife might blow whilst [1] she burst : and having such good conditions, shall the Usurer come upon me with "no cow"? Nay, sir, before I pocket up this word "no cow," my wife's gown goes to the lawyer : why, alas, sir, 'tis as ill a word to me as "no crown" to a king !

[1] Until.

Thras. Well, fellow, go with me, and I'll help thee to a lawyer.

Alc. Marry, and I will, sir. No cow! well, the world goes hard. [*Exeunt.*

Oseas. Where hateful usury
Is counted husbandry;
Where merciless men rob the poor,
And the needy are thrust out of door;
Where gain is held for conscience,
And men's pleasure is all on pence;
Where young gentlemen forfeit their lands,
Through riot, into the usurer's hands;
Where poverty is despis'd, and pity banish'd,
And mercy indeed utterly vanish'd:
Where men esteem more of money than of God;
Let that land look to feel his wrathful rod:
For there is no sin more odious in his sight
Than where usury defrauds the poor of his right.
London, take heed, these sins abound in thee;
The poor complain, the widows wrongèd be;
The gentlemen by subtlety are spoil'd;
The ploughmen lose the crop for which they toil'd:
Sin reigns in thee, O London, every hour:
Repent, and tempt not thus the heavenly power.

ACT THE SECOND

SCENE I.—*The Palace of* RASNI.

Enter REMILIA, *with* ALVIDA *and a train of* Ladies,
in all royalty.

EMIL.. Fair queens, yet handmaids unto
Rasni's love,
Tell me, is not my state as glorious
As Juno's pomp, when tir'd with
heaven's despoil,
Clad in her vestments spotted all
with stars,
She cross'd the silver path unto her Jove?
Is not Remilia far more beauteous,
Rich'd with the pride of nature's excellence,
Than Venus in the brightest of her shine?
My hairs, surpass they not Apollo's locks?
Are not my tresses curlèd with such art
As love delights to hide him in their fair?
Doth not mine eye shine like the morning lamp
That tells Aurora when her love will come?
Have I not stol'n the beauty of the heavens,

And plac'd it on the feature of my face?
Can any goddess make compare with me,
Or match her with the fair Remilia?
  Alvi. The beauties that proud Paris saw from Troy,
Mustering in Ida for the golden ball,
Were not so gorgeous as Remilia.
  Remil. I have trick'd my trammels up with richest
     balm,
And made my perfumes of the purest myrrh :
The precious drugs that Ægypt's wealth affords,
The costly paintings fetch'd from curious Tyre,
Have mended in my face what nature miss'd.
Am I not the earth's wonder in my looks?
  Alvi. The wonder of the earth, and pride of heaven.
  Remil. Look, Alvida, a hair stands not amiss :
For women's locks are trammels of conceit,
Which do entangle Love for all his wiles.
  Alvi. Madam, unless you coy it trick and trim,
And play the civil [1] wanton ere you yield,
Smiting disdain of pleasures with your tongue,
Patting your princely Rasni on the cheek
When he presumes to kiss without consent,
You mar the market : beauty naught avails :
You must be proud; for pleasures hardly got
Are sweet if once attain'd.
  Remil. Fair Alvida,
Thy counsel makes Remilia passing wise.
Suppose that thou wert Rasni's mightiness,
And I Remilia, prince of excellence:
  Alvi. I would be master then of love and thee.
  Remil. " Of love and me! Proud and disdainful
     king,
Dar'st thou presume to touch a deity,
Before she grace thee with a yielding smile?" [2]

---

[1] Grave, sober.   [2] Remilia and Alvida are assuming parts.

G

Alvi. "Tut, my Remilia, be not thou so coy;
Say nay, and take it."[1]

Remil. "Careless and unkind!
Talks Rasni to Remilia in such sort
As if I did enjoy a human form?
Look on thy love, behold mine eyes divine,
And dar'st thou twit me with a woman's fault?
Ah Rasni, thou art rash to judge of me.
I tell thee, Flora oft hath woo'd my lips,
To lend a rose to beautify her spring;
The sea-nymphs fetch their lilies from my cheeks:
Then thou unkind!"—and hereon would I weep.

Alvi. And here would Alvida resign her charge;
For were I but in thought th' Assyrian king,
I needs must 'quite thy tears with kisses sweet,
And crave a pardon with a friendly touch:
You know it, madam, though I teach it not,
The touch I mean, you smile whenas you think it.

Remil. How am I pleas'd to hear thy pretty prate,
According to the humour of my mind!
Ah, nymphs, who fairer than Remilia?
The gentle winds have woo'd me with their sighs,
The frowning air hath clear'd when I did smile;
And when I trac'd upon the tender grass,
Love, that makes warm the centre of the earth,
Lift up his crest to kiss Remilia's foot;
Juno still entertains her amorous Jove
With new delights, for fear he look on me;
The phœnix' feathers are become my fan,
For I am beauty's phœnix in this world.
Shut close these curtains straight, and shadow me,
For fear Apollo spy me in his walks,

---

[1] A proverbial expression. Compare Shakespeare's Richard III.,
Act III. sc. 7: "Play the maid's part,—still answer nay, and
take it."

And scorn all eyes, to see Remilia's eyes.
Nymphs, eunuchs, sing, for Mavors draweth nigh ;
Hide me in closure, let him long to look :
For were a goddess fairer than am I,
I'll scale the heavens to pull her from the place.
     [They draw the curtains, and music plays.
 Alvi. Believe me, though she say that she is fairest,
I think my penny silver by her leave.

Enter RASNI *and* RADAGON, *with* Lords *in pomp, who*
  make a ward about RASNI ; *with them the* Magi *in*
  great pomp.

 Rasni. Magi, for love of Rasni, by your art,
By magic frame an arbour out of hand,
For fair Remilia to disport her in.
Meanwhile, I will bethink me on further pomp. *[Exit.*
  [The Magi *with their rods beat the ground, and from*
    under the same rises a brave arbour ; [1] RASNI
    returns in another suit, while the trumpets
    sound.
 Rasni. Blest be ye, men of art, that grace me thus,
And blessèd be this day where Hymen hies
To join in union pride of heaven and earth !
  [Lightning and thunder, wherewith REMILIA *is*
     strucken.
What wondrous threatening noise is this I hear?
What flashing lightnings trouble our delights?
When I draw near Remilia's royal tent,
I waking dream of sorrow and mishap.
 Radag. Dread not, O king, at ordinary chance ;
These are but common exhalations,
Drawn from the earth, in substance hot and dry,
Or moist and thick, or meteors combust,
Matters and causes incident to time,
    [1] Through a trap in the stage.

Enkindled in the fiery region first.
Tut, be not now a Roman augurer:
Approach the tent, look on Remilia.

   Rasni. Thou hast confirm'd my doubts, kind
      Radagon.—
Now ope, ye folds, where queen of favour sits,
Carrying a net within her curlèd locks,
Wherein the Graces are entangled oft;
Ope like th' imperial gates where Phœbus sits,
Whenas he means to woo his Clytia.
Nocturnal cares, ye blemishers of bliss,
Cloud not mine eyes whilst I behold her face.—
Remilia, my delight !—she answereth not.
    [He draws the curtains, and finds her strucken black
                  with thunder.
How pale ! as if bereav'd in fatal meads,
The balmy breath hath left her bosom quite :
My Hesperus by cloudy death is blent.[1]—
Villains, away, fetch syrups of the Inde,
Fetch balsomo, the kind preserve of life,
Fetch wine of Greece, fetch oils, fetch herbs, fetch all,
To fetch her life, or I will faint and die.
    [They bring in all these, and offer ; naught prevails.
Herbs, oils of Inde, alas, there naught prevails !
Shut are the day-bright eyes that made me see ;
Lock'd are the gems of joy in dens of death.
Yet triumph I on fate, and he on her :
Malicious mistress of inconstancy,
Damn'd be thy name, that hast obscur'd my joy.—
Kings, viceroys, princes, rear a royal tomb
For my Remilia ; bear her from my sight,
Whilst I in tears weep for Remilia.
               [They bear REMILIA's *body out.*
   Radag. What maketh Rasni moody ? loss of one ?
        [1] Destroyed.

As if no more were left so fair as she.
Behold a dainty minion for the nonce,—
Fair Alvida, the Paphlagonian queen :
Woo her, and leave this weeping for the dead.

Rasni. What, woo my subject's wife that honoureth
  me !

Radag. Tut, kings this *meum, tuum* should not know :
Is she not fair ? is not her husband hence ?
Hold, take her at the hands of Radagon ;
A pretty peat [1] to drive your mourn away.

Rasni. She smiles on me, I see she is mine own.——
Wilt thou be Rasni's royal paramour ?

Radag. She blushing yields consent.——Make no dis-
  pute :
The king is sad, and must be gladded straight ;
Let Paphlagonian king go mourn meanwhile.

  [*Thrusts* RASNI *and* ALVIDA *out ; and so they
  all exeunt.*]

Oseas. Pride hath his judgment : London, look about ;
'Tis not enough in show to be devout.
A fury now from heaven to lands unknown
Hath made the prophet speak, not to his own.
Fly, wantons, fly this pride and vain attire,
The seals to set your tender hearts on fire.
Be faithful in the promise you have past,
Else God will plague and punish at the last.
When lust is hid in shroud of wretched life,
When craft doth dwell in bed of married wife,
Mark but the prophet's word that shortly shows. [2]
After death expect for many woes.

---

[1] A form of endearment, equivalent to " pet."
[2] The Quarto reads, " Mark but the Prophets, we that shortly
shows," etc. J. C. Smith suggests " Prophet's woe "; J. C.
Collins, " Prophet, he," etc.

SCENE II.—*A Court of Justice in Nineveh.*

Enter ALCON *and* THRASYBULUS, *with their* Lawyer.

Thras. I need not, sir, discourse unto you the duty of lawyers in tendering the right cause of their clients, nor the conscience you are tied unto by higher command. Therefore suffice, the Usurer hath done me wrong; you know the case; and, good sir, I have strained myself to give you your fees.

Lawyer. Sir, if I should any way neglect so manifest a truth, I were to be accused of open perjury, for the case is evident.

Alc. And truly, sir, for my case, if you help me not for my matter, why, sir, I and my wife are quite undone; I want my mease [1] of milk when I go to my work, and my boy his bread and butter when he goes to school. Master Lawyer, pity me, for surely, sir, I was fain to lay my wife's best gown to pawn for your fees: when I looked upon it, sir, and saw how handsomely it was daubed with statute-lace, [2] and what a fair mockado [3] cape it had, and then thought how handsomely it became my wife,—truly, sir, my heart is made of butter, it melts at the least persecution,—I fell on weeping; but when I thought on the words the Usurer gave me, "no cow," then, sir, I would have stript her into her smock, but I would make him deliver my cow ere I had done: therefore, good Master Lawyer, stand my friend.

Lawyer. Trust me, father, I will do for thee as much as for myself.

---

[1] An old form of " mess."
[2] "The term no doubt has reference to the sumptuary enactments regulating the breadth of the lace which was allowed to be worn."—COLLINS.
[3] Mock-velvet.

Alc. Are you married, sir?

Lawyer. Ay, marry, am I, father.

Alc. Then good's benison light on you and your good wife, and send her that she be never troubled with my wife's disease.

Lawyer. Why, what's thy wife's disease.

Alc. Truly, sir, she hath two open faults, and one privy fault. Sir, the first is, she is too eloquent for a poor man, and hath the words of art, for she will call me rascal, rogue, runagate, varlet, vagabond, slave, knave: why, alas, sir, and these be but holiday-terms, but if you heard her working-day words, in faith, sir, they be rattlers like thunder, sir; for after the dew follows a storm, for then am I sure either to be well buffeted, my face scratched, or my head broken: and therefore, good Master Lawyer, on my knees I ask it, let me not go home again to my wife with this word "no cow"; for then she will exercise her two faults upon me with all extremity.

Lawyer. Fear not, man. But what is thy wife's privy fault?

Alc. Truly, sir, that's a thing of nothing; alas, she, indeed, sir-reverence of your mastership, doth use to break wind in her sleep.—O, sir, here comes the Judge, and the old caitiff the Usurer.

Enter the Judge, *attended, and the* Usurer.

Usurer. Sir, here is forty angels for you, and if at any time you want a hundred pound or two, 'tis ready at your command, or the feeding of three or four fat bullocks: whereas these needy slaves can reward with nothing but a cap and a knee; and therefore I pray you, sir, favour my case.

Judge. Fear not, sir, I'll do what I can for you.

Usurer. What, Master Lawyer, what make you here? mine adversary for these clients?

Lawyer. So it chanceth now, sir.

Usurer. I know you know the old proverb, "He is not wise that is not wise for himself": I would not be disgraced in this action; therefore here is twenty angels; say nothing in the matter, or what you say, say to no purpose, for the Judge is my friend.

Lawyer. Let me alone, I'll fit your purpose.

Judge. Come, where are these fellows that are the plaintiffs? what can they say against this honest citizen our neighbour, a man of good report amongst all men?

Alc. Truly, Master Judge, he is a man much spoken of; marry, every man's cries are against him, and especially we; and therefore I think we have brought our Lawyer to touch him with as much law as will fetch his lands and my cow with a pestilence.

Thras. Sir, I am the other plaintiff, and this is my counsellor: I beseech your honour be favourable to me in equity.

Judge. O, Signor Mizaldo, what can you say in this gentleman's behalf?

Lawyer. Faith, sir, as yet little good.—Sir, tell you your own case to the Judge, for I have so many matters in my head, that I have almost forgotten it.

Thras. Is the wind in that door? Why then, my lord, thus. I took up of this cursed Usurer, for so I may well term him, a commodity of forty pounds, whereof I received ten pound in money, and thirty pound in lute-strings, whereof I could by great friendship make but five pounds: for the assurance of this bad commodity I bound him my land in recognisance: I came at my day, and tendered him his money, and he would not take it: for the redress of my open wrong I crave but justice.

Judge. What say you to this, sir?

Usurer. That first he had no lute-strings of me; for, look you, sir, I have his own hand to my book for the receipt of forty pound.

Thras. That was, sir, but a device of him to colour the statute.

Judge. Well, he hath thine own hand, and we can crave no more in law.—But now, sir, he says his money was tendered at the day and hour.

Usurer. This is manifest contrary, sir, and on that I will depose; for here is the obligation, "to be paid between three and four in the afternoon," and the clock struck four before he offered it, and the words be " between three and four," therefore to be tendered before four.

Thras. Sir, I was there before four, and he held me with brabbling [1] till the clock struck, and then for the breach of a minute he refused my money, and kept the recognisance of my land for so small a trifle.—Good Signor Mizaldo, speak what is law; you have your fee, you have heard what the case is, and therefore do me justice and right: I am a young gentleman, and speak for my patrimony.

Lawyer. Faith, sir, the case is altered; you told me it before in another manner: the law goes quite against you, and therefore you must plead to the Judge for favour.

Thras. [*Aside*]. O execrable bribery!

Alc. Faith, Sir Judge, I pray you let me be the gentleman's counsellor, for I can say thus much in his defence, that the Usurer's clock is the swiftest clock in all the town: 'tis, sir, like a woman's tongue, it goes ever half-an-hour before the time; for when we were gone from him, other clocks in the town struck four.

Judge. Hold thy prating, fellow:—and you, young gentleman, this is my ward: look better another time

[1] Quarrelling, squabbling.

both to your bargains and to the payments; for I must give flat sentence against you, that, for default of tendering the money between the hours, you have forfeited your recognisance, and he to have the land.

Thras. [*Aside*]. O inspeakable injustice!

Alc. [*Aside*]. O monstrous, miserable, moth-eaten Judge!

Judge. Now you, fellow, what have you to say for your matter?

Alc. Master Lawyer, I laid my wife's gown to pawn for your fees: I pray you, to this gear.[1]

Lawyer. Alas, poor man, thy matter is out of my head, and therefore, I pray thee, tell it thyself.

Alc. I hold my cap to a noble,[2] that the Usurer hath given him some gold, and he, chewing it in his mouth, hath got the toothache that he cannot speak.

Judge. Well, sirrah, I must be short, and therefore say on.

Alc. Master Judge, I borrowed of this man thirty shillings, for which I left him in pawn my good cow; the bargain was, he should have eighteen-pence a week, and the cow's milk for usury: now, sir, as soon as I had gotten the money, I brought it him, and broke but a day, and for that he refused his money, and keeps my cow, sir.

Judge. Why, thou hast given sentence against thyself, for in breaking thy day thou hast lost thy cow.

Alc. Master Lawyer, now for my ten shillings.

Lawyer. Faith, poor man, thy case is so bad, I shall but speak against thee.

Alc. 'Twere good, then, I should have my ten shillings again.

Lawyer. 'Tis my fee, fellow, for coming: wouldst thou have me come for nothing?

---

[1] Business.   [2] I bet my cap to a noble (a gold coin).

Alc. Why, then, am I like to go home, not only with no cow, but no gown : this gear goes hard.

Judge. Well, you have heard what favour I can show you : I must do justice.—Come, Master Mizaldo,—and you, sir, go home with me to dinner.

Alc. Why, but, Master Judge, no cow !—and, Master Lawyer, no gown ! Then must I clean run out of the town.

[*Exeunt* Judge, Lawyer, Usurer, *and* Attendants. How cheer you, gentleman ? you cry "no lands" too ; the Judge hath made you a knight for a gentleman, hath dubbed you Sir John Lack-land.

Thras. O miserable time, wherein gold is above God !

Alc. Fear not, man ; I have yet a fetch to get thy lands and my cow again, for I have a son in the court, that is either a king or a king's fellow, and to him will I go and complain on the Judge and the Usurer both.

Thras. And I will go with thee, and entreat him for my case.

Alc. But how shall I go home to my wife, when I shall have nothing to say unto her but "no cow" ? alas, sir, my wife's faults will fall upon me !

Thras. Fear not ; let's go ; I'll quiet her, shalt see.

[*Exeunt.*

Oseas. Fly, judges, fly corruption in your court ;
The judge of truth hath made your judgment short.
Look so to judge that at the latter day
Ye be not judg'd with those that wend astray.
Who passeth judgment for his private gain,
He well may judge he is adjudg'd to pain.

SCENE III.—*A Street near the* King's *Palace.*

Enter ADAM *and his crew of* Ruffians *drunk.*

Adam. Farewell, gentle tapster.—Masters, as good ale
as ever was tapt; look to your feet, for the ale is strong
—Well, farewell, gentle tapster.

First Ruf. [*to Second Ruf.*] Why, sirrah slave, by
heaven's maker, thinkest thou the wench loves thee
best because she laughed on thee? give me but
such another word, and I will throw the pot at
thy head.

Adam. Spill no drink, spill no drink, the ale is good:
I'll tell you what, ale is ale, and so I'll commend me to
you with hearty commendations.—Farewell, gentle
tapster.

Second Ruf. Why, wherefore, peasant, scornest thou
that the wench should love me? look but on her, and
I'll thrust my dagger in thy bosom.

First Ruf. Well, sirrah, well, tha'rt as tha'rt, and so
I'll take thee.

Second Ruf. Why, what am I?

First Ruf. Why, what thou wilt; a slave.

Second Ruf. Then take that, villain, and learn how
thou use me another time.   [*Stabs* First Ruf.

First Ruf. O, I am slain!   [*Dies.*

Second Ruf. That's all one to me, I care not. Now
will I in to my wench, and call for a fresh pot.

                    [*Exit: followed by all except* ADAM.

Adam. Nay, but hear ye, take me with ye, for the ale
is ale.—Cut a fresh toast, tapster, fill me a pot; here is
money, I am no beggar, I'll follow thee as long as the
ale lasts.—A pestilence on the blocks for me, for I might

have had a fall : well, if we shall have no ale, I'll sit me
down : and so farewell, gentle tapster.

[Here he falls over the dead man.

Enter RASNI, ALVIDA, *the* KING OF CILICIA, Lords,
and Attendants.

Rasni. What slaughter'd wretch lies bleeding here his
last,
So near the royal palace of the king ?
Search out if any one be biding nigh,
That can discourse the manner of his death.—
Seat thee, fair Alvida, the fair of fairs ;
Let not the object once offend thine eyes.

First Lord. Here's one sits here asleep, my lord.

Rasni. Wake him, and make inquiry of this thing.

First Lord. Sirrah, you ! hearest thou, fellow ?

Adam. If you will fill a fresh pot, here's a penny, or
else farewell, gentle tapster.

First Lord. He is drunk, my lord.

Rasni. We'll sport with him, that Alvida may laugh.

First Lord. Sirrah, thou fellow, thou must come to
the king.

Adam. I will not do a stroke of work to-day, for the
ale is good ale, and you can ask but a penny for a pot,
no more by the statute.

First Lord. Villain, here's the king ; thou must come
to him.

Adam. The king come to an ale-house !—Tapster, fill
me three pots.—Where's the king ? is this he ?—Give
me your hand, sir : as good ale as ever was tapt ; you
shall drink while your skin crack.

Rasni. But hearest thou, fellow, who killed this man ?

Adam. I'll tell you, sir,—if you did taste of the ale,—
all Nineveh hath not such a cup of ale, it flowers in the

cup, sir; by my troth, I spent eleven pence, beside three races of ginger—

Rasni. Answer me, knave, to my question, how came this man slain?

Adam. Slain! why [the] ale is strong ale, 'tis huffcap;[1] I warrant you, 'twill make a man well.—Tapster, ho! for the king a cup of ale and a fresh toast; here's two races more.

Alvi. Why, good fellow, the king talks not of drink; he would have thee tell him how this man came dead.

Adam. Dead! nay, I think I am alive yet, and will drink a full pot ere night: but hear ye, if ye be the wench that filled us drink, why, so, do your office, and give us a fresh pot; or if you be the tapster's wife, why, so, wash the glass clean.

Alvi. He is so drunk, my lord, there is no talking with him.

Adam. Drunk! nay, then, wench, I am not drunk: th'art shitten quean to call me drunk; I tell thee I am not drunk, I am a smith, I.

Enter the Smith.

First Lord. Sir, here comes one perhaps that can tell.

Smith. God save you, master.

Rasni. Smith, canst thou tell me how this man came dead?

Smith. May it please your highness, my man here and a crew of them went to the ale-house, and came out so drunk that one of them killed another; and now, sir, I am fain to leave my shop, and come to fetch him home.

Rasni. Some of you carry away the dead body: drunken men must have their fits; and, sirrah smith, hence with thy man.

---

[1] Strong ale that makes men swagger and bluster.

Smith. Sirrah, you, rise, come go with me.

Adam. If we shall have a pot of ale, let's have it; here's money; hold, tapster, take my purse.

Smith. Come, then, with me, the pot stands full in the house.

Adam. I am for you, let's go, th'art an honest tapster: we'll drink six pots ere we part.

> [*Exeunt* Smith, ADAM; *and* Attendants *with the dead body.*]

Rasni. Beauteous, more bright than beauty in mine
    eyes,
Tell me, fair sweeting, want'st thou anything
Contain'd within the threefold circle of the world,
That may make Alvida live full content?

Alvi. Nothing, my lord; for all my thoughts are
    pleas'd,
Whenas mine eye surfeits with Rasni's sight.

Enter the KING OF PAPHLAGONIA *malcontent.*

Rasni. Look how thy husband haunts our royal court,
How still his sight breeds melancholy storms.
O, Alvida, I am passing passionate,
And vex'd with wrath and anger to the death!
Mars, when he held fair Venus on his knee,
And saw the limping smith come from his forge,
Had not more deeper furrows in his brow
Than Rasni hath to see this Paphlagon.

Alvi. Content thee, sweet, I'll salve thy sorrow
    straight;
Rest but the ease of all thy thoughts on me,
And if I make not Rasni blithe again,
Then say that women's fancies have no shifts.

K. of Paph. Sham'st thou not, Rasni, though thou
    be'st a king,
To shroud adultery in thy royal seat?

Art thou arch-ruler of great Nineveh,
Who shouldst excel in virtue as in state,
And wrong'st thy friend by keeping back his wife?
Have I not battled in thy troops full oft,
'Gainst Ægypt, Jewry, and proud Babylon,
Spending my blood to purchase thy renown,
And is the guerdon of my chivalry
Ended in this abusing of my wife?
Restore her me, or I will from thy court,
And make discourse of thy adulterous deeds.

Rasni. Why, take her, Paphlagon, exclaim not, man;
For I do prize mine honour more than love.—
Fair Alvida, go with thy husband home.

Alvi. How dare I go, sham'd with so deep misdeed?
Revenge will broil within my husband's breast,
And when he hath me in the court at home,
Then Alvida shall feel revenge for all.

Rasni. What say'st thou, King of Paphlagon, to this?
Thou hear'st the doubt thy wife doth stand upon.
If she hath done amiss, it is my fault;
I prithee, pardon and forget [it] all.

K. of Paph. If that I meant not, Rasni, to forgive,
And quite forget the follies that are past,
I would not vouch her presence in my court;
But she shall be my queen, my love, my life,
And Alvida unto her Paphlagon,
And lov'd, and more belovèd than before.

Rasni. What say'st thou, Alvida, to this?

Alvi. That, will he swear it to my lord the king,
And in a full carouse of Greekish wine
Drink down the malice of his deep revenge,
I will go home and love him new again.

Rasni. What answers Paphlagon?

K. of Paph. That what she hath requested I will do.

Alvi. Go, damosel, fetch me that sweet wine

That stands within my closet on the shelf;
Pour it into a standing-bowl of gold,
But, on thy life, taste not before the king:
Make haste.

                            [*Exit* Female Attendant.
Why is great Rasni melancholy thus?
If promise be not kept, hate all for me.

                   [*Wine brought in by* Female Attendant.
Here is the wine, my lord: first make him swear.

    K. of Paph. By Nineveh's great gods, and Nineveh's
       great king,
My thoughts shall never be to wrong my wife!
And thereon here's a full carouse to her.   [*Drinks.*

    Alvi. And thereon, Rasni, here's a kiss for thee;
Now may'st thou freely fold thine Alvida.

    K. of Paph. O, I am dead! obstruction's of my
       breath!
The poison is of wondrous sharp effect.
Cursèd be all adulterous queans, say I!
And cursing so, poor Paphlagon doth die.   [*Dies.*

    Alvi. Now, have I not salv'd the sorrows of my lord?
Have I not rid a rival of thy loves?
What say'st thou, Rasni, to thy paramour?

    Rasni. That for this deed I'll deck my Alvida
In sendal and in costly sussapine,[1]
Border'd with pearl and India diamond.
I'll cause great Æol perfume all his winds
With richest myrrh and curious ambergris.
Come, lovely minion, paragon for fair,
Come, follow me, sweet goddess of mine eye,
And taste the pleasures Rasni will provide.

                           [*Exeunt.*

---

   [1] Sendal, "a kinde of Cypres stuffe or silke."—*Minsheu, Guide
into the Tongues,* 1617. Sussapine is supposed by Collins to be a
corruption of "gossampine," meaning a cotton cloth.

   H

Oseas. Where whoredom reigns, there murder follows
    fast,
As falling leaves before the winter blast.
A wicked life, train'd up in endless crime,
Hath no regard unto the latter time,
When lechers shall be punish'd for their lust,
When princes plagu'd because they are unjust.
Foresee in time, the warning bell doth toll;
Subdue the flesh, by prayer to save the soul:
London, behold the cause of others' wrack,
And see the sword of justice at thy back:
Defer not off, to-morrow is too late;
By night he comes perhaps to judge thy state.

ACT THE THIRD

SCENE I.—*A Seaport in Judea.*

Enter JONAS.

JONAS. From forth the depth of my
        imprison'd soul
     Steal you, my sighs, [to] testify my
        pain;
     Convey on wings of mine immortal
        tone,
     My zealous prayers unto the starry
throne.
Ah, merciful and just, thou dreadful God!
Where is thine arm to lay revengeful strokes
Upon the heads of our rebellious race?
Lo, Israel, once that flourish'd like the vine,
Is barren laid; the beautiful increase
Is wholly blent, and irreligious zeal
Encampeth there where virtue was enthron'd:
Alas, the while the widow wants relief,
The fatherless is wrong'd by naked need,
Devotion sleeps in cinders of contempt,
Hypocrisy infects the holy priest!
Ah me, for this! woe me, for these misdeeds!

Alone I walk to think upon the world,
And sigh to see thy prophets so contemn'd,
Alas, contemn'd by cursèd Israel!
Yet, Jonas, rest content, 'tis Israel's sin
That causeth this; then muse no more thereon,
But pray amends, and mend thy own amiss.

An Angel *appears to* JONAS.

Angel. Amittai's son, I charge thee muse no more:
I AM hath power to pardon and correct;
To thee pertains to do the Lord's command.
Go girt thy loins, and haste thee quickly hence;
To Nineveh, that mighty city, wend,
And say this message from the Lord of hosts,
Preach unto them these tidings from thy God;—
"Behold, thy wickedness hath tempted me,
And piercèd through the nine-fold orbs of heaven:
Repent, or else thy judgment is at hand."
                    [*This said, the* Angel *vanishes.*

Jonas. Prostrate I lie before the Lord of hosts,
With humble ears intending[1] his behest:
Ah, honour'd be Jehovah's great command!
Then Jonas must to Nineveh repair,
Commanded as the prophet of the Lord.
Great dangers on this journey do await,
But dangers none where heavens direct the course.
What should I deem? I see, yea, sighing see,
How Israel sins, yet knows the way of truth,
And thereby grows the bye-word of the world.
How, then, should God in judgment be so strict
'Gainst those who never heard or knew his power,
To threaten utter ruin of them all?
Should I report this judgment of my God,
I should incite them more to follow sin,

---

[1] Attending to.

And publish to the world my country's blame.
It may not be, my conscience tells me—no.
Ah, Jonas, wilt thou prove rebellious then?
Consider, ere thou fall, what error is.
My mind misgives: to Joppa will I fly,
And for a while to Tharsus shape my course,
Until the Lord unfret his angry brows.

Enter certain Merchants of Tharsus, *a* Master, *and some*
Sailors.

 Master. Come on, brave merchants; now the wind
  doth serve,
And sweetly blows a gale at west-south-west,
Our yards across; our anchor's on the pike;
What, shall we hence, and take this merry gale?
 First Mer. Sailors, convey our budgets straight
  aboard,
And we will recompense your pains at last:
If once in safety we may Tharsus see,
Master, we'll feast these merry mates and thee.
 Master. Meanwhile content yourselves with silly cates;
Our beds are boards, our feasts are full of mirth:
We use no pomp, we are the lords of sea;
When princes sweat in care, we swink [1] of glee.
Orion's shoulders and the Pointers serve
To be our loadstars in the lingering night;
The beauties of Arcturus we behold;
And though the sailor is no bookman held,
He knows more art than ever bookmen read.
 First Sai. By heavens, well said in honour of our
  trade!
Let's see the proudest scholar steer his course,
Or shift his tides, as silly sailors do;
Then will we yield them praise, else never none.

     [1] Toil.

First Mer. Well spoken, fellow, in thine own behalf.
But let us hence: wind tarries none, you wot,
And tide and time let slip is hardly got.

Master. March to the haven, merchants; I follow you.

                           [Exeunt Merchants.

Jonas [*aside*]. Now doth occasion further my desires;
I find companions fit to aid my flight.—
Stay, sir, I pray, and hear a word or two.

Master. Say on, good friend, but briefly, if you
      please;
My passengers by this time are aboard.

Jonas. Whither pretend [1] you to embark yourselves?

Master. To Tharsus, sir, and here in Joppa-haven
Our ship is prest [2] and ready to depart.

Jonas. May I have passage for my money, then?

Master. What not for money? pay ten silverlings, [3]
You are a welcome guest, if so you please.

Jonas [*giving money*]. Hold, take thine hire; I follow
      thee, my friend.

Master. Where is your budget? let me bear it, sir.

Jonas. Go on in peace; who sail as I do now [4]
Put trust in him who succoureth every want.

                              [Exeunt.

Oseas. When prophets, new-inspir'd, presume to force
And tie the power of heaven to their conceits;
When fear, promotion, pride, or simony,
Ambition, subtle craft, their thoughts disguise,
Woe to the flock whereas the shepherd's foul!
For, lo, the Lord at unawares shall plague
The careless guide, because his flocks do stray.
The axe already to the tree is set:
Beware to tempt the Lord, ye men of art.

---

[1] Intend.   [2] Prepared.   [3] Pieces of silver money.
[4] The quartos are unintelligible. This is the conjectural reading
of Mr J. C. Smith, given in Collins' edition.

SCENE II.—*A Public Place in Nineveh.*

Enter ALCON, THRASYBULUS, SAMIA, *and* CLESIPHON.

Cles. Mother, some meat, or else I die for want.

Samia. Ah little boy, how glad thy mother would
Supply thy wants, but naked need denies!
Thy father's slender portion in this world
By usury and false deceit is lost:
No charity within this city bides;
All for themselves, and none to help the poor.

Cles. Father, shall Clesiphon have no relief?

Alc. Faith, my boy, I must be flat with thee, we must
feed upon proverbs now; as "Necessity hath no law,"
"A churl's feast is better than none at all;" for other
remedies have we none, except thy brother Radagon
help us.

Samia. Is this thy slender care to help our child?
Hath nature arm'd thee to no more remorse?[1]
Ah, cruel man, unkind and pitiless!—
Come, Clesiphon, my boy, I'll beg for thee.

Cles. O, how my mother's mourning moveth me!

Alc. Nay, you shall pay me interest for getting the
boy, wife, before you carry him hence: alas, woman,
what can Alcon do more? I'll pluck the belly out of
my heart for thee, sweet Samia; be not so waspish.

Samia. Ah silly man, I know thy want is great,
And foolish I to crave where nothing is.
Haste, Alcon, haste, make haste unto our son;
Who, since he is in favour of the king,
May help this hapless gentleman and us
For to regain our goods from tyrant's hands.

Thras. Have patience, Samia, wait your weal from
heaven:

_____
[1] Compassion.

The gods have rais'd your son, I hope, for this,
To succour innocents in their distress.
Lo, where he comes from the imperial court;
Go, let us prostrate us before his feet.

Alc. Nay, by my troth, I'll never ask my son's blessing;
che trow, cha [1] taught him his lesson to know his father.

Enter RADAGON *attended.* [2]

What, son Radagon! i'faith, boy, how dost thee?
Radag. Villain, disturb me not; I cannot stay.
Alc. Tut, son, I'll help you of that disease quickly,
for I can hold thee: ask thy mother, knave, what cunning I have to ease a woman when a qualm of kindness
comes too near her stomach; let me but clasp mine
arms about her body, and say my prayers in her bosom,
and she shall be healed presently.

Radag. Traitor unto my princely majesty,
How dar'st thou lay thy hands upon a king?
Samia. No traitor, Radagon, but true is he:
What, hath promotion bleared thus thine eye,
To scorn thy father when he visits thee?
Alas, my son, behold with ruthful eyes
Thy parents robb'd of all their worldly weal
By subtle means of usury and guile:
The judge's ears are deaf and shut up close;
All mercy sleeps: then be thou in these plunges [3]
A patron to thy mother in her pains:
Behold thy brother almost dead for food:
O, succour us, that first did succour thee!

Radag. What,   succour   me! false   callet,[4] hence,
     avaunt!
Old dotard, pack! move not my patience:

---

[1] Rustic dialect for "I trow I taught."   [2] The quartos have
"*Enters* RADAGON *solus.*"   [3] Straits   [4] Drab.

I know you not; kings never look so low.

  Samia. You know us not! O Radagon, you know
That, knowing us, you know your parents then;
Thou know'st this womb first brought thee forth to
      light:
I know these paps did foster thee, my son.

  Alc. And I know he hath had many a piece of
bread and cheese at my hands, as proud as he is; that
know I.

  Thras. I wait no hope of succour in this place,
Where children hold their fathers in disgrace.

  Radag. Dare you enforce the furrows of revenge
Within the brows of royal Radagon?
Villain, avaunt! hence, beggars, with your brats!—
Marshal, why whip you not these rogues away,
That thus disturb our royal majesty?

  Cles. Mother, I see it is a wondrous thing,
From base estate for to become a king;
For why, methink, my brother in these fits
Hath got a kingdom, and hath lost his wits.

  Radag. Yet more contempt before my royalty?
Slaves, fetch out tortures worse than Tityus' plagues,
And tear their tongues from their blasphémous heads.

  Thras. I'll get me gone, though wo-begone with grief:
No hope remains :—come, Alcon, let us wend.

  Radag. 'Twere best you did, for fear you catch your
     bane.   [*Exit* THRASYBULUS.

  Samia. Nay, traitor, I will haunt thee to the death :
Ungracious son, untoward, and perverse,
I'll fill the heavens with echoes of thy pride,
And ring in every ear thy small regard,
That dost despise thy parents in their wants;
And breathing forth my soul before thy feet,
My curses still shall haunt thy hateful head,
And being dead, my ghost shall thee pursue.

Enter RASNI, *attended on by his* Magi *and* Kings.

Rasni. How now! what mean these outcries in our
court,
Where naught should sound but harmonies of heaven?
What maketh Radagon so passionate?

Samia. Justice, O king, justice against my son!

Rasni. Thy son! what son?

Samia. This cursèd Radagon.

Radag. Dread monarch, this is but a lunacy,
Which grief and want hath brought the woman to.—
What, doth this passion hold you every moon?

Samia. O, politic in sin and wickedness,
Too impudent for to delude thy prince!—
O Rasni, this same womb first brought him forth:
This is his father, worn with care and age,
This is his brother, poor unhappy lad,
And I his mother, though contemn'd by him.
With tedious toil we got our little good,
And brought him up to school with mickle charge:
Lord, how we joy'd to see his towardness!
And to ourselves we oft in silence said,
This youth when we are old may succour us.
But now preferr'd, and lifted up by thee,
We quite destroy'd by cursèd usury,
He scorneth me, his father, and this child.

Cles. He plays the serpent right, describ'd in Æsop's
tale,
That sought the foster's death, that lately gave him life.

Alc. Nay, an please your majesty-ship, for proof he
was my child, search the parish-book: the clerk will
swear it, his godfathers and godmothers can witness it:
it cost me forty pence in ale and cakes on the wives
at his christening.—Hence, proud king! thou shalt never
more have my blessing!

Rasni [*taking* RADAGON *apart*]. Say sooth in secret,
Radagon,
Is this thy father?
  Radag. Mighty king, he is;
I blushing tell it to your majesty.
  Rasni. Why dost thou, then, contemn him and his
    friends?
  Radag. Because he is a base and abject swain,
My mother and her brat both beggarly,
Unmeet to be allied unto a king.
Should I, that look on Rasni's countenance,
And march amidst his royal equipage,
Embase myself to speak to such as they?
'Twere impious so to impair the love
That mighty Rasni bears to Radagon.
I would your grace would quit them from your sight,
That dare presume to look on Jove's compare.
  Rasni. I like thy pride, I praise thy policy;
Such should they be that wait upon my court:
Let me alone to answer, Radagon.—
Villains, seditious traitors, as you be,
That scandalise the honour of a king,
Depart my court, you stales of impudence,
Unless you would be parted from your limbs!
Too base for to entitle fatherhood
To Rasni's friend, to Rasni's favourite.
  Radag. Hence, begging scold! hence, caitiff clogg'd
    with years!
On pain of death, revisit not the court.
Was I conceiv'd by such a scurvy trull,
Or brought to light by such a lump of dirt?
Go, losel, trot it to the cart and spade!
Thou art unmeet to look upon a king.
Much less to be the father of a king.
  Alc. You may see, wife, what a goodly piece of work

you have made : have I taught you arsmetry, as *additiori multiplicarum*, the rule of three, and all for the begetting of a boy, and to be banished for my labour? O pitiful hearing !—Come, Clesiphon, follow me.

Cles. Brother, beware : I oft have heard it told,
That sons who do their fathers scorn, shall beg when
    they be old.

Radag. Hence, bastard boy, for fear you taste the whip !
                  [Exeunt ALCON *and* CLESIPHON.

Samia. O all you heavens, and you eternal powers,
That sway the sword of justice in your hands
(If mother's curses for her son's contempt
May fill the balance of your fury full),
Pour down the tempest of your direful plagues
Upon the head of cursèd Radagon !
      [A flame of fire appears from beneath ; and RADAGON
                 is swallowed.

So you are just : now triumph, Samia !   *[Exit.*

Rasni. What exorcising charm, or hateful hag,
Hath ravishèd the pride of my delight ?
What tortuous planets, or malevolent
Conspiring power, repining destiny,
Hath made the concave of the earth unclose,
And shut in ruptures lovely Radagon ?
If I be lord commander of the clouds,
King of the earth, and sovereign of the seas,
What daring Saturn, from his fiery den,
Doth dart these furious flames amidst my court ?
I am not chief, there is more great then I :
What, greater than th' Assyrian Satrapes ? [1]
It may not be, and yet I fear there is,
That hath bereft me of my Radagon.

First Magus. Monarch, and potentate of all our pro-
    vinces,

[1] Printed "Satropos," but the word is a title and not a proper name.

Muse not so much upon this accident,
Which is indeed nothing miraculous.
The hill of Sicily, dread sovereign,
Sometime on sudden doth evacuate
Whole flakes of fire, and spews out from below
The smoky brands that Vulcan's bellows drive:
Whether by winds enclosèd in the earth,
Or fracture of the earth by river's force,
Such chances as was this are often seen;
Whole cities sunk, whole countries drownèd quite.
Then muse not at the loss of Radagon,
But frolic with the dalliance of your love.
Let cloths of purple, set with studs of gold,
Embellishèd with all the pride of earth,
Be spread for Alvida to sit upon:
Then thou, like Mars courting the queen of love,
Mayst drive away this melancholy fit.
  Rasni. The proof is good and philosophical;
And more, thy counsel plausible and sweet.—
Come, lords, though Rasni wants his Radagon,
Earth will repay him many Radagons,
And Alvida with pleasant looks revive
The heart that droops for want of Radagon.   [*Exeunt.*
  Oseas. When disobedience reigneth in the child,
And princes' ears by flattery be beguil'd;
When laws do pass by favour, not by truth;
When falsehood swarmeth both in old and youth;
When gold is made a god to wrong the poor,
And charity exil'd from rich men's door;
When men by wit do labour to disprove
The plagues for sin sent down by God above;
When great men's ears are stopt to good advice,
And apt to hear those tales that feed their vice;
Woe to the land! for from the East shall rise
A Lamb of peace, the scourge of vanities,

The judge of truth, the patron of the just,
Who soon will lay presumption in the dust,
And give the humble poor their hearts' desire,
And doom the worldlings to eternal fire:
Repent, all you that hear, for fear of plagues.
O London, this and more doth swarm in thee!
Repent, repent, for why the Lord doth see:
With trembling pray, and mend what is amiss;
The sword of justice drawn already is.

—————————

SCENE III.—*Within the* Smith's *House.*

Enter ADAM *and the* Smith's Wife.

Adam. Why, but hear you, mistress: you know a
woman's eyes are like a pair of pattens, fit to save shoe-
leather in summer, and to keep away the cold in
winter; so you may like your husband with the one eye,
because you are married, and me with the other, because
I am your man. Alas, alas! think, mistress, what a
thing love is: why, it is like to an ostry-faggot,[1] that,
once set on fire, is as hardly quenched as the bird[2]
crocodile driven out of her nest.

S. Wife. Why, Adam, cannot a woman wink but she
must sleep? and can she not love but she must cry it
out at the cross? Know, Adam, I love thee as myself,
now that we are together in secret.

Adam. Mistress, these words of yours are like to a
fox-tail placed in a gentlewoman's fan, which, as it is
light, so it giveth life: O, these words are as sweet as a
lily! whereupon, offering a borachio[3] of kisses to your

---

[1] A faggot in a hostelry, which is kept alight by the guests.
[2] "Bird" is the young of an animal. Adam is talking euphuisti-
cal nonsense.
[3] A leathern bag or bottle for wine.

unseemly personage, I entertain you upon further
acquaintance.

S. Wife. Alas, my husband comes !

Adam. Strike up the drum
And say no words but mum.

Enter the Smith.

Smith. Sirrah you, and you, huswife, well taken together ! I have long suspected you, and now I am glad
I have found you together.

Adam. Truly, sir, and I am glad that I may do you any
way pleasure, either in helping you or my mistress.

Smith. Boy here, and knave, you shall know it
straight; I will have you both before the magistrate,
and there have you surely punished.

Adam. Why, then, master, you are jealous?

Smith. Jealous, knave ! how can I be but jealous, to
see you ever so familiar together? Thou art not only
content to drink away my goods, but to abuse my wife.

Adam. Two good qualities, drunkenness and lechery :
but, master, are you jealous?

Smith. Ay, knave, and thou shalt know it ere I pass,
for I will beswinge thee while this rope will hold.

S. Wife. My good husband, abuse him not, for he
never proffered you any wrong.

Smith. Nay, whore, thy part shall not be behind.

Adam. Why, suppose, master, I have offended you, is
it lawful for the master to beat the servant for all
offences?

Smith. Ay, marry, is it, knave.

Adam. Then, master, will I prove by logic, that seeing
all sins are to receive correction, the master is to be
corrected of the man. And, sir, I pray you, what greater
sin is than jealousy? 'tis like a mad dog that for anger
bites himself : therefore that I may do my duty to you,

good master, and to make a white [1] son of you, I will so beswinge jealousy out of you, as you shall love me the better while you live.

Smith. What, beat thy master, knave?

Adam. What, beat thy man, knave? and, ay, master, and double beat you, because you are a man of credit; and therefore have at you the fairest for forty pence.

[*Beats the* Smith.

Smith. Alas, wife, help, help! my man kills me.

S. Wife. Nay, even as you have baked, so brew: jealousy must be driven out by extremities.

Adam. And that will I do, mistress.

Smith. Hold thy hand, Adam; and not only I forgive and forget all, but I will give thee a good farm to live on.

Adam. Begone, peasant, out of the compass of my further wrath, for I am a corrector of vice; and at night I will bring home my mistress.

Smith. Even when you please, good Adam.

Adam. When I please,—mark the words—'tis a lease-parol,[2] to have and to hold. Thou shalt be mine for ever: and so let's go to the ale-house.   [*Exeunt.*

Oseas. Where servants against masters do rebel,
The commonweal may be accounted hell;
For if the feet the head shall hold in scorn,
The city's state will fall and be forlorn.
This error, London, waiteth on thy state:
Servants, amend, and, masters, leave to hate;
Let love abound, and virtue reign in all;
So God will hold his hand, that threateneth thrall.

---

[1] *White* is an epithet of endearment.
[2] A lease by word of mouth.

ACT THE FOURTH

SCENE I.—*Joppa.*

Enter the Merchants *of Tharsus, the* Master *of the Ship and some* Sailors, *wet from the sea ; with them the* Governor *of Joppa.*

GOV. What strange encounters met you
    on the sea,
    That thus your bark is batter'd by
      the floods,
    And you return thus sea-wreck'd as I
      see?

First Mer. Most mighty Governor, the
    chance is strange,
The tidings full of wonder and amaze,
Which, better than we, our Master can report.

Gov. Master, discourse us all the accident.

Master. The fair Triones with their glimmering light
Smil'd at the foot of clear Bootes' wain,
And in the north, distinguishing the hours,
The loadstar of our course dispers'd his clear ;
When to the seas with blitheful western blasts
We sail'd amain, and let the bowling fly.
Scarce had we gone ten leagues from sight of land,
But, lo, an host of black and sable clouds

'Gan to eclipse Lucina's silver face;
And, with a hurling noise from forth the south,
A gust of wind did rear the billows up.
Then scantled we our sails with speedy hands,
And took our drablers [1] from our bonnets straight,
And severèd our bonnets from the courses:
Our topsails up, we truss our spritsails in;
But vainly strive they that resist the heavens.
For, lo, the waves incense them more and more,
Mounting with hideous roarings from the depth;
Our bark is batter'd by encountering storms,
And well-nigh stemm'd by breaking of the floods.
The steersman, pale and careful, holds his helm,
Wherein the trust of life and safety lay:
Till all at once (a mortal tale to tell)
Our sails were split by Bisa's [2] bitter blast.
Our rudder broke, and we bereft of hope.
There might you see, with pale and ghastly looks,
The dead in thought, and doleful merchants lift
Their eyes and hands unto their country's gods.
The goods we cast in bowels of the sea,
A sacrifice to 'suage proud Neptune's ire.
Only alone a man of Israel,
A passenger, did under hatches lie,
And slept secure, when we for succour pray'd:
Him I awoke, and said, "Why slumberest thou?
Arise, and pray, and call upon thy god;
He will perhaps in pity look on us."
Then cast we lots to know by whose amiss
Our mischief came, according to the guise;
And, lo, the lot did unto Jonas fall,
The Israelite of whom I told you last.

---

[1] "Drabler, an additional piece of canvas, laced to the bottom of the bonnet of a sail, to give it greater depth."—(N. E. D.)
[2] Bisa; the north wind.

Then question we his country and his name;
Who answer'd us, "I am an Hebrew born,
Who fear the Lord of heaven who made the sea,
And fled from him, for which we all are plagu'd:
So, to assuage the fury of my God,
Take me and cast my carcass in the sea;
Then shall this stormy wind and billow cease."
The heavens they know, the Hebrew's God can tell,
How loath we were to execute his will:
But when no oars nor labour might suffice,
We heav'd the hapless Jonas overboard.
So ceas'd the storm, and calmèd all the sea,
And we by strength of oars recover'd shore.

    Gov. A wondrous chance of mighty consequence!
    First Mer. Ah, honour'd be the god that wrought the
        same!
For we have vow'd, that saw his wondrous works,
To cast away profanèd paganism,
And count the Hebrew's god the only god:
To him this offering of the purest gold,
This myrrh and cassia, freely I do yield.

    Master. And on his altar's fume these Turkey cloths,
This gossampine [1] and gold, I'll sacrifice.

    First Sai. To him my heart and thoughts I will addict.
Then suffer us, most mighty Governor,
Within your temples to do sacrifice.

    Gov. You men of Tharsus, follow me.
Who sacrifice unto the God of heaven
Are welcome friends to Joppa's Governor.
                       [Exeunt. A sacrifice.

    Oseas. If warnèd once, the ethnics thus repent,
And at the first their error do lament,
What senseless beasts, devourèd in their sin,
Are they whom long persuasions cannot win!

          [1] Cotton-cloth, or bumbast.

Beware, ye western cities,—where the word
Is daily preachèd, both at church and board,
Where majesty the gospel doth maintain,
Where preachers, for your good, themselves do pain,—
To dally long and still protract the time;
The Lord is just, and you but dust and slime:
Presume not far, delay not to amend;
Who suffereth long, will punish in the end.
Cast thy account, O London, in this case,
Then judge what cause thou hast to call for grace!

SCENE II.—*The Seashore near Nineveh.*

JONAS *is cast out of the Whale's belly upon the Stage.*

Jonas. Lord of the light, thou maker of the world,
Behold, thy hands of mercy rear me up!
Lo, from the hideous bowels of this fish
Thou hast return'd me to the wishèd air!
Lo, here, apparent witness of thy power,
The proud leviathan that scours the seas,
And from his nostrils showers out stormy floods,
Whose back resists the tempest of the wind,
Whose presence makes the scaly troops to shake,
With humble stress of his broad-open'd chaps,
Hath lent me harbour in the raging floods!
Thus, though my sin hath drawn me down to death,
Thy mercy hath restorèd me to life.
Bow ye, my knees; and you, my bashful eyes,
Weep so for grief as you to water would.
In trouble, Lord, I callèd unto thee;
Out of the belly of the deepest hell

I cried, and thou didst hear my voice, O God !
'Tis thou hadst cast me down into the deep :
The seas and floods did compass me about ;
I thought I had been cast from out thy sight ;
The weeds were wrapt about my wretched head ;
I went unto the bottom of the hills :
But thou, O Lord my God, hast brought me up !
On thee I thought whenas my soul did faint :
My prayers did prease [1] before thy mercy-seat.
Then will I pay my vows unto the Lord,
For why salvation cometh from his throne.

The Angel *appears.*

Angel. Jonas, arise, get thee to Nineveh,
And preach to them the preachings that I bade ;
Haste thee to see the will of heaven perform'd.

       [*The* Angel *departs.*

Jonas. Jehovah, I am prest [2] to do thy will.——
What coast is this, and where am I arriv'd ?
Behold sweet Lycus streaming in his bounds,
Bearing the walls of haughty Nineveh,
Whereas three hundred towers do tempt the heaven.
Fair are thy walls, pride of Assyria ;
But, lo, thy sins have piercèd through the clouds !
Here will I enter boldly, since I know
My God commands, whose power no power resists.

         [*Exit.*

Oseas. You prophets, learn by Jonas how to live ;
Repent your sins, whilst he doth warning give.
Who knows his master's will, and doth it not,
Shall suffer many stripes, full well I wot.

---

[1] Press, similar to "mease" for "mess," p. 102.   [2] Ready.

SCENE III.—*The Garden of* RASNI'S *Palace.*

Enter ALVIDA *in rich attire, with the* KING OF CILICIA,
and her Ladies.

Alvi. Ladies, go sit you down amidst this bower,
And let the eunuchs play you all asleep:
Put garlands made of roses on your heads,
And play the wantons whilst I talk a while.
  First Lady. Thou beautiful of all the world, we will.
                              [Ladies *enter the bower.*
  Alvi. King of Cilicia, kind and courteous,
Like to thyself, because a lovely king,
Come, lay thee down upon thy mistress' knee,
And I will sing and talk of love to thee.
  K. of Cil. Most gracious paragon of excellence,
It fits not such an abject prince as I,
To talk with Rasni's paramour and love.
    Alvi. To talk, sweet friend! Who would not talk with
        thee?
O, be not coy! art thou not only fair?
Come, twine thine arms about this snow-white neck,
A love-nest for the great Assyrian king:
Blushing I tell thee, fair Cilician prince,
None but thyself can merit such a grace.
    K. of Cil. Madam, I hope you mean not for to mock
        me.
  Alvi. No, king, fair king, my meaning is to yoke thee.
Hear me but sing of love, then by my sighs,
My tears, my glancing looks, my chang'd cheer,
Thou shalt perceive how I do hold thee dear.
    K. of Cil. Sing, madam, if you please, but love in jest.
    Alvi. Nay, I will love, and sigh at every rest.
                                            [*Sings.*

Beauty, alas, where wast thou born,
Thus to hold thyself in scorn?
Whenas Beauty kiss'd to woo thee,
Thou by Beauty dost undo me:
　　　　　Heigh-ho, despise me not!

I and thou, in sooth, are one,
Fairer thou, I fairer none:
Wanton thou, and wilt thou, wanton,
Yield a cruel heart to plant on?
Do me right, and do me reason;
Cruelty is cursèd treason:
　　　　　Heigh-ho, I love! heigh-ho, I love!
　　　　　Heigh-ho! and yet he eyes me not!

K. of Cil. Madam, your song is passing passionate.
Alvi. And wilt thou not, then, pity my estate?
K. of Cil. Ask love of them who pity may impart.
Alvi. I ask of thee, sweet; thou hast stole my heart.
K. of Cil. Your love is fixèd on a greater king.
Alvi. Tut, women's love it is a fickle thing.
I love my Rasni for his dignity,
I love Cilician king for his sweet eye;
I love my Rasni since he rules the world,
But more I love this kingly little world.
　　　　　[Embraces him.
How sweet he looks! O, were I Cynthia's fere,[1]
And thou Endymion, I should hold thee dear:
Thus should mine arms be spread about thy neck,
　　　　　[Embraces his neck.
Thus would I kiss my love at every beck;
　　　　　[Kisses him.
Thus would I sigh to see thee sweetly sleep,
And if thou wak'dst not soon, thus would I weep;

[1] Companion, therefore—equal.

And thus, and thus, and thus: thus much I love thee.

                          [*Kisses him.*

   K. of Cil. For all these vows, beshrew me if I prove
      ye:

My faith unto my king shall not be fals'd.

   Alvi. Good Lord, how men are coy when they are
      crav'd!

   K. of Cil. Madam, behold our king approacheth nigh,

   Alvi. Thou art Endymion, then, no more: heigh-ho,
      for him I die!

              [*Faints, pointing at the* KING OF CILICIA.

   Enter RASNI, *with his* Kings, Lords, *and* Magi.

   Rasni. What ails the centre of my happiness,

Whereon depends the heaven of my delight?

Thine eyes the motors to command my world,

Thy hands the axier [1] to maintain my world,

Thy smiles the prime and spring-tide of my world,

Thy frowns the winter to afflict the world,

Thou queen of me, I king of all the world!

                 [*She rises as out of a trance.*

   Alvi. Ah feeble eyes, lift up and look on him!

Is Rasni here? then droop no more, poor heart. —

O, how I fainted when I wanted thee!

                    [*Embraces him.*

How fain am I, now I may look on thee!

How glorious is my Rasni, how divine!—

Eunuchs, play hymns to praise his deity:

He is my Jove, and I his Juno am.

   Rasni. Sun-bright as is the eye of summer's day,

Whenas he suits his pennons all in gold

To woo his Leda in a swan-like shape;

Seemly as Galatea for thy white;

            [1] Axis.

Rose-colour'd, lily, lovely, wanton, kind,
Be thou the labyrinth to tangle love,
Whilst I command the crown from Venus' crest,
And pull Orion's girdle from his loins,
Enchas'd with carbuncles and diamonds,
To beautify fair Alvida, my love.—
Play, eunuchs, sing in honour of her name ;
Yet look not, slaves, upon her wooing eyne.
For she is fair Lucina to your king,
But fierce Medusa to your baser eye.
Alvi. What if I slept, where should my pillow be ?
Rasni. Within my bosom, nymph, not on my knee :
Sleep, like the smiling purity of heaven,
When mildest wind is loath to blend [1] the peace ;
Meanwhile my balm shall from thy breath arise ;
And while these closures of thy lamps be shut,
My soul may have his peace from fancy's war.—
This is my Morn, and I her Cephalus :—
Wake not too soon, sweet nymph, my love is won.—
Caitiffs, why stay your strains? why tempt you me ?

Enter the Priests of the Sun, *with mitres on their heads,
carrying fire in their hands.*

First Priest. All hail unto th' Assyrian deity !
Rasni. Priests, why presume you to disturb my
    peace ?
First Priest. Rasni, the Destinies disturb thy peace.
Behold, amidst the adyts [2] of our gods,
Our mighty gods, the patrons of our war,
The ghosts of dead men howling walk about,
Crying "*Væ, Væ*, woe to this city, woe !"
The statues of our gods are thrown down,
And streams of blood our altars do distain.

---

[1] Confound, therefore to destroy.
[2] Adyt ; the innermost sanctuary of a temple.

Alvi. [starting up]. Alas, my lord, what tidings do I
      hear?
Shall I be slain?
    Rasni. Who tempteth Alvida?
Go, break me up the brazen doors of dreams,
And bind me cursèd Morpheus in a chain,
And fetter all the fancies of the night,
Because they do disturb my Alvida.
      [*A hand from out a cloud threatens with a
            burning sword.*

    K. of Cil. Behold, dread prince, a burning sword from
      heaven,
Which by a threatening arm is brandishèd!
    Rasni. What, am I threaten'd, then, amidst my
      throne?
Sages, you Magi, speak; what meaneth this?
    First Magus. These are but clammy exhalations,
Or retrograde conjunctions of the stars,
Or oppositions of the greater lights,
Or radiations finding matter fit,
That in the starry sphere kindled be;
Matters betokening dangers to thy foes,
But peace and honour to my lord the king.
    Rasni. Then frolic, viceroys, kings and potentates;
Drive all vain fancies from your feeble minds.
Priests, go and pray, whilst I prepare my feast,
Where Alvida and I, in pearl and gold,
Will quaff unto our nobles richest wine,
In spite of fortune, fate, or destiny.   [*Exeunt.*
    Oseas. Woe to the trains of women's foolish lust,
In wedlock-rites that yield but little trust,
That vow to one, yet common be to all!
Take warning, wantons; pride will have a fall.
Woe to the land where warnings profit naught!
Who say that nature God's decrees hath wrought;

Who build on fate, and leave the corner-stone,
The God of gods, sweet Christ, the only one.
If such escapes, O London, reign in thee,
Repent, for why each sin shall punish'd be !
Repent, amend, repent, the hour is nigh !
Defer not time ! who knows when he shall die?

SCENE IV.—*A Public Place in Nineveh.*

Enter one clad in Devil's *attire.*

Devil. Longer lives a merry man than a sad; and because I mean to make myself pleasant this night, I have put myself into this attire, to make a clown afraid that passeth this way: for of late there have appeared many strange apparitions, to the great fear and terror of the citizens.—O, here my young master comes.

Enter ADAM *and the* Smith's Wife.

Adam. Fear not, mistress, I'll bring you safe home: if my master frown, then will I stamp and stare ; and if all be not well then, why then to-morrow morn put out mine eyes clean with forty pound.

S. Wife. O, but, Adam, I am afraid to walk so late, because of the spirits that appear in the city.

Adam. What, are you afraid of spirits ? Armed as I am, with ale and nutmegs, turn me loose to all the devils in hell.

S. Wife. Alas, Adam, Adam ! the devil, the devil !

Adam. The devil, mistress ! fly you for your safeguard ;

[*Exit* S. Wife.] let me alone; the devil and I will deal well enough, if he have any honesty at all in him: I'll either win him with a smooth tale, or else with a toast and a cup of ale.

Devil [*singing*].

> *O, O, O, O, fain would I be,*
> *If that my kingdom fulfill'd I might see!*
> *O, O, O, O!*

Adam. Surely this is a merry devil, and I believe he is one of Lucifer's minstrels; hath a sweet voice; now surely, surely, he may sing to a pair of tongs and a bagpipe.

Devil. O, thou art he that I seek for.

Adam. Spritus santus!—Away from me, Satan! I have nothing to do with thee.

Devil. O villain, thou art mine!

Adam. Nominus patrus!—I bless me from thee, and I conjure thee to tell me who thou art!

Devil. I am the spirit of the dead man that was slain in thy company when we were drunk together at the ale.[1]

Adam. By my troth, sir, I cry you mercy; your face is so changed that I had quite forgotten you: well, master devil, we have tossed over many a pot of ale together.

Devil. And therefore must thou go with me to hell.

Adam [*aside*]. I have a policy to shift him, for I know he comes out of a hot place, and I know myself, the smith and the devil hath a dry tooth in his head: therefore will I leave him asleep and run my way.

Devil. Come, art thou ready?

Adam. Faith, sir, my old friend, and now goodman

---

[1] "The ale" here means the ale-house, as it does in Shakespeare's *Two Gentlemen of Verona* (II, 5).

devil, you know you and I have been tossing many a good cup of ale: your nose is grown very rich: what say you, will you take a pot of ale now at my hands? Hell is like a smith's forge, full of water, and yet ever athirst.

Devil. No ale, villain; spirits cannot drink; come, get upon my back, that I may carry thee.[1]

Adam. You know I am a smith, sir: let me look whether you be well shod or no; for if you want a shoe, a remove, or the clinching of a nail, I am at your command.

Devil. Thou hast never a shoe fit for me.

Adam. Why, sir, we shoe horned beasts, as well as you, —[*Aside.*] O good Lord! let me sit down and laugh; hath never a cloven foot; a devil, quoth he! I'll use *Spritus santus* nor *Nominus patrus* no more to him, I warrant you; I'll do more good upon him with my cudgel: now will I sit me down, and become justice of peace to the devil.

Devil. Come, art thou ready?

Adam. I am ready, and with this cudgel I will conjure thee.   [*Beats him.*

Devil. O, hold thy hand! thou killest me, thou killest me!   [*Exit.*

Adam. Then may I count myself, I think, a tall[2] man, that am able to kill a devil. Now who dare deal with me in the parish? or what wench in Nineveh will not love me, when they say, "There goes he that beat the devil?"   [*Exit.*

[1] A famous comic trick in the early plays. Adam is a late figure of the Vice type. Compare *Friar Bacon and Friar Bungay* (V, 2) in which Miles is carried off on a Devil's back.

[2] Bold, brave.

SCENE V.—*A Public Place near the* Usurer's.

Enter THRASYBULUS.

Thras. Loath'd is the life that now enforc'd I lead;
But since necessity will have it so,
(Necessity that doth command the gods),
Through every coast and corner now I pry,
To pilfer what I can to buy me meat.
Here have I got a cloak, not over old,
Which will afford some little sustenance:
Now will I to the broking Usurer,
To make exchange of ware for ready coin.

Enter ALCON, SAMIA, *and* CLESIPHON.

Alc. Wife, bid the trumpets sound, a prize, a prize!
mark the posy: I cut this from a new-married wife, by
the help of a horn-thumb,[1] and a knife,—six shillings,
four pence.

Samia. The better luck ours: but what have we here,
cast apparel? Come away, man, the Usurer is near:
this is dead ware, let it not bide on our hands.

Thras. [*aside*]. Here are my partners in my poverty,
Enforc'd to seek their fortunes as I do:
Alas, that few men should possess the wealth,
And many souls be forc'd to beg or steal!—
Alcon, well met.

Alc. Fellow beggar, whither now?

Thras. To the Usurer, to get gold on commodity.

Alc. And I to the same place, to get a vent for my
villainy. See where the old crust comes: let us salute
him.

[1] An instrument used by pick-pockets in cutting purses.

Enter Usurer.

God-speed, sir : may a man abuse your patience upon a pawn?

Usurer. Friend, let me see it.

Alc. Ecce signum! a fair doublet and hose, new-bought out of the pilferer's shop,—a handsome cloak.

Usurer. How were they gotten?

Thras. How catch the fishermen fish? Master, take them as you think them worth : we leave all to your conscience.

Usurer. Honest men, toward men, good men, my friends, like to prove good members, use me, command me ; I will maintain your credits. There's money : now spend not your time in idleness ; bring me commodity ; I have crowns for you : there is two shillings for thee, and six shillings for thee.   [*Gives money.*

Alc. A bargain.—Now, Samia, have at it for a new smock!—Come, let us to the spring of the best liquor : whilst this lasts, tril-lill!

Usurer. Good fellows, proper fellows, my companions, farewell : I have a pot for you.

Samia [*aside*]. If he could spare it.

Enter JONAS.

Jonas. Repent, ye men of Nineveh, repent !
The day of horror and of torment comes ;
When greedy hearts shall glutted be with fire,
Whenas corruptions veil'd shall be unmask'd,
When briberies shall be repaid with bane,
When whoredoms shall be recompens'd in hell,
When riot shall with vigour be rewarded,
Whenas neglect of truth, contempt of God,
Disdain of poor men, fatherless and sick,

Shall be rewarded with a bitter plague.
Repent, ye men of Nineveh, repent !
The Lord hath spoke, and I do cry it out ;
There are as yet but forty days remaining,
And then shall Nineveh be overthrown :
Repent, ye men of Nineveh, repent !
There are as yet but forty days remaining,
And then shall Nineveh be overthrown.   [*Exit.*

 Usurer. Confus'd in thought, O, whither shall I wend ?
             [*Exit.*
 Thras. My conscience cries that I have done amiss.
             [*Exit.*
 Alc. O God of heaven, 'gainst thee have I offended !
 Samia. Asham'd of my misdeeds, where shall I hide
 me ?
 Cles. Father, methinks this word "repent" is good :
He that punisheth disobedience
Doth hold a scourge for every privy fault.
      [*Exit with* ALCON *and* SAMIA.
 Oseas. Look, London, look ; with inward eyes behold
What lessons the events do here unfold.
Sin grown to pride, to misery is thrall :
The warning-bell is rung, beware to fall.
Ye worldly men, whom wealth doth lift on high,
Beware and fear, for worldly men must die.
The time shall come, where least suspect remains,
The sword shall light upon the wisest brains ;
The head that deems to overtop the sky,
Shall perish in his human policy.
Lo, I have said, when I have said the truth,
When will is law, when folly guideth youth,
When show of zeal is prank'd in robes of zeal,
When ministers powl [1] the pride of commonweal,
When law is made a labyrinth of strife,

   [1] To shave or cut, therefore to pillage, plunder.

When honour yields him friend to wicked life,
When princes hear by others' ears their folly,
When usury is most accounted holy,
If these shall hap, as would to God they might not,
The plague is near : I speak, although I write not.

Enter the Angel.

Angel. Oseas.
Oseas. Lord?
Angel. Now hath thine eyes perus'd these heinous sins,
Hateful unto the mighty Lord of hosts.
The time is come, their sins are waxen ripe,
And though the Lord forewarns, yet they repent not ;
Custom of sin hath harden'd all their hearts.
Now comes revenge, armèd with mighty plagues,
To punish all that live in Nineveh ;
For God is just, as he is merciful,
And doubtless plagues all such as scorn repent.
Thou shalt not see the desolation
That falls unto these cursèd Ninevites,
But shalt return to great Jerusalem,
And preach unto the people of thy God
What mighty plagues are incident to sin,
Unless repentance mitigate His ire :
Rapt in the spirit, as thou wert hither brought,
I'll seat thee in Judæa's provinces.
Fear not, Oseas, then to preach the word.
    Oseas. The will of the Lord be done !
                    [Oseas *is taken away by the* Angel.

K

ACT THE FIFTH.

SCENE I.—*The Palace of* RASNI.

Enter RASNI *with his* Kings, Magi, Lords, *and* Attendants; ALVIDA *and her* Ladies; *to a banquet.*

RASNI. So, viceroys, you have pleas'd
    me passing well;
These curious cates are gracious in
    mine eye,
But these borachios of the richest wine
Make me to think how blithesome we
    will be.—
Seat thee, fair Juno, in the royal throne,
And I will serve thee to see thy face,
That, feeding on the beauty of thy looks,
My stomach and mine eyes may both be fill'd.—
Come, lordings, seat you, fellow-mates at feast,
And frolic, wags; this is a day of glee:
This banquet is for brightsome Alvida.
I'll have them skink [1] my standing bowls with wine,
And no man drink but quaff a whole carouse
Unto the health of beauteous Alvida:

[1] To draw, to pour; here used in the sense of "to fill."

146

For whoso riseth from this feast not drunk,
As I am Rasni, Nineveh's great king,
Shall die the death as traitor to myself,
For that he scorns the health of Alvida.

   K. of Cil. That will I never do, my lord;
Therefore with favour, fortune to your grace,
Carouse unto the health of Alvida.

   Rasni. Gramercy, lording, here I take thy pledge :—
And, Crete, to thee a bowl of Greekish wine,
Here to the health of Alvida.

   K. of Crete. Let come, my lord. Jack skinker, fill it
     full,
A pledge unto the health of heavenly Alvida.

   Rasni. Vassals, attendant on our royal feasts,
Drink you, I say, unto my lover's health :
Let none that is in Rasni's royal court
Go this night safe and sober to his bed.

Enter ADAM.

   Adam. This way he is, and here will I speak with
him.

   First Lord. Fellow, whither pressest thou?

   Adam. I press nobody, sir; I am going to speak with
a friend of mine.

   First Lord. Why, slave, here is none but the king, and
his viceroys.

   Adam. The king! marry, sir, he is the man I would
speak withal.

   First Lord. Why, callest him a friend of thine?

   Adam. Ay, marry, do I, sir; for if he be not my friend,
I'll make him my friend, ere he and I pass,

   First Lord. Away, vassal, begone! thou speak unto
the king!

Adam. Ay, marry, will I, sir; an if he were a king of velvet, I will talk to him.

Rasni. What's the matter there? what noise is that?

Adam. A boon, my liege, a boon, my liege!

Rasni. What is it that great Rasni will not grant,
This day, unto the meanest of his land,
In honour of his beauteous Alvida?
Come hither, swain; what is it that thou cravest?

Adam. Faith, sir, nothing, but to speak a few sentences to your worship.

Rasni. Say, what is it?

Adam. I am sure, sir, you have heard of the spirits that walk in the city here.

Rasni. Ay, what of that?

Adam. Truly, sir, I have an oration to tell you of one of them; and this it is.

Alvi. Why goest not forward with thy tale?

Adam. Faith, mistress, I feel an imperfection in my voice, a disease that often troubles me; but, alas, easily mended; a cup of ale or a cup of wine will serve the turn.

Alvi. Fill him a bowl, and let him want no drink.

Adam. O, what a precious word was that, "And let him want no drink!" [*Drink given to* ADAM.] Well, sir, now I'll tell you forth my tale. Sir, as I was coming alongst the port-royal of Nineveh, there appeared to me a great devil, and as hard-favoured a devil as ever I saw; nay, sir, he was a cuckoldly devil, for he had horns on his head. This devil, mark you now, presseth upon me, and, sir, indeed, I charged him with my pike-staff; but when that would not serve, I came upon him with *Spritus santus,*—why, it had been able to have put Lucifer out of his wits: when I saw my charm would not serve, I was in such a perplexity, that sixpenny-worth of juniper would not have made the place sweet again.

Alvi. Why, fellow, wert thou so afraid?

Adam. O, mistress, had you been there and seen, his very sight had made you shift a clean smock! I promise you, though I were a man, and counted a tall fellow, yet my laundress called me slovenly knave the next day.

Rasni. A pleasant slave.—Forward, sirrah, on with thy tale.

Adam. Faith, sir, but I remember a word that my mistress your bed-fellow spoke.

Rasni. What was that, fellow?

Adam. O, sir, a word of comfort, a precious word— "And let him want no drink."

Rasni. Her word is law; and thou shalt want no drink.   [*Drink given to* ADAM.

Adam. Then, sir, this devil came upon me, and would not be persuaded, but he would needs carry me to hell. I proffered him a cup of ale, thinking, because he came out of so hot a place, that he was thirsty; but the devil was not dry, and therefore the more sorry was I. Well, there was no remedy but I must with him to hell: and at last I cast mine eye aside; if you knew what I spied you would laugh, sir; I looked from top to toe, and he had no cloven feet. Then I ruffled up my hair, and set my cap on the one side, and, sir, grew to be a justice of peace to the devil: at last in a great fume; as I am very choleric, and sometimes so hot in my fustian fumes that no man can abide within twenty yards of me, I start up, and so bombasted the devil, that, sir, he cried out and ran away.

Alvi. This pleasant knave hath made me laugh my fill.

Rasni, now Alvida begins her quaff,
And drinks a full carouse unto her king.

Rasni. A pledge, my love, as hearty as great Jove
Drunk when his Juno heav'd a bowl to him.—

Frolic, my lords ; let all the standards walk ; [1]
Ply it till every man hath ta'en his load.——
How now, sirrah, what cheer? we have no words of you.

Adam. Truly, sir, I was in a brown study about my
mistress.

Alvi. About me ! for what ?

Adam. Truly, mistress, to think what a golden sentence
you did speak : all the philosophers in the world could
not have said more :—" What, come, let him want no
drink." O, wise speech !

Alvi. Villains, why skink you unto this fellow ?
He makes me blithe and merry in my thoughts :
Heard you not that the king hath given command,
That all be drunk this day within his court
In quaffing to the health of Alvida ?

                              [*Drink given to* ADAM.

                    Enter JONAS.

Jonas. Repent, repent, ye men of Nineveh, repent !
The Lord hath spoke, and I do cry it out,
There are as yet but forty days remaining,
And then shall Nineveh be overthrown :
Repent, ye men of Nineveh, repent !

Rasni. What fellow's this, that thus disturbs our feast
With outcries and alarums to repent ?

Adam. O sir, 'tis one Goodman Jonas, that is come
from Jericho ; and surely I think he hath seen some
spirit by the way, and is fallen out of his wits, for he
never leaves crying night nor day. My master heard
him, and he shut up his shop, gave me my indenture,
and he and his wife do nothing but fast and pray.

Jonas. Repent, ye men of Nineveh, repent !

          [1] Let all the standing-bowls go round.

Rasni. Come hither, fellow : what art, and from whence
comest thou ?

Jonas. Rasni, I am a prophet of the Lord,
Sent hither by the mighty God of hosts,
To cry destruction to the Ninevites.
O Nineveh, thou harlot of the world,
I raise thy neighbours round about thy bounds,
To come and see thy filthiness and sin !
Thus saith the Lord, the mighty God of hosts :
Your king loves chambering and wantonness ;
Whoredom and murder do distain his court ;
He favoureth covetous and drunken men ;
Behold, therefore, all like a strumpet foul,
Thou shalt be judg'd and punish'd for thy crime ;
The foe shall pierce the gates with iron ramps,
The fire shall quite consume thee from above,
The houses shall be burnt, the infants slain,
And women shall behold their husbands die.
Thine eldest sister is Samaria.[1]
And Sodom on thy right hand seated is.
Repent, ye men of Nineveh, repent !
The Lord hath spoke, and I do cry it out,
There are as yet but forty days remaining,
And then shall Nineveh be overthrown.

　　　　　　　　　　　　　　　[Offers to depart.

　Rasni. Stay, prophet, stay.

　Jonas. Disturb not him that sent me ;
Let me perform the message of the Lord.　　　*[Exit.*

　Rasni. My soul is buried in the hell of thoughts.—
Ah, Alvida, I look on thee with shame !—
My lords on sudden fix their eyes on ground,
As if dismay'd to look upon the heavens.—
Hence, Magi, who have flattered me in sin !

　　　　　　　　　　　　　　　[Exeunt Magi.

　[1] This is the emendation by J. C. Smith, given in Collins'
edition, of the unintelligible " Lamana " of the quartos.

Horror of mind, disturbance of my soul,
Make me aghast for Nineveh's mishap.
Lords, see proclaim'd, yea, see it straight proclaim'd,
That man and beast, the woman and her child,
For forty days in sack and ashes fast:
Perhaps the Lord will yield, and pity us.—
Bear hence these wretched blandishments of sin,
                          [*Taking off his crown and robe.*
And bring me sackcloth to attire your king:
Away with pomp! my soul is full of woe.—
In pity look on Nineveh, O God!
                  [*Exeunt all except* ALVIDA *and* LADIES.

   Alvi. Assail'd with shame, with horror overborne,
To sorrow sold, all guilty of our sin,
Come, ladies, come, let us prepare to pray.
Alas, how dare we look on heavenly light,
That have despis'd the maker of the same?
How may we hope for mercy from above,
That still despise the warnings from above?
Woe's me, my conscience is a heavy foe.
O patron of the poor oppress'd with sin,
Look, look on me, that now for pity crave!
Assail'd with shame, with horror overborne,
To sorrow sold, all guilty of our sin,
Come, ladies, come, let us prepare to pray.   [*Exeunt.*

   SCENE II.—*A Street near the Temple.*

Enter the Usurer, *with a halter in one hand, a dagger in
                  the other.*[1]

   Usurer. Groaning in conscience, burden'd with my
         crimes,
The hell of sorrow haunts me up and down.

[1] A reminiscence of Kyd's *Spanish Tragedy* (Scene XII), in which
Hieromino enters with a poniard and a rope.

Tread where I list, methinks the bleeding ghosts
Of those whom my corruption brought to naught
Do serve for stumbling-blocks before my steps;
The fatherless and widow wrong'd by me,
The poor oppressèd by my usury,
Methinks I see their hands rear'd up to heaven,
To cry for vengeance of my covetousness.
Whereso I walk, all sigh and shun my way;
Thus am I made a monster of the world:
Hell gapes for me, heaven will not hold my soul.
You mountains, shroud me from the God of truth:
Methinks I see him sit to judge the earth;
See how he blots me out o' the book of life!
O burden, more than Ætna, that I bear!
Cover me, hills, and shroud me from the Lord;
Swallow me, Lycus, shield me from the Lord.
In life no peace: each murmuring that I hear,
Methinks the sentence of damnation sounds,
"Die, reprobate, and hie thee hence to hell."

  [*The* Evil Angel *tempts him, offering the knife and rope.*
What fiend is this that tempts me to the death?
What, is my death the harbour of my rest?
Then let me die:—what second charge is this?
Methinks I hear a voice amidst mine ears,
That bids me stay, and tells me that the Lord
Is merciful to those that do repent.
May I repent? O thou, my doubtful soul,
Thou mayst repent, the judge is merciful!
Hence, tools of wrath, stales[1] of temptation!
For I will pray and sigh unto the Lord;
In sackcloth will I sigh, and fasting pray;
O Lord, in rigour look not on my sins!

   [*He sits down in sackcloth, his hands and eyes*
     reared to heaven.

    [1] Decoys.

Enter ALVIDA *with her* Ladies, *with dispersèd locks.*

Alvi. Come, mournful dames, lay off your broider'd
        locks,
And on your shoulders spread dispersèd hairs:
Let voice of music cease where sorrow dwells:
Clothèd in sackcloth, sigh your sins with me;
Bemoan your pride, bewail your lawless lusts;
With fasting mortify your pamper'd loins:
O, think upon the horror of your sins;
Think, think with me, the burden of your blames!
Woe to thy pomp, false beauty, fading flower,
Blasted by age, by sickness, and by death!
Woe to our painted cheeks, our curious oils,
Our rich array, that foster'd us in sin!
Woe to our idle thoughts, that wound our souls!
O, would to God all nations might receive
A good example by our grievous fall!

    First Lady. You that are planted there where pleasure
        dwells,
And think your pomp as great as Nineveh's,
May fall for sin as Nineveh doth now.

    Alvi. Mourn, mourn, let moan be all your melody,
And pray with me, and I will pray for all :—
O Lord of heaven, forgive us our misdeeds!

    Ladies. O Lord of heaven, forgive us our misdeeds!

    Usurer. O Lord of light, forgive me my misdeeds!

Enter RASNI, *with his* Kings *and* Lords *in sackcloth.*

    K. of Cil. Be not so overcome with grief, O king,
Lest you endanger life by sorrowing so.

    Rasni. King of Cilicia, should I cease my grief,
Whereas my swarming sins afflict my soul?
Vain man, know this, my burden greater is
Than every private subject's in my land.

My life hath been a loadstar unto them,
To guide them in the labyrinth of blame :
Thus I have taught them for to do amiss ;
Then must I weep, my friend, for their amiss.
The fall of Nineveh is wrought by me :
I have maintain'd this city in her shame ;
I have contemn'd the warnings from above ;
I have upholden incest, rape, and spoil ;
'Tis I, that wrought the sin, must weep the sin.
O, had I tears like to the silver streams
That from the Alpine mountains sweetly stream,
Or had I sighs, the treasures of remorse,
As plentiful as Æolus hath blasts,
I then would tempt the heavens with my laments,
And pierce the throne of mercy by my sighs !
    K. of Cil. Heavens are propitious unto faithful prayers.
    Rasni. But after we repent, we must lament,
Lest that a worser mischief doth befall.
O, pray : perhaps the Lord will pity us.—
O God of truth, both merciful and just,
Behold, repentant men, with piteous eyes
We wail the life that we have led before :
O, pardon, Lord ! O, pity Nineveh !
    All. O, pardon, Lord ! O, pity Nineveh !
    Rasni. Let not the infants, dallying on the teat,
For fathers' sins in judgment be oppress'd !
    K. of Cil. Let not the painful mothers big with child,
The innocents, be punish'd for our sin !
    Rasni. O, pardon, Lord ! O, pity Nineveh !
    All. O, pardon, Lord ! O, pity Nineveh !
    Rasni. O Lord of heaven, the virgins weep to thee !
The covetous man sore sorry for his sin,
The prince and poor, all pray before thy throne ;
And wilt thou, then, be wroth with Nineveh ?
    K. of Cil. Give truce to prayer, O king, and rest a space.

Rasni. Give truce to prayers, when times require no
    truce?
No, princes, no. Let all our subjects hie
Unto our temples, where, on humbled knees,
I will expect some mercy from above.

               [They all enter the temple.

SCENE III.—*Outside the City of Nineveh.*

Enter JONAS.

Jonas. This is the day wherein the Lord hath said
That Nineveh shall quite be overthrown;
This is the day of horror and mishap,
Fatal unto the cursèd Ninevites.
These stately towers shall in thy watery bounds,
Swift-flowing Lycus, find their burials:
These palaces, the pride of Assur's kings,
Shall be the bowers of desolation,
Whereas the solitary bird shall sing,
And tigers train their young ones to their nest.
O all ye nations bounded by the west,
Ye happy isles where prophets do abound,
Ye cities famous in the western world,
Make Nineveh a precedent for you!
Leave lewd desires, leave covetous delights,
Fly usury, let whoredom be exil'd,
Lest you with Nineveh be overthrown.
Lo, how the sun's inflamèd torch prevails,
Scorching the parchèd furrows of the earth!.
Here will I sit me down, and fix mine eye
Upon the ruins of yon wretched town;
And, lo, a pleasant shade, a spreading vine,
To shelter Jonas in this sunny heat!
What means my God? the day is done and spent:

Lord, shall my prophecy be brought to naught?
When falls the fire? when will the judge be wroth?
I pray thee, Lord, remember what I said,
When I was yet within my country-land;
Jehovah is too merciful, I fear.
O, let me fly, before a prophet fault!
For thou art merciful, the Lord my God,
Full of compassion, and of sufferance,
And dost repent in taking punishment.
Why stays thy hand? O Lord, first take my life,
Before my prophecy be brought to naught!

      [*A serpent devours the vine.*

Ah, he is wroth! behold, the gladsome vine,
That did defend me from the sunny heat,
Is wither'd quite, and swallow'd by a serpent!
Now furious Phlegon triumphs on my brows,
And heat prevails, and I am faint in heart.

    Enter the Angel.

 Angel. Art thou so angry, Jonas? tell me why.
 Jonas. Jehovah, I with burning heat am plung'd,
And shadow'd only by a silly vine;
Behold, a serpent hath devourèd it:
And lo, the sun, incens'd by eastern wind,
Afflicts me with canicular aspéct.
Would God that I might die! for, well I wot,
'Twere better I were dead then rest alive.
 Angel. Jonas, art thou so angry for the vine?
 Jonas. Yea, I am angry to the death, my God.
 Angel. Thou hast compassion, Jonas, on a vine,
On which thou never labour didst bestow;
Thou never gav'st it life or power to grow,
But suddenly it sprung, and suddenly died:
And should not I have great compassion
On Nineveh, the city of the world,

Wherein there are a hundred thousand souls,
And twenty thousand infants that ne' wot [1]
The right hand from the left, beside much cattle?
O Jonas, look into their temples now,
And see the true contrition of their king,
The subjects' tears, the sinners' true remorse!
Then from the Lord proclaim a mercy-day,
For he is pitiful as he is just.[2]

    Jonas. I go, my God, to finish thy command.
                            [Exit Angel.

O, who can tell the wonders of my God,
Or talk his praises with a fervent tongue?
He bringeth down to hell, and lifts to heaven;
He draws the yoke of bondage from the just,
And looks upon the heathen with piteous eyes:
To him all praise and honour be ascrib'd.
O, who can tell the wonders of my God?
He makes the infant to proclaim his truth,
The ass to speak to save the prophet's life,
The earth and sea to yield increase for man.
Who can describe the compass of his power,
Or testify in terms his endless might?
My ravish'd sprite, O, whither dost thou wend?
Go and proclaim the mercy of my God;
Relieve the careful-hearted Ninevites;
And, as thou wert the messenger of death,
Go bring glad tidings of recover'd grace.   *[Exit.*

SCENE IV.—*Within the City of Nineveh.*

Enter ADAM, *with a bottle of beer in one slop,[3] and a great
piece of beef in another.*

    Adam. Well, Goodman Jonas, I would you had never

---

[1] Know not.   [2] A very faithful paraphrase of chapter 4 of the
book of *Jonah*.   [3] Wide breeches; here breeches pockets.

come from Jewry to this country; you have made me
look like a lean rib of roast beef, or like the picture
of Lent painted upon a red-herring's cob.[1]   Alas,
masters, we are commanded by the proclamation to
fast and pray!, by my troth, I could prettily so-so away
with [2] praying; but for fasting, why, 'tis so contrary to my
nature, that I had rather suffer a short hanging than a
long fasting.   Mark me, the words be these, "Thou shalt
take no manner of food for so many days."   I had as
lief he should have said, "Thou shalt hang thyself for
so many days."   And yet, in faith, I need not find fault
with the proclamation, for I have a buttery and a pantry
and a kitchen about me; for proof, *ecce signum!* this
right slop is my pantry, behold a manchet[3] [*Draws it out*];
this place is my kitchen, for, lo, a piece of beef [*Draws
it out*],—O, let me repeat that sweet word again! "for,
lo, a piece of beef."   This is my buttery, for, see, see,
my friends, to my great joy, a bottle of beer [*Draws it
out*].   Thus, alas, I make shift to wear out this fasting;
I drive away the time.   But there go searchers about
to seek if any man breaks the king's command.   O, here
they be; in with your victuals, Adam.

[*Puts them back into his slops.*

Enter Two Searchers.

First Search. How duly the men of Nineveh keep the
proclamation! how are they armed to repentance!   We
have searched through the whole city, and have not as
yet found one that breaks the fast.

Sec. Search. The sign of the more grace:—but stay,
here sits one, methinks, at his prayers; let us see who
it is.

---

[1] The head of a red-herring.   The term may have become
synonymous with the fish itself.   Adam's meaning cannot be said to
be very clear.   [2] I could endure.   [3] A fine white bread.

First Search. 'Tis Adam, the smith's man.—How now, Adam?

Adam. Trouble me not; "Thou shalt take no manner of food, but fast and pray."

First Search. How devoutly he sits at his orisons! but stay, methinks I feel a smell of some meat or bread about him.

Sec. Search. So thinks me too.—You, sirrah, what victuals have you about you?

Adam. Victuals! O horrible blasphemy! Hinder me not of my prayer, nor drive me not into a choler. Victuals! why, heardest thou not the sentence, "Thou shalt take no food, but fast and pray"?

Sec. Search. Truth, so it should be; but, methinks, I smell meat about thee.

Adam. About me, my friends! these words are actions in the case. About me! no, no, hang those gluttons that cannot fast and pray.

First Search. Well, for all your words, we must search you.

Adam. Search me! take heed what you do; my hose[1] are my castles, 'tis burglary if you break ope a slop; no officer must lift up an iron hatch; take heed, my slops are iron.

[*They search* ADAM.]

Sec. Search. O villain!—see how he hath gotten victuals, bread, beef, and beer, where the king commanded upon pain of death none should eat for so many days, no, not the sucking infant!

Adam. Alas, sir, this is nothing but a *modicum non nocet ut medicus daret*; why, sir, a bit to comfort my stomach.

First Search. Villain, thou shalt be hanged for it.

Adam. These are your words, "I shall be hanged for it"; but first answer me to this question, how many days have we to fast still?

---

[1] Breeches.

Sec. Search. Five days.

Adam. Five days! a long time: then I must be hanged?

First Search. Ay, marry, must thou.

Adam. I am your man, I am for you, sir, for I had rather be hanged than abide so long a fast. What, five days! Come, I'll untruss. Is your halter, and the gallows, the ladder, and all such furniture in readiness?

First Search. I warrant thee, shalt want none of these.

Adam. But hear you, must I be hanged?

First Search. Ay, marry.

Adam. And for eating of meat. Then, friends, know ye by these presents, I will eat up all my meat, and drink up all my drink, for it shall never be said, I was hanged with an empty stomach.

First Search. Come away, knave; wilt thou stand feeding now?

Adam. If you be so hasty, hang yourself an hour, while I come to you, for surely I will eat up my meat.

Sec. Search. Come, let's draw him away perforce.

Adam. You say there is five days yet to fast; these are your words?

Sec. Search. Ay, sir.

Adam. I am for you: come, let's away, and yet let me be put in the Chronicles. [*Exeunt.*

SCENE V.—*The Palace of* RASNI.

Enter JONAS, RASNI, ALVIDA, *the* KING OF CILICIA, *and other* Kings, *royally attended.*

Jonas. Come, careful king, cast off thy mournful
    weeds,
Exchange thy cloudy looks to smoothèd smiles;

L

Thy tears have pierc'd the piteous throne of grace,
Thy sighs, like incense pleasing to the Lord,
Have been peace-offerings for thy former pride:
Rejoice, and praise his name that gave thee peace.
And you, fair nymphs, ye lovely Ninevites,
Since you have wept and fasted 'fore the Lord,
He graciously hath temper'd his revenge:
Beware henceforth to tempt him any more:
Let not the niceness of your beauteous looks
Engraft in you a high-presuming mind;
For those that climb he casteth to the ground,
And they that humble be he lifts aloft.

  Rasni. Lowly I bend with awful bent of eye,
Before the dread Jehovah, God of hosts,
Despising all profane device of man.
Those lustful lures, that whilom led awry
My wanton eyes, shall wound my heart no more;
And she, whose youth in dalliance I abus'd,
Shall now at last become my wedlock-mate.—
Fair Alvida, look not so wo-begone;
If for thy sin thy sorrow do exceed,
Blessèd be thou; come, with a holy band
Let's knit a knot to salve our former shame.

  Alvi. With blushing looks, betokening my remorse,
I lowly yield, my king, to thy behest,
So as this man of God shall think it good.

  Jonas. Woman, amends may never come too late;
A will to practise good is virtuous:
The God of heaven, when sinners do repent,
Doth more rejoice than in ten thousand just.

  Rasni. Then witness, holy prophet, our accord.

  Alvi. Plight in the presence of the Lord thy God.

  Jonas. Blest may you be, like to the flowering sheaves
That play with gentle winds in summer-tide;
Like olive-branches let your children spread.

And as the pines in lofty Lebanon,
Or as the kids that feed on Sepher [1] plains,
So be the seed and offspring of your loins !

Enter the Usurer, THRASYBULUS, *and* ALCON.

Usurer. Come forth, my friends, whom wittingly I
    wrong'd :
Before this man of God receive your due ;
Before our king I mean to make my peace.—
Jonas, behold, in sign of my remorse,
I here restore into these poor men's hands
Their goods which I unjustly have detain'd ;
And may the heavens so pardon my misdeeds
As I am penitent for my offence !
    Thras. And what through want from others I purloin'd,
Behold, O king, I proffer 'fore thy throne,
To be restor'd to such as owe [2] the same.
    Jonas. A virtuous deed, pleasing to God and man.
Would God, all cities drowned in like shame
Would take example of these Ninevites.
    Rasni. Such be the fruits of Nineveh's repent ;
And such for ever may our dealings be,
That he that call'd us home in height of sin
May smile to see our hearty penitence.—
Viceroys, proclaim a fast unto the Lord ;
Let Israel's God be honour'd in our land ;
Let all occasion of corruption die,
For who shall fault therein shall suffer death :—
Bear witness, God, of my unfeignèd zeal.—

---

[1] The quartos give "Lepher," which is unintelligible. This
reading is Dyce's conjecture. It is of little moment that these places
are not plains but mountains.   [2] Own.

Come, holy man, as thou shalt counsel me,
My court and city shall reformèd be.
   Jonas. Wend on in peace, and prosecute this course.
                     [Exeunt all except JONAS.
You islanders, on whom the milder air
Doth sweetly breathe the balm of kind increase,
Whose lands are fatten'd with the dew of heaven,
And made more fruitful than Actæan plains ;
You whom delicious pleasures dandle soft,
Whose eyes are blinded with security,
Unmask yourselves, cast error clean aside.
O London, maiden of the mistress-isle,
Wrapt in the folds and swathing-clouts of shame,
In thee more sins than Nineveh contains !
Contempt of God, despite of reverend age,
Neglect of law, desire to wrong the poor,
Corruption, whoredom, drunkenness, and pride.
Swoll'n are thy brows with impudence and shame,
O proud adulterous glory of the west !
Thy neighbours burn, yet dost thou fear no fire ;
Thy preachers cry, yet dost thou stop thine ears ;
The 'larum rings, yet sleepest thou secure.
London, awake, for fear the Lord do frown :
I set a looking-glass before thine eyes.
O, turn, O, turn, with weeping to the Lord,
And think the prayers and virtues of thy queen
Defer the plague which otherwise would fall !
Repent, O London ! lest for thine offence,
Thy shepherd fail, whom mighty God preserve,
That she may bide the pillar of his church
Against the storms of Romish Anti-Christ !
The hand of mercy overshade her head,
And let all faithful subjects say, Amen !
                               [Exit.

ORLANDO FURIOSO

Two quartos of *Orlando Furioso* are known. Of these, copies of
the first, dated 1594, printed by John Danter for Cuthbert Burby,
are to be found in the British Museum and in the Dyce Library at
South Kensington; copies of the second, dated 1599, and printed by
Simon Stafford for Cuthbert Burby, are to be found in the British
Museum, the Dyce Library and the library of Mr Huth. On the
Stationers' Registers the play is entered, 7th December 1593, to
John Danter, and notice of transfer to Cuthbert Burby is made
under date of 28th May 1594. The play belonged first to the
Queen's players and was probably performed at court, possibly on
St. Stephen's Day, 26th December 1588, though this is conjecture
(*See* Gayley, *Rep. Eng. Com.*, p. 409). Upon the absence of the
Queen's men from court, 26th December 1591 to April 1593, this
play, among others, fell into the hands of the combined Admiral's
and Strange's companies, and was by them performed, as Henslowe
records, 21st February 1592. Greene's name does not appear on
the title-page of the quartos. In *The Defence of Conny-Catching*
(1592), we find the following :—"Master R. G., would it not make
you blush—if you sold *Orlando Furioso* to the Queen's players for
twenty nobles, and when they were in the country, sold the same
play to Lord Admiral's men, for as much more? Was not this
plain coney-catching, M. G. ?" Among the actors in the Admiral
and Strange companies was Edward Alleyn. It so occurs that
there exists at Dulwich College a large portion of the MS. of this
play, containing the part of Orlando, with cues regularly marked,
and with omissions supplied in the handwriting of Alleyn.
Though imperfect, this MS. indicates that the printed edition was
composed from a curtailed and mutilated copy. Greene's play is
based on a free use of Ariosto, and may be considered a parody on
the "mad plays" popular at the time. Reflections of it are to be
found in Peele's *Old Wives' Tale*, in the name Sacripant, and in the
resemblance between ll. 66-69, *Orlando Furioso*, and ll. 885-888,
Old Wives' Tale.

DRAMATIS PERSONÆ

MARSILIUS, Emperor of Africa.
SOLDAN OF EGYPT.
RODOMONT, King of Cuba.
MANDRICARD, King of Mexico.
BRANDIMART, King of the Isles.
SACRIPANT.
ORLANDO.
OGIER.
NAMUS.
OLIVER.
TURPIN.
DUKE OF AQUITAIN.
ROSSILION.
MEDOR.
ORGALIO, page to ORLANDO.
SACRIPANT'S man.
TOM.
RALPH.
Fiddler.
Several of the Twelve Peers of France, whose names are
        not given.   Clowns, Attendants, etc.
ANGELICA, daughter to MARSILIUS.
MELISSA, an enchantress.
Satyrs.

THE HISTORY OF ORLANDO FURIOSO[1]

ACT THE FIRST

SCENE I.—*The Palace of* MARSILIUS.

Enter MARSILIUS *and* ANGELICA, *the* SOLDAN,
RODOMONT, MANDRICARD, BRANDIMART, ORLANDO
and SACRIPANT, *with Attendants.*

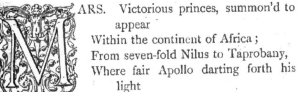

ARS.   Victorious princes, summon'd to
    appear
Within the continent of Africa;
From seven-fold Nilus to Taprobany,
Where fair Apollo darting forth his
    light
Plays on the seas;
From Gades' Islands, where stout Hercules
Emblaz'd his trophies on two posts of brass,
To Tanais, whose swift declining floods
Environ rich Europa to the north;
All fetch'd from out your courts by beauty to this coast,

---

[1] The title in the quartos was "The History of Orlando Furioso,
one of the Twelve Peers of France."

To seek and sue for fair Angelica;
Sith none but one must have this happy prize,
At which you all have levell'd long your thoughts,
Set each man forth his passions how he can,
And let her censure [1] make the happiest man.

Sold. The fairest flower that glories Africa,
Whose beauty Phœbus dares not dash with showers,
Over whose climate never hung a cloud,
But smiling Titan lights the horizon,—
Egypt is mine, and there I hold my state,
Seated in Cairo and in Babylon.
From thence the matchless beauty of Angelica,
Whose hue (as bright as are those silves doves
That wanton Venus mann'th [2] upon her fist),
Forc'd me to cross and cut th' Atlantic seas,
To oversearch the fearful ocean,
Where I arriv'd to etérnize with my lance
The matchless beauty of fair Angelica;
Nor tilt, nor tourney, but my spear and shield
Resounding on their crests and sturdy helms,
Topt high with plumes, like Mars his burgonet,
Enchasing on their curats [3] with my blade,
That none so fair as fair Angelica.
But leaving these such glories as they be,
I love, my lord; let that suffice for me.

Rod. Cuba my seat, a region so enrich'd
With savours sparkling from the smiling heavens,
As those that seek for traffic to my coast
Account it like that wealthy Paradise
From whence floweth Gihon, and swift Euphrates: [4]
The earth within her bowels hath enwrapt,
As in the massy storehouse of the world,

[1] Judgment.
[2] "To man" is a term in falconry, and means to accustom to man, to make tractable.
[3] Cuirasses.   [4] A false quantity.

Millions of gold, as bright as was the shower
That wanton Jove sent down to Danaë.
Marching from thence to manage arms abroad,
I pass'd the triple-parted regiment [1]
That froward Saturn gave unto his sons,
Erecting statues of my chivalry,
Such and so brave as never Hercules
Vow'd for the love of lovely Iole.
But leaving these such glories as they be,
I love, my lord ; let that suffice for me.

  Mand. And I, my lord, am Mandricard of Mexico,
Whose climate, fairer than Iberia's,
Seated beyond the sea of Tripoly,
And richer than the plot Hesperides, [2]
Or that same isle wherein Ulysses' love
Lull'd in her lap the young Telegonus ;
That did but Venus tread a dainty step,
So would she like the land of Mexico,
As, Paphos and brave Cyprus set aside,
With me sweet lovely Venus would abide.
From thence, mounted upon a Spanish bark,
Such as transported Jason to the fleece,
Come from the south, I furrow'd Neptune's seas,
North-east as far as is the frozen Rhine ;
Leaving fair Voya, cross'd up Danuby,
As high as Saba, whose enhancing streams
Cut 'twixt the Tartars and the Russians : [3]
There did I act as many brave attempts,
As did Pirothöus for his Proserpine.
But leaving these such glories as they be,
I love, my lord ; let that suffice for me.

  Brand. The bordering islands, seated here in ken,

---

[1] Dominion.
[2] Here as elsewhere improperly used as the name of a place.
[3] These four lines occur nearly verbatim towards the end of
Peele's *Old Wives' Tale*, ll. 885-8.

Whose shores are sprinkled with rich orient pearl,
More bright of hue than were the margarites [1]
That Cæsar found in wealthy Albion;
The sands of Tagus all of burnish'd gold
Made Thetis never prouder on the clifts [2].
That overpeer the bright and golden shore,
Than do the rubbish of my country seas:
And what I dare, let say the Portingale,
And Spaniard tell, who, mann'd with mighty fleets,
Came to subdue my islands to their king,
Filling our seas with stately argosies,
Carvels and magars, hulks of burden great,
Which Brandimart rebated [3] from his coast,
And sent them home ballas'd with little wealth. [4]
But leaving these such glories as they be,
I love, my lord; let that suffice for me.

    Orl. Lords of the south, and princes of esteem,
Viceroys unto the state of Africa,
I am no king, yet am I princely born,
Descended from the royal house of France,
And nephew to the mighty Charlemagne,
Surnam'd Orlando, the County Palatine.
Swift fame hath sounded to our western seas
The matchless beauty of Angelica,
Fairer than was the nymph of Mercury,
Who, when bright Phœbus mounteth up his coach,
And tracts Aurora in her silver steps,
And sprinkles from the folding of her lap
White lilies, roses, and sweet violets.
Yet thus believe me, princes of the south,
Although my country's love, dearer than pearl
Or mines of gold, might well have kept me back;
The sweet conversing with my king and friends,

---

[1] Pearls.   [2] Cliffs.   [3] Same as French *rebattre*, beat back.
[4] An allusion to the recent repulse of the Spanish Armada.

Left all for love, might well have kept me back;
The seas by Neptune hoisèd to the heavens,
Whose dangerous flaws [1] might well have kept me back;
The savage Moors and Anthropophagi,
Whose lands I pass'd, might well have kept me back;
The doubt of entertainment in the court
When I arriv'd, might well have kept me back;
But so the fame of fair Angelica
Stamp'd in my thoughts the figure of her love,
As neither country, king, or seas, or cannibals,
Could by despairing keep Orlando back.
I list not boast in acts of chivalry
(An humour never fitting with my mind),
But come there forth the proudest champion
That hath suspicion in the Palatine,
And with my trusty sword Durandell,
Single, I'll register upon his helm
What I dare do for fair Angelica.
But leaving these such glories as they be,
I love, my lord;
Angelica herself shall speak for me.

   Mars. Daughter, thou hear'st what love hath here
       alleg'd,
How all these kings, by beauty summon'd here,
Put in their pleas, for hope of diadem,
Of noble deeds, of wealth, and chivalry,
All hoping to possess Angelica.
Sith father's will may hap to aim amiss
(For parents' thoughts in love oft step awry),
Choose thou the man who best contenteth thee,
And he shall wear the Afric crown next me.
For trust me, daughter, like of whom thou please,
Thou satisfied, my thoughts shall be at ease.

   Ang. Kings of the South, viceroys of Africa,

               [1] Blasts.

Sith father's will hangs on his daughter's choice,
And I, as erst Princess Andromache
Seated amidst the crew of Priam's sons,
Have liberty to choose where best I love ;
Must freely say, for fancy hath no fraud,
That far unworthy is Angelica
Of such as deign to grace her with their loves ;
The Soldan with his seat in Babylon,
The Prince of Cuba, and of Mexico,
Whose wealthy crowns might win a woman's will,
Young Brandimart, master of all the isles
Where Neptune planted hath his treasury :
The worst of these men of so high import
As may command a greater dame than I.
But fortune, or some deep-inspiring fate,
Venus, or else the bastard brat of Mars,
Whose bow commands the motions of the mind,
Hath sent proud love to enter such a plea
As nonsuits all your princely evidence,
And flat commands that, maugre majesty,
I choose Orlando, County Palatine.

  Rod. How likes Marsilius of his daughter's choice?

  Mars. As fits Marsilius of his daughter's spouse.

  Rod. Highly thou wrong'st us, King of Africa,
To brave thy neighbour princes with disgrace,
To tie thine honour to thy daughter's thoughts,
Whose choice is like that Greekish giglot's[1] love
That left her lord, Prince Menelaus,
And with a swain made 'scape away to Troy.
What is Orlando but a straggling mate,
Banish'd for some offence by Charlemagne,
Skipp'd from his country as Anchises' son,
And means, as he did to the Carthage Queen,
To pay her ruth and ruin for her love?

       [1] Giglot, a wanton woman.

Orl. Injurious Cuba, ill it fits thy gree
To wrong a stranger with discourtesy.
Were't not the sacred presence of Angelica
Prevails with me, as Venus' smiles with Mars,
To set a supersedeas of my wrath,
Soon should I teach thee what it were to brave.

 Mand. And, Frenchman, were't not 'gainst the law of
   arms,
In place of parley for to draw a sword,
Untaught companion, I would learn you know
What duty 'longs to such a prince as he.

 Orl. Then as did Hector 'fore Achilles' tent,
Trotting his courser softly on the plains,
Proudly dar'd forth the stoutest youth of Greece;
So who stands highest in his own conceit,
And thinks his courage can perform the most,
Let him but throw his gauntlet on the ground,
And I will pawn my honour to his gage,
He shall ere night be met and combated.

 Mars. Shame you not, princes, at this bad agree,
To wrong a stranger with discourtesy?
Believe me, lords, my daughter hath made choice,
And, maugre him that thinks him most aggriev'd,
She shall enjoy the County Palatine.

 Brand. But would these princes follow my advice,
And enter arms as did the Greeks 'gainst Troy,
Nor he, nor thou should'st have Angelica.

 Rod. Let him be thought a dastard to his death,
That will not sell the travails he hath past
Dearer than for a woman's fooleries:
What says the mighty Mandricard?

 Mand. I vow to hie me home to Mexico,
To troop myself with such a crew of men
As shall so fill the downs of Africa
Like to the plains of watery Thessaly,

Whenas an eastern gale, whistling aloft,
Hath overspread the ground with grasshoppers.
Then see, Marsilius, if the Palatine
Can keep his love from falling to our lots,
Or thou canst keep thy country free from spoil.

Mars. Why, think you, lords, with haughty menaces
To dare me out within my palace-gates?
Or hope you to make conquest by constraint
Of that which never could be got by love?
Pass from my court, make haste out of my land,
Stay not within the bounds Marsilius holds;
Lest, little brooking these unfitting braves,
My choler overslip the law of arms,
And I inflict revenge on such abuse.

Rod. I'll beard and brave thee in thy proper town,
And here ensconce myself despite of thee,
And hold thee play till Mandricard return.—
What says the mighty Soldan of Egypt?

Sold. That when Prince Menelaus with all his mates
Had ten years held their siege in Asia,
Folding their wraths in cinders of fair Troy,
Yet, for their arms grew by conceit of love,
Their trophies were but conquest of a girl:
Then trust me, lords, I'll never manage arms
For women's loves that are so quickly lost.

Brand. Tush, my lords, why stand you upon terms?
Let us to our sconce,—and you, my lord, to Mexico.

Orl. Ay, sirs, ensconce ye how you can,
See what we dare, and thereon set your rest.
                    [*Exeunt all except* SACRIPANT *and his* Man.

Sac. [*aside*]. Boast not too much, Marsilius, in thyself,
Nor of contentment in Angelica;
For Sacripant must have Angelica,
And with her Sacripant must have the crown:
By hook or crook I must and will have both.

Ah sweet Revenge, incense their angry minds,
Till, all these princes weltering in their bloods,
The crown do fall to County Sacripant!
Sweet are the thoughts that smother from conceit:
For when I come and set me down to rest,
My chair presents a throne of majesty;
And when I set my bonnet on my head,
Methinks I fit my forehead for a crown;
And when I take my truncheon in my fist,
A sceptre then comes tumbling in my thoughts;
My dreams are princely, all of diadems.
Honour,—methinks the title is too base:
Mighty, glorious, and excellent,—ay, these,
My glorious genius, sound within my mouth;
These please the ear, and with a sweet applause,
Make me in terms coequal with the gods.
Then these, Sacripant, and none but these;
And these, or else make hazard of thy life.
Let it suffice, I will conceal the rest.—
Sirrah!

   Man. My lord?

   Sac. [*aside*]. My lord! How basely was this slave
       brought up,
That knows no titles fit for dignity,
To grace his master with hyperboles!
My lord! Why, the basest baron of fair Africa
Deserves as much: yet County Sacripant
Must he a swain salute with name of lord.—
Sirrah, what thinks the Emperor of my colours,
Because in field I wear both blue and red at once?

   Man. They deem, my lord, your honour lives at peace,
As one that's neuter in these mutinies,
And covets to rest equal friends to both;
Neither envious to Prince Mandricard,
Nor wishing ill unto Marsilius,

   M

That you may safely pass where'er you please,
With friendly salutations from them both.

Sac. Ay, so they guess, but level far awry;
For if they knew the secrets of my thoughts,
Mine emblem sorteth to another sense.
I wear not these as one resolv'd to peace,
But blue and red as enemy to both;
Blue, as hating King Marsilius,
And red, as in revenge to Mandricard:
Foe unto both, friend only to myself,
And to the crown, for that's the golden mark
Which makes my thoughts dream on a diadem.
See'st not thou all men presage I shall be king?
Marsilius sends to me for peace;
Mandricard puts off his cap, ten mile off:
Two things more, and then I cannot miss the crown.

Man. O, what be those, my good lord?

Sac. First must I get the love of fair Angelica.
Now am I full of amorous conceits,
Not that I doubt to have what I desire,
But how I might best with mine honour woo:
Write, or entreat,—fie, that fitteth not;
Send by ambassadors,—no, that's too base;
Flatly command,—ay, that's for Sacripant:
Say thou art Sacripant, and art in love,
And who in Africa dare say the county nay?
O Angelica,
Fairer than Chloris when in all her pride
Bright Maia's son entrapp'd her in the net
Wherewith Vulcan entangled the god of war!

Man. Your honour is so far in contemplation of
Angelica as you have forgot the second in attaining to
the crown.

Sac. That's to be done by poison, prowess, or any
means of treachery, to put to death the traitorous

Orlando.—But who is this comes here? Stand close.

[They retire.

Enter Orgalio.

Org. I am sent on embassage to the right mighty and magnificent, alias, the right proud and pontifical, the County Sacripant; for Marsilius and Orlando, knowing him to be as full of prowess as policy, and fearing lest in leaning to the other faction he might greatly prejudice them, they seek first to hold the candle before the devil, and knowing him to be a Thrasonical mad-cap, they have sent me a Gnathonical [1] companion, to give him lettuce fit for his lips. Now, sir, knowing his astronomical humours, as one that gazeth so high at the stars as he never looketh on the pavement in the streets,—but whist! *lupus est in fabula.*

Sac. [*coming forward*]. Sirrah, thou that ruminatest to thyself a catalogue of privy conspiracies, what art thou?

Org. God save your majesty!

Sac. [*aside*]. My majesty!—Come hither, my well-nutrimented knave; whom takest me to be?

Org. The mighty Mandricard of Mexico.

Sac. [*aside*]. I hold these salutations as ominous; for saluting me by that which I am not, he presageth what I shall be: for so did the Lacedæmonians by Agathocles, who of a base potter wore the kingly diadem.—But why deemest thou me to be the mighty Mandricard of Mexico?

Org. Marry, sir,—

Sac. Stay there: wert thou never in France?

Org. Yes, if it please your majesty.

Sac. So it seems, for there they salute their king by the name of Sir, Monsieur:—but forward.

Org. Such sparks of peerless majesty

---

[1] Thraso and Gnatho were well-known characters in the *Eunuchus* of Terence, and references to them are very common in the works of Elizabethan writers.

From those looks flame, like lightning from the east,
As either Mandricard, or else some greater prince,—

   Sac. [*aside*]. Methinks these salutations make my
      thoughts
To be heroical :—but say, to whom art thou sent?

   Org. To the County Sacripant.

   Sac. Why, I am he.

   Org. It pleaseth your majesty to jest.

   Sac. Whate'er I seem, I tell thee I am he.

   Org. Then may it please your honour, the Emperor
Marsilius, together with his daughter Angelica and
Orlando, entreateth your excellency to dine with them.

   Sac. Is Angelica there?

   Org. There, my good lord.

   Sac. Sirrah.

   Man. My lord?

   Sac. Villain, Angelica sends for me: see that thou
entertain that happy messenger, and bring him in with
thee.   [*Exeunt.*

SCENE II.—*Before the Walls of* RODOMONT'S *Castle.*

Enter ORLANDO, *the* DUKE OF AQUITAIN, *and the*
COUNTY ROSSILION, *with* Soldiers.

   Orl. Princes of France, the sparkling light of fame,
Whose glory's brighter than the burnish'd gates
From whence Latona's lordly son doth march,
When, mounted on his coach tinsell'd with flames,
He triumphs in the beauty of the heavens;
This is the place where Rodomont lies hid:
Here lies he, like the thief of Thessaly,
Which scuds abroad and searcheth for his prey,
And, being gotten, straight he gallops home,
As one that dares not break a spear in field.

But trust me, princes, I have girt his fort,
And I will sack it, or on this castle-wall
I'll write my resolution with my blood :—
Therefore, drum, sound a parle.

        [A parle is sounded, and a Soldier *comes upon*
                    the walls.

    Sol. Who is't that troubleth our sleeps?

    Orl. Why, sluggard, seest thou not Lycaon's son,
The hardy plough-swain unto mighty Jove,
Hath trac'd his silver furrows in the heavens,
And, turning home his over-watchèd team,
Gives leave unto Apollo's chariot?
I tell thee, sluggard, sleep is far unfit
For such as still have hammering in their heads,
But only hope of honour and revenge :
These call'd me forth to rouse thy master up.
Tell him from me, false coward as he is,
That Orlando, the County Palatine,
Is come this morning, with a band of French,
To play him hunt's-up with a point of war ;
I'll be his minstrel with my drum and fife ;
Bid him come forth, and dance it if he dare,
Let fortune throw her favours where she list.

    Sol. Frenchman, between half-sleeping and awake,
Although the misty veil strain'd over Cynthia
Hinders my sight from noting all thy crew,
Yet, for I know thee and thy straggling grooms
Can in conceit build castles in the sky,
But in your actions like the stammering Greek
Which breathes his courage bootless in the air,
I wish thee well, Orlando, get thee gone,
Say that a sentinel did suffer thee ;
For if the round or court-of-guard should hear
Thou or thy men were braying at the walls,
Charles' wealth, the wealth of all his western mines,

Found in the mountains of Transalpine France,
Might not pay ransom to the king for thee.

Orl. Brave sentinel, if nature hath enchas'd
A sympathy of courage to thy tale,
And, like the champion of Andromache,
Thou, or thy master, dare come out the gates,
Maugre the watch, the round, or court-of-guard,
I will attend to abide the coward here.
If not, but still the craven sleeps secure,
Pitching his guard within a trench of stones,
Tell him his walls shall serve him for no proof,
But as the son of Saturn in his wrath
Pash'd [1] all the mountains at Typhœus' head,
And topsy-turvy turn'd the bottom up,
So shall the castle of proud Rodomont.—
And so, brave lords of France, let's to the fight.

　　　　　　　　　　　　　　　　[*Exeunt.*

SCENE III.—*A Battle-field.*

Alarums: RODOMONT *and* BRANDIMART *fly.*
Enter ORLANDO *with* RODOMONT'S *coat.*

Orl. The fox is scap'd, but here's his case:
I miss'd him near; 'twas time for him to trudge.

　　　　　　　[*Enter the* DUKE OF AQUITAIN.
How now, my lord of Aquitain!

Aq. My lord, the court-of-guard is put unto the sword
And all the watch that thought themselves so sure,
So that not one within the castle breathes.

Orl. Come then, let's post amain to find out
　　Rodomont,
And then in triumph march unto Marsilius.　　[*Exeunt.*

　　　　　[1] Hurled, dashed to pieces.

ACT THE SECOND

SCENE I.—*Near the Castle of* MARSILIUS.

Enter MEDOR *and* ANGELICA.

ANG. I marvel, Medor, what my father
    means
    To enter league with County Sacripant?
    Med. Madam, the king your father's
      wise enough;
    He knows the county, like to Cassius,
    Sits sadly dumping, aiming Cæsar's
      death,
Yet crying "Ave" to his majesty.[1]
But, madam, mark awhile, and you shall see
Your father shake him off from secrecy.

   Ang. So much I guess; for when he will'd I should
Give entertainment to the doting earl,
His speech was ended with a frowning smile.

   Med. Madam, see where he comes: I will be gone.

                             [*Exit.*

Enter SACRIPANT *and his* Man.

   Sac. How fares my fair Angelica?

   Ang. Well, that my lord so friendly is in league,

---

[1] In his *Francesco's Fortunes* Greene satirizes "Ave Cæsar" as it occurs in *Edward III.*, presumably by Marlowe.

183

As honour wills him, with Marsilius.

Sac. Angelica, shall I have a word or two with thee?

Ang. What pleaseth my lord for to command?

Sac. Then know, my love, I cannot paint my grief,
Nor tell a tale of Venus and her son,
Reporting such a catalogue of toys:
It fits not Sacripant to be effeminate.
Only give leave, my fair Angelica,
To say, the county is in love with thee.

Ang. Pardon, my lord; my loves are over-past:
So firmly is Orlando printed in my thoughts,
As love hath left no place for any else.

Sac. Why, overweening damsel, see'st thou not
Thy lawless love unto this straggling mate
Hath fill'd our Afric regions full of blood?
And wilt thou still perséver in thy love?
Tush, leave the Palatine, and go with me.

Ang. Brave county, know, where sacred love unites,
The knot of gordian at the shrine of Jove
Was never half so hard or intricate
As be the bands which lovely Venus ties.
Sweet is my love; and, for I love, my lord,
Seek not, unless as Alexander did,
To cut the plough-swain's traces with thy sword,
Or slice the slender fillets of my life:
For else, my lord, Orlando must be mine.

Sac. Stand I on love? Stoop I to Venus' lure,
That never yet did fear the god of war?
Shall men report that County Sacripant
Held lovers' pains for pining passions?
Shall such a siren offer me more wrong
Than they did to the prince of Ithaca?
No; as he his ears, so, county, stop thine eye.
Go to your needle, lady, and your clouts;
Go to such milksops as are fit for love:

I will employ my busy brains for war.

 Ang. Let not, my lord, denial breed offence :
Love doth allow her favours but to one,
Nor can there sit within the sacred shrine
Of Venus more than one installèd heart.
Orlando is the gentleman I love,
And more than he may not enjoy my love.

 Sac. Damsel, begone : fancy[1] hath taken leave ;
Where I took hurt, there have I heal'd myself,
As those that with Achilles' lance were wounded,
Fetch'd help at self-same pointed spear.
Beauty can brave, and beauty hath repulse ;
And, beauty, get ye gone to your Orlando.
         [*Exit* ANGELICA.

 Man. My lord, hath love amated[2] him whose thoughts
Have ever been heroical and brave?
Stand you in dumps, like to the Myrmidon
Trapt in the tresses of Polyxena,
Who, amid the glory of his chivalry,
Sat daunted with a maid of Asia?

 Sac. Thinkst thou my thoughts are lunacies of love?
No, they are brands firèd in Pluto's forge,
Where sits Tisiphone tempering in flames
Those torches that do set on fire revenge.
I lov'd the dame ; but brav'd by her repulse,
Hate calls me on to quittance all my ills ;
Which first must come by offering prejudice
Unto Orlando her belovèd love.

 Man. O, how may that be brought to pass, my
  lord?

 Sac. Thus. Thou see'st that Medor and Angelica
Are still so secret in their private walks,
As that they trace the shady lawnds,
And thickest-shadow'd groves,

   [1] Love.   [2] Confounded, dismayed.

Which well may breed suspicion of some love.
Now, than the French no nation under heaven
Is sooner touch'd with sting of jealousy.

   Man. And what of that, my lord?

   Sac. Hard by, for solace, in a secret grove,
The county once a-day fails not to walk:
There solemnly he ruminates his love.
Upon those shrubs that compass-in the spring,
And on those trees that border-in those walks,
I'll slily have engrav'n on every bark
The names of Medor and Angelica.
Hard by, I'll have some roundelays hung up,
Wherein shall be some posies of their loves,
Fraughted so full of fiery passions
As that the county shall perceive by proof
Medor hath won his fair Angelica.

   Man. Is this all, my lord?

   Sac. No; for thou like to a shepherd shalt be
     cloth'd,
With staff and bottle, like some country-swain
That tends his flocks feeding upon these downs.
Here see thou buzz into the county's ears
That thou hast often seen within these woods
Base Medor sporting with Angelica;
And when he hears a shepherd's simple tale,
He will not think 'tis feign'd.
Then either a madding mood will end his love,
Or worse betide him through fond jealousy.

   Man. Excellent, my lord; see how I will play the
     shepherd.

   Sac. And mark thou how I play the carver:
Therefore be gone, and make thee ready straight.

                    [Exit his Man.

   [SACRIPANT *carves the names and hangs up the*
    roundelays on the trees, and then goes out.

Re-enter his Man *attired like a shepherd.*

Shep. Thus all alone, and like a shepherd's swain,
As Paris, when Œnone lov'd him well,
Forgat he was the son of Priamus,
All clad in grey, sat piping on a reed ;
So I transformèd to this country shape,
Haunting these groves do work my master's will,
To plague the Palatine with jealousy,
And to conceit him with some deep extreme.——
Here comes the man unto his wonted walk.

Enter ORLANDO *and* ORGALIO.

Orl. Orgalio, go see a sentinel be plac'd,
And bid the soldiers keep a court-of-guard,
So to hold watch till secret here alone
I meditate upon the thoughts of love.
    Org. I will, my lord.   [*Exit.*
    Orl. Fair queen of love, thou mistress of delight,
Thou gladsome lamp that wait'st on Phœbe's train,
Spreading thy kindness through the jarring orbs,
That in their union praise thy lasting powers ;
Thou that hast stay'd the fiery Phlegon's course,
And mad'st the coachman of the glorious wain
To droop, in view of Daphne's excellence ;
Fair pride of morn, sweet beauty of the even,[1]
Look on Orlando languishing in love.
Sweet solitary groves, whereas the nymphs
With pleasance laugh to see the satyrs play,
Witness Orlando's faith unto his love.
Tread she these lawnds, kind Flora, boast thy pride.
Seek she for shade, spread, cedars, for her sake.
Fair Flora, make her couch amidst thy flowers.

    [1] At this point the Alleyn manuscript begins.

Sweet crystal springs,
Wash ye with roses when she longs to drink.
Ah, thought, my heaven! ah, heaven, that knows my
      thought!
Smile, joy in her that my content hath wrought.
   Shep. [*aside*]. The heaven of love is but a pleasant
      hell,
Where none but foolish-wise imprison'd dwell.
   Orl. Orlando, what contrarious thoughts be these,
That flock with doubtful motions in thy mind?
Heaven smiles, and trees do boast their summer pride.
What! Venus writes her triumphs here beside.
   Shep. [*aside*]. Yet when thine eye hath seen, thy
      heart shall rue
The tragic chance that shortly shall ensue.
   Orl. [*reads*]. "*Angelica*":—ah, sweet and heavenly
      name,
Life to my life, and essence to my joy!
But, soft! this gordian knot together co-unites
A Medor partner in her peerless love.
Unkind, and will she bend her thoughts to change?
Her name, her writing! Ah foolish and unkind!
No name of hers, unless the brooks relent
To hear her name, and Rhodanus vouchsafe
To raise his moisten'd locks from out the reeds,
And flow with calm alongst his turning bounds:
No name of hers, unless the Zephyr blow
Her dignities alongst Ardenia woods,
Where all the world for wonders do await.
And yet her name! for why Angelica;
But, mix'd with Medor, not Angelica.
Only by me was lov'd Angelica,
Only for me must live Angelica.
I find her drift: perhaps the modest pledge
Of my content hath with a secret smile

And sweet disguise restrain'd her fancy thus,
Figuring Orlando under Medor's name;
Fine drift, fair nymph! Orlando hopes no less.
                                        [*Spies the roundelays.*
Yet more! are Muses masking in these trees,
Framing their ditties in conceited lines,
Making a goddess, in despite of me,
That have no other but Angelica?
    Shep. [*aside*]. Poor hapless man, these thoughts contain thy hell!
    Orl. [*reads*].

> "*Angelica is lady of his heart,*
> *Angelica is substance of his joy,*
> *Angelica is medicine of his smart,*
> *Angelica hath healèd his annoy.*"

Ah, false Angelica!—what, have we more?
                                        [*Reads.*

> "*Let groves, let rocks, let woods, let watery springs,*
> *The cedar, cypress, laurel, and the pine,*
> *Joy in the notes of love that Medor sings*
> *Of those sweet looks, Angelica, of thine.*
> *Then, Medor, in Angelica take delight,*
> *Early, at morn, at noon, at even and night.*"

What, dares Medor court my Venus?
What may Orlando deem?
Aetna, forsake the bounds of Sicily,
For now in me thy restless flames appear.
Refus'd, contemn'd, disdain'd! what worse than these?—
    Orgalio!
                Re-enter ORGALIO.
    Org. My lord?
    Orl. Boy, view these trees carvèd with true love-knots,
The inscription "*Medor and Angelica?*";
And read these verses hung up of their loves:
Now tell me, boy, what dost thou think?

Org. By my troth, my lord, I think Angelica is a woman.

Orl. And what of that?

Org. Therefore unconstant, mutable, having their loves hanging in their eyelids; that as they are got with a look, so they are lost again with a wink. But here's a shepherd; it may be he can tell us news.

Orl. What messenger hath Ate sent abroad
With idle looks to listen my laments?—
Sirrah, who wrongèd happy nature so,
To spoil these trees with this "*Angelica?*"—
Yet in her name, Orlando, they are blest.

Shep. I am a shepherd-swain, thou wandering knight,
That watch my flocks, not one that follow love.

Orl. As follow love! why darest thou dispraise my
      heaven,
Or once disgrace or prejudice her name?
Is not Angelica the queen of love,
Deck'd with the compound wreath of Adon's flowers?
She is.   Then speak, thou peasant, what is he
That dares attempt to court my queen of love,
Or I shall send thy soul to Charon's charge.

Shep. Brave knight, since fear of death enforceth still
To greater minds submission and relent,
Know that this Medor, whose unhappy name
Is mixèd with the fair Angelica's,
Is even that Medor that enjoys her love.
Yon cave bears witness of their kind content;
Yon meadows talk the actions of their joy;
Our shepherds in their songs of solace sing,
"Angelica doth none but Medor love."

Orl. Angelica doth none but Medor love!
Shall Medor, then, possess Orlando's love?
Dainty and gladsome beams of my delight;
Delicious brows, why smile your heavens for those

That, wounding you, prove poor Orlando's foes?
Lend me your plaints, you sweet Arcadian nymphs,
That wont to sing your new-departed loves ;
Thou weeping flood, leavé Orpheus' wail for me ;
And, Titan's nieces, gather all in one
Those fluent springs of your lamenting tears,
And let them stream along my faintful looks.

   Shep. [*aside*]. Now is the fire, late smother'd in suspect,
Kindled, and burns within his angry breast :
Now have I done the will of Sacripant.

   Orl. *Fœmineum servile genus, crudele, superbum* :
Discourteous women, nature's fairest ill,
The woe of man, that first-created curse,
Base female sex, sprung from black Ate's loins,
Proud, disdainful, cruel, and unjust,
Whose words are shaded with enchanting wiles,
Worse than Medusa mateth all our minds ;
And in their hearts sits shameless treachery,
Turning a truthless vile circumference.
O, could my fury paint their furies forth !
For hell's no hell, compared to their hearts,
Too simple devils to conceal their arts ;
Born to be plagues unto the thoughts of men,
Brought for eternal pestilence to the world.

> *O femminile ingegno, di tutti mali sede,*
> *Come ti volgi e muti facilmente,*
> *Contrario oggetto proprio de la fede !*
> *O infelice, O miser chi ti crede !*
> *Importune, superbe, dispettose,*
> *Prive d'amor, di fede e di consiglio,*
> *Timerarie, crudeli, inique, ingrate,*
> *Per pestilenzia eterna al mondo nate.*[1]

[1] The first four of these lines are, with the exception of the last
half of the first line, from the 117th stanza of the twenty-seventh
Canto of Ariosto's *Orlando Furioso* ; the other four are from the
121st stanza of the same Canto.

Villain, what art thou that followest me?

Org. Alas, my lord, I am your servant, Orgalio.

Orl. No, villain, thou art Medor; that rann'st away
  with Angelica.

Org. No, by my troth, my lord, I am Orgalio; ask all
  these people else.

Orl. Art thou Orgalio? tell me where Medor is.

Org. My lord, look where he sits.

Orl. What, sits he here, and braves me too?

Shep. No, truly, sir, I am not he.

Orl. Yes, villain.   [*Draws him in by the leg.*

Org. Help, help, my lord of Aquitain!

Enter the DUKE OF AQUITAIN *and* Soldiers.

O, my lord of Aquitain, the Count Orlando is run
mad, and taking of a shepherd by the heels, rends
him as one would tear a lark! See where he comes,
with a leg on his neck.

Re-enter ORLANDO *with a leg.*

Orl. Villain, provide me straight a lion's skin,
Thou see'st I now am mighty Hercules;
Look where's my massy club upon my neck.
I must to hell to fight with Cerberus,
And find out Medor there or else I die.[1]
You that are the rest, get you quickly away;
Provide ye horses all of burnish'd gold,
Saddles of cork, because I'll have them light;
For Charlemagne the great is up in arms,
And Arthur with a crew of Britons comes
To seek for Medor and Angelica.
    [*So he beateth them all in before him, except* ORGALIO.

[1] A corrupt passage is here supplemented by words from the
Alleyn manuscript.

Enter MARSILIUS.

Org. Ah, my lord, Orlando—

Mars. Orlando! what of Orlando?

Org. He, my lord, runs madding through the woods,
Like mad Orestes in his greatest rage.
Step but aside into the bordering grove,
There shall you see engraven on every tree
The lawless love of Medor and Angelica.
O, see, my lord, not any shrub but bears
The cursèd stamp that wrought the county's rage.
If thou be'st mighty King Marsilius,
For whom the county would adventure life,
Revenge it on the false Angelica.

Mars. Trust me, Orgalio, Theseus in his rage
Did never more revenge his wrong'd Hippolytus
Than I will on the false Angelica.
Go to my court, and drag me Medor forth;
Tear from his breast the daring villain's heart.
Next take that base and damn'd adulteress,—
I scorn to title her with daughter's name,—
Put her in rags, and, like some shepherdess,
Exile her from my kingdom presently.
Delay not, good Orgalio, see it done.

                              [*Exit* ORGALIO.

Enter a Soldier, *with* MANDRICARD *disguised.*

How now, my friend! what fellow hast thou there?

Sol. He says, my lord, that he is servant unto
Mandricard.

Mars. To Mandricard!
It fits me not who sway the diadem,
And rule the wealthy realms of Barbary,
To stain my thoughts with any cowardice.—

   N

Thy master brav'd me to my teeth,
He back'd the Prince of Cuba for my foe;
For which nor he nor his shall 'scape my hands.
No, soldier, think me resolute as he.

Mand. It grieves me much that princes disagree,
Sith black repentance followeth afterward:
But leaving that, pardon me, gracious lord.

Mars. For thou entreat'st, and newly art arriv'd,
And yet thy sword is not imbru'd in blood;
Upon conditions, I will pardon thee,—
That thou shalt never tell thy master, Mandricard,
Nor any fellow-soldier of the camp,
That King Marsilius licens'd thee depart:
He shall not think I am so much his friend,
That he or one of his shall 'scape my hand.

Mand. I swear, my lord, and vow to keep my
   word.

Mars. Then take my banderol[1] of red;
Mine, and none but mine, shall honour thee,
And safe conduct thee to Port Carthagene.

Mand. But say, my lord, if Mandricard were here,
What favour should he find, or life or death?

Mars. I tell thee, friend, it fits not for a king
To prize his wrath before his courtesy.
Were Mandricard, the King of Mexico,
In prison here, and crav'd but liberty,
So little hate hangs in Marsilius' breast,
As one entreaty should quite raze it out.
But this concerns not thee, therefore, farewell.

Mand. Thanks, and good fortune fall to such a king,
As covets to be counted courteous.

   [*Exit* MARSILIUS.

Blush, Mandricard; the honour of thy foe disgraceth
   thee;

---

[1] A streamer attached to a lance.

Thou wrongest him that wisheth thee but well;
Thou bringest store of men from Mexico
To battle him that scorns to injure thee,
Pawning his colours for thy warrantise.
Back to thy ships, and hie thee to thy home;
Budge not a foot to aid Prince Rodomont;
But friendly gratulate these favours found,
And meditate on naught but to be friends.   [*Exeunt.*

ACT THE THIRD

SCENE I.—*The Woods near the Castle of*
MARSILIUS.

Enter ORLANDO *attired like a madman.*

RL. Woods, trees, leaves; leaves,
trees, woods; *tria sequuntur tria.*—
Ho, Minerva! *salve,* good-morrow;
how do you to-day? Tell me,
sweet goddess, will Jove send
Mercury to Calypso, to let me go?
will he? why, then, he's a gentle-
man, every hair o' the head on him.—But, ho, Orgalio!
where art thou, boy?

Enter ORGALIO.

Org. Here, my lord: did you call me?
Orl. No, nor name thee.
Org. Then God be with you.　　　[*Proffers to go in.*
Orl. Nay, prithee, good Orgalio, stay:
Canst thou not tell me what to say?
Org. No, by my troth.

196

Orl. O, this it is ; Angelica is dead.

Org. Why, then, she shall be buried.

Orl. But my Angelica is dead.

Org. Why, it may be so.

Orl. But she's dead and buried.

Org. Ay, I think so.

Orl. Nothing but "I think so," and "It may be so!"

[Beats him.

Org. What do ye mean, my lord?

Orl. Why, shall I tell you that my love is dead, and can ye not weep for her?

Org. Yes, yes, my lord, I will.

Orl. Well, do so, then. Orgalio.

Org. My lord?

Orl. Angelica is dead. [ORGALIO *cries.*] Ah, poor slave! so, cry no more now.

Org. Nay, I have quickly done.

Orl. Orgalio.

Org. My lord?

Orl. Medor's Angelica is dead.

[ORGALIO *cries, and* ORLANDO *beats him again.*

Org. Why do ye beat me, my lord?

Orl. Why, slave, wilt thou weep for Medor's Angelica? thou must laugh for her.

Org. Laugh! yes, I'll laugh all day, an you will.

Orl. Orgalio.

Org. My lord?

Orl. Medor's Angelica is dead.

Org. Ha, ha, ha, ha !

Orl. So, 'tis well now.

Org. Nay, this is easier than the other was.

Orl. Now away! seek the herb moly ;[1] for I must to hell, to seek for Medor and Angelica.

---

[1] See *Odyssey* X. 302, and following. A stock reference in Euphuism.

Org. I know not the herb moly, i'faith.

Orl. Come, I'll lead ye to it by the ears.

Org. 'Tis here, my lord, 'tis here.

Orl. 'Tis indeed. Now to Charon, bid him dress his boat, for he had never such a passenger.

Org. Shall I tell him your name?

Orl. No, then he will be afraid, and not be at home.

[*Exit* ORGALIO.

Enter TOM *and* RALPH.

Tom. Sirrah Ralph, an thou'lt go with me, I'll let thee see the bravest madman that ever thou sawest.

Ralph. Sirrah Tom, I believe 'twas he that was at our town a' Sunday: I'll tell thee what he did, sirrah. He came to our house, when all our folks were gone to church, and there was nobody at home but I, and I was turning of the spit, and he comes in, and bade me fetch him some drink. Now, I went and fetched him some; and ere I came again, by my troth, he ran away with the roast-meat, spit and all, and so we had nothing but porridge to dinner.

Tom. By my troth, that was brave: but, sirrah, he did so course the boys, last Sunday; and if ye call him madman, he'll run after you, and tickle your ribs so with his flap of leather that he hath, as it passeth.[1]

[*They spy* ORLANDO.

Ralph. O, Tom, look where he is! call him madman.

Tom. Madman, madman.

Ralph. Madman, madman.

Orl. What say'st thou, villain? [*Beats them.*
So, now you shall be both my soldiers.

---

[1] A phrase signifying excess; probably "understanding" should be supplied.

Tom. Your soldiers! we shall have a mad captain,
then.

Orl. You must fight against Medor.

Ralph. Yes, let me alone with him for a bloody nose.

Orl. Come, then, and I will give you weapons
straight.   [*Exeunt.*

SCENE II.—*An Open Place in the Woods.*

Enter ANGELICA, *like a poor woman.*

Ang. Thus causeless banish'd from thy native home,
Here sit, Angelica, and rest a while,
For to bewail the fortunes of thy love.

Enter RODOMONT *and* BRANDIMART, *with* Soldiers.

Rod. This way she went, and far she cannot be.

Brand. See where she is, my lord: speak as if you
knew her not.

Rod. Fair shepherdess, for so thy sitting seems,
Or nymph, for less thy beauty cannot be,
What, feed you sheep upon these downs?

Ang. Daughter I am unto a bordering swain,
That tend my flocks within these shady groves.

Rod. Fond girl, thou liest; thou art Angelica.

Brand. Ay, thou art she that wrong'd the Palatine.

Ang. For I am known, albeit I am disguis'd,
Yet dare I turn the lie into thy throat,
Sith thou report'st I wrong'd the Palatine.

Brand. Nay, then, thou shalt be used according
to thy deserts.—Come, bring her to our tents.

Rod. But stay, what drum is this?

Enter ORLANDO *with a drum;* ORGALIO; TOM, RALPH,
and others as Soldiers, *with spits and dripping-pans.*

Brand. Now see, Angelica, the fruits of all your
love.

Orl. Soldiers, this is the city of great Babylon,
Where proud Darius was rebated from :
Play but the men, and I will lay my head,
We'll sack and raze it ere the sun be set.

Tom. Yea, and scratch it too.—March fair, fellow
frying-pan.

Orl. Orgalio, knowest thou the cause of my
laughter?

Org. No, by my troth, nor no wise man else.

Orl. Why, sirrah, to think that if the enemy were fled
ere we come, we'll not leave one of our own soldiers
alive, for we two will kill them with our fists.

Ralph. Foh, come, let's go home again : he'll set
probatum est upon my head-piece anon.

Orl. No, no, thou shalt not be hurt,—nor thee.
Back, soldiers; look where the enemy is.

Tom. Captain, they have a woman amongst them.

Orl. And what of that?

Tom. Why, strike you down the men, and then let me
alone to thrust in the woman.

Orl. No, I am challengèd the single fight.—
Sirrah, is't you challenge me the combat?

Brand. Frantic companion, lunatic and wood,[1]
Get thee hence, or else I vow by heaven,
Thy madness shall not privilege thy life.

Orl. I tell thee, villain, Medor wrong'd me so,
Sith thou art come his champion to the field,
I'll learn thee know I am the Palatine.

[1] Mad.

Alarum : they fight ; ORLANDO *kills* BRANDIMART ; *and
all the rest fly, except* ANGELICA *and* ORGALIO.

Org. Look, my lord, here's one killed.

Orl. Who killed him?

Org. You, my lord, I think.

Orl. I ! no, no, I see who killed him.

[*Goes to* ANGELICA, *and knows her not.*

Come hither, gentle sir, whose prowess hath performed
such an act : think not the courteous Palatine will hinder
that thine honour hath achieved.—Orgalio, fetch me a
sword, that presently this squire may be dubbed a
knight.

Ang. [*aside*]. Thanks, gentle fortune, that sends me
such good hap,

Rather to die by him I love so dear,

Than live and see my lord thus lunatic.

Org. [*giving a sword*]. Here, my lord.

Orl. If thou be'st come of Lancelot's worthy line,
welcome thou art.

Kneel down, sir knight ; rise up, sir knight ;

Here, take this sword, and hie thee to the fight.

[*Exit* ANGELICA *with the sword.*

Now tell me, Orgalio, what dost thou think? will not
this knight prove a valiant squire?

Org. He cannot choose, being of your making.

Orl. But where's Angelica now?

Org. Faith, I cannot tell.

Orl. Villain, find her out,

Or else the torments that Ixion feels,

The rolling stone, the tubs of the Belides—[1]

Villain, wilt thou find her out?

Org. Alas, my lord, I know not where she is.

Orl. Run to Charlemagne, spare for no cost ;

---

[1] Another false quantity.

Tell him, Orlando sent for Angelica.

Org. Faith, I'll fetch you such an Angelica as you
never saw before.   [*Exit.*

Orl. As though that Sagittarius in his pride
Could take brave Leda from stout Jupiter!
And yet, forsooth, Medor, base Medor durst
Attempt to reave Orlando of his love.
Sirrah, you that are the messenger of Jove,
You that can sweep it through the milk-white path
That leads unto the senate-house of Mars,
Fetch me my shield temper'd of purest steel,
My helm forg'd by the Cyclops for Anchises' son
And see if I dare combat for Angelica.

Re-enter ORGALIO *with* TOM[1] *dressed like* ANGELICA.

Org. Come away, and take heed you laugh not.

Tom. No, I warrant you; but I think I had best go
back and shave my beard.

Org. Tush, that will not be seen.

Tom. Well, you will give me the half-crown ye
promised me?

Org. Doubt not of that, man.

Tom. Sirrah, didst not see me serve the fellow a fine
trick, when we came over the market-place?

Org. Why, how was that?

Tom. Why, he comes to me and said, "Gentlewoman,
wilt please you take a pint or a quart?" "No gentlewoman," said I, "but your friend and Dority."

Org. Excellent!—Come, see where my lord is.—My
lord, here is Angelica.

Orl. Mass, thou say'st true, 'tis she indeed.—How
fares the fair Angelica?

---

[1] The designation in the quartos is "the Clown."

Tom. Well, I thank you heartily.

Orl. Why, art thou not that same Angelica,
With brows as bright as fair Erythea
That darks Canopus [1] with her silver hue?

Tom. Yes, forsooth.

Orl. Are not these the beauteous cheeks
Wherein the lily and the native rose
Sit equal-suited with a blushing red?

Tom. He makes a garden-plot in my face.

Orl. Are not, my dear, those [the] radiant eyes,
Whereout proud Phœbus flasheth out his beams?

Tom. Yes, yes, with squibs and crackers bravely.

Orl. You are Angelica?

Tom. Yes, marry, am I.

Orl. Where's your sweetheart Medor?

Tom. Orgalio, give me eighteen-pence, and let me go.

Orl. Speak, strumpet, speak.

Tom. Marry, sir, he is drinking a pint or a quart.

Orl. Why, strumpet, worse than Mars his trothless
       love,
Falser than faithless Cressida! strumpet, thou shalt not
       'scape.   [*Beats him.*

Tom. Come, come, you do not use me like a gentlewoman : an if I be not for you, I am for another.

Orl. Are you? that will I try.

                              [*Beats him out.   Exeunt.*

    [1] Makes Canopus look dark.

ACT THE FOURTH

SCENE I.—*The Camp of the* Twelve Peers of France.

Enter the Twelve Peers of France, *with drum and trumpets.*

GIER. Brave peers of France, sith
we have pass'd the bounds,
Whereby the wrangling billows seek
for straits
To war with Tellus, and her fruitful
mines;
Sith we have furrow'd through those
wandering tides
Of Tyrrhene seas, and made our galleys dance
Upon the Hyperborean billows' crests,
That brave with streams the watery occident;
And found the rich and wealthy Indian clime,
Sought-to by greedy minds for hurtful gold;
Now let us seek to venge the lamp of France
That lately was eclipsèd in Angelica;
Now let us seek Orlando forth, our peer,
Though from his former wits lately estrang'd,
Yet famous in our favours as before;

204

And, sith by chance we all encounter'd be,
Let's seek revenge on her that wrought his wrong.

Namus. But being thus arriv'd in place unknown,
Who shall direct our course unto the court
Where brave Marsilius keeps his royal state?

Ogier. Lo, here, two Indian palmers hard at hand,
Who can perhaps resolve our hidden doubts.

Enter MARSILIUS *and* MANDRICARD *like Palmers.*

Palmers, God speed.

Mars. Lordings, we greet you well.

Ogier. Where lies Marsilius' court, friend, canst thou
tell?

Mars. His court's his camp; the prince is now in arms.

Turpin. In arms! What's he that dares annoy so
great a king?

Mand. Such as both love and fury do confound:
Fierce Sacripant, incens'd with strange desires,
Wars on Marsilius, and, Rodomont being dead,
Hath levied all his men, and traitor-like
Assails his lord and loving sovereign:
And Mandricard, who late hath been in arms
To prosecute revenge against Marsilius,
Is now through favours past become his friend.
Thus stands the state of matchless India.

Ogier. Palmer, I like thy brave and brief discourse;
And, couldst thou bring us to the prince's camp,
We would acknowledge friendship at thy hands.

Mars. Ye stranger lords, why seek ye out Marsilius?

Ogier. In hope that he, whose empire is so large,
Will make both mind and monarchy agree.

Mars. Whence are you, lords, and what request you
here?

Namus. A question over-haughty for thy weed,
Fit for the king himself for to propound.

Mand. O, sir, know that under simple weeds
The gods have mask'd: then deem not with disdain
To answer to this palmer's question,
Whose coat includes perhaps as great as yours.

 Ogier. Haughty their words, their persons full of
  state;
Though habit be but mean, their minds excel.—
Well, palmers, know that princes are in India arriv'd,
Yea, even those western princely peers of France
That through the world adventures undertake,
To find Orlando late incens'd with rage.
Then, palmers, sith you know our styles and state,
Advise us where your king Marsilius is.

 Mars. Lordings of France, here is Marsilius,
That bids you welcome into India,
And will in person bring you to his camp.

 Ogier. Marsilius! and thus disguis'd!

 Mars. Even Marsilius, and thus disguis'd.
But what request these princes at my hand?

 Turpin. We sue for law and justice at thy hand:
We seek Angelica thy daughter out;
That wanton maid, that hath eclips'd the joy
Of royal France, and made Orlando mad.

 Mars. My daughter, lords! why, she is exil'd;
And her griev'd father is content to lose
The pleasance of his age, to countenance law.

 Oliver. Not only exile shall await Angelica,
But death and bitter death shall follow her.
Then yield us right, Marsilius, or our swords
Shall make thee fear to wrong the peers of France.

 Mars. Words cannot daunt me, princes, be assur'd;
But law and justice shall o'er-rule in this,
And I will bury father's name and love.
The hapless maid, banish'd from out my land,
Wanders about in woods and ways unknown:

Her, if ye find, with fury persecute ;
I now disdain the name to be her father.
Lords of France, what would you more of me?
 Ogier. Marsilius, we commend thy princely mind,
And will report thy justice through the world. —
Come, peers of France, let's seek Angelica,
Left for a spoil to our revenging thoughts.   [*Exeunt.*

SCENE II.—*A Grove.*

Enter ORLANDO *like a poet, and* ORGALIO.

 Orl. Orgalio, is not my love like those purple-colour'd
    swans
That gallop by the coach of Cynthia?
 Org. Yes, marry, is she, my lord.
 Orl. Is not her face silver'd like that milk-white shape
That Jove came dancing in to Semele?
 Org. It is, my lord.
 Orl. Then go thy ways, and climb up to the clouds,
And tell Apollo that Orlando sits
Making of verses for Angelica.
And if he do deny to send me down
The shirt which Deianira sent to Hercules,
To make me brave upon my wedding day,
Tell him I'll pass the Alps, and up to Meroe,
(I know he knows that watery lakish hill,)
And pull the harp out of the minstrel's hands,
And pawn it unto lovely Proserpine,
That she may fetch the fair Angelica.

Org. But, my lord, Apollo is asleep, and will not hear
me.

Orl. Then tell him, he is a sleepy knave: but, sirrah,
let nobody trouble me, for I must lie down a while, and
talk with the stars.   [*Lies down and sleeps.*

Enter a Fiddler.

Org. What, old acquaintance! well met.[1]

Fid. Ho, you would have me play Angelica again,
would ye not?

Org. No, but I can tell thee where thou may'st earn
two or three shillings this morning, even with the turning
of a hand.

Fid. Two or three shillings! tush, thou wolt cozen
me, thou: but an thou canst tell where I may earn
a groat, I'll give thee sixpence for thy pains.

Org. Then play a fit of mirth to my lord.

Fid. Why, he is mad still, is he not?

Org. No, no: come, play.

Fid. At which side doth he use to give his reward?

Org. Why, of any side.

Fid. Doth he not use to throw the chamber-pot sometimes? 'Twould grieve me he should wet my fiddle-
strings.

Org. Tush, I warrant thee.

[*The* Fiddler *plays and sings any odd toy,*
and ORLANDO *wakes.*

Orl. Who is this? Shan Cuttelero! heartily welcome,
Shan Cuttelero.

Fid. No, sir, you should have said "Shan the
Fidideldero."

Orl. What, hast thou brought me a sword?

[*Takes away his fiddle.*

---

[1] Fiddler is undoubtedly played by Tom, the clown who had
before played Angelica. See the next speech.

Fid. A sword! no, no, sir, that's my fiddle.

Orl. But dost thou think the temper to be good?
And will it hold, when thus and thus we Medor do
assail?

        [Strikes and beats him with the fiddle.

Fid. Lord, sir, you'll break my living!—*[to* ORGALIO]
You told me your master was not mad.

Orl. Tell me, why hast thou marr'd my sword?
The pummel's well, the blade is curtal short:
Villain, why hast thou made it so?

        [Breaks the fiddle about his head.

Fid. O Lord, sir, will you answer this?   *[Exit.*

Enter MELISSA *with a glass of wine.*

Orl. Orgalio, who is this?

Org. Faith, my lord, some old witch, I think.

Mel. O, that my lord would but conceit[1] my tale!
Then would I speak and hope to find redress.

Orl. Fair Polixena, the pride of Ilion
Fear not Achilles' over-madding boy;
Pyrrhus shall not, etc.—[2]
Souns, Orgalio, why sufferest thou this old trot to come
      so nigh me?

Org. Come, come, stand by, your breath stinks.

Orl. What! be all the Trojans fled?
Then give me some drink.

Mel. Here, Palatine, drink; and ever be thou better
for this draught.

Orl. What's here? The paltry bottle that Darius
      quaff'd?

    *[He drinks, and she charms him with her wand, and
      he lies down to sleep.*

[1] Apprehend, take in.
[2] Signifying that the actor could extemporise as he chose. *Ad lib.*, *ad libitum* would now be the direction.

O

Else would I set my mouth to Tigris' streams,
And drink up overflowing Euphrates.
My eyes are heavy, and I needs must sleep.

    [MELISSA *strikes with her wand, and the* Satyrs *enter*
        with music, and play round about him ; which
        done, they stay ; he awakes and speaks.

What shows are these, that fill mine eyes
With view of such regard as heaven admires
To see my slumbering dreams !
Skies are fulfill'd with lamps of lasting joy,
That boast the pride of haught Latona's son ;
He lighteneth all the candles of the night.
Mnemosyne hath kiss'd the kingly Jove,
And entertain'd a feast within my brains,
Making her daughters'[1] solace on my brow.
Methinks, I feel how Cynthia tunes conceits
Of sad repeat, and melloweth those desires
Which frenzy scarce had ripen'd in my head.
Ate, I'll kiss thy restless cheek a while,
And suffer fruitless passion bide control.

                            [Lies down again.

    Mel. O vos Silvani, Satyri, Faunique, deæque,
Nymphæ Hamadryades, Dryades, Parcæque potentes !
O vos qui colitis lacusque locosque profundos,
Infernasque domus et nigra palatia Ditis !
Tuque Demogorgon, qui noctis fata gubernas,
Qui regis infernum solium, cœlumque, solumque !
Exaudite preces, filiasque auferte micantes ;
In caput Orlandi celestes spargite lymphas,
Spargite, quis misere revocetur rapta per vmbras
Orlandi infelix anima.

    [*Then let the music play before him, and so go forth.*
    Orl. What sights, what shows, what fearful shapes are
        these ?

             [1] The Muses.

More dreadful than appear'd to Hecuba,
When fall of Troy was figur'd in her sleep !
Juno, methought, sent down from heaven by Jove,
Came swiftly sweeping through the gloomy air ;
And calling Iris, sent her straight abroad
To summon Fauns, the Satyrs, and the Nymphs,
The Dryads, and all the demigods,
To secret council ; [and, their] parle past,[1]
She gave them vials full of heavenly dew.
With that, mounted upon her parti-coloured coach,
Being drawn with peacocks proudly through the air,
She flew with Iris to the sphere of Jove.
What fearful thoughts arise upon this show !
What desert grove is this !   How thus disguis'd ?
Where is Orgalio ?

Org. Here, my lord.

Orl. Sirrah, how came I thus disguis'd,
Like mad Orestes, quaintly thus attir'd ?

Org. Like mad Orestes ! nay, my lord, you may
boldly justify the comparison, for Orestes was never so
mad in his life as you were.

Orl. What, was I mad ? what Fury hath enchanted
me ?

Mel. A Fury, sure, worse than Megæra was,
That reft her son from trusty Pylades.

Orl. Why what art thou, some sibyl, or some goddess ?
freely speak.

Mel. Time not affords to tell each circumstance :
But thrice hath Cynthia chang'd her hue,
Since thou, infected with a lunacy,
Hast gadded up and down these lawnds and groves,
Performing strange and ruthful stratagems,
All for the love of fair Angelica,

---

[1] A corrupt passage is here supplemented by four lines from the
Alleyn manuscript.

Whom thou with Medor didst suppose play'd false.
But Sacripant had graven these roundelays,
To sting thee with infecting jealousy:
The swain that told thee of their oft converse,
Was servant unto County Sacripant:
And trust me, Orlando, Angelica,
Though true to thee, is banish'd from the court.
And Sacripant this day bids battle to Marsilius.
The armies ready are to give assail;
And on a hill that overpeers them both
Stand all the worthy matchless peers of France,
Who are in quest to seek Orlando out.
Muse not at this, for I have told thee true:
I am she that curèd thy disease.
Here, take these weapons, given thee by the fates,
And hie thee, county, to the battle straight.

   Orl. Thanks, sacred goddess, for thy helping hand,
Thither will I hie to be reveng'd.

                      [Exeunt.

ACT THE FIFTH

SCENE I.—*A Battle-field.*

Alarums : enter SACRIPANT *crowned, and pursuing*
MARSILIUS *and* MANDRICARD.

AC. Viceroys, you are dead ;
For Sacripant, already crown'd a king,
Heaves up his sword to have your
diadems.

Mars. Traitor, not dead, nor any
whit dismay'd ;
For dear we prize the smallest drop of
blood.

Enter ORLANDO *with a scarf before his face.*

Orl. Stay, princes, 'base not yourselves to combat
such a dog.
Mount on your coursers, follow those that fly,
And let your conquering swords be tainted in their
bloods :
Pass ye for him ; he shall be combated.
        [*Exeunt* MARSILIUS *and* MANDRICARD.
Sac. Why, what art thou that brav'st me thus?

213

Orl. I am, thou see'st, a mercenary soldier,
Homely attir'd, but of so haughty thoughts,
As naught can serve to quench th' aspiring flames,
That burn as do the fires of Sicily,
Unless I win that princely diadem,
That seems so ill upon thy coward's head.

 Sac. Coward!   To arms, sir boy!   I will not brook
  these braves,
If Mars himself, even from his fiery throne
Came arm'd with all his furnitures of war.

       [*They fight, and* SACRIPANT *falls.*
O villain! thou hast slain a prince.

 Orl. Then mayst thou think that Mars himself came
  down,
To vail thy plumes and heave thee from thy pomp.
Proud that thou art, I reck not of thy gree,
But I will have the conquest of my sword,
Which is the glory of thy diadem.

 Sac. These words bewray thou art no base-born
  Moor,
But by descent sprung from some royal line:
Then freely tell me, what's thy name?

 Orl. Nay, first let me know thine.

 Sac. Then know that thou hast slain Prince Sacripant.

 Orl. Sacripant! Then let me at thy dying day entreat,
By that same sphere wherein thy soul shall rest,
If Jove deny not passage to thy ghost,
Thou tell me whether thou wrong'dst Angelica or no?

 Sac. O, that's the sting that pricks my conscience!
O, that's the hell my thoughts abhor to think!
I tell thee, knight, for thou dost seem no less,
That I engrav'd the roundelays on the trees,
And hung the schedules of poor Medor's love,
Intending so to breed debate
Between Orlando and Angelica:

O, thus I wrong'd Orlando and Angelica!
Now tell me, what shall I call thy name?
   Orl. Then dead is the fatal author of my ill.
Base villain, vassal, unworthy of a crown,
Know that the man that struck the fatal stroke
Is Orlando, the County Palatine,
Whom fortune sent to quittance all my wrongs.
Thou foil'd and slain, it now behoves me straight
To hie me fast to massacre thy men :
And so, farewell, thou devil in shape of man.   [*Exit.*
   Sac. Hath Demogorgon, ruler of the fates,
Set such a baleful period on my life
As none might end the days of Sacripant
But mighty Orlando, rival of my love?
Now hold the fatal murderers of men
The sharpen'd knife ready to cut my thread,
Ending the scene of all my tragedy :
This day, this hour, this minute ends the days
Of him that liv'd worthy old Nestor's age.
Phœbus, put on thy sable-suited wreath,
Clad all thy spheres in dark and mourning weeds :
Parch'd be the earth, to drink up every spring :
Let corn and trees be blasted from above ;
Heaven turn to brass, and earth to wedge of steel ;
The world to cinders.　Mars, come thundering down,
And never sheath thy swift-revenging sword,
Till, like the deluge in Deucalion's days,
The highest mountains swim in streams of blood.
Heaven, earth, men, beasts, and every living thing,
Consume and end with County Sacripant!   [*Dies.*

SCENE II.—*The Camp of* MARSILIUS.

Enter MARSILIUS, MANDRICARD, *and the* Twelve Peers *with* ANGELICA.

Mars. Fought is the field, and Sacripant is slain,
With such a massacre of all his men,
As Mars, descending in his purple robe,
Vows with Bellona in whole heaps of blood
To banquet all the demigods of war.

Mand. See, where he lies slaughter'd without the camp,
And by a simple swain, a mercenary,
Who bravely took the combat to himself:
Might I but know the man that did the deed,
I would, my lord, eternize him with fame.

Ogier. Leaving the factious county to his death,
Command, my lord, his body be convey'd[1]
Unto some place, as likes your highness best.
See, Marsilius, posting through Africa,
We have found this straggling girl, Angelica,
Who, for she wrong'd her love Orlando,
Chiefest of the western peers, conversing
With so mean a man as Medor was,
We will have her punish'd by the laws of France,
To end her burning lust in flames of fire.

Mars. Beshrew you, lordings, but you do your worst;
Fire, famine, and as cruel death
As fell to Nero's mother in his rage.

Angelica. Father, if I may dare to call thee so,
And lords of France, come from the western seas,
In quest to find mighty Orlando out,

---

[1] An interesting reminder of the exigencies of Elizabethan stage technique. The scenes represent different localities, but as Sacripant dies at the end of a scene, his body remains on the stage until removed by the best means possible.

Yet, ere I die, let me have leave to say,
Angelica held ever in her thoughts
Most dear the love of County Palatine.
What wretch hath wrong'd us with suspect of lust
I know not, I, nor can accuse the man;
But, by the heavens, whereto my soul shall fly,
Angelica did never wrong Orlando.
I speak not this as one that cares to live,
For why my thoughts are fully malcontent;
And I conjure you by your chivalry,
You quit Orlando's wrong upon Angelica.

Enter ORLANDO, *with a scarf before his face.*

Oliver. Strumpet, fear not, for, by fair Maia's son,
This day thy soul shall vanish up in fire,
As Semele, when Juno wil'd the trull
To entertain the glory of her love.

Orl. Frenchman, for so thy quaint array imports,
Be thou a peer, or be thou Charlemagne,
Or hadst thou Hector's or Achilles' heart,
Or never-daunted thoughts of Hercules,
That did in courage far surpass them all,
I tell thee, sir, thou liest in thy throat,—
The greatest brave Transalpine France can brook,—
In saying that sacred Angelica
Did offer wrong unto the Palatine.
I am a common mercenary soldier;
Yet, for I see my princess is abus'd
By new-come stragglers from a foreign coast,
I dare the proudest of these western lords
To crack a blade in trial of her right.

Mand. Why, foolish-hardy, daring, simple groom,
Follower of fond-conceited[1] Phaëton,

----

[1] Silly-minded.

Know'st thou to whom thou speak'st?

Mars. Brave soldier, for so much thy courage says,
These men are princes, dipt within the blood
Of kings most royal, seated in the west,
Unfit to accept a challenge at your hand!
Yet thanks that thou wouldst in thy lord's defence
Fight for my daughter; but her guilt is known.

Ang. Ay, rest thee, soldier, Angelica is false,—
False, for she hath no trial of her right:
Soldier, let me die for the 'miss [1] of all.
Wert thou as stout as was proud Theseus,
In vain thy blade should offer my defence;
For why these be the champions of the world,
Twelve Peers of France that never yet were foil'd.

Orl. How, madam, the Twelve Peers of France!
Why, let them be twelve devils of hell,
What I have said, I'll pawn my sword,
To seal it on the shield of him that dares,
Malgrado [2] of his honour, combat me.

Oliver. Marry, sir, that dare I.

Orl. Y'ar' [3] a welcome man, sir.

Turpin. Chastise the groom, Oliver, and learn him
know
We are not like the boys of Africa.

Orl. Hear you, sir? You that so peremptorily bade
him fight,
Prepare your weapons, for your turn is next:
'Tis not one champion can discourage me.
Come, are ye ready?

[*He fights first with one, and then with the other,
and overcomes them both.*

So stand aside:—and, madam, if my fortune last it out,
I'll guard your person with Twelve Peers of France.

[1] Amiss, fault.   [2] In spite of, notwithstanding.
[3] Orlando is adapting his language to his disguise.

Ogier. [aside]. O Ogier, how canst thou stand, and
    see a slave
Disgrace the house of France?—Sirrah, prepare you;
For angry Nemesis sits on my sword to be reveng'd.
              [*They fight a good while, and then breathe.*
Ogier. Howe'er disguis'd in base or Indian shape,
Ogier can well discern thee by thy blows;
For either thou art Orlando or the devil.
   Orl. [taking off his scarf]. Then, to assure you that I
    am no devil,
Here's your friend and companion, Orlando.
   Ogier. And none can be more glad than Ogier is,
That he hath found his cousin in his sense.
   Oliver. Whenas I felt his blows upon my shield,
My teeth did chatter, and my thoughts conceiv'd,
Who might this be, if not the Palatine.
   Turpin. So had I said, but that report did tell
My lord was troubled with a lunacy.
   Orl. So was I, lordings; but give me leave awhile,
Humbly as Mars did to his paramour,
So to submit to fair Angelica.—
Pardon thy lord, fair saint Angelica,
Whose love, stealing by steps into extremes,
Grew by suspect to causeless lunacy.
   Ang. O no, my lord, but pardon my amiss;
For had not Orlando lov'd Angelica,
Ne'er had my lord fall'n into these extremes,
Which we will parley private to ourselves.
Ne'er was the Queen of Cyprus half so glad
As is Angelica to see her lord,
Her dear Orlando, settled in his sense.
   Orl. Thanks, my sweet love.—
But why stand the Prince of Africa,
And Mandricard the King of Mexico,
So deep in dumps, when all rejoice beside?

First know, my lord, I slaughter'd Sacripant;
I am the man that did the slave to death;
Who frankly there did make confession,
That he engrav'd the roundelays on the trees,
And hung the schedules of poor Medor's love,
Intending by suspect to breed debate
Deeply 'twixt me and fair Angelica:
His hope had hap, but we had all the harm;
And now revenge, leaping from out the seat
Of him that may command stern Nemesis,
Hath pour'd those treasons justly on his head.
What saith my gracious lord to this?

  Mars. I stand amaz'd, deep over-drench'd with joy,
To hear and see this unexpected end:
So well I rest content.—Ye peers of France,
Sith it is prov'd Angelica is clear,
Her and my crown I freely will bestow
Upon Orlando, the County Palatine.

  Orl. Thanks my good lord.—And now, my friends of
      France,
Frolic, be merry: we will hasten home,
So soon as King Marsilius will consent
To let his daughter wend with us to France.
Meanwhile we'll richly rig up all our fleet
More brave [1] than was that gallant Grecian keel
That brought away the Colchian fleece of gold:
Our sails of sendal [2] spread into the wind;
Our ropes and tacklings all of finest silk,
Fetch'd from the native looms of labouring worms,
The pride of Barbary, and the glorious wealth
That is transported by the western bounds;
Our stems cut out of gleaming ivory;

---

[1] Splendid.
[2] "A kinde of Cipres stuffe or silke." Minsheu, *Guide into the Tongues*, 1617.

Our planks and sides fram'd out of cypress-wood,
That bears the name of Cyparissus' change,
To burst the billows of the ocean-sea,
Where Phœbus dips his amber tresses oft,
And kisses Thetis in the day's decline ;
That Neptune proud shall call his Tritons forth
To cover all the ocean with a calm :
So rich shall be the rubbish of our barks,
Ta'en here for ballass to the ports of France,
That Charles himself shall wonder at the sight.
Thus, lordings, when our banquetings be done,
And Orlando espousèd to Angelica,
We'll furrow through the moving ocean,
And cheerly frolic with great Charlemagne.

[Exeunt omnes.

FRIAR BACON AND
FRIAR BUNGAY

OF *Friar Bacon and Friar Bungay* there are three quartos, dated 1594, 1630 and 1655. The first quarto was published by Edward White, and 14th May 1594, the play is entered by the publisher on the *Stationers' Registers*. The two exemplars of this quarto are in the British Museum and in Bridgewater House. In Henslowe's *Diary*, *Friar Bacon* heads the list of plays by my Lord Strange's men in an entry for 19th February 1592. At this time it was not a new play. Between this date and 6th May it was performed by Strange's men once every three weeks, and once a week between the following 10th January and 30th January. 1st April 1594, it was taken over by the original owners, the Queen's players, who were then acting with Sussex' players, and was performed 1st and 5th April at the Rose Theatre. Presumably it was sent to press by the Queen's men. At Christmas 1602 Middleton wrote a Prologue and Epilogue for a performance of the play by the Admiral's men at Court, for which he received five shillings. After this the play was probably kept in the possession of the Admiral's players, for the 1630 title-page indicates its performance by the Palsgrave's men. In no sense a plagiarism, the play is strictly a rival of Marlowe's *Dr. Faustus*, and it must have been performed within a year after Marlowe's play appeared in 1587. With *James IV.* it represents Greene's dramatic workmanship at its best. A few months after the appearance of the play it was parodied in *Fair Em, The Miller's Daughter of Manchester*. Greene's play is based on a romance written at the end of the sixteenth century, and probably accessible to both Greene and Marlowe. The "wall of brass" is common to both plays, and comes in each case directly from the source-book, the *Famous History of Friar Bacon*. This popular old story, of which the earliest extant edition is dated 1630, is now accessible in Thoms' *Early English Prose Romances*, Vol. I. To his source-material Greene added, probably out of his own head, the character of Margaret and her touching love-story. For the historical portions of the play there is no warrant in actual events.

DRAMATIS PERSONÆ

KING HENRY THE THIRD.
EDWARD, PRINCE OF WALES, his son.
EMPEROR OF GERMANY.
KING OF CASTILE.
DUKE OF SAXONY.
LACY, Earl of Lincoln.
WARREN, Earl of Sussex.
ERMSBY, a Gentleman.
RALPH SIMNELL, the King's Fool.
FRIAR BACON.
MILES, Friar Bacon's poor scholar.
FRIAR BUNGAY.
JAQUES VANDERMAST.
BURDEN,
MASON,   } Doctors of Oxford.
CLEMENT,
LAMBERT, } Gentlemen.
SERLSBY,
Two Scholars, their sons.
Keeper.
KEEPER'S FRIEND.
THOMAS, } Clowns.
RICHARD,
Constable.
A Post.
Lords, Clowns, etc.
ELINOR, daughter to the King of Castile.
MARGARET, the Keeper's daughter.
JOAN, a country wench.
Hostess of the Bell at Henley.
A Devil.
Spirit in the shape of HERCULES.

THE HONOURABLE HISTORY OF FRIAR BACON AND FRIAR BUNGAY.

ACT THE FIRST.

SCENE I.—*At Framlingham.*

Enter PRINCE EDWARD *malcontented, with* LACY, WARREN, ERMSBY, *and* RALPH SIMNELL.

ACY. Why looks my lord like to a
  troubled sky,
When heaven's bright shine is
  shadowed with a fog?
Alate we ran the deer, and through
  the lawnds
Stripp'd [1] with our nags the lofty frolic
bucks
That scudded 'fore the teasers [2] like the wind :
Ne'er was the deer of merry Fressingfield
So lustily pull'd down by jolly mates,
Nor shar'd the farmers such fat venison,
So frankly dealt, this hundred years before ;

[1] Outstripped.   [2] Hunting-dogs.

227

Nor have I seen my lord more frolic in the chase,
And now chang'd to a melancholy dump.

War. After the prince got to the keeper's lodge,
And had been jocund in the house awhile,
Tossing off ale and milk in country cans;
Whether it was the country's sweet content,
Or else the bonny damsel fill'd us drink,
That seem'd so stately in her stammel [1] red,
Or that a qualm did cross his stomach then,
But straight he fell into his passions.

Erms. Sirrah Ralph, what say you to your master,
Shall he thus all amort [2] live malcontent?

Ralph. Hearest thou, Ned?—Nay, look if he will
speak to me!

P. Edw. What say'st thou to me, fool?

Ralph. I prithee, tell me, Ned, art thou in love with
the Keeper's daughter?

P. Edw. How if I be, what then?

Ralph. Why then, sirrah, I'll teach thee how to deceive
love.

P. Edw. How, Ralph?

Ralph. Marry, Sirrah Ned, thou shalt put on my cap
and my coat and my dagger, and I will put on thy
clothes and thy sword; and so thou shalt be my fool.

P. Edw. And what of this?

Ralph. Why, so thou shalt beguile Love; for Love
is such a proud scab, that he will never meddle with
fools nor children. Is not Ralph's counsel good, Ned?

P. Edw. Tell me, Ned Lacy, didst thou mark the
maid,
How lovely in her country weeds she look'd?
A bonnier wench all Suffolk cannot yield:—
All Suffolk! nay, all England holds none such.

Ralph. Sirrah Will Ermsby, Ned is deceived.

---

[1] A coarse woolen cloth.   [2] For *alamort:* dejected.

Erms. Why, Ralph?

Ralph. He says all England hath no such, and I say, and I'll stand to it, there is one better in Warwickshire.

War. How provest thou that, Ralph?

Ralph. Why, is not the abbot a learned man, and hath read many books, and thinkest thou he hath not more learning than thou to choose a bonny wench? yes, I warrant thee, by his whole grammar.

Erms. A good reason, Ralph.

P. Edw. I tell thee, Lacy, that her sparkling eyes
Do lighten forth sweet love's alluring fire;
And in her tresses she doth fold the looks
Of such as gaze upon her golden hair:
Her bashful white, mix'd with the morning's red,
Luna doth boast upon her lovely cheeks;
Her front is beauty's table, where she paints
The glories of her gorgeous excellence;
Her teeth are shelves of precious margarites,[1]
Richly enclos'd with ruddy coral cleeves.[2]
Tush, Lacy, she is beauty's over-match,
If thou survey'st her curious imagery.

Lacy. I grant, my lord, the damsel is as fair
As simple Suffolk's homely towns can yield;
But in the court be quainter[3] dames than she,
Whose faces are enrich'd with honour's taint,
Whose beauties stand upon the stage of fame,
And vaunt their trophies in the courts of love.

P. Edw. Ah, Ned, but hadst thou watch'd her as
    myself,
And seen the secret beauties of the maid,
Their courtly coyness were but foolery.

Erms. Why, how watch'd you her, my lord?

P. Edw. Whenas she swept like Venus through the
   house,—

---

[1] Pearls.   [2] Cliffs.   [3] Rarer.

And in her shape fast folded up my thoughts,—
Into the milk-house went I with the maid,
And there amongst the cream-bowls she did shine
As Pallas 'mongst her princely huswifery:
She turn'd her smock over her lily arms,
And div'd them into milk to run her cheese;
But whiter than the milk her crystal skin,
Checkèd with lines of azure, made her blush,[1]
That art or nature durst bring for compare.
Ermsby, if thou hadst seen, as I did note it well,
How beauty play'd the huswife, how this girl,
Like Lucrece, laid her fingers to the work,
Thou wouldst, with Tarquin, hazard Rome and all
To win the lovely maid of Fressingfield.

Ralph. Sirrah Ned, wouldst fain have her?

P. Edw. Ay, Ralph.

Ralph. Why, Ned, I have laid the plot in my head;
thou shalt have her already.

P. Edw. I'll give thee a new coat, an learn me that.

Ralph. Why, Sirrah Ned, we'll ride to Oxford to
Friar Bacon: O, he is a brave scholar, sirrah; they
say he is a brave necromancer, that he can make women
of devils, and he can juggle cats into costermongers.

P. Edw. And how then, Ralph?

Ralph. Marry, Sirrah, thou shalt go to him: and because thy father Harry shall not miss thee, he shall turn
me into thee; and I'll to the court, and I'll prince it out;
and he shall make thee either a silken purse full of gold,
or else a fine wrought smock.

P. Edw. But how shall I have the maid?

Ralph. Marry, sirrah, if thou be'st a silken purse full
of gold, then on Sundays she'll hang thee by her side,
and you must not say a word. Now, sir, when she comes
into a great prease of people, for fear of the cutpurse, on

---

[1] Made that woman blush. That, etc.

a sudden she'll swap thee into her plackerd;[1] then,
sirrah, being there, you may plead for yourself.

Erms. Excellent policy!

P. Edw. But how if I be a wrought smock?

Ralph. Then she'll put thee into her chest and lay
thee into lavender, and upon some good day she'll put
thee on; and at night when you go to bed, then being
turned from a smock to a man, you may make up the
match.

Lacy. Wonderfully wisely counselled, Ralph.

P. Edw. Ralph shall have a new coat.

Ralph. God thank you when I have it on my back,
Ned.

P. Edw. Lacy, the fool hath laid a perfect plot;
For why our country Margaret is so coy,
And stands so much upon her honest points,
That marriage or no market with the maid.
Ermsby, it must be necromantic spells
And charms of art that must enchain her love,
Or else shall Edward never win the girl.
Therefore, my wags, we'll horse us in the morn,
And post to Oxford to this jolly friar:
Bacon shall by his magic do this deed.

War. Content, my lord; and that's a speedy way
To wean these headstrong puppies from the teat.

P. Edw. I am unknown, not taken for the prince;
They only deem us frolic courtiers,
That revel thus among our liege's game:
Therefore I have devis'd a policy.
Lacy, thou know'st next Friday is Saint James',
And then the country flocks to Harleston fair:
Then will the Keeper's daughter frolic there,
And over-shine the troop of all the maids,
That come to see and to be seen that day.

[1] Pocket.

Haunt thee disguis'd among the country-swains,
Feign thou'rt a farmer's son, not far from thence,
Espy her loves, and who she liketh best ;
Cote [1] him, and court her to control the clown ;
Say that the courtier 'tirèd all in green,
That help'd her handsomely to run her cheese,
And fill'd her father's lodge with venison,
Commends him, and sends fairings to herself.
Buy something worthy of her parentage,
Not worth her beauty ; for, Lacy, then the fair
Affords no jewel fitting for the maid :
And when thou talk'st of me, note if she blush :
O, then she loves ; but if her cheeks wax pale,
Disdain it is.   Lacy, send how she fares,
And spare no time nor cost to win her loves.

    Lacy. I will, my lord, so execute this charge,
As if that Lacy were in love with her.

    P. Edw. Send letters speedily to Oxford of the news.

    Ralph. And, Sirrah Lacy, buy me a thousand thousand
million of fine bells.

    Lacy. What wilt thou do with them, Ralph ?

    Ralph. Marry, every time that Ned sighs for the
Keeper's daughter, I'll tie a bell about him : and so
within three or four days I will send word to his father
Harry, that his son, and my master Ned, is become
Love's morris-dance.

    P. Edw. Well, Lacy, look with care unto thy charge,
And I will haste to Oxford to the friar,
That he by art, and thou by secret gifts
Mayst make me lord of merry Fressingfield.

    Lacy. God send your honour your heart's desire.
                         [*Exeunt.*

---

    [1] Pass by, outstrip.

SCENE II.—FRIAR BACON'S *cell at Brazen-nose.*

Enter FRIAR BACON, *and* MILES *with books under his arm; with them* BURDEN, MASON *and* CLEMENT.

Bacon. Miles, where are you?

Miles. Hic sum, doctissime et reverendissime doctor.

Bacon. Attulisti nos libros meos de necromantia?

Miles. Ecce quam bonum et quam jucundum habitare libros in vnum!

Bacon. Now, masters of our academic state,
That rule in Oxford, viceroys in your place,
Whose heads contain maps of the liberal arts,
Spending your time in depth of learnèd skill,
Why flock you thus to Bacon's secret cell,
A friar newly stall'd in Brazen-nose?
Say what's your mind, that I may make reply.

Burd. Bacon, we hear, that long we have suspect,
That thou art read in magic's mystery;
In pyromancy, to divine by flames;
To tell, by hydromantic, ebbs and tides;
By aeromancy to discover doubts,
To plain out questions, as Apollo did.

Bacon. Well, Master Burden, what of all this?

Miles. Marry, sir, he doth but fulfil, by rehearsing of these names, the fable of the Fox and the Grapes: that which is above us pertains nothing to us.

Burd. I tell thee, Bacon, Oxford makes report,
Nay, England, and the court of Henry says
Thou'rt making of a brazen head by art,
Which shall unfold strange doubts and aphorisms,
And read a lecture in philosophy;
And, by the help of devils and ghastly fiends,
Thou mean'st, ere many years or days be past,

To compass England with a wall of brass

   Bacon. And what of this?

   Miles. What of this, master! why he doth speak mystically; for he knows, if your skill fail to make a brazen head, yet Mother Waters' strong ale will fit his turn to make him have a copper nose.

   Clem. Bacon, we come not grieving at thy skill,
But joying that our académy yields
A man suppos'd the wonder of the world;
For if thy cunning work these miracles,
England and Europe shall admire thy fame,
And Oxford shall in characters of brass,
And statues, such as were built up in Rome,
Etérnize Friar Bacon for his art.

   Mason. Then, gentle friar, tell us thy intent.

   Bacon. Seeing you come as friends unto the friar,
Resolve [1] you, doctors, Bacon can by books
Make storming Boreas thunder from his cave,
And dim fair Luna to a dark eclipse.
The great arch-ruler, potentate of hell,
Trembles when Bacon bids him, or his fiends,
Bow to the force of his pentageron.[2]
What art can work, the frolic friar knows;
And therefore will I turn my magic books,
And strain out necromancy to the deep.
I have contriv'd and fram'd a head of brass
(I made Belcephon hammer out the stuff),
And that by art shall read philosophy:
And I will strengthen England by my skill,
That if ten Cæsars liv'd and reign'd in Rome,
With all the legions Europe doth contain,
They should not touch a grass of English ground:
The work that Ninus rear'd at Babylon,

---

[1] Be you assured.
[2] The magical five-rayed star used as a defence against demons.

The brazen walls fram'd by Semiramis,
Carv'd out like to the portal of the sun,
Shall not be such as rings the English strand
From Dover to the market-place of Rye.

Burd. Is this possible?

Miles. I'll bring ye two or three witnesses.

Burd. What be those?

Miles. Marry, sir, three or four as honest devils and
good companions as any be in hell.

Mason. No doubt but magic may do much in this;
For he that reads but mathematic rules
Shall find conclusions that avail to work
Wonders that pass the common sense of men.

Burd. But Bacon roves a bow beyond his reach,
And tells of more than magic can perform;
Thinking to get a fame by fooleries.
Have I not pass'd as far in state of schools,
And read of many secrets? yet to think
That heads of brass can utter any voice,
Or more, to tell of deep philosophy,
This is a fable Æsop had forgot.

Bacon. Burden, thou wrong'st me in detracting thus;
Bacon loves not to stuff himself with lies:
But tell me 'fore these doctors, if thou dare,
Of certain questions I shall move to thee.

Burd. I will: ask what thou can.

Miles. Marry, sir, he'll straight be on your pick-pack,
to know whether the feminine or the masculine gender
be most worthy.

Bacon. Were you not yesterday Master Burden, at
Henley upon the Thames?

Burd. I was: what then?

Bacon. What book studied you thereon all night?

Burd. I! none at all; I read not there a line.

Bacon. Then, doctors, Friar Bacon's art knows naught.

Clem. What say you to this, Master Burden? doth he not touch you?

Burd. I pass not of [1] his frivolous speeches.

Miles. Nay, Master Burden, my master, ere he hath done with you, will turn you from a doctor to a dunce, and shake you so small, that he will leave no more learning in you than is in Balaam's ass.

Bacon. Masters, for that learn'd Burden's skill is deep,
And sore he doubts of Bacon's cabalism,
I'll show you why he haunts to Henley oft:
Not, doctors, for to taste the fragrant air,
But there to spend the night in alchemy,
To multiply with secret spells of art;
Thus private steals he learning from us all.
To prove my sayings true, I'll show you straight
The book he keeps at Henley for himself.

Miles. Nay, now my master goes to conjuration, take heed.

Bacon. Masters, stand still, fear not, I'll show you but his book.

[*Conjures.*

Per omnes deos infernales, Belcephon!

Enter Hostess *with a shoulder of mutton on a spit, and a* Devil.

Miles. O, master, cease your conjuration, or you spoil all; for here's a she-devil come with a shoulder of mutton on a spit: you have marred the devil's supper; but no doubt he thinks our college fare is slender, and so hath sent you his cook with a shoulder of mutton, to make it exceed.

Hostess. O, where am I, or what's become of me?

Bacon. What art thou?

Hostess. Hostess at Henley, mistress of the Bell.

[1] Care not for.

Bacon. How camest thou here?

Hostess. As I was in the kitchen 'mongst the maids,
Spitting the meat against supper for my guess,[1]
A motion mov'd me to look forth of door:
No sooner had I pried into the yard,
But straight a whirlwind hoisted me from thence,
And mounted me aloft unto the clouds.
As in a trance I thought nor fearèd naught,
Nor know I where or whither I was ta'en,
Nor where I am, nor what these persons be.

Bacon. No? know you not Master Burden?

Hostess. O, yes, good sir, he is my daily guest.—
What, Master Burden! 'twas but yesternight
That you and I at Henley play'd at cards.

Burd. I know not what we did.—A pox of all conjuring friars!

Clem. Now, jolly friar, tell us, is this the book that
Burden is so careful to look on?

Bacon. It is.—But, Burden, tell me now,
Think'st thou that Bacon's necromantic skill
Cannot perform his head and wall of brass,
When he can fetch thine hostess in such post?

Miles. I'll warrant you, master, if Master Burden could
conjure as well as you, he would have his book every
night from Henley to study on at Oxford.

Mason. Burden, what, are you mated[2] by this frolic
        friar?—
Look how he droops; his guilty conscience
Drives him to 'bash and makes his hostess blush.

Bacon. Well, mistress, for I will not have you miss'd,
You shall to Henley to cheer up your guests
'Fore supper gin.—Burden, bid her adieu;
Say farewell to your hostess 'fore she goes.—
Sirrah, away, and set her safe at home.

---

[1] Guests.   [2] Confounded,

Hostess. Master Burden, when shall we see you at Henley?

[*Exeunt* Hostess *and* Devil.

Burd. The devil take thee and Henley too.

Miles. Master, shall I make a good motion?

Bacon. What's that?

Miles. Marry, sir, now that my hostess is gone to provide supper, conjure up another spirit, and send Doctor Burden flying after.

Bacon. Thus, rulers of our academic state,
You have seen the friar frame his art by proof;
And as the college callèd Brazen-nose[1]
Is under him, and he the master there,
So surely shall this head of brass be fram'd,
And yield forth strange and uncouth aphorisms;
And hell and Hecate shall fail the friar,
But I will circle England round with brass.

Miles. So be it, *et nunc et semper;* amen.

[*Exeunt.*

SCENE III.—*Harleston Fair.*

Enter MARGARET *and* JOAN; THOMAS, RICHARD, *and other Clowns; and* LACY *disguised in country apparel.*

Thom. By my troth, Margaret, here's a weather is able to make a man call his father "whoreson": if this weather hold, we shall have hay good cheap, and butter and cheese at Harleston will bear no price.

Mar. Thomas, maids when they come to see the fair Count not to make a cope[2] for dearth of hay:

---

[1] In Bacon's day Brasenose College was not in existence.
[2] Bargain.

When we have turn'd our butter to the salt,
And set our cheese safely upon the racks,
Then let our fathers price it as they please.
We country sluts of merry Fressingfield
Come to buy needless naughts to make us fine,
And look that young men should be frank this day,
And court us with such fairings as they can.
Phœbus is blithe, and frolic looks from heaven,
As when he courted lovely Semele,
Swearing the pedlers shall have empty packs,
If that fair weather may make chapmen buy.

Lacy. But, lovely Peggy, Semele is dead,
And therefore Phœbus from his palace pries,
And, seeing such a sweet and seemly saint,
Shows all his glories for to court yourself.

Mar. This is a fairing, gentle sir, indeed,
To soothe me up with such smooth flattery ;
But learn of me, your scoff's too broad before.—
Well, Joan, our beauties must abide their jests ;
We serve the turn in jolly Fressingfield.

Joan. Margaret, a farmer's daughter for a farmer's son :
I warrant you, the meanest of us both
Shall have a mate to lead us from the church.
                    [LACY *whispers* MARGARET *in the ear.*
But, Thomas, what's the news? what, in a dump?
Give me your hand, we are near a pedler's shop ;
Out with your purse, we must have fairings now.

Thom. Faith, Joan, and shall: I'll bestow a fairing on
you, and then we will to the tavern, and snap off a pint
of wine or two.

Mar. Whence are you, sir? of Suffolk? for your terms
Are finer than the common sort of men.

Lacy. Faith, lovely girl, I am of Beccles by,
Your neighbour, not above six miles from hence,
A farmer's son, that never was so quaint

But that he could do courtesy to such dames.
But trust me, Margaret, I am sent in charge,
From him that revell'd in your father's house,
And fill'd his lodge with cheer and venison,
'Tirèd in green: he sent you this rich purse,
His token that he help'd you run your cheese,
And in the milkhouse chatted with yourself.

Mar. To me? you forget yourself.

Lacy. Women are often weak in memory.

Mar. O, pardon, sir, I call to mind the man:
'Twere little manners to refuse his gift,
And yet I hope he sends it not for love;
For we have little leisure to debate of that.

Joan. What, Margaret! blush not: maids must have
their loves.

Thom. Nay, by the mass, she looks pale as if she were
angry.

Rich. Sirrah, are you of Beccles? I pray, how doth
Goodman Cob? my father bought a horse of him.—I'll
tell you, Margaret, 'a were good to be a gentleman's jade,
for of all things the foul hilding could not abide a dung-
cart.

Mar. [*aside*].   How different is this farmer from the
        rest,
That erst as yet have pleas'd my wandering sight!
His words are witty, quicken'd with a smile,
His courtesy gentle, smelling of the court;
Facile and debonair in all his deeds;
Proportion'd as was Paris, when, in grey,
He courted Œnon in the vale by Troy.
Great lords have come and pleaded for my love:
Who but the Keeper's lass of Fressingfield?
And yet methinks this farmer's jolly son
Passeth the proudest that hath pleas'd mine eye.
But, Peg, disclose not that thou art in love,

And show as yet no sign of love to him,
Although thou well wouldst wish him for thy love:
Keep that to thee till time doth serve thy turn,
To show the grief wherein thy heart doth burn.——
Come, Joan and Thomas, shall we to the fair?——
You, Beccles man, will not forsake us now?

   Lacy. Not whilst I may have such quaint girls as you.

   Mar. Well, if you chance to come by Fressingfield,
Make but a step into the Keeper's lodge;
And such poor fare as woodmen can afford,
Butter and cheese, cream and fat venison,
You shall have store, and welcome therewithal.

   Lacy. Gramercies, Peggy; look for me ere long.

                          [*Exeunt.*

Q

ACT THE SECOND

SCENE I.—*The Court at Hampton House.*

Enter KING HENRY THE THIRD, *the* EMPEROR OF
GERMANY, *the* KING OF CASTILE, ELINOR, *and*
VANDERMAST.

. HEN. Great men of Europe, monarchs
of the West,
Ring'd with the walls of old Oceanus,
Whose lofty surge is like the battlements
That compass'd high-built Babel in
with towers,—
Welcome, my lords, welcome, brave
western kings,
To England's shore, whose promontory-cleeves
Show Albion is another little world;
Welcome says English Henry to you all;
Chiefly unto the lovely Elinor,
Who dar'd for Edward's sake cut through the seas,
And venture as Agenor's damsel through the deep,
To get the love of Henry's wanton son.
 K. of Cast. England's rich monarch, brave Planta-
genet,
The Pyren Mounts swelling above the clouds,

That ward the wealthy Castile in with walls,
Could not detain the beauteous Elinor;
But hearing of the fame of Edward's youth,
She dar'd to brook Neptunus' haughty pride,
And bide the brunt of froward Æolus:
Then may fair England welcome her the more.

   Elin. After that English Henry by his lords
Had sent Prince Edward's lovely counterfeit,
A present to the Castile Elinor,
The comely portrait of so brave a man,
The virtuous fame discoursèd of his deeds,
Edward's courageous resolution,
Done at the Holy Land 'fore Damas'[1] walls,
Led both mine eye and thoughts in equal links,
To like so of the English monarch's son,
That I attempted perils for his sake.

   Emp. Where is the prince, my lord?

   K. Hen. He posted down, not long since, from the
      court,
To Suffolk side, to merry Framlingham,
To sport himself amongst my fallow deer:
From thence, by packets sent to Hampton House,
We hear the prince is ridden, with his lords,
To Oxford, in the acadèmy there
To hear dispute amongst the learnèd men.
But we will send forth letters for my son,
To will him come from Oxford to the court.

   Emp. Nay, rather, Henry, let us, as we be,
Ride for to visit Oxford with our train.
Fain would I see your universities,
And what learn'd men your acadèmy yields.
From Hapsburg have I brought a learnèd clerk,
To hold dispute with English orators:
This doctor, surnam'd Jaques Vandermast,

---

[1] Edward could not have fought before Damascus.

A German born, pass'd into Padua,
To Florence and to fair Bologna,
To Paris, Rheims, and stately Orleans,
And, talking there with men of art, put down
The chiefest of them all in aphorisms,
In magic, and the mathematic rules :
Now let us, Henry, try him in your schools.

 K. Hen. He shall, my lord ; this motion likes me well.
We'll progress straight to Oxford with our trains,
And see what men our académy brings.—
And, wonder Vandermast, welcome to me :
In Oxford shalt thou find a jolly friar,
Call'd Friar Bacon, England's only flower :
Set him but non-plus in his magic spells,
And make him yield in mathematic rules,
And for thy glory I will bind thy brows,
Not with a poet's garland made of bays,
But with a coronet of choicest gold.
Whilst then we set to Oxford with our troops,
Let's in and banquet in our English court. [*Exeunt.*

SCENE II.—*A Street in Oxford.*

Enter RALPH SIMNELL *in* PRINCE EDWARD'S *apparel;*
 and PRINCE EDWARD, WARREN, *and* ERMSBY
 disguised.

 Ralph. Where be these vacabond knaves, that they
attend no better on their master ?

 P. Edw. If it please your honour, we are all ready at
an inch.

 Ralph. Sirrah Ned, I'll have no more post-horse to
ride on : I'll have another fetch.

Erms. I pray you, how is that, my lord?

Ralph. Marry, sir, I'll send to the Isle of Ely for four or five dozen of geese, and I'll have them tied six and six together with whip-cord: now upon their backs will I have a fair field-bed with a canopy; and so, when it is my pleasure, I'll flee into what place I please. This will be easy.

War. Your honour hath said well: but shall we to Brazen-nose College before we pull off our boots?

Erms. Warren, well motioned; we will to the friar before we revel it within the town.—Ralph, see you keep your countenance like a prince.

Ralph. Wherefore have I such a company of cutting[1] knaves to wait upon me, but to keep and defend my countenance against all mine enemies? have you not good swords and bucklers?

Enter FRIAR BACON *and* MILES.

Erms. Stay, who comes here?

War. Some scholar; and we'll ask him where Friar Bacon is.

Bacon. Why, thou arrant dunce, shall I never make thee a good scholar? doth not all the town cry out and say, Friar Bacon's subsizer is the greatest blockhead in all Oxford? why, thou canst not speak one word of true Latin.

Miles. No, sir? yes! what is this else? *Ego sum tuus homo,* "I am your man;" I warrant you, sir, as good Tully's phrase as any is in Oxford.

Bacon. Come on, sirrah; what part of speech is *Ego?*

Miles. *Ego,* that is "I"; marry, *nomen substantivo.*

Bacon. How prove you that?

[1] Swaggering.

Miles. Why, sir, let him prove himself an 'a will; I can be heard, felt and understood.

Bacon. O gross dunce!　　　　　　　[*Beats him.*

P. Edw. Come, let us break off this dispute between these two.—Sirrah, where is Brazen-nose College?

Miles. Not far from Coppersmith's Hall.

P. Edw. What, dost thou mock me?

Miles. Not I, sir, but what would you at Brazen-nose?

Erms. Marry, we would speak with Friar Bacon.

Miles. Whose men be you?

Erms. Marry, scholar, here's our master.

Ralph. Sirrah, I am the master of these good fellows; mayst thou not know me to be a lord by my reparrel?

Miles. Then here's good game for the hawk; for here's the master-fool, and a covey of coxcombs: one wise man, I think, would spring you all.

P. Edw. Gog's wounds! Warren, kill him.

War. Why, Ned, I think the devil be in my sheath; I cannot get out my dagger.

Erms. Nor I mine: swones,[1] Ned, I think I am bewitched.

Miles. A company of scabs! the proudest of you all draw your weapon, if he can.—[*Aside*]. See how boldly I speak, now my master is by.

P. Edw. I strive in vain; but if my sword be shut
And conjur'd fast by magic in my sheath,
Villain, here is my fist.

　　　　　　　[*Strikes* MILES *a box on the ear.*

Miles. O, I beseech you conjure his hands too, that he may not lift his arms to his head, for he is light-fingered!

Ralph. Ned, strike him; I'll warrant thee by mine honour.

Bacon. What! means the English prince to wrong my man?

---

[1] Equivalent to "'swounds," "God's wounds."

P. Edw. To whom speakest thou?

Bacon. To thee.

P. Edw. Who art thou?

Bacon. Could you not judge, when all your swords
    grew fast,
That Friar Bacon was not far from hence?
Edward, King Henry's son and Prince of Wales,
Thy fool disguis'd cannot conceal thyself:
I know both Ermsby and the Sussex Earl,
Else Friar Bacon had but little skill.
Thou com'st in post from merry Fressingfield,
Fast-fancied[1] to the Keeper's bonny lass,
To crave some succour of the jolly friar:
And Lacy, Earl of Lincoln, hast thou left,
To treat fair Margaret to allow thy loves;
But friends are men, and love can baffle lords;
The earl both woos and courts her for himself.

War. Ned, this is strange; the friar knoweth all.

Erms. Apollo could not utter more than this.

P. Edw. I stand amaz'd to hear this jolly friar,
Tell even the very secrets of my thoughts:—
But, learnèd Bacon, since thou know'st the cause
Why I did post so fast from Fressingfield,
Help, friar, at a pinch, that I may have
The love of lovely Margaret to myself,
And, as I am true Prince of Wales, I'll give
Living and lands to strength thy college state.

War. Good friar, help the prince in this.

Ralph. Why, servant Ned, will not the friar do it?—
Were not my sword glued to my scabbard by conjuration,
I would cut off his head, and make him do it by force.

Miles. In faith, my lord, your manhood and your sword
is all alike; they are so fast conjured that we shall never
see them.

                    [1] Tied by love.

Erms. What, doctor, in a dump ! tush, help the prince,
And thou shalt see how liberal he will prove.

Bacon. Crave not such actions greater dumps than
          these?
I will, my lord, strain out my magic spells ;
For this day comes the earl to Fressingfield,
And 'fore that night shuts in the day with dark,
They'll be betrothèd each to other fast.
But come with me ; we'll to my study straight,
And in a glass prospective[1] I will show.
What's done this day in merry Fressingfield.

P. Edw. Gramercies, Bacon ; I will quite thy pain.

Bacon. But send your train, my lord, into the town :
My scholar shall go bring them to their inn ;
Meanwhile we'll see the knavery of the earl.

P. Edw. Warren, leave me :—and, Ermsby, take the
          fool :
Let him be master and go revel it,
Till I and Friar Bacon talk awhile.

War. We will, my lord.

Ralph. Faith, Ned, and I'll lord it out till thou comest ;
I'll be Prince of Wales over all the black-pots[2] in Oxford.
                                        [*Exeunt.*

SCENE III.—FRIAR BACON'S *Cell.*

FRIAR BACON *and* PRINCE EDWARD *go into the study.*[3]

Bacon. Now, frolic Edward, welcome to my cell ;
Here tempers Friar Bacon many toys,

---

[1] A glass which reflects magically distant or future events and
scenes.   [2] Leathern wine-jugs.
[3] "After Bacon and Edward had walked a few paces about (or
perhaps towards the back of) the stage, the audience were to
suppose that the scene was changed to the interior of Bacon's cell."
—DYCE.

And holds this place his consistory-court,
Wherein the devils plead homage to his words.
Within this glass prospective thou shalt see
This day what's done in merry Fressingfield
'Twixt lovely Peggy and the Lincoln Earl.

    P. Edw. Friar, thou glad'st me : now shall Edward try
How Lacy meaneth to his sovereign lord.

    Bacon. Stand there and look directly in the glass.

        Enter MARGARET *and* FRIAR BUNGAY.[1]

What sees my lord ?
    P. Edw. I see the Keeper's lovely lass appear,
As brightsome as the paramour of Mars,
Only attended by a jolly friar.

    Bacon. Sit still, and keep the crystal in your eye.

    Mar. But tell me, Friar Bungay, is it true,
That this fair, courteous, country swain,
Who says his father is a farmer nigh,
Can be Lord Lacy, Earl of Lincolnshire ?

    Bun. Peggy, 'tis true, 'tis Lacy for my life,
Or else mine art and cunning both do fail,
Left by Prince Edward to procure his loves ;
For he in green, that holp you run your cheese,
Is son to Henry, and the Prince of Wales.

    Mar. Be what he will, his lure is but for lust :
But did Lord Lacy like poor Margaret,
Or would he deign to wed a country lass,
Friar, I would his humble handmaid be,
And for great wealth quite him with courtesy.

    Bun. Why, Margaret, dost thou love him ?

---

[1] " Perhaps the curtain which concealed the upper stage . . . was withdrawn, discovering Margaret and Bungay standing there, and when the representation in the glass was supposed to be over, the curtain was drawn back again."—DYCE.

Mar. His personage, like the pride of vaunting Troy,
Might well avouch to shadow Helen's rape :
His wit is quick and ready in conceit,
As Greece afforded in her chiefest prime :
Courteous, ah friar, full of pleasing smiles !
Trust me, I love too much to tell thee more ;
Suffice to me he's England's paramour.

Bun. Hath not each eye that view'd thy pleasing face
Surnamèd thee Fair Maid of Fressingfield?

Mar. Yes, Bungay, and would God the lovely earl
Had that *in esse,* that so many sought.

Bun. Fear not, the friar will not be behind
To show his cunning to entangle love.

P. Edw. I think the friar courts the bonny wench ;
Bacon, methinks he is a lusty churl.

Bacon. Now look, my lord.

Enter LACY *disguised as before.*

P. Edw. Gog's wounds, Bacon, here comes Lacy !
Bacon. Sit still, my lord, and mark the comedy.
Bun. Here's Lacy, Margaret, step aside awhile
[*Retires with* MARGARET.
Lacy. Daphne, the damsel that caught Phœbus fast,
And lock'd him in the brightness of her looks,
Was not so beauteous in Apollo's eyes
As is fair Margaret to the Lincoln Earl.
Recant thee, Lacy, thou art put in trust :—
Edward, thy sovereign's son, hath chosen thee,
A secret friend, to court her for himself,
And dar'st thou wrong thy prince with treachery ?—
Lacy, love makes no exception of a friend,
Nor deems it of a prince but as a man.
Honour bids thee control him in his lust ;
His wooing is not for to wed the girl,
But to entrap her and beguile the lass.

Lacy, thou lov'st; then brook not such abuse,
But wed her, and abide thy prince's frown:
For better die, than see her live disgrac'd.

Mar. Come, friar, I will shake him from his dumps.——
                                   [*Comes forward.*
How cheer you, sir? a penny for your thought:
You're early up, pray God it be the near.[1]
What, come from Beccles in a morn so soon?

Lacy. Thus watchful are such men as live in love,
Whose eyes brook broken slumbers for their sleep.
I tell thee, Peggy, since last Harleston fair
My mind hath felt a heap of passions.

Mar. A trusty man, that court it for your friend:
Woo you still for the courtier all in green?——
[*Aside.*] I marvel that he sues not for himself.

Lacy. Peggy, I pleaded first to get your grace for
    him;
But when mine eyes survey'd your beauteous looks,
Love, like a wag, straight div'd into my heart,
And there did shrine the idea of yourself.
Pity me, though I be a farmer's son,
And measure not my riches, but my love.

Mar. You are very hasty; for to garden well,
Seeds must have time to sprout before they spring:
Love ought to creep as doth the dial's shade,
For timely ripe is rotten too-too soon.

Bun. [*coming forward*]. *Deus hic;* room for a merry
    friar!
What, youth of Beccles, with the Keeper's lass?
'Tis well; but tell me, hear you any news.

Mar. No, friar: what news?

Bun. Hear you not how the pursuivants do post
With proclamations through each country-town?

Lacy. For what, gentle friar? tell the news.

---

[1] An allusion to the proverb, " Early up and never the nearer."

Bun. Dwell'st thou. in Beccles, and hear'st not of
  these news?
Lacy, the Earl of Lincoln, is late fled
From Windsor court, disguisèd like a swain,
And lurks about the country here unknown.
Henry suspects him of some treachery,
And therefore doth proclaim in every way,
That who can take the Lincoln Earl shall have,
Paid in the Exchequer, twenty thousand crowns.

Lacy. The Earl of Lincoln! friar, thou art mad:
It was some other; thou mistak'st the man:
The Earl of Lincoln! why, it cannot be.

Mar. Yes, very well, my lord, for you are he:
The Keeper's daughter took you prisoner:
Lord Lacy, yield, I'll be your gaoler once.

P. Edw. How familiar they be, Bacon!

Bacon. Sit still, and mark the sequel of their loves.

Lacy. Then am I double prisoner to thyself:
Peggy, I yield; but are these news in jest?

Mar. In jest with you, but earnest unto me;
For why these wrongs do wring me at the heart.
Ah, how these earls and noblemen of birth
Flatter and feign to forge poor women's ill.

Lacy. Believe me, lass, I am the Lincoln Earl:
I not deny but, 'tirèd thus in rags,
I liv'd disguis'd to win fair Peggy's love.

Mar. What love is there where wedding ends not
  love?

Lacy. I meant, fair girl, to make thee Lacy's wife.

Mar. I little think that earls will stoop so low.

Lacy. Say, shall I make thee countess ere I sleep?

Mar. Handmaid unto the earl, so please himself:
A wife in name, but servant in obedience.

Lacy. The Lincoln Countess, for it shall be so:
I'll plight the bands and seal it with a kiss.

P. Edw. Gog's wounds, Bacon, they kiss! I'll stab
   them.

Bacon. O, hold your hands, my lord it is the glass

P. Edw. Choler to see the traitors gree so well
Made me think the shadows substances.

Bacon. 'Twere a long poniard, my lord, to reach
   between
Oxford and Fressingfield; but sit still and see more.

Bun. Well, Lord of Lincoln, if your loves be knit,
And that your tongues and thoughts do both agree,
To avoid ensuing jars, I'll hamper up the match.
I'll take my portace[1] forth, and wed you here:
Then go to bed and seal up your desires.

Lacy. Friar, content.—Peggy, how like you this?

Mar. What likes my lord is pleasing unto me.

Bun. Then hand-fast hand, and I will to my book.

Bacon. What sees my lord now?

P. Edw. Bacon, I see the lovers hand in hand,
The friar ready with his portace there
To wed them both: then am I quite undone.
Bacon, help now, if e'er thy magic serv'd:
Help, Bacon; stop the marriage now,
If devils or necromancy may suffice,
And I will give thee forty thousand crowns.

Bacon. Fear not, my lord, I'll stop the jolly friar
For mumbling up his orisons this day.

Lacy. Why speak'st not, Bungay? Friar to thy book.
            [BUNGAY *is mute, crying* "Hud, hud."

Mar. How look'st thou, friar, as a man distraught?
Reft of thy senses, Bungay? show by signs
If thou be dumb, what passion holdeth thee.

Lacy. He's dumb indeed. Bacon hath with his
   devils
Enchanted him, or else some strange disease

---

[1] Breviary, portable prayer-book.

Or apoplexy hath possess'd his lungs :
But, Peggy, what he cannot with his book
We'll 'twixt us both unite it up in heart.

 Mar. Else let me die, my lord, a miscreant.

 P. Edw. Why stands Friar Bungay so amaz'd?

 Bacon. I have struck him dumb, my lord ; and, if
  your honour please
I'll fetch this Bungay straightway from Fressingfield,
And he shall dine with us in Oxford here.

 P. Edw. Bacon, do that, and thou contentest me.

 Lacy. Of courtesy, Margaret, let us lead the friar
Unto thy father's lodge, to comfort him
With broths, to bring him from this hapless trance.

 Mar. Or else, my lord, we were passing unkind
To leave the friar so in his distress.

  Enter a Devil, *who carries off* BUNGAY *on his back.*

O, help, my lord ! a devil, a devil, my lord !
Look how he carries Bungay on his back !
Let's hence, for Bacon's spirits be abroad.

        [*Exit with* LACY.

 P. Edw. Bacon, I laugh to see the jolly friar
Mounted upon the devil, and how the earl
Flees with his bonny lass for fear.
As soon as Bungay is at Brazen-nose,
And I have chatted with the merry friar,
I will in post hie me to Fressingfield,
And quite these wrongs on Lacy ere't be long.

 Bacon. So be it, my lord : but let us to our dinner ;
For ere we have taken our repast awhile,
We shall have Bungay brought to Brazen-nose.

         [*Exeunt.*

SCENE IV.—*The Regent House at Oxford.*

Enter BURDEN, MASON, *and* CLEMENT.

Mason. Now that we are gathered in the Regent
    House,
It fits us talk about the king's repair;
For he, troop'd with all the western kings,
That lie along'st the Dantzic seas by east,
North by the clime of frosty Germany,
The Almain monarch and the Saxon duke,
Castile and lovely Elinor with him,
Have in their jests resolv'd for Oxford town.
    Burd. We must lay plots of stately tragedies,
Strange comic shows, such as proud Roscius
Vaunted before the Roman Emperors,
To welcome all the western potentates.
    Clem. But more; the king by letters hath foretold
That Frederick, the Almain emperor,
Hath brought with him a German of esteem,
Whose surname is Don Jaques Vandermast,
Skilful in magic and those secret arts.
    Mason. Then must we all make suit unto the friar,
To Friar Bacon, that he vouch this task,
And undertake to countervail in skill
The German; else there's none in Oxford can
Match and dispute with learnèd Vandermast.
    Burd. Bacon, if he will hold the German play,
Will teach him what an English friar can do:
The devil, I think, dare not dispute with him.
    Clem. Indeed, Mas doctor, he [dis]pleasur'd you,
In that he brought your hostess, with her spit,
From Henley, posting unto Brazen-nose.
    Burd. A vengeance on the friar for his pains!

But leaving that, let's hie to Bacon straight,
To see if he will take this task in hand.

Clem. Stay, what rumour is this? the town is up in a mutiny: what hurly-burly is this?

Enter a Constable, *with* RALPH SIMNELL, WARREN, ERMSBY, *still disguised as before, and* MILES.

Cons. Nay, masters, if you were ne'er so good, you shall before the doctors to answer your misdemeanour.

Burd. What's the matter, fellow?

Cons. Marry, sir, here's a company of rufflers,[1] that, drinking in the tavern, have made a great brawl, and almost killed the vintner.

Miles. Salve, Doctor Burden![2]
This lubberly lurden,
Ill-shap'd and ill-fac'd,
Disdain'd and disgrac'd,
What he tells unto *vobis*
Mentitur de nobis.

Burd. Who is the master and chief of this crew?

Miles. Ecce asinum mundi
Figura rotundi,
Neat, sheat, and fine,
As brisk as a cup of wine.

Burd. [*to* RALPH]. What are you?

Ralph. I am, father doctor, as a man would say, the bell-wether of this company: these are my lords, and I the Prince of Wales.

Clem. Are you Edward, the king's son?

Ralph. Sirrah Miles, bring hither the tapster that drew the wine, and, I warrant, when they see how soundly I have broke his head, they'll say 'twas done by no less man than a prince.

---

[1] Bullies.　　　　[2] Skeltonical verse.

Mason. I cannot believe that this is the Prince of Wales.

War. And why so, sir?

Mason. For they say the prince is a brave and a wise gentleman.

War. Why, and think'st thou, doctor, that he is not
    so?
Dar'st thou detract and derogate from him,
Being so lovely and so brave a youth?

Erms. Whose face, shining with many a sugar'd smile,
Bewrays that he is bred of princely race.

Miles. And yet, master doctor,
To speak like a proctor,
And tell unto you
What is veriment and true:
To cease of this quarrel,
Look but on his apparel;
Then mark but my talis,
He is great Prince of Walis,
The chief of our *gregis*,
And *filius regis*:
Then 'ware what is done,
For he is Henry's white [1] son.

Ralph. Doctors, whose doting night-caps are not capable of my ingenious dignity, know that I am Edward Plantagenet, whom if you displease, will make a ship that shall hold all your colleges, and so carry away the university with a fair wind to the Bankside in Southwark.—How sayest thou, Ned Warren, shall I not do it?

War. Yes, my good lord; and, if it please your lordship, I will gather up all your old pantofles,[2] and with the cork make you a pinnace of five hundred ton, that shall serve the turn marvellous well, my lord.

Erms. And I, my lord, will have pioners to under-

---

[1] A term of endearment.   [2] Loose shoes.

R

mine the town, that the very gardens and orchards be
carried away for your summer walks.

Miles. And I, with *scientia*
And great *diligentia,*
Will conjure and charm,
To keep you from harm ;
That *utrum horum mavis,*
Your very great *navis,*
Like Barclay's ship,[1]
From Oxford do skip
With colleges and schools,
Full-loaden with fools.
Quid dicis ad hoc,
Worshipful *Domine* Dawcock ?[2]

   Clem. Why, hare-brain'd courtiers, are you drunk or
       mad,
To taunt us up with such scurrility?
Deem you us men of base and light esteem,
To bring us such a fop for Henry's son?—
Call out the beadles and convey them hence
Straight to Bocardo :[3] let the roisters lie
Close clapt in bolts, until their wits be tame.

   Erms. Why, shall we to prison, my lord?

   Ralph. What sayest, Miles, shall I honour the prison
with my presence?

   Miles. No, no : out with your blades,
And hamper these jades ;
Have a flurt and a crash,

---

[1] The allusion is to Alexander Barclay's English version (1509) of
Sebastian Brant's *Narrenschiff.*
[2] "An expression borrowed from the author whose style is here
imitated—

        " *Construas hoc,*
        Domine Dawcocke !
       'Ware the Hauke, Skelton."—DYCE.

[3] A prison in the old north gate of Oxford, so named after one of
the moods of the third syllogistic figure.

Now play revel-dash,
And teach these sacerdos
That the Bocardos,
Like peasants and elves,
Are meet for themselves.

Mason. To the prison with them, constable.

War. Well, doctors, seeing I have sported me
With laughing at these mad and merry wags,
Know that Prince Edward is at Brazen-nose,
And this, attirèd like the Prince of Wales,
Is Ralph, King Henry's only lovèd fool;
I, Earl of Sussex, and this Ermsby,
One of the privy-chamber to the king;
Who, while the prince with Friar Bacon stays,
Have revell'd it in Oxford as you see.

Mason. My lord, pardon us, we knew not what you
            were:
But courtiers may make greater scapes than these.
Wilt please your honour dine with me to-day?

War. I will, Master doctor, and satisfy the vintner for
his hurt; only I must desire you to imagine him all this
forenoon the Prince of Wales.

Mason. I will, sir.

Ralph. And upon that I will lead the way; only I will
have Miles go before me, because I have heard Henry
say that wisdom must go before majesty.   [*Exeunt.*

ACT THE THIRD

SCENE I.—*At Fressingfield.*

Enter PRINCE EDWARD *with his poniard in his hand,*
LACY *and* MARGARET,

EDW. Lacy, thou canst not shroud thy
traitorous thoughts,
Nor cover, as did Cassius, all thy wiles;
For Edward hath an eye that looks as
far
As Lyncæus from the shores of Græcia.
Did I not sit in Oxford by the friar,
And see thee court the maid of Fressingfield,
Sealing thy flattering fancies with a kiss?
Did not proud Bungay draw his portace forth,
And joining hand in hand had married you,
If Friar Bacon had not struck him dumb,
And mounted him upon a spirit's back,
That we might chat at Oxford with the friar?
Traitor, what answer'st? is not all this true?

Lacy. Truth all, my lord; and thus I make reply.
At Harleston fair, there courting for your grace,

Whenas mine eye survey'd her curious shape,
And drew the beauteous glory of her looks
To dive into the centre of my heart,
Love taught me that your honour did but jest,
That princes were in fancy but as men;
How that the lovely maid of Fressingfield
Was fitter to be Lacy's wedded wife,
Than concubine unto the Prince of Wales.

   P. Edw. Injurious Lacy, did I love thee more
Than Alexander his Hephæstion?
Did I unfold the passions of my love,
And lock them in the closet of thy thoughts?
Wert thou to Edward second to himself,
Sole friend and partner of his secret loves?
And could a glance of fading beauty break
Th' enchainèd fetters of such private friends?
Base coward, false, and too effeminate
To be corrival with a prince in thoughts!
From Oxford have I posted since I din'd,
To quite a traitor 'fore that Edward sleep.

   Mar. 'Twas I, my lord, not Lacy, stept awry:
For oft he su'd and courted for yourself,
And still woo'd for the courtier all in green;
But I, whom fancy made but over-fond,
Pleaded myself with looks as if I lov'd;
I fed mine eye with gazing on his face,
And still bewitch'd lov'd Lacy with my looks;
My heart with sighs, mine eyes pleaded with tears,
My face held pity and content at once;
And more I could not cipher-out by signs
But that I lov'd Lord Lacy with my heart.
Then, worthy Edward, measure with thy mind
If women's favours will not force men fall,
If beauty, and if darts of piercing love,
Are not of force to bury thoughts of friends.

P. Edw. I tell thee, Peggy, I will have thy loves:
Edward or none shall conquer Margaret.
In frigates bottom'd with rich Sethin planks,
Topt with the lofty firs of Lebanon,
Stemm'd and encas'd with burnish'd ivory,
And overlaid with plates of Persian wealth,
Like Thetis shalt thou wanton on the waves,
And draw the dolphins to thy lovely eyes,
To dance lavoltas[1] in the purple streams:
Sirens, with harps and silver psalteries,
Shall wait with music at thy frigate's stem,
And entertain fair Margaret with their lays.
England and England's wealth shall wait on thee;
Britain shall bend unto her prince's love,
And do due homage to thine excellence,
If thou wilt be but Edward's Margaret.

Mar. Pardon, my lord: if Jove's great royalty
Sent me such presents as to Danaë;
If Phœbus 'tirèd in Latona's webs,
Came courting from the beauty of his lodge;
The dulcet tunes of frolic Mercury,—
Not all the wealth heaven's treasury affords,—
Should make me leave Lord Lacy or his love.

P. Edw. I have learn'd at Oxford, there, this point
of schools,—
Ablata causa, tollitur effectus:
Lacy—the cause that Margaret cannot love
Nor fix her liking on the English prince—
Take him away, and then the effects will fail.
Villain, prepare thyself: for I will bathe
My poniard in the bosom of an earl.

Lacy. Rather than live, and miss fair Margaret's love,
Prince Edward, stop not at the fatal doom,
But stab it home: end both my loves and life.

Mar. Brave Prince of Wales, honour'd for royal deeds,

---

[1] A dance resembling the waltz or polka.

'Twere sin to stain fair Venus' courts with blood;
Love's conquest ends, my lord, in courtesy:
Spare Lacy, gentle Edward; let me die,
For so both you and he do cease your loves.

P. Edw. Lacy shall die as traitor to his lord.

Lacy. I have deserv'd it, Edward; act it well.

Mar. What hopes the prince to gain by Lacy's death?

P. Edw. To end the loves 'twixt him and Margaret.

Mar. Why, thinks King Henry's son that Margaret's
        love
Hangs in th' uncertain balance of proud time?
That death shall make a discord of our thoughts?
No, stab the earl, and 'fore the morning sun
Shall vaunt him thrice over the lofty east,
Margaret will meet her Lacy in the heavens.

Lacy. If aught betides to lovely Margaret
That wrongs or wrings her honour from content,
Europe's rich wealth nor England's monarchy
Should not allure Lacy to over-live:
Then, Edward, short my life and end her loves.

Mar. Rid me, and keep a friend worth many loves.

Lacy. Nay, Edward, keep a love worth many friends.

Mar. An if thy mind be such as fame hath blaz'd,
Then, princely Edward, let us both abide
The fatal resolution of thy rage:
Banish thou fancy, and embrace revenge,
And in one tomb knit both our carcases,
Whose hearts were linkèd in one perfect love.

P. Edw. [*aside.*] Edward, art thou that famous Prince
        of Wales,
Who at Damasco beat the Saracens,
And brought'st home triumph on thy lance's point?
And shall thy plumes be pull'd by Venus down?
Is't princely to dissever lover's leagues,
To part such friends as glory in their loves?

Leave, Ned, and make a virtue of this fault,
And further Peg and Lacy in their loves:
So in subduing fancy's passion,
Conquering thyself, thou gett'st the richest spoil.—
Lacy, rise up. Fair Peggy, here's my hand:
The Prince of Wales hath conquer'd all his thoughts,
And all his loves he yields unto the earl.
Lacy, enjoy the maid of Fressingfield;
Make her thy Lincoln Countess at the church,
And Ned, as he is true Plantagenet,
Will give her to thee frankly for thy wife.

Lacy. Humbly I take her of my sovereign,
As if that Edward gave me England's right,
And rich'd me with the Albion diadem.

Mar. And doth the English prince mean true?
Will he vouchsafe to cease his former loves,
And yield the title of a country maid
Unto Lord Lacy?

P. Edw. I will, fair Peggy, as I am true lord.

Mar. Then, lordly sir, whose conquest is as great,
In conquering love, as Cæsar's victories,
Margaret, as mild and humble in her thoughts
As was Aspasia unto Cyrus self,
Yields thanks, and, next Lord Lacy, doth enshrine
Edward the second secret in her heart.

P. Edw. Gramercy, Peggy:—now that vows are past,
And that your loves are not to be revolt,[1]
Once, Lacy, friends again. Come, we will post
To Oxford; for this day the king is there,
And brings for Edward Castile Elinor.
Peggy, I must go see and view my wife:
I pray God I like her as I loved thee.
Beside, Lord Lincoln, we shall hear dispute
'Twixt Friar Bacon and learn'd Vandermast.

---

[1] Overturned; literal transference from the Latin.

Peggy, we'll leave you for a week or two.

Mar. As it please Lord Lacy : but love's foolish looks
Think footsteps miles, and minutes to be hours.

Lacy. I'll hasten, Peggy, to make short return.——
But please your honour go unto the lodge,
We shall have butter, cheese, and venison ;
And yesterday I brought for Margaret
A lusty bottle of neat claret-wine :
Thus can we feast and entertain your grace.

P. Edw. 'Tis cheer, Lord Lacy, for an Emperor,
If he respect the person and the place :
Come, let us in ; for I will all this night
Ride post until I come to Bacon's cell.

[*Exeunt.*

SCENE II.—*At Oxford.*

Enter KING HENRY, *the* EMPEROR, *the* KING OF
CASTILE, ELINOR, VANDERMAST, *and* BUNGAY.

Emp. Trust me, Plantagenet, these Oxford schools
Are richly seated near the river-side :
The mountains full of fat and fallow deer,
The battling [1] pastures lade [2] with kine and flocks,
The town gorgeous with high-built colleges,
And scholars seemly in their grave attire,
Learnèd in searching principles of art.——
What is thy judgment, Jaques Vandermast?

Van. That lordly are the buildings of the town,
Spacious the rooms, and full of pleasant walks ;
But for the doctors, how that they be learnèd,

[1] Nourishing to cattle, productive.   [2] Laden.

It may be meanly, for aught I can hear,
Bun. I tell thee, German, Hapsburg holds none such
None read so deep as Oxenford contains:
There are within our academic state
Men that may lecture it in Germany
To all the doctors of your Belgic schools.

 K. Hen. Stand to him, Bungay, charm this Vandermast,
And I will use thee as a royal king.

 Van. Wherein dar'st thou dispute with me?

 Bun. In what a doctor and a friar can.

 Van. Before rich Europe's worthies put thou forth
The doubtful question unto Vandermast.

 Bun. Let it be this,—Whether the spirits of pyromancy
or geomancy, be most predominant in magic?

 Van. I say, of pyromancy.

 Bun. And I, of geomancy.

 Van. The cabalists that write of magic spells,
As Hermes,[1] Melchie,[2] and Pythagoras,
Affirm that, 'mongst the quadruplicity
Of elemental essence, *terra* is but thought
To be a *punctum* squared to[3] the rest;
And that the compass of ascending elements
Exceed in bigness as they do in height;
Judging the concave circle of the sun
To hold the rest in his circumference.
If, then, as Hermes says, the fire be greatest,
Purest, and only giveth shape to spirits,
Then must these dæmones that haunt that place
Be every way superior to the rest.

 Bun. I reason not of elemental shapes,
Nor tell I of the concave latitudes,
Noting their essence nor their quality,
But of the spirits that pyromancy calls,

---

 [1] Trismegistus. [2] Porphyry. [3] An atom compared with.

And of the vigour of the geomantic fiends.
I tell thee, German, magic haunts the ground,
And those strange necromantic spells
That work such shows and wondering in the world
Are acted by those geomantic spirits
That Hermes calleth *terræ filii*.
The fiery spirits are but transparent shades,
That lightly pass as heralds to bear news;
But earthly fiends, clos'd in the lowest deep,
Dissever mountains, if they be but charg'd,
Being more gross and massy in their power.

   Van. Rather these earthly geomantic spirits
Are dull and like the place where they remain;
For when proud Lucifer fell from the heavens,
The spirits and angels that did sin with him,
Retain'd their local essence as their faults,
All subject under Luna's continent:
They which offended less hung in the fire,
And second faults did rest within the air;
But Lucifer and his proud-hearted fiends
Were thrown into the centre of the earth,
Having less understanding than the rest,
As having greater sin and lesser grace.
Therefore such gross and earthly spirits do serve
For jugglers, witches, and vile sorcerers;
Whereas the pyromantic genii
Are mighty, swift, and of far-reaching power.
But grant that geomancy hath most force;
Bungay, to please these mighty potentates,
Prove by some instance what thy art can do.

   Bun. I will.

   Emp. Now, English Harry, here begins the game;
We shall see sport between these learnèd men.

   Van. What wilt thou do?

   Bun. Show thee the tree, leav'd with refinèd gold,

Whereon the fearful dragon held his seat,
That watch'd the garden call'd Hesperides,
Subdu'd and won by conquering Hercules.

Here BUNGAY *conjures, and the Tree appears with the*
Dragon shooting fire.

Van. Well done!
K. Hen. What say you, royal lordings, to my friar?
Hath he not done a point of cunning skill?
Van. Each scholar in the necromantic spells
Can do as much as Bungay hath perform'd.
But as Alcmena's bastard raz'd this tree,
So will I raise him up as when he liv'd,
And cause him pull the dragon from his seat,
And tear the branches piecemeal from the root.—
Hercules! *Prodi, prodi,* Hercules!

HERCULES *appears in his lion's skin.*

Her. Quis me vult?
Van. Jove's bastard son, thou Libyan Hercules,
Pull off the sprigs from off the Hesperian tree,
As once thou didst to win the golden fruit.
Her. Fiat.   [*Begins to break the branches.*
Van. Now, Bungay, if thou canst by magic charm
The fiend, appearing like great Hercules,
From pulling down the branches of the tree,
Then art thou worthy to be counted learnèd.
Bun. I cannot.
Van. Cease, Hercules, until I give thee charge.—
Mighty commander of this English isle,
Henry, come from the stout Plantagenets,
Bungay is learn'd enough to be a friar;
But to compare with Jaques Vandermast,
Oxford and Cambridge must go seek their cells

To find a man to match him in his art.
I have given non-plus to the Paduans,
To them of Sien, Florence, and Bologna,
Rheims, Louvain, and fair Rotterdam,
Frankfort, Lutrech,[1] and Orleans :
And now must Henry, if he do me right,
Crown me with laurel, as they all have done.

Enter BACON.

Bacon. All hail to this royal company,
That sit to hear and see this strange dispute !—
Bungay, how stand'st thou as a man amaz'd ?
What, hath the German acted more than thou ?
    Van. What art thou that question'st thus ?
    Bacon. Men call me Bacon.
    Van. Lordly thou look'st, as if that thou wert learn'd ;
Thy countenance, as if science held her seat
Between the circled arches of thy brows.
    K. Hen. Now, monarchs, hath the German found his
        match.
    Emp. Bestir thee, Jaques, take not now the foil,
Lest thou dost lose what foretime thou didst gain.
    Van. Bacon, wilt thou dispute ?
    Bacon. No, unless he were more learn'd than Vander-
        mast ;
For yet, tell me, what hast thou done ?
    Van. Rais'd Hercules to ruinate that tree,
That Bungay mounted by his magic spells.
    Bacon. Set Hercules to work.
    Van. Now, Hercules, I charge thee to thy task ;
Pull off the golden branches from the root.
    Her. I dare not ; see'st thou not great Bacon here,
Whose frown doth act more than thy magic can ?

[1] Possibly the reference is to Lutetia (Paris) rather than Utrecht,
which was not yet a university town.

Van. By all the thrones, and dominations,
Virtues, powers, and mighty hierarchies,
I charge thee to obey to Vandermast.

Her. Bacon, that bridles headstrong Belcephon,
And rules Asmenoth, guider of the north,
Binds me from yielding unto Vandermast.

K. Hen. How now, Vandermast! have you met with
your match?

Van. Never before was't known to Vandermast
That men held devils in such obedient awe.
Bacon doth more than art, or else I fail.

Emp. Why, Vandermast, art thou overcome?—
Bacon, dispute with him, and try his skill.

Bacon. I came not, monarchs, for to hold dispute
With such a novice as is Vandermast;
I came to have your royalties to dine
With Friar Bacon here in Brazen-nose:
And, for this German troubles but the place,
And holds this audience with a long suspence,
I'll send him to his académy hence.—
Thou, Hercules, whom Vandermast did raise,
Transport the German unto Hapsburg straight,
That he may learn by travail, 'gainst the spring,
More secret dooms and aphorisms of art.
Vanish the tree, and thou away with him!

[*Exit* HERCULES *with* VANDERMAST *and the Tree.*

Emp. Why, Bacon, whither dost thou send him?

Bacon. To Hapsburg: there your highness at return
Shall find the German in his study safe.

K. Hen. Bacon, thou hast honour'd England with thy
skill,
And made fair Oxford famous by thine art:
I will be English Henry to thyself;—
But tell me, shall we dine with thee to-day?

Bacon. With me, my lord; and while I fit my cheer,

See where Prince Edward comes to welcome you,
Gracious as the morning-star of heaven.

[*Exit.*

Enter PRINCE EDWARD, LACY, WARREN, ERMSBY.

Emp. Is this Prince Edward, Henry's royal son?
How martial is the figure of his face!
Yet lovely and beset with amorets.[1]
   K. Hen. Ned, where hast thou been?
   P. Edw. At Framlingham, my lord, to try your bucks
If they could scape the teasers or the toil.
But hearing of these lordly potentates
Landed, and progress'd up to Oxford town,
I posted to give entertain to them:
Chief to the Almain monarch; next to him,
And joint with him, Castile and Saxony
Are welcome as they may be to the English court.
Thus for the men: but see, Venus appears,
Or one that overmatcheth Venus in her shape!
Sweet Elinor, beauty's high-swelling pride,
Rich nature's glory, and her wealth at once,
Fair of all fairs, welcome to *Albion;*
Welcome to me, and welcome to thine own,
If that thou deign'st the welcome from myself.
   Elin. Martial Plantagenet, Henry's high-minded son,
The mark that Elinor did count her aim,
I lik'd thee 'fore I saw thee: now I love,
And so as in so short a time I may;
Yet so as time shall never break that so:
And therefore so accept of Elinor.
   K. of Cast. Fear not, my lord, this couple will agree,
If love may creep into their wanton eyes:—
And therefore, Edward, I accept thee here,
Without suspence, as my adopted son.

[1] Love-kindling looks.

K. Hen. Let me that joy in these consorting greets,
And glory in these honours done to Ned,
Yield thanks for all these favours to my son,
And rest a true Plantagenet to all.

Enter MILES *with a cloth and trenchers and salt.*

Miles. Salvete, omnes reges,
That govern your *greges*
In Saxony and Spain,
In England and in Almain!
For all this frolic rabble
Must I cover the table
With trenchers, salt, and cloth;
And then look for your broth.

    Emp. What pleasant fellow is this?

    K. Hen. 'Tis, my lord, Doctor Bacon's poor scholar.

    Miles. [*aside*] My master hath made me sewer of these great lords; and, God knows, I am as serviceable at a table as a sow is under an apple-tree: 'tis no matter; their cheer shall not be great, and therefore what skills where the salt stand, before or behind?[1]   [*Exit.*

    K. of Cast. These scholars know more skill in axioms,
How to use quips and sleights of sophistry,
Than for to cover courtly for a king.

Re-enter MILES *with a mess of pottage and broth;
and, after him,* BACON.

    Miles. Spill, sir? why, do you think I never carried twopenny chop before in my life?—
By you leave, *nobile decus,*
For here comes Doctor Bacon's *pecus,*

---

    [1] "The salt-cellar, generally a very large and massive one, stood in the middle of the table; guests of superior rank always sat above it towards the upper part of the table, those of inferior rank below it towards the bottom."—COLLINS.

Being in his full age
To carry a mess of pottage.

   Bacon. Lordings, admire not if your cheer be this,
For we must keep our academic fare;
No riot where philosophy doth reign :
And therefore, Henry, place these potentates,
And bid them fall unto their frugal cates.

   Emp. Presumptuous friar! what, scoff'st thou at a
      king?
What, dost thou taunt us with thy peasant's fare,
And give us cates fit for country swains?—
Henry, proceeds this jest of thy consent,
To twit us with a pittance of such price?
Tell me, and Frederick will not grieve thee long.

   K. Hen. By Henry's honour, and the royal faith
The English monarch beareth to his friend,
I knew not of the friar's feeble fare,
Nor am I pleas'd he entertains you thus.

   Bacon. Content thee, Frederick, for I show'd the cates
To let thee see how scholars use to feed;
How little meat refines our English wits :—
Miles, take away, and let it be thy dinner.

   Miles. Marry, sir, I will.
This day shall be a festival-day with me,
For I shall exceed in the highest degree.   [*Exit.*

   Bacon. I tell thee, monarch, all the German peers
Could not afford thy entertainment such,
So royal and so full of majesty,
As Bacon will present to Frederick.
The basest waiter that attends thy cups
Shall be in honours greater than thyself ;
And for thy cates, rich Alexandria drugs,[1]
Fetch'd by carvels from Ægypt's richest straits,
Found in the wealthy strand of Africa,

               [1] Spices.

S

Shall royalize the table of my king;
Wines richer than th' Ægyptian courtesan
Quaff'd to Augustus' kingly countermatch,
Shall be carous'd in English Henry's feast;
Candy shall yield the richest of her canes;
Persia, down her Volga by canoes,
Send down the secrets of her spicery;
The Afric dates, mirabolans [1] of Spain,
Conserves, and suckets [2] from Tiberias,
Cates from Judæa, choicer that the lamp
That firèd Rome with sparks of gluttony,
Shall beautify the board for Frederick:
And therefore grudge not at a friar's feast.

SCENE III.—*At Fressingfield.*

Enter LAMBERT *and* SERLSBY *with the* Keeper.

  Lam. Come, frolic Keeper of our liege's game,
Whose table spread hath other venison
And jacks of wines to welcome passengers,
Know I'm in love with jolly Margaret,
That overshines our damsels as the moon
Darkeneth the brightest sparkles of the night.
In Laxfield here my land and living lies:
I'll make thy daughter jointer of it all,
So thou consent to give her to my wife;
And I can spend five-hundred marks a year.
  Serl. I am the lands-lord, Keeper, of thy holds,
By copy all thy living lies in me;
Laxfield did never see me raise my due:

---

[1] Dried plums.   [2] Sugar plums.

I will enfeoff fair Margaret in all,
So she will take her to a lusty squire.

 Keep. Now, courteous gentles, if the Keeper's girl
Hath pleas'd the liking fancy of you both,
And with her beauty hath subdu'd your thoughts,
'Tis doubtful to decide the question.
It joys me that such men of great esteem
Should lay their liking on this base estate,
And that her state should grow so fortunate
To be a wife to meaner men than you:
But sith such squires will stoop to keeper's fee,
I will, to avoid displeasure of you both,
Call Margaret forth, and she shall make her choice.

 Lam. Content, Keeper ; send her unto us.
           [*Exit* Keeper.
Why, Serlsby, is thy wife so lately dead,
Are all thy loves so lightly passèd over,
As thou canst wed before the year be out ?

 Serl. I live not, Lambert, to content the dead,
Nor was I wedded but for life to her :
The grave ends and begins a married state.

Enter MARGARET.

 Lam. Peggy, the lovely flower of all towns,
Suffolk's fair Helen, and rich England's star,
Whose beauty, temper'd with her huswifery,
Makes England talk of merry Fressingfield !

 Serl. I cannot trick it up with poesies,
Nor paint my passions with comparisons,
Nor tell a tale of Phœbus and his loves :
But this believe me,—Laxfield here is mine,
Of ancient rent seven-hundred pounds a year ;
And if thou canst but love a country squire,
I will enfeoff thee, Margaret, in all :
I cannot flatter ; try me, if thou please.

Mar. Brave neighbouring squires, the stay of Suffolk's
    clime,
A keeper's daughter is too base in gree
To match with men accounted of such worth :
But might I not displease, I would reply.
    Lam. Say, Peggy ; naught shall make us discontent.
    Mar. Then, gentles, note that love hath little stay,
Nor can the flames that Venus sets on fire
Be kindled but by fancy's motion :
Then pardon, gentles, if a maid's reply
Be doubtful, while I have debated with myself,
Who, or of whom, love shall constrain me like.
    Serl. Let it be me ; and trust me, Margaret,
The meads environ'd with the silver streams,
Whose battling pastures fatten all my flocks,
Yielding forth fleeces stapled with such wool,
As Lemnster cannot yield more finer stuff,
And forty kine with fair and burnish'd heads,
With strouting [1] dugs that paggle to the ground,
Shall serve thy dairy, if thou wed with me.
    Lam. Let pass the country wealth, as flocks and kine,
And lands that wave with Ceres' golden sheaves,
Filling my barns with plenty of the fields ;
But, Peggy, if thou wed thyself to me,
Thou shalt have garments of embroider'd silk,
Lawns, and rich net-works for thy head-attire :
Costly shall be thy fair habiliments,
If thou wilt be but Lambert's loving wife.
    Mar. Content you, gentles, you have proffer'd fair,
And more than fits a country maid's degree :
But give me leave to counsel me a time,
For fancy blooms not at the first assault ;
Give me but ten days' respite, and I will reply,
Which or to whom myself affectionates.

        [1] Protuberant.

Serl. Lambert, I tell thee thou'rt importunate;
Such beauty fits not such a base esquire:
It is for Serlsby to have Margaret.

Lam. Think'st thou with wealth to overreach me?
Serlsby, I scorn to brook thy country braves:
I dare thee, coward, to maintain this wrong,
At dint of rapier, single in the field.

Serl. I'll answer, Lambert, what I have avouch'd.—
Margaret, farewell; another time shall serve.

[Exit.

Lam. I'll follow.—Peggy, farewell to thyself;
Listen how well I'll answer for thy love.

[Exit.

Mar. How fortune tempers lucky haps with frowns,
And wrongs me with the sweets of my delight!
Love is my bliss, and love is now my bale.
Shall I be Helen in my froward fates,
As I am Helen in my matchless hue,
And set rich Suffolk with my face afire?
If lovely Lacy were but with his Peggy,
The cloudy darkness of his bitter frown
Would check the pride of these aspiring squires.
Before the term of ten days be expir'd,
Whenas they look for answer of their loves,
My lord will come to merry Fressingfield,
And end their fancies and their follies both:
Till when, Peggy, be blithe and of good cheer.

Enter a Post *with a letter and a bag of gold.*

Post. Fair, lovely damsel, which way leads this path?
How might I post me unto Fressingfield?
Which footpath leadeth to the Keeper's lodge?

Mar. Your way is ready, and this path is right:
Myself do dwell hereby in Fressingfield;

And if the Keeper be the man you seek,
I am his daughter: may I know the cause?

  Post. Lovely, and once belovèd of my lord,—
No marvel if his eye was lodg'd so low,
When brighter beauty is not in the heavens,—
The Lincoln Earl hath sent you letters here,
And, with them, just an hundred pounds in gold.
Sweet, bonny wench, read them, and make reply.

                   [Gives letter and bag.

  Mar. The scrolls that Jove sent Danaë,
Wrapt in rich closures of fine burnish'd gold,
Were not more welcome than these lines to me.
Tell me, whilst that I do unrip the seals,
Lives Lacy well? how fares my lovely lord?

  Post. Well, if that wealth may make men to live well.

  Mar. [*reads.*] *The blooms of the almond-tree grow in a
night, and vanish in a morn; the flies hæmeræ, fair
Peggy, take life with the sun, and die with the dew; fancy
that slippeth in with a gaze, goeth out with a wink; and
too timely loves have ever the shortest length. I write this
as thy grief, and my folly, who at Fressingfield loved that
which time hath taught me to be but mean dainties: eyes
are dissemblers, and fancy is but queasy; therefore know,
Margaret, I have chosen a Spanish lady to be my wife,
chief waiting-woman to the Princess Elinor; a lady fair,
and no less fair than thyself, honourable and wealthy. In
that I forsake thee, I leave thee to thine own liking; and
for thy dowry I have sent thee an hundred pounds; and
ever assure thee of my favour, which shall avail thee and
thine much. Farewell.*

               Not thine, nor his own,
                     Edward Lacy.

Fond Ate, doomer of bad-boding fates,
That wraps proud fortune in thy snaky locks,
Did'st thou enchant my birthday with such stars

As lighten'd mischief from their infancy?
If heavens had vow'd, if stars had made decree,
To show on me their froward influence,
If Lacy had but lov'd, heavens, hell, and all
Could not have wrong'd the patience of my mind.

  Post. It grieves me, damsel; but the earl is forc'd
To love the lady by the king's command.

  Mar. The wealth combin'd within the English shelves,[1]
Europe's commander, nor the English king,
Should not have mov'd the love of Peggy from her lord.

  Post. What answer shall I return to my lord?

  Mar. First, for thou cam'st from Lacy whom I lov'd,—
Ah, give me leave to sigh at every thought!—
Take thou, my friend, the hundred pound he sent;
For Margaret's resolution craves no dower:
The world shall be to her as vanity;
Wealth, trash; love, hate; pleasure, despair:
For I will straight to stately Framlingham,
And in the abbey there be shorn a nun,
And yield my loves and liberty to God.
Fellow, I give thee this, not for the news,
For those be hateful unto Margaret,
But for thou'rt Lacy's man, once Margaret's love.

  Post. What I have heard, what passions I have seen,
I'll make report of them unto the earl.

  Mar. Say that she joys his fancies be at rest,
And prays that his misfortune may be hers.

                                      [Exeunt.

[1] Cliffs.

ACT THE FOURTH

SCENE I.—FRIAR BACON'S *Cell.*

FRIAR BACON *draws the curtains and is discovered, lying on a bed,*[1] *with a white stick in one hand, a book in the other, and a lamp lighted beside him; and the* Brazen Head, *and* MILES *with weapons by him.*

BACON. Miles, where are you?

Miles. Here, sir.

Bacon. How chance you tarry so long?

Miles. Think you that the watching of the Brazen Head craves no furniture? I warrant you, sir, I have so armed myself that if all your devils come, I will not fear them an inch.

Bacon. Miles, thou know'st that I have divèd into hell,
And sought the darkest palaces of fiends;

[1] The stage direction is, "*Enter Friar Bacon drawing the curtains, with a white stick, a book in his hand,*" etc.

280

That with my magic spells great Belcephon
Hath left his lodge and kneelèd at my cell;
The rafters of the earth rent from the poles,
And three-form'd Luna hid her silver looks,
Trembling upon her concave continent,
When Bacon read upon his magic book.
With seven years' tossing necromantic charms,
Poring upon dark Hecat's principles,
I have fram'd out a monstrous head of brass,
That, by the enchanting forces of the devil,
Shall tell out strange and uncouth aphorisms,
And girt fair England with a wall of brass.
Bungay and I have watch'd these threescore days,
And now our vital spirits crave some rest:
If Argus liv'd, and had his hundred eyes,
They could not over watch Phobetor's night.
Now, Miles, in thee rests Friar Bacon's weal:
The honour and renown of all his life
Hangs in the watching of this Brazen Head;
Therefore I charge thee by the immortal God,
That holds the souls of men within his fist,
This night thou watch; for ere the morning-star
Sends out his glorious glister on the north,
The head will speak: then, Miles, upon thy life,
Wake me; for then by magic art I'll work
To end my seven years' task with excellence.
If that a wink but shut thy watchful eye,
Then farewell Bacon's glory and his fame!
Draw close the curtains, Miles: now, for thy life,
Be watchful, and—   [*Falls asleep.*

Miles. So; I thought you would talk yourself asleep
anon; and 'tis no marvel, for Bungay on the days, and
he on the nights, have watch'd just these ten and fifty
days: now this is the night, and 'tis my task, and no
more.   Now, Jesus bless me, what a goodly head it is!

and a nose! you talk of *nos autem glorificare;*[1] but
here's a nose that I warrant may be called *nos autem
populare* for the people of the parish. Well, I am
furnished with weapons: now, sir, I will set me down
by a post, and make it as good as a watchman to wake
me, if I chance to slumber. I thought, Goodman Head,
I would call you out of your *memento* . . . Passion o'
God, I have almost broke my pate! [*A great noise.*]
Up, Miles, to your task; take your brown-bill[2] in your
hand; here's some of your master's hobgoblins abroad.

The Brazen Head. Time is.

Miles. Time is! Why, Master Brazen-head, have you
such a capital nose, and answer you with syllables,
"Time is"? Is this all my master's cunning, to spend
seven years' study about "Time is"? Well, sir, it may
be we shall have some better orations of it anon: well,
I'll watch you as narrowly as ever you were watched,
and I'll play with you as the nightingale with the slow-
worm; I'll set a prick against my breast. Now rest
there, Miles.—Lord have mercy upon me, I have almost
killed myself! [*A great noise*]. Up, Miles; list how
they rumble.

The Brazen Head. Time was.

Miles. Well, Friar Bacon, you have spent your seven
years' study well, that can make your head speak but two
words at once, "Time was." Yea, marry, time was when
my master was a wise man, but that was before he began
to make the Brazen Head. You shall lie while your arse
ache, an your Head speak no better. Well, I will watch,
and walk up and down, and be a peripatetian and a
philosopher of Aristotle's stamp. [*A great noise.*]
What, a fresh noise? Take thy pistols in hand,
Miles.

[1] Greene uses the same pun in *A Looking Glass*, Act I. scene 2.
[2] A watchman's pike or halbert.

The Brazen Head. Time is past.

[*A lightning flashes forth, and a hand appears that breaks down the* Head *with a hammer.*

Miles. Master, master, up! hell's broken loose; your Head speaks; and there's such a thunder and lightning, that I warrant all Oxford is up in arms. Out of your bed, and take a brown-bill in your hand; the latter day is come.

Bacon. Miles, I come. O passing warily watch'd! Bacon will make thee next himself in love.
When spake the head?

Miles. When spake the head! did not you say that he should tell strange principles of philosophy? Why, sir, it speaks but two words at a time.

Bacon. Why, villain, hath it spoken oft?

Miles. Oft! ay, marry, hath it, thrice: but in all those three times it hath uttered but seven words.

Bacon. As how?

Miles. Marry, sir, the first time he said, "Time is," as if Fabius Cumentator¹ should have pronounced a sentence; [the second time] he said "Time was"; and the third time with thunder and lightning, as in great choler, he said, "Time is past."

Bacon. 'Tis past indeed. Ah, villain! time is past: My life, my fame, my glory, all are past.—
Bacon, the turrets of thy hope are ruin'd down,
Thy seven years' study lieth in the dust:
Thy Brazen Head lies broken through a slave,
That watch'd, and would not when the Head did will.—
What said the Head first?

Miles. Even, sir, "Time is."

Bacon. Villain, if thou hadst call'd to Bacon then,
If thou hadst watch'd, and wak'd the sleepy friar,
The Brazen Head had utter'd aphorisms,

¹ Miles' blundering reminiscences of "Cunctator."

And England had been circled round with brass:
But proud Asmenoth, ruler of the north,
And Demogorgon, master of the fates,
Grudge that a mortal man should work so much.
Hell trembled at my deep-commanding spells,
Fiends frown'd to see a man their over-match;
Bacon might boast more than a man might boast:
But now the braves of Bacon have an end,
Europe's conceit of Bacon hath an end,
His seven years' practice sorteth to ill end:
And, villain, sith my glory hath an end,
I will appoint thee to some fatal end.
Villain, avoid! get thee from Bacon's sight!
Vagrant, go roam and range about the world,
And perish as a vagabond on earth.

  Miles. Why, then, sir, you forbid me your service?

  Bacon. My service, villain! with a fatal curse,
That direful plagues and mischief fall on thee.

  Miles. 'Tis no matter, I am against you with the old
proverb—"The more the fox is curst[1] the better he fares."
God be with you, sir; I'll take but a book in my hand,
a wide-sleeved gown on my back, and a crowned cap on
my head, and see if I can want promotion.   [*Exit.*

  Bacon. Some fiend or ghost haunt on thy weary steps,
Until they do transport thee quick to hell:
For Bacon shall have never merry day,
To lose the fame and honour of his Head.   [*Exit.*

---

  [1] Miles is here punning on "coursed."

SCENE II.—*At Court.*

Enter the EMPEROR, *the* KING OF CASTILE, KING
HENRY, ELINOR, PRINCE EDWARD, LACY, *and*
RALPH SIMNELL.

Emp. Now, lovely prince, the prime of Albion's
    wealth,
How fare the Lady Elinor and you?
What, have you courted and found Castile fit
To answer England in equivalence?
Will 't be a match 'twixt bonny Nell and thee?

  P. Edw. Should Paris enter in the courts of Greece,
And not lie fetter'd in fair Helen's looks?
Or Phœbus scape those piercing amorets,
That Daphne glanced at his deity?
Can Edward, then, sit by a flame and freeze,
Whose heat puts Helen and fair Daphne down?
Now, monarchs, ask the lady if we gree.

  K. Hen. What, madam, hath my son found grace
    or no?

  Elin. Seeing, my lord, his lovely counterfeit,
And hearing how his mind and shape agreed,
I came not, troop'd with all this warlike train,
Doubting of love, but so affectionate,
As Edward hath in England what he won in Spain.

  K. of Cast. A match, my lord; these wantons needs
    must love:
Men must have wives, and women will be wed:
Let's haste the day to honour up the rites.

  Ralph. Sirrah Harry, shall Ned marry Nell?

  K. Hen. Ay, Ralph; how then?

  Ralph. Marry, Harry, follow my counsel: send for
Friar Bacon to marry them for he'll so conjure him and

her with his necromancy, that they shall love together
like pig and lamb whilst they live.

K. of Cast. But hearest thou, Ralph, art thou content
to have Elinor to thy lady?

Ralph. Ay, so she will promise me two things.

K. of Cast. What's that, Ralph?

Ralph. That she will never scold with Ned, nor fight
with me.—Sirrah Harry, I have put her down with a
thing unpossible.

K. Hen. What's that, Ralph?

Ralph. Why, Harry, didst thou ever see that a woman
could both hold her tongue and her hands? No! but
when egg-pies grow on apple-trees, then will thy grey
mare prove a bag-piper.

Emp. What say the Lord of Castile and the Earl of
Lincoln, that they are in such earnest and secret talk?

K. of Cast. I stand, my lord, amazed at his talk,
How he discourseth of the constancy
Of one surnam'd, for beauty's excellence,
The Fair Maid of merry Fressingfield.

K. Hen. 'Tis true, my lord, 'tis wondrous for to hear;
Her beauty passing Mars's paramour,
Her virgin's right as rich as Vesta's was:
Lacy and Ned have told me miracles.

K. of Cast. What says Lord Lacy? shall she be his
wife?

Lacy. Or else Lord Lacy is unfit to live.—
May it please your highness give me leave to post
To Fressingfield, I'll fetch the bonny girl,
And prove in true appearance at the court,
What I have vouchèd often with my tongue.

K. Hen. Lacy, go to the 'querry of my stable,
And take such coursers as shall fit thy turn:
Hie thee to Fressingfield, and bring home the lass:
And, for her fame flies through the English coast,

If it may please the Lady Elinor,
One day shall match your excellence and her.

Elin. We Castile ladies are not very coy;
Your highness may command a greater boon:
And glad were I to grace the Lincoln Earl
With being partner of his marriage-day.

P. Edw. Gramercy, Nell, for I do love the lord,
As he that's second to myself in love,

Ralph. You love her?—Madam Nell, never believe
him you, though he swears he loves you.

Elin. Why, Ralph?

Ralph. Why, his love is like unto a tapster's glass that
is broken with every touch; for he loved the fair maid
of Fressingfield once out of all ho.[1]—Nay, Ned, never
wink upon me: I care not, I.

K. Hen. Ralph tells all; you shall have a good
    secretary of him.—
But, Lacy, haste thee post to Fressingfield;
For ere thou hast fitted all things for her state,
The solemn marriage-day will be at hand.

Lacy. I go, my lord.   [*Exit.*

Emp. How shall we pass this day, my lord?

K. Hen. To horse, my lord; the day is passing fair:
We'll fly the partridge, or go rouse the deer.
Follow, my lords; you shall not want for sport.

                     [*Exeunt.*

SCENE III.—Friar Bacon's *Cell.*

Enter, to Friar Bacon *in his cell,* Friar Bungay.

Bun. What means the friar that frolick'd it of late,
To sit as melancholy in his cell,
As if he had neither lost nor won to-day?

           ' Beyond all measure.

Bacon. Ah, Bungay, my Brazen Head is spoil'd,
My glory gone, my seven years' study lost !
The fame of Bacon, bruited through the world,
Shall end and perish with this deep disgrace.

Bun. Bacon hath built foundation of his fame
So surely on the wings of true report,
With acting strange and uncouth miracles,
As this cannot infringe what he deserves.

Bacon. Bungay, sit down, for by prospective skill
I find this day shall fall out ominous :
Some deadly act shall 'tide me ere I sleep :
But what and wherein little can I guess,
My mind is heavy, whatso'er shall hap.   [*Knocking within.*
Who's that knocks ?

Bun. Two scholars that desire to speak with you.

Bacon. Bid them come in.——

Enter two Scholars.

Now, my youths, what would you have ?

First Schol. Sir, we are Suffolkmen and neighbouring
          friends :
Our fathers in their countries lusty squires ;
Their lands adjoin : in Cratfield mine doth dwell,
And his in Laxfield.   We are college-mates,
Sworn brothers, as our fathers live as friends.

Bacon. To what end is all this ?

Second Schol. Hearing your worship kept within your
          cell
A glass prospective, wherein men might see
Whatso their thoughts or hearts' desire could wish,
We come to know how that our fathers fare.

Bacon. My glass is free for every honest man.
Sit down, and you shall see ere long,

How or in what state your friendly fathers live.
Meanwhile, tell me your names.
   First Schol. Mine Lambert.
   Second Schol. And mine Serlsby.
   Bacon. Bungay, I smell there will be a tragedy.

Enter LAMBERT *and* SERLSBY, *with rapiers and daggers.*[1]

   Lam. Serlsby, thou hast kept thine hour like a man:
Thou'rt worthy of the title of a squire,
That durst, for proof of thy affection
And for thy mistress' favour, prize[2] thy blood.
Thou know'st what words did pass at Fressingfield,
Such shameless braves as manhood cannot brook:
Ay, for I scorn to bear such piercing taunts,
Prepare thee, Serlsby; one of us will die.
   Serl. Thou see'st I single [meet] thee [in] the field,
And what I spake, I'll maintain with my sword:
Stand on thy guard, I cannot scold it out.
And if thou kill me, think I have a son,
That lives in Oxford in the Broadgates-hall,
Who will revenge his father's blood with blood.
   Lam. And, Serlsby, I have there a lusty boy,
That dares at weapon buckle with thy son,
And lives in Broadgates too, as well as thine:
But draw thy rapier, for we'll have a bout.
   Bacon. Now, lusty younkers, look within the glass,
And tell me if you can discern your sires.
   First Schol. Serlsby, 'tis hard; thy father offers wrong,
To combat with my father in the field.
   Second Schol. Lambert, thou liest, my father's is th'
      abuse,
   And thou shalt find it, if my father harm.

---

[1] These are discovered in the upper stage just as Margaret and
Friar Bungay were discovered in Act. II. scene 3.
[2] Venture.

T

Bun. How goes it, sirs?

First Schol. Our fathers are in combat hard by
    Fressingfield.

Bacon. Sit still, my friends, and see the event.

Lam. Why stand'st thou, Serlsby? doubt'st thou of
    thy life?

A veney, [1] man! fair Margaret craves so much.

Serl. Then this for her.

First Schol. Ah, well thrust!

Second Schol. But mark the ward.

    [LAMBERT *and* SERLSBY *fight and stab each other.*

Lam. O, I am slain!   [*Dies.*

Serl. And I,—Lord have mercy on me!   [*Dies.*

First Schol. My father slain!—Serlsby, ward that.

Second Schol. And so is mine!—Lambert, I'll quite
thee well.

    [*The two* Scholars *stab each other and die.*

Bun. O strange stratagem!

Bacon. See, friar, where the fathers [2] both lie dead!—
Bacon, thy magic doth effect this massacre:
This glass prospective worketh many woes;
And therefore seeing these brave lusty Brutes,[3]
These friendly youths, did perish by thine art,
End all thy magic and thine art at once.
The poniard that did end their fatal lives,
Shall break the cause efficient of their woes.
So fade the glass, and end with it the shows
That necromancy did infuse the crystal with.

    [*Breaks the glass.*

Bun. What means learn'd Bacon thus to break his
    glass?

Bacon. I tell thee, Bungay, it repents me sore

---

[1] A bout.
[2] Dyce suggests that Greene here meant "scholars." Gayley
suggests that Bacon may have taken the glass.   [3] Britons.

That ever Bacon meddled in this art.
The hours I have spent in pyromantic spells,
The fearful tossing in the latest night
Of papers full of necromantic charms,
Conjuring and adjuring devils and fiends,
With stole and alb and strange pentageron ;
The wresting of the holy name of God,
As Soter, Eloim, and Adonai,
Alpha, Manoth, and Tetragrammaton,
With praying to the five-fold powers of heaven,
Are instances that Bacon must be damn'd,
For using devils to countervail his God.—
Yet, Bacon, cheer thee, drown not in despair :
Sins have their salves, repentance can do much :
Think Mercy sits where Justice holds her seat,
And from those wounds those bloody Jews did pierce,
Which by thy magic oft did bleed afresh,
From thence for thee the dew of mercy drops,
To wash the wrath of high Jehovah's ire,
And make thee as a new-born babe from sin.—
Bungay, I'll spend the remnant of my life
In pure devotion, praying to my God
That he would save what Bacon vainly lost.

                        [*Exeunt.*

With stone and old and sore
The wreckin of the holy mass of
As that holy and sore
Shall Margaret all sore
With pining of the seem of saven
As I through and that seem of saven
In which

ACT THE FIFTH

SCENE I.—*A Meadow near the Keeper's Lodge.*

Enter MARGARET *in nun's apparel, the* Keeper, *and their*
Friend.

EEPER. Margaret, be not so headstrong
in these vows :
O, bury not such beauty in a cell,
That England hath held famous for
the hue !
Thy father's hair, like to the silver
blooms

That beautify the shrubs of Africa,
Shall fall before the dated time of death,
Thus to forgo his lovely Margaret.
   Mar. Ah, father, when the harmony of heaven
Soundeth the measures of a lively faith,
The vain illusions of this flattering world
Seem odious to the thoughts of Margaret.
I lovèd once,—Lord Lacy was my love ;

And now I hate myself for that I lov'd,
And doted more on him than on my God:
For this I scourge myself with sharp repents.
But now the touch of such aspiring sins
Tells me all love is lust but love of heavens ;
That beauty us'd for love is vanity :
The world contains naught but alluring baits,
Pride, flattery, and inconstant thoughts.
To shun the pricks of death, I leave the world,
And vow to meditate on heavenly bliss,
To live in Framlingham a holy nun,
Holy and pure in conscience and in deed ;
And for to wish all maids to learn of me
To seek heaven's joy before earth's vanity.

   Friend. And will you then, Margaret, be shorn a nun,
and so leave us all?

   Mar. Now farewell, world, the engine of all woe !
Farewell to friends and father ! welcome Christ !
Adieu to dainty robes ! this base attire
Better befits an humble mind to God
Than all the show of rich habiliments.
Farewell, O love, and, with fond love, farewell
Sweet Lacy, whom I lov'd once so dear !
Ever be well, but never in my thoughts,
Lest I offend to think on Lacy's love :
But even to that, as to the rest, farewell !

Enter LACY, WARREN *and* ERMSBY, *booted and spurred.*

   Lacy. Come on, my wags, we're near the Keeper's
      lodge.
Here have I oft walk'd in the watery meads,
And chatted with my lovely Margaret.
   War. Sirrah Ned, is not this the Keeper?
   Lacy. 'Tis the same.

Erms. The old lecher hath gotten holy mutton[1] to
him; a nun, my lord.

Lacy. Keeper, how far'st thou? holla, man, what cheer?
How doth Peggy, thy daughter and my love?

Keeper. Ah, good my lord! O, woe is me for Peggy!
See where she stands clad in her nun's attire,
Ready for to be shorn in Framlingham:
She leaves the world because she left your love.
O, good my lord, persuade her if you can!

Lacy. Why, how now, Margaret! what, a malcontent?
A nun? what holy father taught you this,
To task yourself to such a tedious life
As die a maid? 'twere injury to me
To smother up such beauty in a cell.

Mar. Lord Lacy, thinking of my former miss,
How fond the prime of wanton years were spent
In love (O, fie upon that fond conceit,
Whose hap and essence hangeth in the eye!),
I leave both love and love's content at once,
Betaking me to him that is true love,
And leaving all the world for love of him.

Lacy. Whence, Peggy, comes this metamorphosis?
What, shorn a nun, and I have from the court
Posted with coursers to convey thee hence
To Windsor, where our marriage shall be kept!
Thy wedding robes are in the tailor's hands.
Come, Peggy, leave these peremptory vows.

Mar. Did not my lord resign his interest,
And make divorce 'twixt Margaret and him?

Lacy. 'Twas but to try sweet Peggy's constancy.
But will fair Margaret leave her love and lord?

Mar. Is not heaven's joy before earth's fading bliss,
And life above sweeter than life in love?

Lacy. Why, then, Margaret will be shorn a nun?

[1] *Mutton* is a cant term for a prostitute.

Mar. Margaret hath made a vow which may not be
    revok'd.

War. We cannot stay, my lord; an if she be so
    strict,

Our leisure grants us not to woo afresh.

Erms. Choose you, fair damsel,—yet the choice is
    yours,——

Either a solemn nunnery or the court,

God or Lord Lacy: which contents you best,

To be a nun, or else Lord Lacy's wife?

Lacy. A good motion.—Peggy, your answer must be
    short.

Mar. The flesh is frail; my lord doth know it well,

That when he comes with his enchanting face,

Whate'er betide I cannot say him nay.

Off goes the habit of a maiden's heart,

And, seeing fortune will, fair Framlingham,

And all the show of holy nuns, farewell!

Lacy for me, if he will be my lord.

Lacy. Peggy, thy lord, thy love, thy husband.

Trust me, by truth of knighthood, that the king

Stays for to marry matchless Elinor,

Until I bring thee richly to the court,

That one day may both marry her and thee.—

How say'st thou, Keeper? art thou glad of this?

Keeper. As if the English king had given

The park and deer of Fressingfield to me.

Erms. I pray thee, my lord of Sussex, why art thou
in a brown study?

War. To see the nature of women; that be they
never so near God, yet they love to die in a man's
arms.

Lacy. What have you fit for breakfast? We have
    hied

And posted all this night to Fressingfield.

Mar. Butter and cheese, and umbles of a deer,
Such as poor keepers have within their lodge.
  Lacy. And not a bottle of wine?
  Mar. We'll find one for my lord.
  Lacy. Come, Sussex, let us in : we shall have more,
For she speaks least, to hold her promise sure.

[Exeunt.

SCENE II.—F<small>RIAR</small> B<small>ACON</small>'s Cell.

Enter a Devil.

Dev. How restless are the ghosts of hellish spirits,
When every charmer with his magic spells,
Calls us from nine-fold-trenchèd Phlegethon,
To scud and over-scour the earth in post
Upon the speedy wings of swiftest winds !
Now Bacon hath rais'd me from the darkest deep,
To search about the world for Miles his man,
For Miles, and to torment his lazy bones
For careless watching of his Brazen Head.
See where he comes : O, he is mine !

Enter M<small>ILES</small> in a gown and a corner-cap.

Miles. A scholar, quoth you ! marry, sir, I would I
had been made a bottle-maker when I was made a
scholar ; for I can get neither to be a deacon, reader,
nor schoolmaster, no, not the clerk of a parish. Some
call me dunce ; another saith, my head is as full of Latin
as an egg's full of oatmeal : thus I am tormented, that
the devil and Friar Bacon haunt me.—Good Lord,
here's one of my master's devils ! I'll go speak to him.
—What, Master Plutus, how cheer you ?

Dev. Dost thou know me?

Miles. Know you, sir! why, are not you one of my master's devils, that were wont to come to my master, Doctor Bacon, at Brazen-nose?

Dev. Yes, marry, am I.

Miles. Good Lord, Master Plutus, I have seen you a thousand times at my master's, and yet I had never the manners to make you drink. But, sir, I am glad to see how conformable you are to the statute.—I warrant you, he's as yeomanly a man as you shall see: mark you, masters, here's a plain, honest man, without welt or guard.[1]—But I pray you, sir, do you come lately from hell?

Dev. Ay, marry: how then?

Miles. Faith, 'tis a place I have desired long to see: have you not good tippling-houses there? may not a man have a lusty fire there, a pot of good ale, a pair[2] of cards, a swinging piece of chalk, and a brown toast that will clap a white waistcoat on a cup of good drink?

Dev. All this you may have there.

Miles. You are for me, friend, and I am for you. But I pray you, may I not have an office there?

Dev. Yes, a thousand: what would'st thou be?

Miles. By my troth, sir, in a place where I may profit myself. I know hell is a hot place, and men are marvellous dry, and much drink is spent there; I would be a tapster.

Dev. Thou shalt.

Miles. There's nothing lets me from going with you, but that 'tis a long journey, and I have never a horse.

Dev. Thou shalt ride on my back.

Miles. Now surely here's a courteous devil, that, for

---

[1] *Welt* and *guard* are synonymous: without facing or ornament, as these are against the statute. [2] A pack.

to pleasure his friend, will not stick to make a jade of himself.—But I pray you, goodman friend, let me move a question to you.

Dev. What's that?

Miles. I pray you, whether is your pace a trot or an amble?

Dev. An amble.

Miles. 'Tis well; but take heed it be not a trot: but 'tis no matter, I'll prevent it.   [*Puts on spurs.*

Dev. What dost?

Miles. Marry, friend, I put on my spurs; for if I find your pace either a trot or else uneasy, I'll put you to a false gallop; I'll make you feel the benefit of my spurs.

Dev. Get up upon my back.

[M**ILES** *mounts on the* Devil's *back.*

Miles. O Lord, here's even a goodly marvel, when a man rides to hell on the devil's back!

[*Exeunt, the* Devil *roaring.*

SCENE III.—*At Court.*

Enter the E**MPEROR** *with a pointless sword; next the* K**ING** **OF** C**ASTILE** *carrying a sword with a point;* L**ACY** *carrying the globe;* W**ARREN** *carrying a rod of gold with a dove on it;* [1] E**RMSBY** *with a crown and sceptre;* P**RINCESS** E**LINOR** *with* M**ARGARET**, *Countess of Lincoln, on her left hand;* P**RINCE** E**DWARD**; K**ING** H**ENRY**; F**RIAR** B**ACON**; *and* Lords *attending.*

P. Edw. Great potentates, earth's miracles for state, Think that Prince Edward humbles at your feet,

---

[1] "The 'curtana' or 'pointless sword' of mercy; the 'pointed sword' of justice; the 'golden rod' of equity."—G**AYLEY**.

And, for these favours, on his martial sword
He vows perpetual homage to yourselves,
Yielding these honours unto Elinor.
 K. Hen. Gramercies, lordings; old Plantagenet,
That rules and sways the Albion diadem,
With tears discovers these conceivèd joys,
And vows requital, if his men-at-arms,
The wealth of England, or due honours done
To Elinor, may quite his favourites.
But all this while what say you to the dames
That shine like to the crystal lamps of heaven?
 Emp. If but a third were added to these two,
They did surpass those gorgeous images
That gloried Ida with rich beauty's wealth.
 Mar. 'Tis I, my lords, who humbly on my knee
Must yield her orisons to mighty Jove
For lifting up his handmaid to this state;
Brought from her homely cottage to the court,
And grac'd with kings, princes, and emperors,
To whom (next to the noble Lincoln Earl)
I vow obedience, and such humble love
As may a handmaid to such mighty men.
 P. Elin. Thou martial man that wears the Almain
   crown,
And you the western potentates of might,
The Albion princess, English Edward's wife,
Proud that the lovely star of Fressingfield,
Fair Margaret, Countess to the Lincoln Earl,
Attends on Elinor,—gramercies, lord, for her,—
'Tis I give thanks for Margaret to you all,
And rest for her due bounden to yourselves.
 K. Hen. Seeing the marriage is solémnizèd,
Let's march in triumph to the royal feast.—
But why stands Friar Bacon here so mute?
 Bacon. Repentant for the follies of my youth,

That magic's secret mysteries misled,
And joyful that this royal marriage
Portends such bliss unto this matchless realm.

    K. Hen. Why, Bacon, what strange event shall happen
        to this land?
Or what shall grow from Edward and his Queen?

    Bacon. I find [1] by deep prescience of mine art,
Which once I temper'd in my secret cell,
That here where Brute did build his Troynovant,
From forth the royal garden of a king
Shall flourish out so rich and fair a bud,
Whose brightness shall deface proud Phœbus' flower,
And overshadow Albion with her leaves.
Till then Mars shall be master of the field,
But then the stormy threats of wars shall cease:
The horse shall stamp as careless of the pike,
Drums shall be turn'd to timbrels of delight;
With wealthy favours plenty shall enrich
The strand that gladded wandering Brute to see;
And peace from heaven shall harbour in these leaves,
That, gorgeous, beautify this matchless flower:
Apollo's heliotropion then shall stoop,
And Venus' hyacinth shall vail her top;
Juno shall shut her gilliflowers up,
And Pallas' bay-shall 'bash her brightest green;
Ceres' carnation, in consort with those,
Shall stoop and wonder at Diana's rose.

    K. Hen. This prophecy is mystical.—
But, glorious commanders of Europa's love,
That make fair England like that wealthy isle
Circled with Gihon and swift Euphrates,
In royalizing Henry's Albion
With presence of your princely mightiness,—
Let's march: the tables all are spread,

---

[1] Here begins a compliment to Queen Elizabeth.

And viands, such as England's wealth affords,
Are ready set to furnish out the boards.
You shall have welcome, mighty potentates:
It rests to furnish up this royal feast,
Only your hearts be frolic; for the time
Craves that we taste of naught but jouissance.
Thus glories England over all the west.

                           [*Exeunt Omnes.*

Omne tulit punctum qui miscuit utile dulci.

JAMES THE FOURTH

THREE of Greene's plays, *A Looking-Glass, Orlando Furioso* and *Friar Bacon*, are known to have been printed in 1594. Two plays, *James IV.* and *Friar Bacon*, were entered on the Stationers' Registers on the same day, 14th May 1594. It is altogether probable that the first printing of *James IV.* occurred in the same year, though no trace of such an edition has been found. The earliest extant Quarto is dated 1598, and was printed by Thomas Creede. Of this two copies are known, one in the British Museum and one in the South Kensington Museum. Lowndes records a reprint of 1599, but none such has been discovered. The play is not mentioned by Henslowe, and there is no record of its performance. The text of the Quarto of 1598 is in very poor state, and shows indications that the play was either published from a stage copy or that type was set by dictation. In V. 3, the King of England is called Arius, though elsewhere he is given his own title. In II. 2 and III. 2, Ateukin is called Gnatho ; in V. 2, Ateukin and Gnatho appear together. This last duplication of Ateukin and his Terentian prototype is held by Fleay to indicate another hand in the composition of the play. Gnatho here, however, stands instead of Jaques. It should be noticed that in the original story by Cinthio, the Capitano is equivalent to both Ateukin and Jaques. The confusion probably arose then from an uncertainty in Greene's mind as to names rather than from double authorship. In the hasty first composition Greene probably used the well-known dramatic type-name for "sycophant," and was later careless in substituting the name of his choice. The plot of the play is taken, as indicated by Mr P. A. Daniel in 1881, from the first novel of the third decade of Cinthio's *Hecatommithi*. The play makes no pretence to historical accuracy, and the title itself, in so far as it refers to Flodden Field, is misleading. Nevertheless the play is by some held to be "the finest Elizabethan historical play outside of Shakespeare." By its acted prologue and interplay it served as a model for Shakespeare's *Taming of the Shrew* and *Midsummer Night's Dream.*

DRAMATIS PERSONÆ.

KING OF ENGLAND.
LORD PERCY
SAMLES.
KING OF SCOTS.
LORD DOUGLAS.
LORD MORTON.
LORD ROSS.
BISHOP OF ST ANDREWS.
LORD EUSTACE.
SIR BARTRAM.
SIR CUTHBERT ANDERSON.
ATEUKIN.
JAQUES.
A Lawyer.
A Merchant.
A Divine.
SLIPPER, } sons to BOHAN.
NANO, a dwarf, }
ANDREW.
Purveyor, Herald, Scout, Huntsmen, Soldiers, Revellers, etc.
DOROTHEA, Queen of Scots.
COUNTESS OF ARRAN.
IDA, her daughter.
LADY ANDERSON.
Ladies, etc.
OBERON, King of Fairies.
BOHAN.
Antics, Fairies, etc.

JAMES THE FOURTH[1]

THE INDUCTION.

Music playing within. Enter after OBERON, *King
of Fairies, an* Antic,[2] *who dance about a tomb
placed conveniently on the stage; out of which
suddenly starts up, as they dance,* BOHAN, *a Scot,
attired like a ridstall*[3] *man, from whom the
Antics fly.* OBERON *remains.*

OH. Ah say, what's thou?

Ober. Thy friend, Bohan.

Boh. What wot I or reck I that?
whay, guid man, I reck no friend nor
ay reck no foe; als ene to me. Git
thee ganging, and trouble not may
whayet,[4] or ays gar[5] thee recon me
nene of thay friend, by the Mary
mass, sall I!

[1] The complete title of the 1598 edition was, "The Scottish History
of James the Fourth, Slain at Flodden. Intermixed with a pleasant
comedy, presented by Oberon King of Fairies."

[2] "A technical term for the burlesque dance of an anti-masque,
and there being several performers takes a plural verb."—W. W.
Greg, *Modern Language Review,* I., p. 248.

[3] Collins defines this, after Skeat, as a stableman, a stable-cleaner,

[4] My quiet.   [5] I'll make.

Ober. Why, angry Scot, I visit thee for love; then what moves thee to wrath?

Boh. The de'il a whit reck I thy love; for I know too well that true love took her flight twenty winter sence to heaven, whither till ay can, weel I wot, ay sal ne'er find love: an thou lovest me, leave me to myself. But what were those puppets that hopped and skipped about me year whayle?[1]

Ober. My subjects.

Boh. Thay subjects! whay, art thou a king?

Ober. I am.

Boh. The de'il thou art! whay, thou lookest not so big as the King of Clubs, nor so sharp as the King of Spades, nor so fain as the King a Daymonds: be the mass, ay take thee to be the king of false hearts; therefore I rid [2] thee away, or ayse so curry your kingdom that you's be glad to run to save your life.

Ober. Why, stoical Scot, do what thou darest to me: here is my breast, strike.

Boh. Thou wilt not threap [3] me, this whinyard [4] has gard many better men to lope then thou! [*Tries to draw his sword.*] But how now! Gos sayds, what, will't not out? Whay, thou witch, thou de'il! Gad's fute, may whinyard!

Ober. Why, pull, man; but what an 'twere out, how then?

Boh. This, then,—thou weart best be gone first; for ay'l so lop thy limbs that thou's go with half a knave's carcass to the de'il.

Ober. Draw it out: now strike, fool, canst thou not?

Boh. Bread ay gad, what de'il is in me? Whay, tell me, thou skipjack, what art thou?

Ober. Nay, first tell me what thou wast from thy birth,

[1] Erewhile. Greene's Scottish dialect is not very accurate.
[2] Advise.   [3] Contradict.   [4] Sword, dagger.

what thou hast passed hitherto, why thou dwellest in a tomb and leavest the world; and then I will release thee of these bonds; before, not.

Boh. And not before! then needs must, needs sall. I was born a gentleman of the best blood in all Scotland, except the king. When time brought me to age, and death took my parents, I became a courtier; where, though ay list not praise myself, ay engraved the memory of Bohan on the skin-coat of some of them, and revelled with the proudest.

Ober. But why, living in such reputation, didst thou leave to be a courtier?

Boh. Because my pride was vanity, my expense loss, my reward fair words and large promises, and my hopes spilt; for that after many years' service one outran me; and what the de'il should I then do there? No, no; flattering knaves, that can cog and prate fastest, speed best in the court.

Ober. To what life didst thou then betake thee?

Boh. I then changed the court for the country, and the wars for a wife: but I found the craft of swains more vile than the knavery of courtiers, the charge of children more heavy than servants, and wives' tongues worse than the wars itself; and therefore I gave o'er that, and went to the city to dwell; and there I kept a great house with small cheer, but all was ne'er the near.[1]

Ober. And why?

Boh. Because, in seeking friends, I found table-guests to eat me and my meat, my wife's gossips to bewray the secrets of my heart, kindred to betray the effect of my life: which when I noted,—the court ill, the country worse, and the city worst of all,—in good time my wife died, ay would she had died twenty winter sooner, by

[1] Never the nearer: a favourite phrase with old writers.

the mass!——leaving my two sons[1] to the world, and
shutting myself into this tomb, where, if I die, I am sure
I am safe from wild beasts, but, whilst I live, cannot be
free from ill company. Besides, now I am sure, gif all
my friends fail me, I sall have a grave of mine own pro-
viding. This is all. Now, what art thou?

Ober. Oberon, King of Fairies, that loves thee because
thou hatest the world; and, to gratulate thee, I brought
these antics to show thee some sport in dancing, which
thou hast loved well.

Boh. Ha, ha, ha! thinkest thou those puppets can
please me? whay, I have two sons, that with one Scottish
jig shall break the necks of thy antics.

Ober. That I would fain see.

Boh. Why, thou shalt.—Ho, boys!

Enter SLIPPER *and* NANO.

Haud your clacks,[2] lads; trattle not for thy life, but
gather up your legs, and dance me forthwith a jig worth
the sight.

Slip. Why, I must talk, an I die for't: wherefore was
my tongue made?

Boh. Prattle, an thou darest, one word more, and ais
dab this whinyard in thy wemb.

Ober. Be quiet, Bohan. I'll strike him dumb, and
his brother too; their talk shall not hinder our jig.—Fall
to it; dance, I say, man!

Boh. Dance, Humer, dance, ay rid thee.

[*The two dance a jig devised for the nonst.*
Now get you to the wide world with more than my father
gave me; that's learning enough both kinds, knavery
and honesty; and that I gave you, spend at pleasure.

Ober. Nay, for their sport I will give them this gift:

---

[1] Some words are wanting here.
[2] Hold you your chattering.

to the dwarf I give a quick wit, pretty of body, and awarrant his preferment to a prince's service, where by his wisdom he shall gain more love than common; and to loggerhead your son I give a wandering life, and promise he shall never lack, and avow that, if in all distresses he call upon me, to help him. Now let them go.

[*Exeunt* SLIPPER *and* NANO *with courtesies.*

Boh. Now, king, if thou be a king, I will show thee whay I hate the world by demonstration. In the year fifteen hundred and twenty, was in Scotland a king, over-ruled with parasites, misled by lust, and many circumstances too long to trattle on now, much like our court of Scotland this day. That story have I set down. Gang with me to the gallery, and I'll show thee the same in action by guid fellows of our country-men; and then, when thou see'st that, judge if any wise man would not leave the world if he could.

Ober. That will I see: lead, and I'll follow thee.

[*Exeunt.*

Laus Deo detur in æternum.

ACT THE FIRST

SCENE I.—*The Court at Edinburgh.*

Enter the KING OF ENGLAND, *the* KING OF SCOTS, QUEEN DOROTHEA, *the* COUNTESS OF ARRAN, IDA, *and* Lords; *with them* ATEURIN, *aloof.*

. OF SCOTS. Brother of England, since our neighbouring lands
And near alliance do invite our loves,
The more I think upon our last accord,
The more I grieve your sudden parting hence.
First, laws of friendship did confirm our peace;
Now both the seal of faith and marriage-bed,
The name of father, and the style of friend;
These force in me affection full confirm'd;
So that I grieve—and this my hearty grief
The heavens record, the world may witness well—
To lose your presence, who are now to me
A father, brother, and a vowèd friend.
    K. of Eng. Link all these lovely styles, good king, in one:

And since thy grief exceeds in my depart,
I leave my Dorothea to enjoy
Thy whole compact [of] loves and plighted vows.
Brother of Scotland, this is my joy, my life,
Her father's honour, and her country's hope,
Her mother's comfort, and her husband's bliss:
I tell thee, king, in loving of my Doll,
Thou bind'st her father's heart, and all his friends,
In bands of love that death cannot dissolve.

  K. of Scots. Nor can her father love her like to me,
My life's light, and the comfort of my soul.—
Fair Dorothea, that wast England's pride,
Welcome to Scotland; and, in sign of love,
Lo, I invest thee with the Scottish crown.—
Nobles and ladies, stoop unto your queen,
And trumpets sound, that heralds may proclaim
Fair Dorothea peerless Queen of Scots.

  All. Long live and prosper our fair Queen of Scots!
               [They install and crown her.

  Q. Dor. Thanks to the King of Kings for my dignity;
Thanks to my father, that provides so carefully;
Thanks to my lord and husband for this honour;
And thanks to all that love their king and me.

  All Long live fair Dorothea, our true queen!
  K. of Eng. Long shine the sun of Scotland in her
      pride,
Her father's comfort, and fair Scotland's bride!
But, Dorothea, since I must depart,
And leave thee from thy tender mother's charge,
Let me advise my lovely daughter first
What best befits her in a foreign land.
Live, Doll, for many eyes shall look on thee
With care of honour and the present state;
For she that steps to height of majesty
Is even the mark whereat the enemy aims:

Thy virtues shall be construèd to vice,
Thine affable discourse to abject mind ;
If coy, detracting tongues will call thee proud :
Be therefore wary in this slippery state ;
Honour thy husband, love him as thy life,
Make choice of friends—as eagles of their young—
Who soothe no vice, who flatter not for gain,
But love such friends as do the truth maintain.
Think on these lessons when thou art alone,
And thou shalt live in health when I am gone.

Q. Dor. I will engrave these precepts in my heart :
And as the wind with calmness wooes you hence,
Even so I wish the heavens, in all mishaps,
May bless my father with continual grace.

K. of Eng. Then, son, farewell :
The favouring winds invite us to depart.
Long circumstance in taking princely leaves
Is more officious than convenient.
Brother of Scotland, love me in my child :
You greet me well, if so you will her good.

K. of Scots. Then, lovely Doll, and all that favour me,
Attend to see our English friends at sea :
Let all their charge depend upon my purse :
They are our neighbours, by whose kind accord
We dare attempt the proudest potentate.
Only, fair countess, and your daughter, stay ;
With you I have some other thing to say.

[*Exeunt, in all royalty, the* KING OF ENGLAND,
QUEEN DOROTHEA *and* Lords.

[*Aside*]. So let them triumph that have cause to joy :
But, wretched king, thy nuptial knot is death,
Thy bride the breeder of thy country's ill ;
For thy false heart dissenting from thy hand,
Misled by love, hath made another choice,—
Another choice, even when thou vow'd'st thy soul

To Dorothea, England's choicest pride.
O, then thy wandering eyes bewitch'd thy heart!
Even in the chapel did thy fancy change,
When, perjur'd man, though fair Doll had thy hand,
The Scottish Ida's beauty stale thy heart:
Yet fear and love have tied thy ready tongue
From babbling forth the passions of thy mind,
'Less fearful silence have in subtle looks
Bewray'd the treason of my new-vow'd love.
Be fair and lovely, Doll; but here's the prize,
That lodgeth here, and enter'd through mine eyes:
Yet, howso'er I love, I must be wise.—
Now, lovely countess, what reward or grace
May I employ on you for this your zeal,
And humble honours, done us in our court,
In entertainment of the English king?

    Count. of A. It was of duty, prince, that I have done;
And what in favour may content me most,
Is, that it please your grace to give me leave
For to return unto my country-home.

    K. of Scots. But, lovely Ida, is your mind the same?

    Ida. I count of court, my lord, as wise men do,
'Tis fit for those that know what 'longs thereto:
Each person to his place; the wise to art,
The cobbler to his clout, the swain to cart.

    K. of Scots. But, Ida, you are fair, and beauty shines,
And seemeth best, where pomp her pride refines.

    Ida. If beauty, as I know there's none in me,
Were sworn my love, and I his life should be,
The farther from the court I were remov'd,
The more, I think, of heaven I were belov'd.

    K. of Scots. And why?

    Ida. Because the court is counted Venus' net,
Where gifts and vows for stales [1] are often set:

---

    [1] Decoys.

None, be she chaste as Vesta, but shall meet
A curious tongue to charm her ears with sweet.

K. of Scots. Why, Ida, then I see you set at naught
The force of love.

Ida. In sooth, this is my thought,
Most gracious king,—that they that little prove,
Are mickle blest, from bitter sweets of love.
And weel I wot, I heard a shepherd sing,
That, like a bee, love hath a little sting:
He lurks in flowers, he percheth on the trees,
He on kings' pillows bends his pretty knees;
The boy is blind, but when he will not spy,
He hath a leaden foot and wings to fly:
Beshrew me yet, for all these strange effects,
If I would like the lad that so infects.

 K. of Scots. [*aside*]. Rare wit, fair face, what heart
  could more desire?
But Doll is fair and doth concern thee near:
Let Doll be fair, she is won; but I must woo
And win fair Ida; there's some choice in two.—
But, Ida, thou art coy.

Ida. And why, dread king?

K. of Scots. In that you will dispraise so sweet a thing
As love.   Had I my wish—

Ida. What then?

K. of Scots. Then would I place
His arrow here, his beauty in that face.

Ida. And were Apollo mov'd and rul'd by me,
His wisdom should be yours, and mine his tree.

K. of Scots. But here returns our train.

  Re-enter QUEEN DOROTHEA *and* Lords.

       Welcome, fair Doll!
How fares our father? is he shipp'd and gone?

Q. Dor. My royal father is both shipp'd and gone :
God and fair winds direct him to his home !

K. of Scots. Amen, say I.—[*Aside*]. Would thou wert
with him too !
Then might I have a fitter time to woo.—
But, countess, you would be gone, therefore, farewell,—
Yet, Ida, if thou wilt, stay thou behind
To accompany my queen :
But if thou like the pleasures of the court,—
[*Aside*]. Or if she lik'd me, though she left the court,—
What should I say ? I know not what to say.—
You may depart :—and you, my courteous queen,
Leave me a space ; I have a weighty cause
To think upon :—[*Aside*]. Ida, it nips me near ;
It came from thence, I feel it burning here.

[*Exeunt all except the* KING OF SCOTS *and* ATEUKIN.

Now am I free from sight of common eye,
Where to myself I may disclose the grief
That hath too great a part in mine affects.

Ateu. [*aside*]. And now is my time by wiles and
words to rise,
Greater than those that think themselves more wise.

K. of Scots. And first, fond king, thy honour doth
engrave
Upon thy brows the drift of thy disgrace.
Thy new-vow'd love, in sight of God and men,
Links thee to Dorothea during life ;
For who more fair and virtuous than thy wife ?
Deceitful murderer of a quiet mind,
Fond love, vile lust, that thus misleads us men
To vow our faiths, and fall to sin again !
But kings stoop not to every common thought :
Ida is fair and wise, fit for a king ;
And for fair Ida will I hazard life,
Venture my kingdom, country, and my crown :

Such fire hath love to burn a kingdom down.
Say Doll dislikes that I estrange my love;
Am I obedient to a woman's look?
Nay, say her father frown when he shall hear
That I do hold fair Ida's love so dear:
Let father frown and fret, and fret and die,
Nor earth nor heaven shall part my love and I.—
Yea, they shall part us, but we first must meet,
And woo and win, and yet the world not see't.—
Yea, there's the wound, and wounded with that
    thought,
So let me die, for all my drift is naught!
    Ateu. [*coming forward*]. Most gracious and imperial
        majesty,—
[*Aside*] A little flattery more were but too much.
    K. of Scots. Villain, what art thou
That thus dar'st interrupt a prince's secrets?
    Ateu. Dread king, thy vassal is a man of art,
Who knows, by constellation of the stars,
By oppositions and by dire aspécts,
The things are past and those that are to come.
    K. of Scots. But where's thy warrant to approach my
        presence?
    Ateu. My zeal, and ruth to see your grace's wrong,
Make me lament I did detract [1] so long.
    K. of Scots. If thou know'st thoughts, tell me, what
        mean I now?
    Ateu. I'll calculate the cause
Of those your highness' smiles, and tell your thoughts.
    K. of Scots. But lest thou spend thy time in idleness,
And miss the matter that my mind aims at,
Tell me: what star was opposite when that was thought?
                    [*Strikes him on the ear.*
    Ateu. 'Tis inconvenient, mighty potentate,
            [1] Hold back.

Whose looks resemble Jove in majesty,
To scorn the sooth of science with contempt.
I see in those imperial looks of yours
The whole discourse of love : Saturn combust,
With direful looks, at your nativity
Beheld fair Venus in her silver orb :
I know, by certain axioms I have read,
Your grace's griefs, and further can express
Her name that holds you thus in fancy's bands.

   K. of Scots. Thou talkest wonders.

   Ateu. Naught but truth, O king.
'Tis Ida is the mistress of your heart,
Whose youth must take impression of affects ;
For tender twigs will bow, and milder minds
Will yield to fancy, be they follow'd well.

   K. of Scots. What god art thou, compos'd in human
      shape,
Or bold Trophonius, to decide our doubts ?
How know'st thou this ?

   Ateu. Even as I know the means
To work your grace's freedom and your love.
Had I the mind, as many courtiers have,
To creep into your bosom for your coin,
And beg rewards for every cap and knee,
I then would say, " If that your grace would give
This lease, this manor, or this patent seal'd,
For this or that I would effect your love :"
But Ateukin is no parasite, O prince.
I know your grace knows scholars are but poor ;
And therefore, as I blush to beg a fee,
Your mightiness is so magnificent,
You cannot choose but cast some gift apart,
To ease my bashful need that cannot beg.
As for your love, O, might I be employ'd,
How faithfully would Ateukin compass it !

But princes rather trust a smoothing tongue
Than men of art that can accept the time.
   K. of Scots. Ateukin,—if so thy name, for so thou
     say'st,—
Thine art appears in entrance of my love;
And, since I deem thy wisdom match'd with truth,
I will exalt thee; and thyself alone
Shalt be the agent to dissolve my grief.
Sooth is, I love, and Ida is my love;
But my new marriage nips me near, Ateukin,
For Dorothea may not brook th' abuse.
   Ateu. These lets are but as motes against the sun,
Yet not so great; like dust before the wind,
Yet not so light. Tut, pacify your grace:
You have the sword and sceptre in your hand;
You are the king, the state depends on you;
Your will is law. Say that the case were mine:
Were she my sister whom your highness loves,
She should consent, for that our lives, our goods,
Depend on you; and if your queen repine,
Although my nature cannot brook of blood,
And scholars grieve to hear of murderous deeds,—
But if the lamb should let the lion's way,
By my advice the lamb should lose her life.
Thus am I bold to speak unto your grace,
Who am too base to kiss your royal feet;
For I am poor, nor have I land nor rent,
Nor countenance here in court; but for my love,
Your grace shall find none such within the realm.
   K. of Scots. Wilt thou effect my love? shall she be mine?
   Ateu. I'll gather moly, crocus, and the herbs
That heal the wounds of body and the mind;
I'll set out charms and spells; naught else shall be left
To tame the wanton if she shall rebel:
Give me but tokens of your highness' trust.

K. of Scots. Thou shalt have gold, honour, and wealth
    enough ;
Win my love, and I will make thee great.
  Ateu. These words do make me rich, most noble
    prince ;.
I am more proud of them than any wealth.
Did not your grace suppose I flatter you,
Believe me, I would boldly publish this ;—
Was never eye that saw a sweeter face,
Nor never ear that heard a deeper wit :
O God, how I am ravish'd in your worth.!
  K. of Scots. Ateukin, follow me ; love must have ease.
  Ateu. I'll kiss your highness' feet ; march when you
    please.   *[Exeunt.*

SCENE II.—*Public Place in Edinburgh.*

Enter SLIPPER, NANO, *and* ANDREW, *with their bills,
ready written, in their hands.*

  And. Stand back, sir ; mine shall stand highest.
  Slip. Come under mine arm, sir, or get a footstool ;
or else, by the light of the moon, I must come to it.
  Nano. Agree, my masters ; every man to his height :
though I stand lowest, I hope to get the best master.
  And. Ere I will stoop to a thistle, I will change turns ;
as good luck comes on the right hand as the left : here's
for me.
  Slip. And me.
  Nano. And mine.   *[They set up their bills.*
  And. But tell me, fellows, till better occasion come,
do you seek masters?

  X

Slip. ⎱
Nano. ⎰ We do.

And. But what can you do worthy preferment?

Nano. Marry, I can smell a knave from a rat.

Slip. And I can lick a dish before a cat.

And. And I can find two fools unsought,—how like you that?

But, in earnest now, tell me: of what trades are you two?

Slip. How mean you that, sir, of what trade? Marry, I'll tell you, I have many trades: the honest trade when I needs must; the filching trade when time serves; the cozening trade as I find occasion. And I have more qualities: I cannot abide a full cup unkissed, a fat capon uncarved, a full purse unpicked, nor a fool to prove a justice as you do.

And. Why, sot, why callest thou me fool?

Nano. For examining wiser than thyself.

And. So doth many more than I in Scotland.

Nano. Yea, those are such as have more authority than wit, and more wealth than honesty.

Slip. This is my little brother with the great wit; 'ware him!—But what canst thou do, tell me, that art so inquisitive of us?

And. Anything that concerns a gentleman to do, that can I do.

Slip. So you are of the gentle trade?

And. True.

Slip. Then, gentle sir, leave us to ourselves, for here comes one as if he would lack a servant ere he went.

[ANDREW *stands aside.*

Enter ATEUKIN.

Ateu. Why, so, Ateukin, this becomes thee best:
Wealth, honour, ease, and angels in thy chest.

Now may I say, as many often sing,
" No fishing to [1] the sea, nor service to a king."
Unto this high promotion doth belong
Means to be talk'd of in the thickest throng.
And first, to fit the humours of my lord,
Sweet lays and lines of love I must record ;
And such sweet lines and love-lays I'll indite,
As men may wish for, and my liege delight :
And next, a train of gallants at my heels,
That men may say, the world doth run on wheels ;
For men of art, that rise by indirection
To honour and the favour of their king,
Must use all means to save what they have got,
And win their favours whom they never knew.
If any frown to see my fortunes such,
A man must bear a little,—not too much !
But, in good time !—these bills portend, I think,
That some good fellows do for service seek.   [*Reads.*

*If any gentleman, spiritual or temporal, will entertain
out of his service, a young stripling of the age of thirty
years, that can sleep with the soundest, eat with the
hungriest, work with the sickest, lie with the loudest, face
with the proudest, etc., that can wait in a gentleman's
chamber when his master is a mile off, keep his stable
when 'tis empty, and his purse when 'tis full, and hath
many qualities worse than all these, let him write his
name and go his way, and attendance shall be given.*
By my faith, a good servant : which is he ?

Slip. Truly, sir, that am I.

Ateu. And why dost thou write such a bill ? Are all
these qualities in thee ?

Slip. O Lord, ay, sir, and a great many more, some
better, some worse, some richer, some poorer. Why,
sir, do you look so ? do they not please you ?

    " To " is here used in the sense of " compared with."

Ateu. Truly, no, for they are naught, and so art thou: if thou hast no better qualities, stand by.

Slip. O, sir, I tell the worst first; but, an you lack a man, I am for you: I'll tell you the best qualities I have.

Ateu. Be brief, then.

Slip. If you need me in your chamber, I can keep the door at a whistle; in your kitchen, turn the spit, and lick the pan, and make the fire burn; but if in the stable,—

Ateu. Yea, there would I use thee.

Slip. Why, there you kill me, there am I! and turn me to a horse and a wench, and I have no peer.

Ateu. Art thou so good in keeping a horse? I pray thee, tell me how many good qualities hath a horse.

Slip. Why, so, sir: a horse hath two properties of a man, that is, a proud heart, and a hardy stomach; four properties of a lion, a broad breast, a stiff docket,—hold your nose, master,—a wild countenance, and four good legs; nine properties of a fox, nine of a hare, nine of an ass, and ten of a woman.

Ateu. A woman! why, what properties of a woman hath a horse?

Slip. O, master, know you not that? Draw your tables,[1] and write what wise I speak. First, a merry countenance; second, a soft pace; third, a broad forehead; fourth, broad buttocks; fifth, hard of ward; sixth, easy to leap upon; seventh, good at long journey; eighth, moving under a man; ninth, always busy with the mouth; tenth, ever chewing on the bridle.

Ateu. Thou art a man for me: what's thy name?

Slip. An ancient name, sir, belonging to the chamber and the night-gown: guess you that.

Ateu. What's that? Slipper?

[1] Tablets, memorandum books.

Slip. By my faith, well guessed; and so 'tis indeed. You'll be my master?

Ateu. I mean so.

Slip. Read this first.

Ateu. [*reads*]. *Pleaseth it any gentleman to entertain a servant of more wit than stature, let them subscribe, and attendance shall be given.*

What of this?

Slip. He is my brother, sir; and we two were born together, must serve together, and will die together, though we be both hanged.

Ateu. What's thy name?

Nano. Nano.

Ateu. The etymology of which word is "a dwarf." Are not thou the old stoic's son that dwells in his tomb?

Slip. } We are.
Nano. }

Ateu. Thou art welcome to me. Wilt thou give thyself wholly to be at my disposition?

Nano. In all humility I submit myself.

Ateu. Then will I deck thee princely, instruct thee courtly, and present thee to the queen as my gift. Art thou content?

Nano. Yes, and thank your honour too.

Slip. Then welcome, brother, and follow now.

And. [*coming forward*]. May it please your honour to abase your eye so low as to look either on my bill or myself?

Ateu. What are you?

And. By birth a gentleman; in profession a scholar; and one that knew your honour in Edinburgh, before your worthiness called you to this reputation: by me, Andrew Snoord.

Ateu. Andrew, I remember thee; follow me, and we

will confer further; for my weighty affairs for the king
command me to be brief at this time.—Come on, Nano.
—Slipper, follow.   [*Exeunt.*

SCENE III.—Sir Bartram's *Castle.*

Enter Sir Bartram, *with* Eustace, *and others,*
booted.

Sir Bar. But tell me, lovely Eustace, as thou lov'st
        me,
Among the many pleasures we have pass'd,
Which is the rifest in thy memory,
To draw thee over to thine ancient friend?
    Eust. What makes Sir Bartram thus inquisitive?
Tell me, good knight, am I welcome or no?
    Sir Bar. By sweet Saint Andrew and may sale[1] I
        swear,
As welcome is my honest Dick to me
As morning's sun, or as the watery moon
In merkest night, when we the borders track.
I tell thee, Dick, thy sight hath clear'd my thoughts
Of many baneful troubles that there woon'd:[2]
Welcome to Sir Bartram as his life!
Tell me, bonny Dick: hast got a wife?
    Eust. A wife! God shield, Sir Bartram, that were ill,
To leave my wife and wander thus astray:
But time and good advice, ere many years,
May chance to make my fancy bend that way.
What news in Scotland? therefore came I hither,
To see your country and to chat together.

---

        [1] My soul.   [2] Dwelt.

Sir Bar. Why, man, our country's blithe, our king is
    well,
Our queen so-so, the nobles well and worse,
And weel are they that are about the king,
But better are the country gentlemen:
And I may tell thee, Eustace, in our lives
We old men never saw so wondrous change.
But leave this trattle, and tell me what news
In lovely England with our honest friends.

Eust. The king, the court, and all our noble friends
Are well; and God in mercy keep them so!
The northern lords and ladies hereabouts,
That know I came to see your queen and court,
Commend them to my honest friend Sir Bartram,—
And many others that I have not seen.
Among the rest, the Countess Elinor,
From Carlisle, where we merry oft have been,
Greets well my lord, and hath directed me,
By message, this fair lady's face to see.

                              [Shows a portrait.

Sir Bar. I tell thee, Eustace, 'less mine old eyes
    daze,
This is our Scottish moon and evening's pride;
This is the blemish of your English bride.
Who sail by her, are sure of wind at will;
Her face is dangerous, her sight is ill:
And yet, in sooth, sweet Dick, it may be said,
The king hath folly, there's virtue in the maid.

Eust. But knows my friend this portrait? be advis'd.

Sir Bar. Is it not Ida, the Countess of Arran's
    daughter's?

Eust. So was I told by Elinor of Carlisle:
But tell me, lovely Bartram: is the maid
Evil-inclin'd, misled, or concubine
Unto the king or any other lord?

Sir Bar. Should I be brief and true, than thus, my
    Dick :
All England's grounds yield not a blither lass,
Nor Europe can surpass her for her gifts
Of virtue, honour, beauty, and the rest :
But our fond king, not knowing sin in lust,
Makes love by endless means and precious gifts ;
And men that see it dare not say't, my friend,
But we may wish that it were otherwise.
But I rid thee to view the picture still,
For by the person's sight there hangs some ill.

Eust. O, good Sir Bartram, you suspect I love
(Then were I mad) her whom I never saw.
But, howsoe'er, I fear not enticings :
Desire will give no place unto a king :
I'll see her whom the world admires so much,
That I may say with them, " There lives none
    such."

Sir Bar. Be Gad, and sall both see and talk with
    her ;
And, when thou'st done, whate'er her beauty be,
I'll warrant thee her virtues may compare
With the proudest she that waits upon your queen.

               Enter Servant.

Serv. My lady entreats your worship in to supper.
Sir Bar. Guid, bonny Dick, my wife will tell thee
more :
Was never no man in her book before ;
Be Gad, she's blithe, fair, lewely,[1] bonny, etc.[2]
                        [Exeunt.

---

[1] Greene probably intended a Scotch dialect form of "lovely."
[2] The player was expected to extemporise until off the stage.

CHORUS.[1]

Enter BOHAN *and* OBERON ; *to them a round of*
Fairies, *or some pretty dance.*

Boh. Be Gad, gramercies, little king, for this ;
This sport is better in my exile life
Than ever the deceitful werld could yield.

Ober. I tell thee, Bohan, Oberon is king
Of quiet, pleasure, profit, and content,
Of wealth, of honour, and of all the world ;
Tied to no place,—yet all are tied to one.
Live thou this life, exil'd from world and men,
And I will show thee wonders ere we part.

Boh. Then mark my story, and the strange doubts
That follow flatterers, lust, and lawless will,
And then say I have reason to forsake
The world and all that are within the same.
Go shroud us in our harbour, where we'll see
The pride of folly, as it ought to be.   [*Exeunt.*

After the first Act.

I.

Ober. Here see I good fond actions in thy jig
And means to paint the world's inconstant ways :
But turn thine ene, see what I can command.

Enter two battles, strongly fighting, the one led by
SEMIRAMIS, *the other by* STABROBATES : *she flies, and*
her crown is taken, and she hurt.

Boh. What gars this din of mirk and baleful harm,
Where every wean is all betaint with blood?

Ober. This shows thee, Bohan, what is worldly pomp :
Semiramis, the proud Assyrian queen,

[1] The scene between Bohan and Oberon may properly be entitled
"Chorus," as such scenes appear at the end of each act with the
exception of the fifth. The relationship of the three dumb shows
with the play as a whole and with each other has not been
explained. In many places the text is hopelessly corrupt.

When Ninus died, did levy in her wars
Three millions of footmen to the fight,
Five hundred thousand horse, of armèd cars
A hundred thousand more; yet in her pride
Was hurt and conquered by Stabrobates.
Then what is pomp?

Boh. I see thou art thine ene,
Thou bonny king, if princes fall from high:
My fall is past, until I fall to die.
Now mark my talk, and prosecute my jig.

2.

Ober. How should these crafts withdraw thee from
the world?
But look, my Bohan, pomp allureth.

Enter CYRUS, *Kings humbling themselves; himself crowned
by Olive Pat* [1] : *at last dying, laid in a marble tomb
with this inscription:*
"Whoso thou be that passest [by],—
For I know one shall pass,—know I
Am Cyrus of Persia, and I pray
Leave me not thus like a clod of clay
Wherewith my body is covered."   [*All exeunt.*

Enter the King *in great pomp, who reads it, and
issueth, crying,* "Ver meum."

Boh. What meaneth this?

Ober. Cyrus of Persia,
Mighty in life, within a marble grave
Was laid to rot; whom Alexander once
Beheld entomb'd, and weeping did confess,
Nothing in life could 'scape from wretchedness:
Why, then, boast men?

Boh. What reck I, then, of life,

[1] The entire passage is so corrupt as to be unintelligible,

Who make the grave my home, the earth my wife?
But mark me more.

3.

Boh. I can no more; my patience will not warp
To see these flatterers how they scorn and carp.
Ober. Turn but thy head.

Enter four Kings *carrying crowns,* Ladies *presenting
odours to* Potentate *enthroned, who suddenly is slain
by his* Servants *and thrust out; and so they eat.*
[*Exeunt.*

Boh. Sike is the werld; but whilk is he I saw?
Ober. Sesostris, who was conqueror of the world,
Slain at the last and stamp'd on by his slaves.
Boh. How blest are peur men, then, that know their
graves !
Now mark the sequel of my jig.

[4.] [1]

Boh. An he weel meet ends. The mirk and sable night
Doth leave the peering morn to pry abroad ;
Thou nill me stay : hail, then, thou pride of kings !
I ken the world, and wot well worldly things.
Mark thou my jig, in mirkest terms that tells
The loath of sins and where corruption dwells.
Hail me ne mere with shows of guidly sights ;
My grave is mine,—that rids me from despites.

[5.]

Boh. Accept my jig, guid king, and let me rest ;
The grave with guid men is a gay-built nest.
Ober. The rising sun doth call me hence away ;
Thanks for thy jig, I may no longer stay :
But if my train did wake thee from thy rest
So shall they sing thy lullaby to nest.   [*Exeunt.*

[1] Manly's readjustment of a corrupt passage, based upon a
suggestion by Kittredge, has been accepted.

ACT THE SECOND

SCENE I.—*Porch to the Castle of the* COUNTESS
OF ARRAN.

The COUNTESS OF ARRAN *and* IDA *discovered sitting
at work.*

A Song.[1]

COUNT OF A. Fair Ida, might you
    choose the greatest good,
'Midst all the world in blessings
    that abound,
Wherein, my daughter, should your
    liking be?
    Ida. Not in delights, or pomp, or
majesty.

Count of A. And why?

Ida. Since these are means to draw the mind
From perfect good, and make true judgment blind.

Count of A. Might you have wealth and fortune's
    richest store?

Ida. Yet would I, might I choose, be honest-poor;
For she that sits at fortune's feet a-low

---

[1] The song is not inserted. It was not necessarily composed by
the author of the play.

332

Is sure she shall not taste a further woe;
But those that prank on top of fortune's ball
Still fear a change, and, fearing, catch a fall.

 Count of A. Tut, foolish maid, each one contemneth
  need.

 Ida. Good reason why, they know not good indeed.

 Count of A. Many, marry, then, on whom distress
  doth lour.

 Ida. Yes, they that virtue deem an honest dower.
Madam, by right this world I may compare
Unto my work, wherein with heedful care
The heavenly workman plants with curious hand—
As I with needle draw—each thing on land
Even as he list: some men like to the rose
Are fashion'd fresh; some in their stalks do close,
And, born, do sudden die; some are but weeds,
And yet from them a secret good proceeds:
I with my needle, if I please, may blot
The fairest rose within my cambric plot;
God with a beck can change each worldly thing,
The poor to earth, the beggar to the king.
What, then, hath man wherein he well may boast,
Since by a beck he lives, a lour[1] is lost?

 Count of A. Peace, Ida, here are strangers near at
  hand.

    Enter EUSTACE *with letters.*

 Eust. Madam, God speed!

 Count of A. I thank you, gentle squire.

 Eust. The country Countess of Northumberland
Doth greet you well; and hath requested me
To bring these letters to your ladyship.
       [Delivers the letters.

       Frown.

Count of A. I thank her honour, and yourself, my
 friend.   [*Peruses them.*
I see she means you good, brave gentleman.—
Daughter, the Lady Elinor salutes
Yourself as well as me : then for her sake
'Twere good you entertain'd that courtier well.
 Ida. As much salute as may become my sex,
And he in virtue can vouchsafe to think,
I yield him for the courteous countess' sake.—
Good sir, sit down : my mother here and I
Count time misspent an endless vanity.
 Eust. [*aside*]. Beyond report, the wit, the fair, the
  shape !—
What work you here, fair mistress ? may I see it ?
 Ida. Good sir, look on : how like you this compáct ?
 Eust. Methinks in this I see true love in act :
The woodbines with their leaves do sweetly spread,
The roses blushing prank them in their red ;
No flower but boasts the beauties of the spring ;
This bird hath life indeed, if it could sing.
What means, fair mistress, had you in this work ?
 Ida. My needle, sir.
 Eust. In needles, then, there lurk
Some hidden grace, I deem, beyond my reach.
 Ida. Not grace in them, good sir, but those that
  teach.
 Eust. Say that your needle now were Cupid's sting,—
[*Aside*]. But, ah, her eye must be no less,
In which is heaven and heavenliness,
In which the food of God is shut,
Whose powers the purest minds do glut !
 Ida. What if it were ?
 Eust. Then see a wondrous thing ;
I fear me you would paint in Tereus' heart
Affection in his power and chiefest part.

Ida. Good Lord, sir, no! for hearts but prickèd soft
Are wounded sore, for so I hear it oft.

    Eust. What recks the wound, where but your happy
        eye
May make him live whom Jove hath judg'd to die?

    Ida. Should life and death within this needle lurk,
I'll prick no hearts, I'll prick upon my work.

Enter ATEUKIN *and* SLIPPER.

    Count of A. Peace, Ida, I perceive the fox at hand.

    Eust. The fox! why, fetch your hounds, and chase
        him hence.

    Count of A. O, sir, these great men bark at small
        offence.
Come, will it please you enter, gentle sir?

[They offer to go out.

    Ateu. Stay, courteous ladies; favour me so much
As to discourse a word or two apart.

    Count of A. Good sir, my daughter learns this rule of
        me,
To shun resort and strangers' company;
For some are shifting mates that carry letters;
Some, such as you, too good because our betters.

    Slip. Now, I pray you, sir, what akin are you to a
pickerel?

    Ateu. Why, knave?

    Slip. By my troth, sir, because I never knew a proper
situation fellow of your pitch fitter to swallow a gudgeon.

    Ateu. What meanest thou by this?

    Slip. "Shifting fellow," sir,—these be thy words; [1]
"shifting fellow": this gentlewoman, I fear me, knew
your bringing up.

    Ateu. How so?

<hr>

[1] Words that describe you.

Slip. Why, sir, your father was a miller, that could
shift for a peck of grist in a bushel, and you a fair-
spoken gentleman, that can get more land by a lie than
an honest man by his ready money.

Ateu. Caitiff, what sayest thou?

Slip. I say, sir, that if she call you shifting knave, you
shall not put her to the proof.

Ateu. And why?

Slip. Because, sir, living by your wit as you do, shifting
is your letters-patents: it were a hard matter for me to
get my dinner that day wherein my master had not sold
a dozen of devices, a case of cogs, and a suit of shifts,[1] in
the morning. I speak this in your commendation, sir,
and, I pray you, so take it.

Ateu. If I live, knave, I will be revenged. What
gentleman would entertain a rascal thus to derogate from
his honour?   [*Beats him.*

Ida. My lord, why are you thus impatient?

Ateu. Not angry, Ida; but I teach this knave
How to behave himself among his betters.—
Behold, fair countess, to assure your stay,
I here present the signet of the king,
Who now by me, fair Ida, doth salute you:
And since in secret I have certain things
In his behalf, good madam, to impart,
I crave your daughter to discourse apart.

Count of A. She shall in humble duty be addrest [2]
To do his highness' will in what she may.

Ida. Now, gentle sir, what would his grace with
    me?

Ateu. Fair, comely nymph, the beauty of your face,
Sufficient to bewitch the heavenly powers,
Hath wrought so much in him, that now of late
He finds himself made captive unto love;

---

[1] Cozener's terms.   [2] Prepared, ready.

And though his power and majesty require
A straight command before an humble suit,
Yet he his mightiness doth so abase
As to entreat your favour, honest maid.

  Ida. Is he not married, sir, unto our queen?

  Ateu. He is.

  Ida. And are not they by God accurs'd,
That sever them whom he hath knit in one?

  Ateu. They be: what then? we seek not to displace
The princess from her seat; but, since by love
The king is made your own, he is resolv'd
In private to accept your dalliance,
In spite of war, watch, or worldly eye.

  Ida. O, how he talks, as if he should not die!
As if that God in justice once could wink
Upon that fault I am asham'd to think!

  Ateu. Tut, mistress, man at first was born to err;
Women are all not formèd to be saints:
'Tis impious for to kill our native king,
Whom by a little favour we may save.

  Ida. Better, than live unchaste, to lie in grave.

  Ateu. He shall erect your state, and wed you well.

  Ida. But can his warrant keep my soul from hell?

  Ateu. He will enforce, if you resist his suit.

  Ida. What tho?[1]   The world may shame to him
    account,
To be a king of men and worldly pelf,
Yet hath no power to rule and guide himself.

  Ateu. I know you, gentle lady, and the care
Both of your honour and his grace's health
Makes me confusèd in this dangerous state.

  Ida. So counsel him, but soothe thou not his sin:
'Tis vain allurement that doth make him love:
I shame to hear, be you asham'd to move.

             [1] What then?

   Y

Count of A. [*aside*]. I see my daughter grows
    impatient:
I fear me, he pretends some bad intent.

Ateu. Will you despise the king and scorn him so?

Ida. In all allegiance I will serve his grace,
But not in lust: O, how I blush to name it!

Ateu. [*aside*]. An endless work is this: how should I
frame it?   [*They discourse privately.*

Slip. O, mistress, may I turn a word upon you?

Count of A. Friend, what wilt thou?

Slip. O, what a happy gentlewoman be you truly! the
world reports this of you, mistress, that a man can no
sooner come to your house but the butler comes with a
black-jack and says, "Welcome, friend, here's a cup of
the best for you": verily, mistress, you are said to have
the best ale in all Scotland.

Count of A. Sirrah, go fetch him drink. [*Servant
brings drink*]. How likest thou this?

Slip. Like it, mistress! why, this is quincy quarie,
pepper de watchet, single goby, of all that ever I tasted!
I'll prove in this ale and toast the compass of the whole
world. First, this is the earth,—it lies in the middle, a
fair brown toast, a goodly country for hungry teeth to
dwell upon; next, this is the sea, a fair pool for a dry
tongue to fish in: now come I, and, seeing the world is
naught, I divide it thus; and, because the sea cannot stand
witnout the earth, as Aristotle saith, I put them both
into their first chaos, which is my belly: and so,
mistress, you may see your ale is become a miracle.

Eust. A merry mate, madam, I promise you.

Count of A. Why sigh you, sirrah?

Slip. Truly, madam, to think upon the world, which,
since I denounced it, keeps such a rumbling in my
stomach, that, unless your cook give it a counterbuff
with some of your roasted capons or beef, I fear me I

shall become a loose body, so dainty, I think, I shall
neither hold fast before nor behind.

Count of A. Go take him in, and feast this merry
　swain.—

Sirrah, my cook is your physician;
He hath a purge for to digest the world.

　　　　　　　　　　　[*Exeunt* SLIPPER *and* Servant.

Ateu. Will you not, Ida, grant his highness this?

Ida. As I have said, in duty I am his:
For other lawless lusts that ill beseem him,
I cannot like, and good I will not deem him.

Count of A. Ida, come in:—and, sir, if so you please,
Come, take a homely widow's entertain.

Ida. If he have no great haste, he may come nigh;
If haste, though he be gone, I will not cry.

　　[*Exeunt* COUNTESS OF ARRAN, IDA, *and* EUSTACE.

Ateu. I see this labour lost, my hope in vain;
Yet will I try another drift again.　　　[*Exit.*

SCENE II.—*The Court at Edinburgh.*

Enter, one by one, the BISHOP OF ST ANDREWS, DOUGLAS,
　MORTON, *and others, one way;* QUEEN DOROTHEA
　with NANO, *another way.*

Bp. of St And. [*aside*]. O wrack of commonweal! O
　　wretched state!

Doug. [*aside*]. O hapless flock, whereas the guide is
　　blind!

Mort. [*aside*]. O heedless youth, where counsel is
　　despis'd!　　　　　　[*They are all in a muse.*

Q. Dor. Come, pretty knave, and prank it by my
          side;
Let's see your best attendance out of hand.

Nano. Madam, although my limbs are very small,
My heart is good; I'll serve you therewithal.

Q. Dor. How, if I were assail'd, what couldst thou
          do?

Nano. Madam, call help, and boldly fight it too:
Although a bee be but a little thing,
You know, fair queen, it hath a bitter sting.

Q. Dor. How couldst thou do me good, were I in
          grief?

Nano. Counsel, dear princess, is a choice relief:
Though Nestor wanted force, great was his wit;
And though I am but weak, my words are fit.

Bp. of St And. [*aside*]. Like to a ship upon the ocean-
          seas,
Tost in the doubtful stream, without a helm,
Such is a monarch without good advice.
I am o'erheard: cast rein upon thy tongue;
Andrews, beware; reproof will breed a scar.

Mort. Good-day, my lord.

Bp. of St And. Lord Morton, well y-met.—
Whereon deems Lord Douglas all this while?

Doug. Of that which yours and my poor heart doth
          break,
Although fear shuts our mouths, we dare not speak.

Q. Dor. [*aside*]. What mean these princes sadly to
          consult?
Somewhat, I fear, betideth them amiss,
They are so pale in looks, so vex'd in mind.—
In happy hour, the noble Scottish peers,
Have I encounter'd you: what makes you mourn?

Bp. of St And. If we with patience may attention gain,
Your grace shall know the cause of all our grief.

Q. Dor. Speak on, good father: come and sit by me:
I know thy care is for the common good.

  Bp. of St And. As fortune, mighty princess, reareth some
To high estate and place in commonweal,
So by divine bequest to them is lent
A riper judgment and more searching eye,
Whereby they may discern the common harm ;
For where our fortunes in the world are most,
Where all our profits rise and still increase,
There is our mind, thereon we meditate,—
And what we do partake of good advice,
That we employ for to concern the same.
To this intent, these nobles and myself,
That are, or should be, eyes of commonweal,
Seeing his highness' reckless course of youth,
His lawless and unbridled vein in love,
His too intentive trust to flatterers,
His abject care of counsel and his friends,
Cannot but grieve ; and, since we cannot draw
His eye or judgment to discern his faults,
Since we have spoke and counsel is not heard,
I, for my part,—let others as they list,—
Will leave the court, and leave him to his will,
Lest with a ruthful eye I should behold
His overthrow, which, sore I fear, is nigh.

  Q. Dor. Ah, father, are you so estrang'd from love,
From due allegiance to your prince and land,
To leave your king when most he needs your help?
The thrifty husbandmen are never wont,
That see their lands unfruitful, to forsake them ;
But, when the mould is barren and unapt,
They toil, they plow, and make the fallow fat :
The pilot in the dangerous seas is known ;
In calmer waves the silly sailor strives.
Are you not members, lords, of commonweal,

And can your head, your dear anointed king,
Default, ye lords, except yourselves do fail?
O, stay your steps, return and counsel him!

Doug. Men seek not moss upon a rolling stone,
Or water from the sieve, or fire from ice,
Or comfort from a reckless monarch's hands.
Madam, he sets us light, that serv'd in court,
In place of credit, in his father's days:
If we but enter presence of his grace,
Our payment is a frown, a scoff, a frump;
Whilst flattering Gnatho[1] pranks it by his side,
Soothing the careless king in his misdeeds:
And, if your grace consider your estate,
His life should urge you too, if all be true.

Q. Dor. Why, Douglas, why?

Doug. As if you have not heard
His lawless love to Ida grown of late,
His careless estimate of your estate.

Q. Dor. Ah, Douglas, thou misconster'st his intent!
He doth but tempt his wife, he tries my love:
This injury pertains to me, not to you.
The king is young; and, if he step awry,
He may amend, and I will love him still.
Should we disdain our vines because they sprout
Before their time? or young men, if they strain
Beyond their reach? No; vines that bloom and spread
Do promise fruits, and young men that are wild
In age grow wise. My friends and Scottish peers,
If that an English princess may prevail,
Stay, stay with him: lo, how my zealous prayer
Is plead with tears! fie, peers, will you hence?

Bp. of St And. Madam, 'tis virtue in your grace to
plead;

---

[1] Gnatho is the parasite in the *Eunuchus* of Terence. Here
and elsewhere in this play the name refers specifically to Ateukin.

But we, that see his vain untoward course,
Cannot but fly the fire before it burn,
And shun the court before we see his fall.

 Q. Dor. Will you not stay? then, lordings, fare you
  well.
Though you forsake your king, the heavens, I hope,
Will favour him through mine incessant prayer.

 Nano. Content you, madam ; thus old Ovid sings,
'Tis foolish to bewail recureless things.

 Q. Dor. Peace, dwarf; these words my patience
  move.

 Nano. Although you charm my speech, charm not
  my love.

      [*Exeunt* QUEEN DOROTHEA *and* NANO.

Enter the KING OF SCOTS ; *the* Nobles, *spying him
  as they are about to go off, return.*

 K. of Scots. Douglas, how now! why changest thou
  thy cheer?

 Doug. My private troubles are so great, my liege,
As I must crave your license for awhile,
For to intend mine own affairs at home.

 K. of Scots. You may depart. [*Exit* DOUGLAS.] But
  why is Morton sad?

 Mort. The like occasion doth import me too :
So I desire your grace to give me leave.

 K. of Scots. Well, sir, you may betake you to your
  ease.

        [*Exit* MORTON.

[*Aside*]. When such grim sirs are gone, I see no let
To work my will.

 Bp. of St And. What, like the eagle, then,
With often flight wilt thou thy feathers lose?
O king, canst thou endure to see thy court

Of finest wits and judgments dispossess'd,
Whilst cloaking craft with soothing climbs so high
As each bewails ambition is so bad?
Thy father left thee with estate and crown,
A learnèd council to direct thy course:
These carelessly, O king, thou castest off,
To entertain a train of sycophants.
Thou well may'st see, although thou wilt not see,
That every eye and ear both sees and hears
The certain signs of thine incontinence.
Thou art allied unto the English king
By marriage;—a happy friend indeed,
If usèd well; if not, a mighty foe.
Thinketh your grace, he can endure and brook
To have a partner in his daughter's love?
Thinketh your grace, the grudge of privy wrongs
Will not procure him change his smiles to threats?
O, be not blind to good! call home your lords,
Displace these flattering Gnathoes, drive them hence!
Love and with kindness take your wedlock wife;
Or else, which God forbid, I fear a change:
Sin cannot thrive in courts without a plague.

   K. of Scots. Go pack thou too, unless thou mend thy
     talk!
On pain of death, proud bishop, get you gone,
Unless you headless mean to hop away!

   Bp. of St And. Thou God of heaven, prevent my
     country's fall!   [*Exit with other* Nobles.

   K. of Scots. These stays and lets to pleasure plague
     my thoughts,
Forcing my grievous wounds anew to bleed;
But care that hath transported me so far,
Fair Ida, is dispers'd in thought of thee,
Whose answer yields me life or breeds my death.
Yond comes the messenger of weal or woe.

Enter ATEUKIN.[1]

Ateukin, what news?

Ateu. The adamant, O king, will not be fil'd
But by itself, and beauty that exceeds
By some exceeding favour must be wrought :
Ida is coy as yet, and doth repine,
Objecting marriage, honour, fear and death :
She's holy-wise, and too precise for me.

K. of Scots. Are these thy fruits of wit, thy sight in art,
Thine eloquence, thy policy, thy drift,—
To mock thy prince?　Then, caitiff, pack thee hence,
And let me die devourèd in my love !

Ateu. Good lord, how rage gainsayeth reason's
　　　power !
My dear, my gracious, and belovèd prince,
The essence of my soul, my god on earth, .
Sit down and rest yourself: appease your wrath,
Lest with a frown ye wound me to the death.
O, that I were included in my grave,
That either now, to save my prince's life,
Must counsel cruelty, or lose my king !

K. of Scots. Why, sirrah, is there means to move her
　　　mind ?

Ateu. O, should I not offend my royal liege,—

K. of Scots. Tell all, spare naught, so I may gain my
　　　love.

Ateu. Alas, my soul, why art thou torn in twain,
For fear thou talk a thing that should displease?

K. of Scots. Tut, speak whatso thou wilt, I pardon
　　　thee.

Ateu. How kind a word, how courteous is his grace !
Who would not die to succour such a king?
My liege, this lovely maid of modest mind

　　　　　　[1] Printed "Gnatho."

Could well incline to love, but that she fears
Fair Dorothea's power: your grace doth know,
Your wedlock is a mighty let to love.
Were Ida sure to be your wedded wife,
That then the twig would bow you might command:
Ladies love presents, pomp, and high estate.

 K. of Scots. Ah, Ateukin, how should we displace this
  let?

 Ateu. Tut, mighty prince,—O, that I might be whist![1]
 K. of Scots. Why dalliest thou?

 Ateu. I will not move my prince!
I will prefer his safety 'fore my life.
Hear me, O king! 'tis Dorothea's death
Must do you good.

 K. of Scots. What, murder of my queen!
Yet, to enjoy my love, what is my queen?
O, but my vow and promise to my queen!
Ay, but my hope to gain a fairer queen:
With how contrarious thoughts am I withdrawn!
Why linger I 'twixt hope and doubtful fear?
If Dorothea die, will Ida love?

 Ateu. She will, my lord.

 K. of Scots. Then let her die: devise, advise the
  means;
All likes me well that lends me hope in love.

 Ateu. What, will your grace consent? Then let me
  work.
There's here in court a Frenchman, Jaques call'd
A fit performer of our enterprise,
Whom I by gifts and promise will corrupt
To slay the queen, so that your grace will seal
A warrant for the man, to save his life.

 K. of Scots. Naught shall he want; write thou, and I
  will sign:

<hr>

[1] Silent.

And, gentle Gnatho, if my Ida yield,
Thou shalt have what thou wilt; I'll give thee straight
A barony, an earldom, for reward.

Ateu. Frolic, young king, the lass shall be your own:
I'll make her blithe and wanton by my wit.

[*Exeunt.*

CHORUS [1]

Enter BOHAN *and* OBERON.

Boh. So, Oberon, now it begins to work in kind.
The ancient lords by leaving him alone,
Disliking of his humours and despite,
Let him run headlong, till his flatterers,
Soliciting his thoughts of lawless lust
With vile persuasions and alluring words,
Make him make way by murder to his will.
Judge, fairy king, hast heard a greater ill?

Ober. Nor seen more virtue in a country maid.
I tell thee, Bohan, it doth make me sorry,
To think the deeds the king means to perform.

Boh. To change that humour, stand and see the rest:
I trow my son Slipper will show's a jest.

Enter SLIPPER *with a companion,* boy *or* wench, *dancing*
a hornpipe, and dance out again.

Now after this beguiling of our thoughts,
And changing them from sad to better glee,
Let's to our cell, and sit and see the rest,
For, I believe, this jig will prove no jest.   [*Exeunt.*

[1] The text of this Chorus is very corrupt.

ACT THE THIRD

SCENE I.—*Edinburgh.*

Enter SLIPPER *one way, and* SIR BARTRAM *another way.*

SIR BAR. Ho, fellow! stay, and let me speak with thee.

Slip. Fellow! friend, thou dost disbuse me; I am a gentleman.

Sir Bar. A gentleman! how so?

Slip. Why, I rub horses, sir.

Sir Bar. And what of that?

Slip. O simple-witted! mark my reason. They that do good service in the commonweal are gentlemen; but such as rub horses do good service in the commonweal; ergo, tarbox, master courtier, a horse-keeper is a gentleman.

Sir Bar. Here is overmuch wit, in good earnest. But, sirrah, where is thy master?

Slip. Neither above ground nor under ground, drawing out red into white, swallowing that down without chawing that was never made without treading.

Sir Bar. Why, where is he, then?

Slip. Why, in his cellar, drinking a cup of neat and brisk claret, in a bowl of silver. O, sir, the wine runs

trillill down his throat, which cost the poor vintner many
a stamp before it was made. But I must hence, sir, I
have haste.

Sir Bar. Why, whither now, I prithee?

Slip. Faith, sir, to Sir Silvester, a knight, hard by,
upon my master's errand, whom I must certify this, that
the lease of East Spring shall be confirmed; and therefore must I bid him provide trash, for my master is no
friend without money.

Sir Bar. [*aside*]. This is the thing for which I su'd so
long,
This is the lease which I, by Gnatho's means,
Sought to possess by patent from the king;
But he, injurious man, who lives by crafts,
And sells king's favours for who will give most,
Hath taken bribes of me, yet covertly
Will sell away the thing pertains to me:
But I have found a present help, I hope,
For to prevent his purpose and deceit.——
Stay, gentle friend.

Slip. A good word; thou hast won me: this word is
like a warm caudle to a cold stomach.

Sir Bar. Sirrah, wilt thou, for money and reward,
Convey me certain letters, out of hand,
From out thy master's pocket?

Slip. Will I, sir? why, were it to rob my father, hang
my mother, or any such like trifles, I am at your commandment, sir. What will you give me, sir?

Sir Bar. A hundred pounds.

Slip. I am your man: give me earnest. I am dead
at a pocket, sir; why, I am a lifter, master, by my
occupation.

Sir Bar. A lifter! what is that?

Slip. Why, sir, I can lift a pot as well as any man,
and pick a purse as soon as any thief in my country.

Sir Bar. Why, fellow, hold; here is earnest, ten pound to assure thee. [*Gives money*]. Go, despatch, and bring it me to yonder tavern thou seest; and assure thyself, thou shalt both have thy skin full of wine and the rest of thy money.

Slip. I will, sir.—Now room for a gentleman, my masters! who gives me money for a fair new angel,[1] a trim new angel? [*Exeunt.*

SCENE II.—*The Same.*

Enter ANDREW *and* Purveyor.

Pur. Sirrah, I must needs have your master's horses: the king cannot be unserved.

And. Sirrah, you must needs go without them, because my master must be served.

Pur. Why, I am the king's purveyor, and I tell thee I will have them.

And. I am Ateukin's servant, Signior Andrew, and I say, thou shalt not have them.

Pur. Here's my ticket; deny it if thou darest.

And. There is the stable; fetch them out if thou darest.

Pur. Sirrah, sirrah, tame your tongue, lest I make you.

And. Sirrah, sirrah, hold your hand, lest I bum[2] you.

Pur. I tell thee, thy master's geldings are good, and therefore fit for the king.

And. I tell thee, my master's horses have galled backs, and therefore cannot fit the king. Purveyor, purveyor,

---

[1] A piece of money worth from 6*s.* to 10*s.* Puns upon the several meanings of the word were frequent.

[2] Strike, beat.

purvey thee of more wit : darest thou presume to wrong my Lord Ateukin, being the chiefest man in court ?

Pur. The more unhappy commonweal where flatterers are chief in court.

And. What sayest thou ?

Pur. I say thou art too presumptuous, and the officers shall school thee.

And. A fig for them and thee, purveyor ! They seek a knot in a ring that would wrong my master or his servants in this court.

Enter JAQUES.

Pur. The world is at a wise pass when nobility is afraid of a flatterer.

Jaq. Sirrah, what be you that *parley contre Monsieur* my Lord Ateukin ? *en bonne foi*, prate you against Sir *Altesse*, me maka your *tête* to leap from your shoulders, *per ma foi c'y ferai-je ?*

And. O, signior captain, you show yourself a forward and friendly gentleman in my master's behalf : I will cause him to thank you.

Jaq. Poltron, speak me one *parola* against my *bon gentilhomme*, I shall *estamp* your guts, and thump your backa, that you *no point* manage this ten hours.

Pur. Sirrah, come open me the stable, and let me have the horses ;—and, fellow, for all your French brags, I will do my duty.

And. I'll make garters of thy guts, thou villain, if thou enter this office.

Jaq. Mort Dieu, take me that cappa *pour votre labeur :* be gone, villain, in the *mort.*   [*Exit.*

Pur. What, will you resist me, then ? Well, the council, fellow, shall know of your insolency.

And. Tell them what thou wilt, and eat that I can best spare from my back-parts, and get you gone with a vengeance.   [*Exit* Purveyor.

Enter ATEUKIN.

Ateu. Andrew.

And. Sir?

Ateu. Where be my writings I put in my pocket last night?

And. Which, sir? your annotations upon Machiavel?

Ateu. No, sir; the letters-patents for East Spring.

And. Why, sir, you talk wonders to me, if you ask that question.

Ateu. Yea, sir, and will work wonders too with you, unless you find them out: villain, search me them out, and bring them me, or thou art but dead.

And. A terrible word in the latter end of a sessions. Master, were you in your right wits yesternight?

Ateu. Dost thou doubt it?

And. Ay, and why not, sir? for the greatest clerks are not the wisest, and a fool may dance in a hood, as well as a wise man in a bare frock: besides, such as give themselves to philautia,[1] as you do, master, are so choleric of complexion that that which they burn in fire over night they seek for with fury the next morning. Ah, I take care of your worship! this commonweal should have a great loss of so good a member as you are.

Ateu. Thou flatterest me.

And. Is it flattery in me, sir, to speak you fair? what is it, then, in you to dally with the king?

Ateu. Are you prating, knave? I will teach you better nurture! Is this the care you have of my wardrobe, of my accounts, and matters of trust?

---

[1] φιλαυτία, self-love, Collier's emendation of a meaningless passage in the quartos.

And. Why, alas, sir, in times past your garments have been so well inhabited as your tenants would give no place to a moth to mangle them; but since you are grown greater, and your garments more fine and gay, if your garments are not fit for hospitality, blame your pride and commend my cleanliness: as for your writings, I am not for them, nor they for me.

Ateu. Villain, go, fly, find them out: if thou losest them, thou losest my credit.

And. Alas, sir, can I lose that you never had?

Ateu. Say you so? then hold, feel you that you never felt. [*Beats him.*

Re-enter JAQUES.

Jaq. O monsieur, *ayez patience:* pardon your *pauvre valet:* me be at your commandment.

Ateu. Signior Jaques, well met; you shall command me.—Sirrah, go cause my writings be proclaimed in the market-place; promise a great reward to them that find them; look where I supped and everywhere.

And. I will, sir—[*aside*]. Now are two knaves well met, and three well parted: if thou conceive mine enigma, gentlemen,[1] what shall I be, then? faith, a plain harp-shilling.[2] [*Exit.*

Ateu. Sieur Jaques, this our happy meeting rids
Your friends and me of care and grievous toil;
For I, that look into deserts of men,
And see among the soldiers in this court
A noble forward mind, and judge thereof,
Cannot but seek the means to raise them up

[1] The word "gentlemen" is addressed to the audience.
[2] An Irish coin below the value of the earliest shilling, so called from having a harp on it.

Z

Who merit credit in the commonweal.
To this intent, friend Jaques, I have found
A means to make you great, and well-esteem'd
Both with the king and with the best in court:
For I espy in you a valiant mind,
Which makes me love, admire, and honour you.
To this intent, if so your trust, and faith,
Your secrecy be equal with your force,
I will impart a service to thyself,
Which if thou dost effect, the king, myself,
And what or he, or I with him, can work,
Shall be employ'd in what thou wilt desire.

Jaq. Me sweara by my ten bones, my signior, to be loyal to your lordship's intents, affairs: yea, my *monseigneur, que non ferai-je pour* your pleasure? By my sworda, me be no *babillard*.[1]

Ateu. Then hoping on thy truth, I prithee see
How kind Ateukin is to forward thee.
Hold [*giving money*], take this earnest-penny of my love,
And mark my words: the king, by me, requires
No slender service, Jaques, at thy hands.—
Thou must by privy practice make away
The queen, fair Dorothea, as she sleeps,
Or how thou wilt, so she be done to death:
Thou shalt not want promotion here in court.

Jaq. Stabba the woman! *par ma foi, monseigneur,* me thrusta my weapon into her belly, so me may be guard *par le roi.* Me do your service: but me no be hanged *pour* my labour?

Ateu. Thou shalt have warrant, Jaques, from the king:
None shall outface, gainsay, and wrong my friend.
Do not I love thee, Jaques? fear not, then:
I tell thee, whoso toucheth thee in aught
Shall injure me: I love, I tender thee:

----

[1] Babbler, chatterer.

Thou art a subject fit to serve his grace.
Jaques, I had a written warrant once,
But that, by great misfortune, late is lost.
Come, wend we to Saint Andrews, where his grace
Is now in progress, where he shall assure
Thy safety, and confirm thee to the act.
   Jaq. We will attend your nobleness.

                                [*Exeunt.*

SCENE III.—*The Palace of the* KING OF SCOTS.

Enter QUEEN DOROTHEA, SIR BARTRAM, NANO,
        ROSS, Ladies, *and* Attendants.

   Q. Dor. Thy credit, Bartram, in the Scottish court,
Thy reverend years, the strictness of thy vows,
All these are means sufficient to persuade;
But love, the faithful link of loyal hearts,
That hath possession of my constant mind,
Exiles all dread, subdueth vain suspect.
Methinks no craft should harbour in that breast
Where majesty and virtue are install'd:
Methinks my beauty should not cause my death.
   Sir Bar. How gladly, sovereign princess, would I err,
And bide my shame to save your royal life!
'Tis princely in yourself to think the best,
To hope his grace is guiltless of this crime:
But if in due prevention you default,
How blind are you that were forewarn'd before!
   Q. Dor. Suspicion without cause deserveth blame.
   Sir Bar. Who see, and shun not, harms, deserve the
       same.

Behold the tenor of this traitorous plot.

[Gives warrant.

Q. Dor. What should I read? Perhaps he wrote it
     not.

Sir Bar. Here is his warrant, under seal and sign,
To Jaques, born in France, to murder you.

Q. Dor. Ah, careless king, would God this were not
     thine!
What though I read? ah, should I think it true?

Ross. The hand and seal confirm the deed is his.

Q. Dor. What know I though if now he thinketh
     this?

Nano. Madam, Lucretius saith that to repent
Is childish, wisdom to prevent.

Q. Dor. What tho?

Nano. Then cease your tears, that have dismay'd you,
And cross the foe before he have betray'd you.

Sir Bar. What need these long suggestions in this
     cause,
When every circumstance confirmeth truth?
First, let the hidden mercy from above
Confirm your grace, since by a wondrous means
The practice of your dangers came to light:
Next, let the tokens of approved truth
Govern and stay your thoughts, too much seduc'd,
And mark the sooth, and listen the intent.
Your highness knows, and these my noble lords
Can witness this, that whilst your husband's sire
In happy peace possess'd the Scottish crown,
I was his sworn attendant here in court;
In dangerous fight I never fail'd my lord;
And since his death, and this your husband's reign,
No labour, duty, have I left undone,
To testify my zeal unto the crown.
But now my limbs are weak, mine eyes are dim,

Mine age unwieldly and unmeet for toil,
I came to court, in hope, for service past,
To gain some lease to keep me, being old.
There found I all was upsy-turvy turn'd,
My friends displac'd, the nobles loth to crave:
Then sought I to the minion of the king,
Ateukin, who, allur'd by a bribe,
Assur'd me of the lease for which I sought.
But see the craft! when he had got the grant,
He wrought to sell it to Sir Silvester,
In hope of greater earnings from his hands.
In brief, I learn'd his craft, and wrought the means,
By one his needy servants for reward,
To steal from out his pocket all the briefs;
Which he perform'd, and with reward resign'd.
Them when I read,—now mark the power of God,—
I found this warrant seal'd among the rest,
To kill your grace, whom God long keep alive!
Thus, in effect, by wonder are you sav'd:
Trifle not, then, but seek a speedy flight;
God will conduct your steps, and shield the right.

  Q. Dor. What should I do? ah, poor unhappy queen,
Born to endure what fortune can contain!
Alas, the deed is too apparent now!
But, O mine eyes, were you as bent to hide
As my poor heart is forward to forgive,
Ah cruel king, my love would thee acquit!
O, what avails to be allied and match'd
With high estates, that marry but in show?
Were I baser born, my mean estate
Could warrant me from this impendent harm:
But to be great and happy, these are twain.
Ah, Ross, what shall I do? how shall I work?

  Ross. With speedy letters to your father send,
Who will revenge you and defend your right.

Q. Dor. As if they kill not me, who with him fight!
As if his breast be touch'd, I am not wounded!
As if he wail'd, my joys were not confounded!
We are one heart, though rent by hate in twain;
One soul, one essence doth our weal contain:
What, then, can conquer him, that kills not me?

Ross. If this advice displease, then, madam, flee.

Q. Dor. Where may I wend or travel without fear?

Ross. Where not, in changing this attire you wear?

Q. Dor. What, shall I clad me like a country maid?

Nano. The policy is base, I am afraid.

Q. Dor. Why, Nano?

Nano. Ask you why? What, may a queen
March forth in homely weed, and be not seen?
The rose, although in thorny shrubs she spread,
Is still the rose, her beauties wax not dead;
And noble minds, although the coat be bare,
Are by their semblance known, how great they are.

Sir Bar. The dwarf saith true.

Q. Dor. What garments lik'st thou, than?

Nano. Such as may make you seem a proper man.

Q. Dor. He makes me blush and smile, though I am
    sad.

Nano. The meanest coat for safety is not bad.

Q. Dor. What, shall I jet[1] in breeches, like a squire?
Alas, poor dwarf, thy mistress is unmeet.

Nano. Tut, go me thus, your cloak before your
    face,
Your sword uprear'd with quaint and comely grace:
If any come and question what you be,
Say you "A man," and call for witness me.

Q. Dor. What, should I swear a sword? to what
    intent?

Nano. Madam, for show; it is an ornament:

               ¹ Strut.

If any wrong you, draw : a shining blade
Withdraws a coward thief that would invade.

  Q. Dor. But, if I strike, and he should strike again,
What should I do? I fear I should be slain.

  Nano. No, take it single on your dagger so :
I'll teach you, madam, how to ward a blow.

  Q. Dor. How little shapes much substance may
      include !—
Sir Bartram, Ross, ye ladies, and my friends,
Since presence yields me death, and absence life,
Hence will I fly, disguisèd like a squire,
As one that seeks to live in Irish wars :
You, gentle Ross, shall furnish my depart.

  Ross. Yea, prince, and die with you with all my
      heart !
Vouchsafe me, then, in all extremest states
To wait on you and serve you with my best.

  Q. Dor. To me pertains the woe : live then in rest.
Friends, fare you well : keep secret my depart :
Nano alone shall my attendant be.

  Nano. Then, madam, are you mann'd, I warrant ye !
Give me a sword, and, if there grow debate,
I'll come behind, and break your enemy's pate.

  Ross. How sore we grieve to part so soon away !

  Q. Dor. Grieve not for those that perish if they
      stay.

  Nano. The time in words misspent is little worth ;
Madam, walk on, and let them bring us forth.

                    [Exeunt.

CHORUS

Enter BOHAN.

  Boh. So, these sad motions make the fairy sleep ;
And sleep he shall in quiet and content :

For it would make a marble melt and weep,
To see these treasons 'gainst the innocent.
But, since she 'scapes by flight to save her life,
The king may chance repent she was his wife.
The rest is ruthful; yet, to beguile the time,
'Tis interlac'd with merriment and rhyme.

[*Exit.*

ACT THE FOURTH

SCENE I.—*On the King's Preserves.*

After a noise of horns and shoutings, enter certain
Huntsmen (*if you please, singing*) *one way; another*
way ATEUKIN *and* JAQUES.

TEU. Say, gentlemen, where may we
    find the king?
      First Hunts. Even here at hand,
      on hunting;
    And at this hour he taken hath a
      stand,
    To kill a deer.
Ateu. A pleasant work in hand.
Follow your sport, and we will seek his grace.
   First Hunts. When such him seek, it is a woful case.
          [*Exeunt* Huntsmen *one way*, ATEUKIN *and*
                JACQUES *another.*

SCENE II.—*Near the Castle of the* COUNTESS *of* ARRAN.

Enter the COUNTESS OF ARRAN, IDA *and* EUSTACE.

Count. of A. Lord Eustace, as your youth and virtuous
    life
Deserve a far more fair and richer wife,

So, since I am a mother, and do wit
What wedlock is, and that which 'longs to it,
Before I mean my daughter to bestow,
'Twere meet that she and I your state did know.

 Eust. Madam, if I consider Ida's worth,
I know my portions merit none so fair,
And yet I hold in farm and yearly rent
A thousand pound, which may her state content.

  Count. of A. But what estate, my lord, shall she
   possess?

 Eust. All that is mine, grave countess, and no less.—
But, Ida, will you love?

 Ida. I cannot hate.

 Eust. But will you wed?

 Ida. 'Tis Greek to me, my lord:
I'll wish you well, and thereon take my word.

  Eust. Shall I some sign of favour, then, receive?

 Ida. Ay, if her ladyship will give me leave.

 Count. of A. Do what thou wilt.

 Ida. Then, noble English peer,
Accept this ring, wherein my heart is set;
A constant heart, with burning flames be-fret,
But under-written this, *O morte dura:*
Hereon whenso you look with eyes *pura,*
The maid you fancy most will favour you.

 Eust. I'll try this heart, in hope to find it true.

   Enter certain Huntsmen *and* Ladies.

 First Hunts. Widow countess, well y-met;[1]
Ever may thy joys be many;—
Gentle Ida, fair beset,
Fair and wise, not fairer any;
Frolic huntsmen of the game
Will you well, and give you greeting.

  [1] This lyrical passage was undoubtedly sung.

Ida. Thanks, good woodman, for the same,
And our sport, and merry meeting.
    First Hunts. Unto thee we do present
Silver hart with arrow wounded.
    Eust. [*aside*]. This doth shadow my lament,
[With] both fear and love confounded.
    Ladies. To the mother of the maid,
Fair as the lilies, red as roses,
Even so many goods are said,
As herself in heart supposes.
    Count. of A. What are you, friends, that thus do wish
        us well?
    First Hunts. Your neighbours nigh, that have on
        hunting been,
Who, understanding of your walking forth,
Prepar'd this train to entertain you with :
This Lady Douglas, this Sir Egmond is.
    Count. of A. Welcome, ye ladies, and thousand thanks
        for this.
Come, enter you a homely widow's house,
And if mine entertainment please you, let us feast.
    First Hunts. A lovely lady never wants a guest.
            [*Exeunt* COUNTESS OF ARRAN, Huntsmen,
                        and Ladies.
    Eust. Stay, gentle Ida, tell me what you deem,
What doth this hart, this tender hart beseem?
    Ida. Why not, my lord, since nature teacheth art
To senseless beasts to cure their grievous smart ;
Dictamnum [1] serves to close the wound again.
    Eust. What help for those that love?
    Ida. Why, love again.
    Eust. Were I the hart,—
    Ida. Then I the herb would be :
You shall not die for help ; come, follow me.   [*Exeunt.*
    [1] See *Æneid* XII., 411 ; a favourite allusion of the Euphuists.

SCENE III.—*A Public Place near the Palace.*

Enter ANDREW *and* JAQUES.

Jaq. *Mon dieu*, what *malheur* be this! me come a the chamber, Signior Andrew, *mon dieu*; taka my poniard *en ma main* to give the *estocade* to the *damoisella*: *par ma foi*, there was no person; *elle s'est en allée.*

And. The worse luck, Jaques: but because I am thy friend, I will advise thee somewhat towards the attainment of the gallows.

Jaq. Gallows! what be that?

And. Marry, sir, a place of great promotion, where thou shalt by one turn above ground rid the world of a knave, and make a goodly ensample for all bloody villains of thy profession.

Jaq. *Que dites vous*, Monsieur Andrew?

And. I say, Jaques, thou must keep this path, and hie thee; for the queen, as I am certified, is departed with her dwarf, apparelled like a squire. Overtake her, Frenchman, stab her: I'll promise thee, this doublet shall be happy.

Jaq. *Pourquoi?*

And. It shall serve a jolly gentleman, Sir Dominus Monseigneur Hangman.

Jaq. *C'est tout un*; me will rama *pour la monnoie.*

[*Exit.*

And. Go, and the rot consume thee!—O, what a trim world is this! My master lives by cozening the king, I by flattering him; Slipper, my fellow, by stealing, and I by lying: is not this a wily accord, gentlemen?[1] This last night, our jolly horsekeeper, being well steeped

---

[1] Again addressed to the audience.

in liquor, confessed to me the stealing of my master's
writings, and his great reward. Now dare I not bewray
him, lest he discover my knavery; but this have I
wrought: I understand he will pass this way, to provide
him necessaries; but, if I and my fellows fail not, we will
teach him such a lesson as shall cost him a chief place
on Pennyless Bench[1] for his labour. But yond he
comes.   [*Stands aside.*

Enter SLIPPER, *with a* Tailor, *a* Shoemaker, *and a*
Cutler.

Slip. Tailor.

Tai. Sir?

Slip. Let my doublet be white northern, five groats
the yard: I tell thee, I will be brave.

Tai. It shall, sir.

Slip. Now, sir, cut it me like the battlements of a
custard, full of round holes; edge me the sleeves with
Coventry blue, and let the linings be of tenpenny lockram.

Tai. Very good, sir.

Slip. Make it the amorous cut, a flap before.

Tai. And why so? that fashion is stale.

Slip. O, friend, thou art a simple fellow. I tell thee,
a flap is a great friend to a storrie; it stands him instead
of clean napery; and, if a man's shirt be torn, it is a
present penthouse to defend him from a clean huswife's
scoff.

Tai. You say sooth, sir.

Slip. [*giving money*]. Hold, take thy money; there is
seven shillings for the doublet, and eight for the breeches:
seven and eight; by'rlady, thirty-six is a fair deal of
money.

Tai. Farewell, sir.

---

[1] A church seat for loungers, the original in Carfax Church,
Oxford. To sit on Pennyless Bench indicated extreme poverty.

Slip. Nay, but stay, tailor.

Tai. Why, sir?

Slip. Forget not this special make : let my back-parts be well lined, for there come many winter-storms from a windy belly, I tell thee. [*Exit* Tailor]. Shoemaker.

Shoe. Gentleman, what shoe will it please you to have?

Slip. A fine, neat calves'-leather, my friend.

Shoe. O, sir, that is too thin, it will not last you.

Slip. I tell thee, it is my near kinsman, for I am Slipper, which hath his best grace in summer to be suited in calves'[1] skins. Goodwife Calf was my grand-mother, and Goodman Netherleather mine uncle; but my mother, good woman, alas, she was a Spaniard, and being well tanned and dressed by a good fellow, an Englishman, is grown to some wealth : as, when I have but my upper-parts clad in her husband's costly Spanish leather, I may be bold to kiss the fairest lady's foot in this country.

Shoe. You are of high birth, sir; but have you all your mother's marks on you?

Slip. Why, knave?

Shoe. Because, if thou come of the blood of the Slippers, you should have a shoemaker's awl thrust through your ear.

Slip. [*giving money*]. Take your earnest, friend, and be packing, and meddle not with my progenitors. [*Exit* Shoemaker]. Cutler.

Cut. Here, sir.

Slip. I must have a reaper and digger.[2]

Cut. A rapier and dagger, you mean, sir?

---

[1] Kittredge's emendation. For the unintelligible "lakus" of the quarto one would accept Collier's conjecture "Jack-ass," were it not for the fact, enunciated by Collins (after N. E. D.), that this word was unknown before the eighteenth century.

[2] Collier's emendation for "a rapier and dagger," it being clear that Slipper has miscalled the weapons.

Slip. Thou sayest true; but it must have a very fair edge.

Cut. Why so, sir?

Slip. Because it may cut by himself, for truly, my friend, I am a man of peace, and wear weapons but for fashion.

Cut. Well, sir, give me earnest, I will fit you.

Slip. [*giving money*]. Hold, take it: I betrust thee, friend; let me be well armed.

Cut. You shall. [*Exit.*

Slip. Now what remains? there's twenty crowns for house, three crowns for household-stuff, sixpence to buy a constable's staff; nay, I will be the chief of my parish. There wants nothing but a wench, a cat, a dog, a wife, and a servant, to make an whole family. Shall I marry with Alice, Goodman Grimshawe's daughter? she is fair, but indeed her tongue is like clocks on Shrove Tuesday, always out of temper. Shall I wed Sisley of the Whighton? O, no! she is like a frog in a parsley-bed; as skittish as an eel: if I seek to hamper her, she will horn me. But a wench must be had, Master Slipper; yea, and shall be, dear friend.

And. [*aside*]. I now will drive him from his contemplations.—O, my mates, come forward: the lamb is unpent, the fox shall prevail.

Enter three Antics, *who dance round, and take*
Slipper *with them.*

Slip. I will, my friend, and I thank you heartily: pray, keep your courtesy: I am yours in the way of an hornpipe.—[*Aside*]. They are strangers; I see they understand not my language: wee, wee.—[1]

[*Whilst they are dancing,* ANDREW *takes away*
SLIPPER'S *money, and the other* Antics *depart.*

Nay, but, my friends, one hornpipe further! a refluence

---

[1] So also in the quarto, line 5, scene v. of this act, French "oui" is spelled "wee."

back, and two doubles forward! What, not one cross-point against Sundays? What, ho, sirrah, you gone? you with the nose like an eagle, an you be a right Greek, one turn more.—Thieves, thieves! I am robbed! thieves! Is this the knavery of fiddlers? Well, I will then bind the whole credit of their occupation on a bag-piper, and he for my money. But I will after, and teach them to caper in a halter, that have cozened me of my money. [*Exit.*

SCENE IV.—*The Forest near Edinburgh.*

Enter QUEEN DOROTHEA *in man's apparel, and* NANO.

Q. Dor. Ah, Nano, I am weary of these weeds,
Weary to wield this weapon that I bear,
Weary of love from whom my woe proceeds,
Weary of toil, since I have lost my dear.
O weary life, where wanteth no distress,
But every thought is paid with heaviness!
  Nano. Too much of weary, madam: if you please,
Sit down, let weary die, and take your ease.
  Q. Dor. How look I, Nano? like a man or no?
  Nano. If not a man, yet like a manly shrow.[1]
  Q. Dor. If any come and meet us on the way,
What should we do, if they enforce us stay?
  Nano. Set cap a-huff, and challenge him the field:
Suppose the worst, the weak may fight to yield.
  Q. Dor. The battle, Nano, in this troubled mind
Is far more fierce than ever we may find.
The body's wounds by medicines may be eas'd,
But griefs of mind, by salves are no appeas'd.

[1] Shrew.

Nano. Say, madam, will you hear your Nano sing?

Q. Dor. Of woe, good boy, but of no other thing.

Nano. What if I sing of fancy?[1] will it please?

Q. Dor. To such as hope success such notes breed ease.

Nano. What if I sing, like Damon, to my sheep?

Q. Dor. Like Phillis, I will sit me down to weep.

Nano. Nay, since my songs afford such pleasure small,
I'll sit me down, and sing you none at all.

Q. Dor. O, be not angry, Nano!

Nano. Nay, you loathe
To think on that which doth content us both.

Q. Dor. And how?

Nano. You scorn disport when you are weary,
And loathe my mirth, who live to make you merry.

Q. Dor. Danger and fear withdraw me from delight.

Nano. 'Tis virtue to contemn false fortune's spite.

Q. Dor. What should I do to please thee, friendly squire?

Nano. A smile a-day is all I will require;
And, if you pay me well the smiles you owe me,
I'll kill this cursèd care, or else beshrow me.

Q. Dor. We are descried; O, Nano, we are dead!

Enter JAQUES, *his sword drawn.*

Nano. Tut, yet you walk, you are not dead indeed.
Draw me your sword, if he your way withstand,
And I will seek for rescue out of hand.

Q. Dor. Run, Nano, run, prevent thy princess' death.

Nano. Fear not, I'll run all danger out of breath.

[*Exit.*

Jaq. Ah, you *calletta!* you *strumpetta! Maitressa Doretie, êtes vous surprise?* Come, say your paternoster, *car vous êtes morte, par ma foi.*

[1] Love.

2 A

Q. Dor. Callet! me strumpet! Caitiff as thou art!
But even a princess born, who scorns thy threats:
Shall never Frenchman say an England maid
Of threats of foreign force will be afraid.

Jaq. You no *dire votres prières? morbleu, mechante femme,* guarda your breasta there : me make you die on my Morglay.[1]

Q. Dor. God shield me, helpless princess and a wife,
And save my soul, although I lose my life!
     [*They fight, and she is sore wounded.*
Ah, I am slain! some piteous power repay
This murderer's cursèd deed, that doth me slay!

Jaq. Elle est tout morte. Me will run *pour* a wager, for fear me be *surpris* and *pendu* for my labour. *Bien, je m'en allerai au roi lui dire mes affaires. Je serai un chevalier* for this day's travail.   [*Exit.*

[*Re-enter* NANO, *with* SIR CUTHBERT ANDERSON, *his sword drawn, and* Servants.

Sir Cuth. Where is this poor distressèd gentleman?
Nano. Here laid on ground, and wounded to the
  death.
Ah, gentle heart, how are these beauteous looks
 Dimm'd by the tyrant cruelties of death!
O weary soul, break thou from forth my breast,
And join thee with the soul I honour'd most!

Sir Cuth. Leave mourning, friend, the man is yet alive.
Some help me to convey him to my house:
There will I see him carefully recur'd,
And send privy search to catch the murderer.

Nano. The God of heaven reward thee, courteous
  knight!
    [*Exeunt, bearing out* QUEEN DOROTHEA.

---

[1] The sword of Sir Bevis of Southampton; the common synonym for a sword.

SCENE V.—*Another part of the Forest.*

Enter the King of Scots, Jaques, Ateukin, Andrew;
   Jaques *running with his sword one way, the* King
   with his train *another way.*

K. of Scots. Stay, Jaques, fear not, sheath thy murder-
      ing blade :
Lo, here thy king and friends are come abroad
To save thee from the terrors of pursuit.
What, is she dead?
   Jaq. Oui, *Monsieur, elle* is *blessée par la tête* over *les
épaules :* I warrant, she no trouble you.
   Ateu. O, then, my liege, how happy art thou grown,
How favour'd of the heavens, and blest by love !
Methinks I see fair Ida in thine arms,
Craving remission for her late contempt ;
Methinks I see her blushing steal a kiss,
Uniting both your souls by such a sweet ;
And you, my king, suck nectar from her lips.
Why, then, delays your grace to gain the rest
You long desir'd? why lose we forward time?
Write, make me spokesman now, vow marriage :
If she deny you favour, let me die.
   And. Mighty and magnificent potentate, give credence
to mine honourable good lord, for I heard the midwife
swear at his nativity that the fairies gave him the property
of the Thracian stone ; for who toucheth it is exempted
from grief, and he that heareth my master's counsel is
already possessed of happiness ; nay, which is more
miraculous, as the nobleman in his infancy lay in his
cradle, a swarm of bees laid honey on his lips in token
of his eloquence, for *melle dulcior fluit oratio.*

Ateu. Your grace must bear with imperfections:
This is exceeding love that makes him speak.

K. of Scots. Ateukin, I am ravish'd in conceit,
And yet depress'd again with earnest thoughts.
Methinks, this murder soundeth in mine ear
A threatening noise of dire and sharp revenge:
I am incens'd with grief, yet fain would joy.
What may I do to end me of these doubts?

Ateu. Why, prince, it is no murder in a king
To end another's life to save his own:
For you are not as common people be,
Who die and perish with a few men's tears;
But if you fail, the state doth whole default,
The realm is rent in twain in such a loss.
And Aristotle holdeth this for true,
Of evils needs we must choose the least:
Then better were it, that a woman died
Than all the help of Scotland should be blent.
'Tis policy, my liege, in every state,
To cut off members that disturb the head:
And by corruption generation grows,
And contraries maintain the world and state.

K. of Scots. Enough, I am confirm'd. Ateukin,
          come,
Rid me of love, and rid me of my grief;
Drive thou the tyrant from this tainted breast,
Then may I triumph in the height of joy.
Go to mine Ida, tell her that I vow
To raise her head, and make her honours great:
Go to mine Ida, tell her that her hairs
Shall be embellishèd with orient pearls,
And crowns of sapphires compassing her brows,
Shall war with those sweet beauties of her eyes:
Go to mine Ida, tell her that my soul
Shall keep her semblance closèd in my breast;

And I, in touching of her milk-white mould,
Will think me deified in such a grace.
I like no stay: go write, and I will sign:
Reward me Jaques ; give him store of crowns.
And, Sirrah Andrew, scout thou here in court,
And bring me tidings, if thou canst perceive
The least intent of muttering in my train ;
For either those that wrong thy lord or thee
Shall suffer death.

 Ateu. How much, O mighty king,
Is thy Ateukin bound to honour thee !—
Bow thee, Andrew, bend thine sturdy knees ;
Seest thou not here thine only God on earth?

      [*Exit the* KING.

 Jaq. Mais où est mon argent, seigneur ?

 Ateu. Come, follow me. His grace, I see, is mad,[1]
That thus on sudden he hath left us here.—
Come, Jaques: we will have our packet soon despatch'd,
And you shall be my mate upon the way.

 Jaq. Comme vous plaira, monsieur.

    [*Exeunt* ATEUKIN *and* JAQUES.

 And. Was never such a world, I think, before,
When sinners seem to dance within a net ;
The flatterer and the murderer, they grow big ;
By hook or crook promotion now is sought.
In such a world, where men are so misled,
What should I do, but, as the proverb saith,
Run with the hare, and hunt with the hound?
To have two means beseems a witty man.
Now here in court I may aspire and climb
By subtlety, for my master's death :
And, if that fail, well fare another drift ;
I will, in secret, certain letters send
Unto the English king, and let him know

---

 [1] Manly's suggested emendation of the meaningless " His grave,
I see, is made," of the quarto.

The order of his daughter's overthrow,
That, if my master crack his credit here,
As I am sure long flattery cannot hold,
I may have means within the English court
To 'scape the scourge that waits on bad advice.

　　　　　　　　　　　　　　　　[Exit.

CHORUS

Enter BOHAN *and* OBERON.

Ober. Believe me, bonny Scot, these strange events
Are passing pleasing ; may they end as well.
Boh. Else say that Bohan hath a barren skull,
If better motions yet than any past
Do not, more glee to make, the fairy greet.
But my small son made pretty handsome shift
To save the queen his mistress, by his speed.
Ober. Yea, and yon laddie, for his sport he made,
Shall see, when least he hopes, I'll stand his friend,
Or else he capers in a halter's end.
Boh. What, hang my son ! I trow not, Oberon :
I'll rather die than see him woebegone.

　　　Enter a round, or some dance, at pleasure.

Ober. Bohan, be pleas'd, for, do they what they will,
Here is my hand, I'll save thy son from ill.

　　　　　　　　　　　　　　　　[Exeunt.

ACT THE FIFTH

SCENE I.—*Castle of* SIR CUTHBERT ANDERSON.

Enter QUEEN DOROTHEA *in man's apparel and in a nightgown,* LADY ANDERSON, *and* NANO; *and* SIR CUTHBERT ANDERSON *behind.*

ADY AND. My gentle friend, beware, in taking air,
    Your walks grow not offensive to your wounds.

    Q. Dor. Madam, I thank you of your courteous care:
    My wounds are well-nigh clos'd, though sore they are.

Lady And. Methinks these closèd wounds should breed more grief,
Since open wounds have cure, and find relief.

    Q. Dor. Madam, if undiscover'd wounds you mean,
They are not cur'd, because they are not seen.

    Lady And. I mean the wounds which do the heart subdue.

    Nano. O, that is love: Madam, speak I not true?

             [SIR CUTHBERT ANDERSON *overhears.*

    Lady And. Say it were true, what salve for such a sore?

Nano. Be wise, and shut such neighbours out of door.
Lady And. How if I cannot drive him from my
  breast?
Nano. Then chain him well, and let him do his best.
Sir Cuth. [*aside*]. In ripping up their wounds, I see
  their wit;
But if these wounds be cur'd, I sorrow it.
Q. Dor. Why are you so intentive to behold
My pale and woful looks, by care controll'd?
Lady And. Because in them a ready way is found
To cure my care and heal my hidden wound.
Nano. Good master, shut your eyes, keep that
  conceit;
Surgeons give coin to get a good receipt.
Q. Dor. Peace, wanton son; this lady did amend
My wounds; mine eyes her hidden griefs shall end.
Nano. Look not too much, it is a weighty case
Whereas a man puts on a maiden's face;
For many times, if ladies 'ware them not,
A nine months' wound, with little work is got.
Sir Cuth. [*aside*]. I'll break off their dispute, lest love
  proceed
From covert smiles, to perfect love indeed.
         [*Comes forward.*
Nano. The cat's abroad, stir not, the mice be still.
Lady And. Tut, we can fly such cats, when so we
  will.
Sir Cuth. How fares my guest? take cheer, naught
  shall default,
That either doth concern your health or joy:
Use me; my house, and what is mine is yours.
Q. Dor. Thanks, gentle knight; and, if all hopes be
  true,
I hope ere long to do as much for you.
Sir Cuth. Your virtue doth acquit me of that doubt:

But, courteous sir, since troubles call me hence,
I must to Edinburgh unto the king,
There to take charge, and wait him in his wars.—
Meanwhile, good madam, take this squire in charge,
And use him so as if it were myself.

   Lady And. Sir Cuthbert, doubt not of my diligence :
Meanwhile, till your return, God send you health.

   Q. Dor. God bless his grace, and, if his cause be
     just,
Prosper his wars ; if not, he'll mend, I trust.
Good sir, what moves the king to fall to arms ?

   Sir Cuth. The King of England forageth his land,
And hath besieg'd Dunbar with mighty force.
What other news are common in the court.
Read you these letters, madam ; [*giving letters to* LADY
     ANDERSON] tell the squire
The whole affairs of state, for I must hence.

   Q. Dor. God prosper you, and bring you back from
     thence !

             [*Exit* SIR CUTHBERT ANDERSON.
Madam, what news ?

   Lady And. They say the queen is slain.

   Q. Dor. Tut, such reports more false than truth
     contain.

   Lady And. But these reports have made his nobles
     leave him.

   Q. Dor. Ah, careless men, and would they so deceive
     him ?

   Lady And. The land is spoil'd, the commons fear the
     cross ;
All cry against the king, their cause of loss :
The English king subdues and conquers all.

   Q. Dor. Alas, this war grows great on causes small !

   Lady And. Our court is desolate, our prince alone,
Still dreading death.

Q. Dor. Woe's me, for him I mourn!
Help, now help, a sudden qualm
Assails my heart!

Nano. Good madam, stand his friend:
Give us some liquor to refresh his heart.

    Lady And. Daw thou him up,[1] and I will fetch thee
        forth
Potions of comfort, to repress his pain.   [*Exit.*

    Nano. Fie, princess, faint on every fond report!
How well-nigh had you open'd your estate!
Cover these sorrows with the veil of joy,
And hope the best; for why this war will cause
A great repentance in your husband's mind.

    Q. Dor. Ah, Nano, trees live not without their
        sap,
And Clytie cannot blush but on the sun;
The thirsty earth is broke with many a gap,
And lands are lean where rivers do not run:
Where soul is reft from that it loveth best,
How can it thrive or boast of quiet rest?
Thou know'st the prince's loss must be my death,
His grief, my grief; his mischief must be mine.
O, if thou love me, Nano, hie to court!
Tell Ross, tell Bartram, that I am alive;
Conceal thou yet the place of my abode:
Will them, even as they love their queen,
As they are chary of my soul and joy,
To guard the king, to serve him as my lord.
Haste thee, good Nano, for my husband's care
Consumeth me, and wounds me to the heart.

    Nano. Madam, I go, yet loth to leave you here.

    Q. Dor. Go thou with speed: even as thou hold'st me
        dear,
Return in haste.   [*Exit* NANO.

---

[1] Revive, resuscitate him.

Re-enter LADY ANDERSON.

Lady And. Now, sir, what cheer? come taste this
    broth I bring.

Q. Dor. My grief is past, I feel no further sting.

Lady And. Where is your dwarf? why hath he left
    you, sir?

Q. Dor. For some affairs : he is not travell'd far.

Lady And. If so you please, come in and take your
    rest.

Q. Dor. Fear keeps awake a discontented breast.

                             [*Exeunt.*

SCENE II.—*Porch to the Castle of the*
    COUNTESS OF ARRAN.

After a solemn service, enter from the COUNTESS OF
    ARRAN'S *house a service, with musical songs of
    marriages, or a mask, or pretty triumph : to them*
    ATEUKIN *and* JAQUES.

Ateu. What means this triumph, friend? why are these
    feasts?

First Revel. Fair Ida, sir, was married yesterday
Unto Sir Eustace, and for that intent
We feast and sport it thus to honour them :
An, if you please, come in and take your part ;
My lady is no niggard of her cheer.

                        [*Exeunt* Revellers.

Jaq. Monseigneur, why be you so sadda? *faites bonne
    chere : foutre de ce monde !*

Ateu. What, was I born to be the scorn of kin?
To gather feathers like to a hopper-crow,

And lose them in the height of all my pomp?
Accursèd man, now is my credit lost!
Where are my vows I made unto the king?
What shall become of me, if he shall hear
That I have caus'd him kill a virtuous queen,
And hope in vain for that which now is lost?
Where shall I hide my head? I know the heavens
Are just and will revenge; I know my sins
Exceed compare. Should I proceed in this,
This Eustace must amain be made away.
O, were I dead, how happy should I be!

Jaq. Est ce donc à tel point votre etat? faith, then
adieu, Scotland, adieu, Signior Ateukin: me will homa
to France, and no be hanged in a strange country.

[*Exit.*

Ateu. Thou dost me good to leave me thus alone,
That galling grief and I may yoke in one.
O, what are subtle means to climb on high,
When every fall swarms with exceeding shame?
I promis'd Ida's love unto the prince,
But she is lost, and I am false forsworn.
I practis'd Dorothea's hapless death,
And by this practice have commenc'd a war.
O cursèd race of men, that traffic guile,
And, in the end, themselves and kings beguile!
Asham'd to look upon my prince again,
Asham'd of my suggestions and advice,
Asham'd of life, asham'd that I have err'd,
I'll hide myself, expecting for [1] my shame.
Thus God doth work with those that purchase fame
By flattery, and make their prince their game. [*Exit.*

---

[1] Waiting for.

SCENE III.—*The English Camp before Dunbar.*

Enter the KING OF ENGLAND, LORD PERCY, SAMLES,
and others.

K. of Eng.[1] Thus far, ye English peers, have we
   display'd
Our waving ensigns with a happy war;
Thus nearly hath our furious rage reveng'd
My daughter's death upon the traitorous Scot.
And now before Dunbar our camp is pitch'd;
Which, if it yield not to our compromise,
The plough shall furrow where the palace stood,
And fury shall enjoy so high a power
That mercy shall be banish'd from our swords.

Enter DOUGLAS *and others on the walls.*

Doug. What seeks the English king?
K. of Eng. Scot, open those gates, and let me enter
   in:
Submit thyself and thine unto my grace,
Or I will put each mother's son to death,
And lay this city level with the ground.
Doug. For what offence, for what default of ours,
Art thou incens'd so sore against our state?
Can generous hearts in nature be so stern
To prey on those that never did offend?
What though the lion, king of brutish race,
Through outrage sin, shall lambs be therefore slain?

---

[1] "To the speeches of the King of England throughout this scene
is prefixed *Arius.* Collier remarks, *History of English Dramatic
Poetry,* iii. 161, 'It is a singular circumstance that the King of
England is called *Arius,* as if Greene at the time he wrote had some
scruple in naming Henry VIII. on account of the danger of giving
offence to the Queen and Court.'"—COLLINS.

Or is it lawful that the humble die
Because the mighty do gainsay the right?
O English king, thou bearest in thy crest
The king of beasts, that harms not yielding ones:
The roseal cross is spread within thy field,
A sign of peace, not of revenging war.
Be gracious, then, unto this little town;
And, though we have withstood thee for awhile
To show allegiance to our liefest liege,
Yet, since we know no hope of any help,
Take us to mercy, for we yield ourselves.

    K. of Eng. What, shall I enter, then, and be your
        lord?

    Doug. We will submit us to the English king.

    [*They descend, open the gates, and humble themselves.*

    K. of Eng. Now life and death dependeth on my
        sword:

This hand now rear'd, my Douglas, if I list,
Could part thy head and shoulders both in twain;
But, since I see thee wise and old in years,
True to thy king, and faithful in his wars,
Live thou and thine. Dunbar is too-too small
To give an entrance to the English king:
I, eagle-like, disdain these little fowls,
And look on none but those that dare resist.
Enter your town, as those that live by me:
For others that resist, kill, forage, spoil.
Mine English soldiers, as you love your king,
Revenge his daughter's death, and do me right.

                            [*Exeunt.*

SCENE IV.—*Near the Scottish Camp.*

Enter a Lawyer, *a* Merchant, *and a* Divine.

Law. My friends, what think you of this present state?
Were ever seen such changes in a time?
The manners and the fashions of this age
Are, like the ermine-skin, so full of spots,
As sooner may the Moor be washèd white
Than these corruptions banish'd from this realm.
    Merch. What sees Mas Lawyer in this state amiss?
    Law. A wresting power that makes a nose of wax
Of grounded law, a damn'd and subtle drift
In all estates to climb by others' loss;
An eager thirst of wealth, forgetting truth.
Might I ascend unto the highest states,
And by descent discover every crime,
My friends, I should lament, and you would grieve
To see the hapless ruins of this realm.
    Div. O lawyer, thou hast curious eyes to pry
Into the secret maims of their estate;
But if thy veil of error were unmask'd,
Thyself should see your sect do maim her most.
Are you not those that should maintain the peace,
Yet only are the patrons of our strife?
If your profession have his ground and spring
First from the laws of God, then country's right,
Not any ways inverting nature's power,
Why thrive you by contentions? why devise you
Clauses, and subtle reasons to except?
Our state was first, before you grew so great,
A lantern to the world for unity:
Now they that are befriended and are rich
Oppress the poor: come Homer without coin,

He is not heard.   What shall we term this drift?
To say the poor man's cause is good and just,
And yet the rich man gains the best in law?
It is your guise (the more the world laments)
To coin provisos to beguile your laws;
To make a gay pretext of due proceeding,
When you delay your common-pleas for years.
Mark what these dealings lately here have wrought:
The crafty men have purchas'd great men's lands;
They powl,[1] they pinch, their tenants are undone;
If these complain, by you they are undone;
You fleece them of their coin, their children beg,
And many want, because you may be rich:
This scar is mighty, Master Lawyer.
Now war hath gotten head within this land,
Mark but the guise.   The poor man that is wrong'd
Is ready to rebel; he spoils, he pills;
We need no foes to forage that we have:
The law, say they, in peace consumèd us,
And now in war we will consume the law.
Look to this mischief, lawyers: conscience knows
You live amiss; amend it, lest you end!

    Law. Good Lord, that these divines should see so far
In others' faults, without amending theirs!
Sir, sir, the general defaults in state
(If you would read before you did correct)
Are, by a hidden working from above,
By their successive changes still remov'd.
Were not the law by contraries maintain'd,
How could the truth from falsehood be discern'd?
Did we not taste the bitterness of war,
How could we know the sweet effects of peace?
Did we not feel the nipping winter-frosts,
How should we know the sweetness of the spring?

[1] Pillage, plunder.

Should all things still remain in one estate,
Should not in greatest arts some scars be found?
Were all upright, nor chang'd, what world were this?
A chaos, made of quiet, yet no world,
Because the parts thereof did still accord:
This matter craves a variance, not a speech.
But, Sir Divine, to you: look on your maims,
Divisions, sects, your simonies, and bribes,
Your cloaking with the great for fear to fall,—
You shall perceive you are the cause of all.
Did each man know there was a storm at hand,
Who would not clothe him well, to shun the wet?
Did prince and peer, the lawyer and the least,
Know what were sin, without a partial gloss,
We'd need no long discovery then of crimes,
For each would mend, advis'd by holy men.
Thus [I] but slightly shadow out your sins;
But, if they were depainted out of life,
Alas, we both had wounds enough to heal!

   Merch. None of you both, I see, but are in fault;
Thus simple men, as I, do swallow flies.
This grave divine can tell us what to do;
But we may say, " Physician, mend thyself."
This lawyer hath a pregnant wit to talk;
But all are words, I see no deeds of worth.

   Law. Good merchant, lay your fingers on your
       mouth;
Be not a blab, for fear you bite yourself.
What should I term your state, but even the way
To every ruin in this commonweal?
You bring us in the means of all excess,
You rate it and retail it as you please;
You swear, forswear, and all to compass wealth;
Your money is your god, your hoard your heaven;
You are the groundwork of contention.

   2 B

First, heedless youth by you is over-reach'd ;
We are corrupted by your many crowns :
The gentlemen, whose titles you have bought,
Lose all their fathers' toil within a day,
Whilst Hob your son, and Sib your nutbrown child,
Are gentlefolks, and gentles are beguil'd.
This makes so many noble minds to stray,
And take sinister courses in the state.

Enter a Scout.

Scout. My friends, be gone, an if you love your lives !
The King of England marcheth here at hand :
Enter the camp, for fear you be surpris'd.
Div. Thanks, gentle scout,—God mend that is amiss,
And place true zeal whereas corruption is !   [*Exeunt.*

SCENE V.—*Castle of* SIR CUTHBERT ANDERSON.

Enter QUEEN DOROTHEA *in man's apparel,* LADY
ANDERSON, *and* NANO.

Q. Dor. What news in court, Nano ? let us know it.
Nano. If so you please, my lord, I straight will
      show it :
The English king hath all the borders spoil'd,
Hath taken Morton prisoner, and hath slain
Seven thousand Scottish lads not far from Tweed.
Q. Dor. A woful murder and a bloody deed !
Nano. The king, our liege, hath sought by many
      means

For to appease his enemy by prayers:
Naught will prevail unless he can restore
Fair Dorothea, long supposèd dead:
To this intent he hath proclaimèd late,
That whosoe'er return the queen to court
Shall have a thousand marks for his reward.

   Lady And. He loves her, then, I see, although
      enforc'd,
That would bestow such gifts for to regain her.
Why sit you sad, good sir? be not dismay'd.

   Nano. I'll lay my life, this man would be a maid.

   Q. Dor. [*aside to Nano*]. Fain would I show myself,
      and change my tire.

   Lady And. Whereon divine you, sir?

   Nano. Upon desire.
Madam, mark but my skill. I'll lay my life,
My master here, will prove a married wife.

   Q. Dor. [*aside to Nano*]. Wilt thou bewray me, Nano?

   Nano [*aside to Dor.*]. Madam, no:
You are a man, and like a man you go:
But I, that am in speculation seen,[1]
Know you would change your state to be a queen.

   Dor. [*aside to Nano*]. Thou art not, dwarf, to learn
      thy mistress' mind:
Fain would I with thyself disclose my kind,
But yet I blush.

   Nano [*aside to Dor.*]. What? blush you, madam, than,[2]
To be yourself, who are a feignèd man?[3]

   Lady And. Deceitful beauty, hast thou scorn'd me so?

   Nano. Nay, muse not, madam, for he tells you true.

   Lady And. Beauty bred love, and love hath bred my
      shame.

   Nano. And women's faces work more wrongs than
      these:

_____
[1] Tried, skilled.   [2] Then.   [3] From this point the scene is confused.

Take comfort, madam, to cure your disease.
And yet he loves a man as well as you,
Only this difference, he cannot fancy two.

   Lady And. Blush, grieve, and die in thine insatiate
     lust.

   Q. Dor. Nay, live, and joy that thou hast won a friend,
That loves thee as his life by good desert.

   Lady And. I joy, my lord, more than my tongue can
     tell :
Though not as I desir'd, I love you well.
But modesty, that never blush'd before,
Discover my false heart : I say no more.
Let me alone.

   Q. Dor. Good Nano, stay awhile.
Were I not sad, how kindly could I smile,
To see how fain I am to leave this weed !
And yet I faint to show myself indeed :
But danger hates delay ; I will be bold.—
Fair lady, I am not [as you] suppose,
A man, but even that queen, more hapless I,
Whom Scottish king appointed hath to die ;
I am the hapless princess, for whose right,
These kings in bloody wars revenge despite ;
I am that Dorothea whom they seek,
Yours bounden for your kindness and relief ;
And, since you are the means that save my life,
Yourself and I will to the camp repair,
Whereas your husband shall enjoy reward,
And bring me to his highness once again.

   Lady And. Pardon, most gracious princess, if you
     please,
My rude discourse and homely entertain ;
And, if my words may savour any worth,
Vouchsafe my counsel in this weighty cause :
Since that our liege hath so unkindly dealt,

Give him no trust, return unto your sire ;
There may you safely live in spite of him.
  Q. Dor. Ah lady, so would worldly counsel work ;
But constancy, obedience, and my love,
In that my husband is my lord and chief,
These call me to compassion of his state :
Dissuade me not, for virtue will not change.
  Lady And. What wondrous constancy is this I hear !
If English dames their husbands love so dear,
I fear me in the world they have no peer.
  Nano. Come, princess, wend, and let us change your
    weed :
I long to see you now a queen indeed.   [*Exeunt.*

———————

SCENE VI.—*Camp of the* KING OF SCOTS.

Enter the KING OF SCOTS, *the* English Herald, *and*
Lords.

  K. of Scots. He would have parley, lords. Herald, say
    he shall,
And get thee gone. Go, leave me to myself.
                    [*Exit* Herald.—*Lords retire.*
'Twixt love and fear, continual is the war ;
The one assures me of my Ida's love,
The other moves me for my murder'd queen :
Thus find I grief of that whereon I joy,
And doubt in greatest hope, and death in weal.
Alas, what hell may be compar'd with mine,
Since in extremes my comforts do consist !
War then will cease, when dead ones are reviv'd ;

Some then will yield when I am dead for hope.—
Who doth disturb me?

         Enter ANDREW *and* SLIPPER.

Andrew?
   And. Ay, my liege.
   K. of Scots. What news?
   And. I think my mouth was made at first
To tell these tragic tales, my liefest lord.
   K. of Scots. What, is Ateukin dead? tell me the worst
   And. No, but your Ida—shall I tell him all?—
Is married late—ah, shall I say to whom?—
My master sad—for why he shames the court—
Is fled away; ah, most unhappy flight!
Only myself—ah, who can love you more!—
To show my duty,—duty past belief,—
Am come unto your grace, O gracious liege,
To let you know—O, would it were not thus!—
That love is vain and maids soon lost and won.
   K. of Scots. How have the partial heavens, then, dealt
     with me,
Boding my weal, for to abase my power!
Alas, what thronging thoughts do me oppress!
Injurious love is partial in my right,
And flattering tongues, by whom I was misled,
Have laid a snare, to spoil my state and me.
Methinks I hear my Dorothea's ghost
Howling revenge for my accursèd hate:
The ghosts of those my subjects that are slain
Pursue me, crying out, "Woe, woe to lust!"
The foe pursues me at my palace-door,
He breaks my rest, and spoils me in my camp.
Ah, flattering brood of sycophants, my foes!
First shall my dire revenge begin on you.—
I will reward thee, Andrew.

Slip. Nay, sir, if you be in your deeds of charity, remember me. I rubbed Master Ateukin's horse-heels when he rid to the meadows.

K. of Scots. And thou shalt have thy recompense for
    that.—
Lords, bear them to the prison, chain them fast,
Until we take some order for their deaths.

                                   [Lords *seize them.*

And. If so your grace in such sort give rewards,
Let me have naught; I am content to want.

Slip. Then, I pray, sir, give me all; I am as ready for a reward as an oyster for a fresh tide; spare not me, sir.

K. of Scots. Then hang them both as traitors to the
    king.

Slip. The case is altered, sir: I'll none of your gifts. What, I take a reward at your hands, master! faith, sir, no; I am a man of a better conscience.

K. of Scots. Why dally you? Go draw them hence away.

Slip. Why, alas, sir, I will go away.—I thank you, gentle friends; I pray you spare your pains: I will not trouble his honour's mastership; I'll run away.

K. of Scots. Why stay you? move me not. Let search
    be made
For vile Ateukin: whoso finds him out
Shall have five hundred marks for his reward.
Away with them, lords!

Enter OBERON *and* Antics, *and carry away* SLIPPER;
    he makes pots[1] and sports, and scorns. ANDREW
    is removed.

Troops, about my tent!
Let all our soldiers stand in battle 'ray;
For, lo, the English to their parley come.

                   [1] Grimaces.

March over bravely, first the English host, the sword
carried before the King *by* PERCY; *the Scottish*
on the other side, with all their pomp, bravely.

What seeks the King of England in this land?

    K. of Eng. False, traitorous Scot, I come for to
       revenge

My daughter's death ; I come to spoil thy wealth,
Since thou hast spoil'd me of my marriage joy ;
I come to heap thy land with carcases,
That this thy thirsty soil, chok'd up with blood,
May thunder forth revenge upon thy head ;
I come to quit thy loveless love with death :
In brief, no means of peace shall e'er be found,
Except I have my daughter or thy head.

    K. of Scots. My head, proud king ! abase thy
       pranking plumes :

So striving fondly, mayst thou catch thy grave.
But, if true judgment do direct thy course,
This lawful reason should divert the war :
Faith, not by my consent thy daughter died.

    K. of Eng. Thou liest, false Scot ! thy agents have
       confess'd it.

These are but fond delays : thou canst not think
A means to reconcile me for thy friend.
I have thy parasite's confession penn'd ;
What, then, canst thou allege in thy excuse?

    K. of Scots. I will repay the ransom for her blood.

    K. of Eng. What, think'st thou, caitiff, I will sell my
       child ?

No ; if thou be a prince and man-at-arms,
In single combat come and try thy right,
Else will I prove thee recreant to thy face.

    K. of Scots. I seek no combat, false injurious king.
But, since thou needless art inclin'd to war,

Do what thou dar'st ; we are in open field :
Arming my battle, I will fight with thee.

 K. of Eng. Agreed.—Now trumpets, sound a dreadful charge.
Fight for your princess, brave Englishmen !

 K. of Scots. Now for your lands, your children, and
  your wives,
My Scottish peers, and lastly for your king !

*Alarum sounded ; both the battles offer to meet, and just
 as the kings are joining battle, enter* SIR CUTHBERT
 ANDERSON *and* LADY ANDERSON ; *with them enters*
 QUEEN DOROTHEA, *richly attired, who stands con-*
 cealed, and NANO.

 Sir Cuth. Stay, princes, wage not war: a privy
  grudge
'Twixt such as you, most high in majesty,
Afflicts both nocent and the innocent.
How many swords, dear princes, see I drawn !
The friend against his friend, a deadly feud ;
A desperate division in those lands
Which, if they join in one, command the world.
O, stay ! with reason mitigate your rage ;
And let an old man, humbled on his knees,
Entreat a boon, good princes, of you both.

 K. of Eng. I condescend, for why thy reverend years
Import some news of truth and consequence.

 K. of Scots. I am content, for, Anderson, I know
Thou art my subject and dost mean me good.

 Sir Cuth. But by your gracious favours grant me this,
To swear upon your swords to do me right.

 K. of Eng. See, by my sword, and by a prince's faith,
In every lawful sort I am thine own.

 K. of Scots. And, by my sceptre and the Scottish
  crown,

I am resolv'd to grant thee thy request.

Sir Cuth. I see you trust me, princes, who repose
The weight of such a war upon my will.
Now mark my suit.   A tender lion's whelp,
This other day, came straggling in the woods,
Attended by a young and tender hind,
In courage haught, yet 'tirèd like a lamb.
The prince of beasts had left this young in keep,
To foster up as love-mate and compeer,
Unto the lion's mate, a neighbour-friend :
This stately guide, seducèd by the fox,
Sent forth an eager wolf, bred up in France,
That gripp'd the tender whelp and wounded it.
By chance, as I was hunting in the woods,
I heard the moan the hind made for the whelp :
I took them both, and brought them to my house.
With chary care I have recur'd the one ;
And since I know the lions are at strife
About the loss and damage of the young,
I bring her home ; make claim to her who list.

                           [*Discovers* QUEEN DOROTHEA.

Q. Dor. I am the whelp, bred by this lion up,
This royal English king, my happy sire :
Poor Nano is the hind that tended me.
My father, Scottish king, gave me to thee,
A hapless wife : thou, quite misled by youth,
Hast sought sinister loves and foreign joys.
The fox Ateukin, cursèd parasite,
Incens'd your grace to send the wolf abroad,
The French-born Jaques, for to end my days :
He, traitorous man, pursu'd me in the woods,
And left me wounded ; where this noble knight
Both rescu'd me and mine, and sav'd my life.
Now keep thy promise : Dorothea lives ;
Give Anderson his due and just reward :

And since, you kings, your wars began by me,
Since I am safe, return, surcease your fight.

  K. of Scots. Durst I presume to look upon those eyes
Which I have tirèd with a world of woes ?
Or did I think submission were enough,
Or sighs might make an entrance to thy soul,
You heavens, you know how willing I would weep ;
You heavens can tell how glad I would submit ;
You heavens can say how firmly I would sigh.

    Q. Dor. Shame me not, prince, companion in thy
        bed :
Youth hath misled,—tut, but a little fault :
'Tis kingly to amend what is amiss.
Might I with twice as many pains as these
Unite our hearts, then should my wedded lord
See how incessant labours I would take.—
My gracious father, govern your affects :
Give me that hand, that oft hath blest this head,
And clasp thine arms, that have embrac'd this [neck],
About the shoulders of my wedded spouse.
Ah, mighty prince, this king and I am one !
Spoil thou his subjects, thou despoilest me ;
Touch thou his breast, thou dost attaint this heart :
O, be my father, then, in loving him !

  K. of Eng. Thou provident kind mother of increase,
Thou must prevail ; ah, Nature, thou must rule !
Hold, daughter, join my hand and his in one ;
I will embrace him for to favour thee :
I call him friend, and take him for my son.

    Q. Dor. Ah, royal husband, see what God hath
        wrought !
Thy foe is now thy friend.—Good men-at-arms,
Do you the like.—These nations if they join,
What monarch, with his liege-men, in this world,
Dare but encounter you in open field ?

K. of Scots. All wisdom, join'd with godly piety!—
Thou English king, pardon my former youth;
And pardon, courteous queen, my great misdeed;
And, for assurance of mine after-life,
I take religious vows before my God,
To honour thee for father, her for wife.
   Sir Cuth. But yet my boons, good princes, are not
      pass'd.
First, English king, I humbly do request,
That by your means our princess may unite
Her love unto mine aldertruest love,[1]
Now you will love, maintain, and help them both.
   K. of Eng. Good Anderson, I grant thee thy request.
   Sir Cuth. But you, my prince, must yield me mickle
      more.
You know your nobles are your chiefest stays,
And long time have been banish'd from your court:
Embrace and reconcile them to yourself;
They are your hands, whereby you ought to work.
As for Ateukin and his lewd compeers,
That sooth'd you in your sins and youthly pomp,
Exile, torment, and punish such as they;
For greater vipers never may be found
Within a state than such aspiring heads,
That reck not how they climb, so that they climb.
   K. of Scots. Guid knight, I grant thy suit.—First I
      submit,
And humbly crave a pardon of your grace:—
Next, courteous queen, I pray thee by thy loves
Forgive mine errors past, and pardon me.—
My lords and princes, if I have misdone
(As I have wrong'd indeed both you and yours),
Hereafter, trust me, you are dear to me.
As for Ateukin, whoso finds the man,

     [1] Truest love of all.

Let him have martial law, and straight be hang'd,
As all his vain abettors now are dead.
And Anderson our treasurer shall pay
Three thousand marks for friendly recompense.

    Nano. But, princes, whilst you friend it thus in one,
Methinks of friendship Nano shall have none.

        Q. Dor. What would my dwarf, that I will not
           bestow?

        Nano. My boon, fair queen, is this,—that you would
           go:
Although my body is but small and neat,
My stomach, after toil, requireth meat:
An easy suit, dread princess; will you wend?

        K. of Scots. Art thou a pigmy-born, my pretty friend?

        Nano. Not so, great king, but Nature, when she
           fram'd me,
Was scant of earth, and Nano therefore nam'd me;
And, when she saw my body was so small,
She gave me wit to make it big withal.

        K. of Scots. Till time when —

        Q. Dor. Eat, then.

        K. of Scots. My friend, it stands with wit
To take repast when stomach serveth it.

        Q. Dor.[1] Thy policy, my Nano, shall prevail.—
Come, royal father, enter we my tent:—
And, soldiers, feast it, frolic it, like friends:—
My princes, bid this kind and courteous train
Partake some favours of our late accord.
Thus wars have end, and, after dreadful hate,
Men learn at last to know their good estate.

                              [*Exeunt omnes.*

---

   [1] By dramatic convention this speech should belong to the King
of Scots.

GEORGE-A-GREENE,
THE PINNER OF
WAKEFIELD

THE first Quarto of *George-a-Greene* was printed in 1599 by Simon Stafford for Cuthbert Burby. It had been entered by Burby on the Stationers' Registers four years earlier, 1st April 1595, as an interlude. Henslowe's first notice of the play occurs for 29th December 1593, at which date it was performed by Sussex' men at the Rose, these players possibly having secured the play from the Queen's players. Henslowe records five performances between 29th December 1593 and 22nd January 1594, sometimes under the major title, and sometimes under the title *The Pinner of Wakefield*. The play was reprinted in Dodsley's *Old Plays* in 1744. Neither on the title-page, nor on the Stationers' Registers, nor by Henslowe, is the name of the author mentioned. For long it was supposed that the play was by John Heywood. It was finally assigned to Greene through the discovery by Collier of a copy of the Quarto of 1599 with the following notes on the title-page :—

"Written by . . . a minister who act[ed] th[e] piñers pt in it himselfe. Teste W. Shakespea[re].

Ed. Juby saith that yᵉ play was made by Ro. Gree[ne]."

These notes are in different hands, and as against the adverse testimony of internal structure, their evidence in favour of Greene's authorship is of slight weight. With the exception of the episode of the King of Scotland and Jane a' Barley the play is founded on a romance, *The Famous History of George-a-Greene*, etc., first printed in 1706 by an editor, N. W., from a MS. now in Sion College. Whether there was a printed Elizabethan version, or the author of the play used the MS., it is now impossible to say. The romance is now reprinted in Thoms' *Early English Prose Romances*, Vol. II. In the Bodleian Library there is a black-letter romance of 1632, treating the same subject, but its story is evidently not the basis of the play. The Quarto of the play, which is owned by the Duke of Devonshire, is very poorly printed, and many scenes have been curtailed.

DRAMATIS PERSONÆ

EDWARD, King of England.
JAMES, King of Scotland.
EARL OF KENDAL.
EARL OF WARWICK.
LORD BONFIELD.
LORD HUMES.
SIR GILBERT ARMSTRONG.
SIR NICHOLAS MANNERING.
GEORGE-A-GREENE.
MUSGROVE.
CUDDY, his son.
NED-A-BARLEY.
GRIME.
ROBIN HOOD.
MUCH, the Miller's son.
SCARLET.
JENKIN, George-a-Greene's man.
WILY, George-a-Greene's boy.
JOHN.
Justice.
Townsmen, Shoemakers, Soldiers, Messengers, etc.
JANE-A-BARLEY
BETTRIS, daughter to Grime.
MAID MARIAN.

GEORGE-A-GREENE, THE PINNER[1] OF WAKEFIELD.

ACT THE FIRST

SCENE I.—*At Bradford.*

Enter the EARL OF KENDAL; *with him* LORD BONFIELD, SIR GILBERT ARMSTRONG, SIR NICHOLAS MANNERING, *and* JOHN.

KEN. Welcome to Bradford, martial
    gentlemen,
Lord Bonfield, and Sir Gilbert Arm-
    strong both;
And all my troops, even to my basest
    groom,
Courage and welcome! for the day is
ours.
Our cause is good, 'tis for the land's avail:
Then let us fight, and die for England's good.
  All. We will, my lord.

---

[1] One who impounds stray cattle.

Ken. As I am Henry Momford, Kendal's earl,
You honour me with this assent of yours;
And here upon my sword I make protest
For to relieve the poor or die myself.
And know, my lords, that James, the King of Scots,
Wars hard upon the borders of this land:
Here is his post.—Say, John Taylor, what news with
   King James?

John. War, my lord, [I] tell, and good news, I trow;
for King Jamy vows to meet you the twenty-sixth of this
month, God willing; marry, doth he, sir.

Ken. My friends, you see what we have to win.—
Well, John, commend me to King James, and tell him,
I will meet him the twenty-sixth of this month,
And all the rest; and so, farewell.   [*Exit* JOHN.
Bonfield, why stand'st thou as a man in dumps?
Courage! for, if I win, I'll make thee duke:
I, Henry Momford will be king myself;
And I will make thee Duke of Lancaster,
And Gilbert Armstrong Lord of Doncaster.

Bon. Nothing, my lord, makes me amaz'd at all,
But that our soldiers find our victuals scant.
We must make havoc of those country-swains;
For so will the rest tremble and be afraid,
And humbly send provision to your camp.

Arm. My Lord Bonfield gives good advice:
They make a scorn, and stand upon the king;
So what is brought is sent from them perforce;
Ask Mannering else.

Ken. What say'st thou, Mannering?

Man. Whenas I show'd your high commission,
They made this answer,
Only to send provision for your horses.

Ken. Well, hie thee to Wakefield, bid the town
To send me all provision that I want,

Lest I, like martial Tamburlaine, lay waste
Their bordering countries, and leaving none alive
That contradicts my commission.

Man. Let me alone ;
My lord, I'll make them vail [1] their plumes ;
For whatsoe'er he be, the proudest knight,
Justice, or other, that gainsay'th your word,
I'll clap him fast, to make the rest to fear.

Ken. Do so, Nick : hie thee thither presently,
And let us hear of thee again to-morrow.

Man. Will you not remove, my lord ?

Ken. No, I will lie at Bradford all this night
And all the next.—Come, Bonfield, let us go,
And listen out some bonny lasses here.   *[Exeunt.*

SCENE II.—*At Wakefield.*

Enter the Justice, Townsmen, GEORGE-A-GREENE, *and*
SIR NICHOLAS MANNERING *with his commission.*

Jus. Master Mannering, stand aside, whilst we confer
What is best to do.—Townsmen of Wakefield,
The Earl of Kendal here hath sent for victuals ;
And in aiding him we show ourselves no less
Than traitors to the king ; therefore
Let me hear, townsmen, what is your consents.

First Towns. Even as you please, we are all content.

Jus. Then, Master Mannering, we are resolv'd—

Man. As how ?

[1] Lower.

Jus. Marry, sir, thus.
We will send the Earl of Kendal no victuals,
Because he is a traitor to the king;
And in aiding him we show ourselves no less.

Man. Why, men of Wakefield, are you waxen
    mad,
That present danger cannot whet your wits,
Wisely to make provision of yourselves?
The earl is thirty thousand men strong in power,
And what town soever him resist,
He lays it flat and level with the ground.
Ye silly men, you seek your own decay:
Therefore send my lord such provision as he wants,
So he will spare your town,
And come no nearer Wakefield than he is.

Jus. Master Mannering, you have your answer; you
    may be gone.

Man. Well, Woodroffe, for so I guess is thy name,
I'll make thee curse thy overthwart denial;
And all that sit upon the bench this day shall rue
The hour they have withstood my lord's commission.

Jus. Do thy worst, we fear thee not.

Man. See you these seals? before you pass the town,
I will have all things my lord doth want,
In spite of you.

Geo. Proud dapper Jack, vail bonnet to the bench
That represents the person of the king;
Or, sirrah, I'll lay thy head before thy feet.

Man. Why, who art thou?

Geo. Why, I am George-a-Greene,
True liege-man to my king,
Who scorns that men of such esteem as these
Should brook the braves of any traitorous squire.
You of the bench, and you, my fellow-friends,
Neighbours, we subjects all unto the king;

We are English born, and therefore Edward's friends,
Vow'd unto him even in our mothers' womb,
Our minds to God, our hearts unto our king:
Our wealth, our homage, and our carcases,
Be all King Edward's.   Then, sirrah, we
Have nothing left for traitors, but our swords,
Whetted to bathe them in your bloods, and die
'Gainst you, before we send you any victuals.

    Jus. Well spoken, George-a-Greene!

    First Towns. Pray let George-a Greene speak for us.

    Geo. Sirrah, you get no victuals here,
Not if a hoof of beef would save your lives.

    Man. Fellow, I stand amaz'd at thy presumption.
Why, what art thou that dar'st gainsay my lord,
Knowing his mighty puissance and his stroke?
Why, my friend, I come not barely of myself;
For, see, I have a large commission.

    Geo. Let me see it, sirrah [*Takes the commission*].
        Whose seals be these?

    Man. This is the Earl of Kendal's seal-at-arms;
This Lord Charnel Bonfield's;
And this Sir Gilbert Armstrong's.

    Geo. I tell thee, sirrah, did good King Edward's son
Seal a commission 'gainst the king his father,
Thus would I tear it in despite of him,
                [*Tears the commission.*
Being traitor to my sovereign.

    Man. What, hast thou torn my lord's commission?
Thou shalt rue it, and so shall all Wakefield.

    Geo. What, are you in choler? I will give you pills
To cool your stomach.   Seest thou these seals?
Now, by my father's soul,
Which was a yeoman when he was alive,
Eat them, or eat my dagger's point, proud squire.

    Man. But thou dost but jest, I hope.

Geo. Sure that shall you see before we two part.

Man. Well, an there be no remedy, so, George :

       [*Swallows one of the seals.*

One is gone ; I pray thee, no more now.

 Geo. O, sir, if one be good, the others cannot hurt.

    [Mannering *swallows the other two seals.*

So, sir ; now you may go tell the Earl of Kendal,

Although I have rent his large commission,

Yet of courtesy I have sent all his seals

Back again by you.

 Man. Well, sir, I will do your errand.   [*Exit.*

 Geo. Now let him tell his lord that he hath spoke

With George-a-Greene,

Hight Pinner of merry Wakefield town,

That hath physic for a fool,

Pills for a traitor that doth wrong his sovereign.

Are you content with this that I have done?

 Jus. Ay, content, George ;

For highly hast thou honour'd Wakefield town

In cutting off proud Mannering so short.

Come, thou shalt be my welcome guest to-day ;

For well thou hast deserv'd reward and favour.   [*Exeunt.*

     SCENE III.—*In Westmoreland.*

     Enter Musgrove *and* Cuddy.

 Cud. Now, gentle father, list unto thy son,

And for my mother's love,

That erst was blithe and bonny in thine eye,

Grant one petition that I shall demand.

Mus. What is that, my Cuddy?

Cud. Father, you know the ancient enmity of late
Between the Musgroves and the wily Scots,
Whereof they have oath
Not to leave one alive that strides a lance.
O father, you are old, and, waning, age unto the
      grave:
Old William Musgrove, which whilom was thought
The bravest horseman in all Westmoreland,
Is weak, and forc'd to stay his arm upon a staff,
That erst could wield a lance.
Then, gentle father, resign the hold to me;
Give arms to youth, and honour unto age.

Mus. Avaunt, false-hearted boy! my joints do quake
Even with anguish of thy very words.
Hath William Musgrove seen an hundred years?
Have I been fear'd and dreaded of the Scots,
That, when they heard my name in any road,[1]
They fled away, and posted thence amain,
And shall I die with shame now in mine age?
No, Cuddy, no: thus resolve I,
Here have I liv'd, and here will Musgrove die.
                     [Exeunt.

SCENE IV.—*At Bradford.*

Enter LORD BONFIELD, SIR GILBERT ARMSTRONG,
      GRIME, *and* BETTRIS.

Bon. Now, gentle Grime, God-a-mercy for our good
    cheer;

[1] Inroad.

Our fare was royal, and our welcome great:
And sith so kindly thou hast entertain'd us,
If we return with happy victory,
We will deal as friendly with thee in recompense.

   Grime. Your welcome was but duty, gentle lord ;
For wherefore have we given us our wealth,
But   to   make   our   betters   welcome   when   they
     come ?
[*Aside*]. O, this goes hard when traitors must be
     flatter'd !
But life is sweet, and I cannot withstand it :
God, I hope, will revenge the quarrel of my king.

   Arm. What said you, Grime?
   Grime. I say, Sir Gilbert, looking on my daughter,
I curse the hour that e'er I got the girl;
For, sir, she may have many wealthy suitors,
And yet she disdains them all,
To have poor George-a-Greene unto her husband.

   Bon. On that, good Grime, I am talking with thy
     daughter ;
But she, in quirks and quiddities of love,
Sets me to school, she is so over-wise.—
But, gentle girl, if thou wilt forsake the Pinner
And be my love, I will advance thee high ;
To dignify those hairs of amber hue,
I'll grace them with a chaplet made of pearl,
Set with choice rubies, sparks, and diamonds,
Planted upon a velvet hood, to hide that head
Wherein two sapphires burn like sparkling fire :
This will I do, fair Bettris, and far more,
If thou wilt love the Lord of Doncaster.

   Bet. Heigh-ho! my heart is in a higher place,
Perhaps on the earl, if that be he.
See where he comes, or angry, or in love,
For why his colour looketh discontent.

Enter the EARL OF KENDAL *and* SIR NICHOLAS
MANNERING.

Ken. Come, Nick, follow me.

Bon. How now, my lord! what news?

Ken. Such news, Bonfield, as will make thee laugh,
And fret thy fill, to hear how Nick was us'd.
Why, the Justices stand on their terms:
Nick, as you know, is haughty in his words;
He laid the law unto the Justices
With threatening braves, that one look'd on another,
Ready to stoop; but that a churl came in,
One George-a-Greene, the Pinner of the town,
And with his dagger drawn laid hands on Nick,
And by no beggars swore that we were traitors,
Rent our commission, and upon a brave
Made Nick to eat the seals or brook the stab:
Poor Mannering, afraid, came posting hither straight.

Bet. O lovely George, fortune be still thy friend!
And as thy thoughts be high, so be thy mind
In all accords, even to thy heart's desire!

Bon. What says fair Bettris?

Grime. My lord, she is praying for George-a-Greene:
He is the man, and she will none but him.

Bon. But him! why, look on me, my girl:
Thou know'st, that yesternight I courted thee,
And swore at my return to wed with thee.
Then tell me, love, shall I have all thy fair?

Bet. I care not for earl, nor yet for knight,
Nor baron that is so bold;
For George-a-Greene, the merry Pinner,
He hath my heart in hold.[1]

---

[1] In ballad style, though not found in the ballad " The Jolly Pinder of Wakefield."

Bon. Bootless, my lord, are many vain replies:
Let us hie us to Wakefield, and send her the Pinner's
      head.

Ken. It shall be so.—Grime, gramercy,
Shut up thy daughter, bridle her affects;[1]
Let me not miss her when I make return;
Therefore look to her, as to thy life, good Grime.

Grime. I warrant you, my lord.

Ken. And, Bettris,
Leave a base Pinner, for to love an earl.

              [*Exeunt* GRIME *and* BETTRIS.

Fain would I see this Pinner George-a-Greene.
It shall be thus:
Nick Mannering shall lead on the battle,
And we three will go to Wakefield in some disguise:
But howsoever, I'll have his head to-day.   [*Exeunt.*

         [1] Affections.

ACT THE SECOND

SCENE I.—*Before* SIR JOHN-A-BARLEY'S
Castle.

Enter JAMES, KING OF SCOTS, LORD HUMES, *with*
Soldiers, *and* JOHN.

JAMES. Why, Johnny, then the Earl
of Kendal is blithe,
And hath brave men that troop
along with him?
John. Ay, marry, my liege,
And hath good men that come
along with him,
And vows to meet you at Scrasblesea, God willing.
K. James. If good Saint Andrew lend King Jamy
leave,
I will be with him at the 'pointed day.

Enter NED.

But, soft!—Whose pretty boy art thou?
Ned. Sir, I am son unto Sir John-a-Barley,
Eldest, and all that e'er my mother had;
Edward my name.

K. James. And whither art thou going, pretty Ned?

Ned. To seek some birds, and kill them, if I can:
And now my schoolmaster is also gone,
So have I liberty to ply my bow;
For when he comes, I stir not from my book.

K. James. Lord Humes, but mark the visage of this
     child:
By him I guess the beauty of his mother;
None but Leda could breed Helena.——
Tell me, Ned, who is within with thy mother?

Ned. Naught but herself and household servants, sir:
If you would speak with her, knock at this gate.

K. James. Johnny, knock at that gate.

                         [JOHN *knocks at the gate.*

Enter JANE-A-BARLEY *upon the walls.*

Jane. O, I'm betray'd! What multitudes be these?

K. James. Fear not, fair Jane, for all these men are
     mine,
And all thy friends, if thou be friend to me:
I am thy lover, James the King of Scots,
That oft have su'd and woo'd with many letters,
Painting my outward passions with my pen,
Whenas my inward soul did bleed for woe.
Little regard was given to my suit;
But haply thy husband's presence wrought it:
Therefore, sweet Jane, I fitted me to time,
And, hearing that thy husband was from home,
Am come to crave what long I have desir'd.

Ned. Nay, soft you, sir! you get no entrance here,
That seek to wrong Sir John-a-Barley so,
And offer such dishonour to my mother.

K. James. Why, what dishonour, Ned?

Ned. Though young,
Yet often have I heard my father say,

No greater wrong than to be made cuckold.
Were I of age, or were my body strong,
Were he ten kings, I would shoot him to the heart
That should attempt to give Sir John the horn.—
Mother, let him not come in:
I will go lie at Jocky Miller's house.

    K. James. Stay him.

    Jane. Ay, well said; Ned, thou hast given the king
        his answer;
For were the ghost of Cæsar on the earth,
Wrapp'd in the wonted glòry of his honour,
He should not make me wrong my husband so.
But good King James is pleasant, as I guess,
And means to try what humour I am in;
Else would he never have brought an host of men,
To have them witness of his Scottish lust.

    K. James. Jane, in faith, Jane,—

    Jane. Never reply,
For I protest by the highest holy God,
That doometh just revenge for things amiss,
King James, of all men, shall not have my love.

    K. James. Then list to me: Saint Andrew be my
        boot,
But I'll raze thy castle to the very ground,
Unless thou open the gate, and let me in.

    Jane. I fear thee not, King Jamy: do thy worst.
This castle is too strong for thee to scale;
Besides, to-morrow will Sir John come home.

    K. James. Well, Jane, since thou disdain'st King
        James's love,
I'll draw thee on with sharp and deep extremes;
For, by my father's soul, this brat of thine
Shall perish here before thine eyes,
Unless thou open the gate, and let me in.

    Jane. O deep extremes! my heart begins to break:

My little Ned looks pale for fear.—
Cheer thee, my boy, I will do much for thee.
   Ned. But not so much as to dishonour me.
   Jane. An if thou diest, I cannot live, sweet Ned.
   Ned. Then die with honour, mother, dying chaste.
   Jane. I am armed :
My husband's love, his honour, and his fame,
Join[1] victory by virtue.   Now, King James,
If mother's tears cannot allay thine ire,
Then butcher him, for I will never yield :
The son shall die before I wrong the father.
   K. James. Why, then, he dies.

     Alarum within.   Enter a Messenger.

   Mess. My lord, Musgrove is at hand.
   K. James. Who, Musgrove ?   The devil he is !   Come,
     my horse !   [*Exeunt.*

SCENE II.—*The Same.*

Enter MUSGROVE *with* KING JAMES *prisoner ;* JANE-A-
           BARLEY *on the walls.*

  Mus. Now, King James, thou art my prisoner.
   K. James. Not thine, but fortune's prisoner.

        Enter CUDDY.

   Cud. Father, the field is ours : their colours we have
     seiz'd,
And Humes is slain ; I slew him hand to hand.
   Mus. God and Saint George !
   Cud. O father, I am sore athirst !

       [1] For " enjoin."

Jane. Come in, young Cuddy, come and drink thy fill :
Bring in King Jamy with you as a guest ;
For all this broil was 'cause he could not enter.

> [*Exit above.—Exeunt below, the others.*

SCENE III.—*At Wakefield.*

Enter GEORGE-A-GREENE.

Geo. The sweet content of men that live in love
Breeds fretting humours in a restless mind ;
And fancy, being check'd by fortune's spite,
Grows too impatient in her sweet desires ;
Sweet to those men whom love leads on to bliss,
But sour to me whose hap is still amiss.

Enter JENKIN.

Jen. Marry, amen, sir.

Geo. Sir, what do you cry "amen" at?

Jen. Why, did not you talk of love?

Geo. How do you know that?

Jen. Well, though I say it that should not say it, there are few fellows in our parish so nettled with love as I have been of late.

Geo. Sirrah, I thought no less, when the other morning you rose so early to go to your wenches. Sir, I had thought you had gone about my honest business.

Jen. Trow, you have hit it ; for, master, be it known to you, there is some good-will betwixt Madge the souce-wife[1] and I ; marry, she hath another lover.

---

[1] A woman who sells "souce" or brine for pickling.

2 D

Geo. Can'st thou brook any rivals in thy love?

Jen. A rider! no, he is a sow-gelder and goes afoot.
But Madge 'pointed to meet me in your wheat-close.

Geo. Well, did she meet you there?

Jen. Never make question of that.   And first I saluted
her with a green gown, and after fell as hard a-wooing as
if the priest had been at our backs to have married us.

Geo. What, did she grant?

Jen. Did she grant! never make question of that.
And she gave me a shirt-collar wrought over with no
counterfeit stuff.

Geo. What, was it gold?

Jen. Nay, 'twas better than gold.

Geo. What was it?

Jen. Right Coventry blue.   We had no sooner come
there but wot you who came by?

Geo. No: who?

Jen. Clim the sow-gelder.

Geo. Came he by?

Jen. He spied Madge and I sit together: he leapt
from his horse, laid his hand on his dagger, and began
to swear.   Now I seeing he had a dagger, and I nothing
but this twig in my hand, I gave him fair words and said
nothing.   He comes to me, and takes me by the bosom.
"You whoreson slave," said he, "hold my horse, and
look he take no cold in his feet."   "No, marry, shall
he, sir," quoth I; "I'll lay my cloak underneath him."
I took my cloak, spread it all along, and his horse on
the midst of it.

Geo. Thou clown, didst thou set his horse upon thy
cloak?

Jen. Ay, but mark how I served him.   Madge and he
was no sooner gone down into the ditch, but I plucked
out my knife, cut four holes in my cloak, and made his
horse stand on the bare ground.

Geo. 'Twas well done. Now, sir, go and survey my fields: if you find any cattle in the corn, to pound with them.

Jen. And if I find any in the pound, I shall turn them out.   [*Exit.*

Enter the EARL OF KENDAL, LORD BONFIELD, SIR
    GILBERT ARMSTRONG, *all disguised, with a train
    of men.*

Ken. Now we have put the horses in the corn,
Let us stand in some corner for to hear
What braving terms the Pinner will breathe
When he spies our horses in the corn.

[*Retires with the others.*

Re-enter JENKIN *blowing his horn.*

Jen. O master, where are you? we have a prize.

Geo. A prize! what is it?

Jen. Three goodly horses in our wheat-close.

Geo. Three horses in our wheat-close! whose be they?

Jen. Marry, that's a riddle to me; but they are there; velvet [1] horses, and I never saw such horses before. As my duty was, I put off my cap, and said as followeth: "My masters, what do you make in our close?" One of them, hearing me ask what he made there, held up his head and neighed, and after his manner laughed as heartily as if a mare had been tied to his girdle. "My masters," said I, "it is no laughing matter; for, if my master take you here, you go as round as a top to the pound." Another untoward jade, hearing me threaten him to the pound and to tell you of them, cast up both his heels, and let such a monstrous great fart, that was as much as in his language to say, "A fart for

[1] "Allusions to velvet as being costly, fine, and luxurious are very common in the Elizabethan writers."—COLLINS.

the pound, and a fart for George-a-Greene!" Now I,
hearing this, put on my cap, blew my horn, called them
all jades, and came to tell you.

Geo. Now, sir, go and drive me those three horses to
the pound.

Jen. Do you hear? I were best to take a constable
with me.

Geo. Why so?

Jen. Why, they, being gentlemen's horses, may stand
on their reputation, and will not obey me.

Geo. Go, do as I bid you, sir.

Jen. Well, I may go.

The EARL OF KENDAL, LORD BONFIELD, *and*
SIR GILBERT ARMSTRONG *come forward.*

Ken. Whither away, sir?

Jen. Whither away! I am going to put the horses in
　　the pound.

Ken. Sirrah, those three horses belong to us,
And we put them in,
And they must tarry there and eat their fill.

Jen. Stay, I will go tell my master.—Hear you,
master? we have another prize : those three horses be
in your wheat-close still, and here be three geldings more.

Geo. What be these?

Jen. These are the masters of the horses.

Geo. Now, gentlemen (I know not your degrees,
But more you cannot be, unless you be kings,)
Why wrong you us of Wakefield with your horses?
I am the Pinner, and, before you pass,
You shall make good the trespass they have done.

Ken. Peace, saucy mate, prate not to us :
I tell thee, Pinner, we are gentlemen.

Geo. Why, sir, so may I, sir, although I give no arms.

Ken. Thou! how art thou a gentleman?

Jen. And such is my master, and he may give as good
arms as ever your great-grandfather could give.

Ken. Pray thee, let me hear how.

Jen. Marry, my master may give for his arms the
picture of April in a green jerkin, with a rook on one
fist and an horn on the other: but my master gives
his arms the wrong way, for he gives the horn on
his fist; and your grandfather, because he would not
lose his arms, wears the horn on his own head.

Ken. Well, Pinner, sith our horses be in,
In spite of thee they now shall feed their fill,
And eat until our leisures serve to go.

Geo. Now, by my father's soul,
Were good King Edward's horses in the corn,
They shall amend the scath, or kiss the pound;
Much more yours, sir, whatsoe'er you be.

Ken. Why, man, thou knowest not us:
We do belong to Henry Momford, Earl of Kendal;
Men that, before a month be full expir'd,
Will be King Edward's betters in the land.

Geo. King Edward's betters! Rebel, thou liest!
[*Strikes him.*

Bon. Villain, what hast thou done? thou hast
struck an earl.

Geo. Why, what care I? a poor man that is true,
Is better than an earl, if he be false.
Traitors reap no better favours at my hands.

Ken. Ay, so methinks; but thou shalt dear aby ¹ this
blow.—
Now or never lay hold on the Pinner!

All the train comes forward.

Geo. Stay, my lords, let us parley on these broils:

¹ Pay the penalty for.

Not Hercules against two, the proverb is,
Nor I against so great a multitude.—
[*Aside*].   Had not your troops come marching as they
        did,
I would have stopt your passage unto London:
But now I'll fly to secret policy.
    Ken. What dost thou murmur, George?
    Geo. Marry, this, my lord; I muse,
If thou be Henry Momford, Kendal's earl,
That thou wilt do poor George-a-Greene this wrong,
Ever to match me with a troop of men.
    Ken. Why dost thou strike me, then?
    Geo. Why, my lord, measure me but by yourself:
Had you a man had serv'd you long,
And heard your foe misuse you behind your back,
And would not draw his sword in your defence,
You would cashier him.
Much more, King Edward is my king:
And before I'll hear him so wrong'd,
I'll die within this place,
And maintain good whatsoever I have said.
And, if I speak not reason in this case,
What I have said I'll maintain in this place.
    Bon. A pardon, my lord, for this Pinner;
For, trust me, he speaketh like a man of worth.
    Ken. Well, George, wilt thou leave Wakefield and
        wend with me,
I'll freely put up all and pardon thee.
    Geo. Ay, my lord, considering me one thing,
You will leave these arms, and follow your good king.
    Ken. Why, George, I rise not against King Edward,
But for the poor that is oppress'd by wrong;
And, if King Edward will redress the same,
I will not offer him disparagement,
But otherwise; and so let this suffice.

Thou hear'st the reason why I rise in arms :
Now, wilt thou leave Wakefield and wend with me,
I'll make thee captain of a hardy band,
And, when I have my will, dub thee a knight.

Geo. Why, my lord, have you any hope to win?

Ken. Why, there is a prophecy doth say,
That King James and I shall meet at London,
And make the king vail bonnet to us both.

Geo. If this were true, my lord, this were a mighty
reason.

Ken. Why, it is a miraculous prophecy, and cannot
fail.

Geo. Well, my lord, you have almost turned me.—
Jenkin, come hither.

Jen. Sir ?

Geo. Go your ways home, sir,
And drive me those three horses home unto my
house,
And pour them down a bushel of good oats.

Jen. Well, I will.—[*Aside*]. Must I give these scurvy
horses oats?   [*Exit.*

Geo. Will it please you to command your train
aside ?

Ken. Stand aside.   [*The train retires.*

Geo. Now list to me :
Here in a wood, not far from hence,
There dwells an old man in a cave alone,
That can foretell what fortunes shall befall you,
For he is greatly skilful in magic art.
Go you three to him early in the morning,
And question him : if he says good,
Why, then, my lord, I am the foremost man
Who will march up with your camp to London.

Ken. George, thou honourest me in this. But where
shall we find him out?

Geo. My man shall conduct you to the place ;
But, good my lord, tell me true what the wise man saith.

Ken. That will I, as I am Earl of Kendal.

Geo. Why, then, to honour George a-Greene the more,
Vouchsafe a piece of beef at my poor house ;
You shall have wafer-cakes your fill,
A piece of beef hung up since Martlemas :
If that like you not, take what you bring, for me.

Ken. Gramercies, George.   [*Exeunt.*

ACT THE THIRD

SCENE I.—*Before* GRIME'S *house in Bradford.*

Enter GEORGE-A-GREENE'S *boy* WILY, *disguised as a woman.*

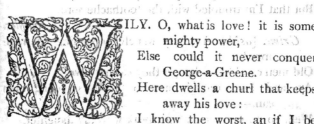

WILY. O, what is love! it is some
mighty power,
Else could it never conquer
George-a-Greene.
Here dwells a churl that keeps
away his love :
I know the worst, an if I be
espied,
'Tis but a beating ; and if I by this means
Can get fair Bettris forth her father's door,
It is enough.
Venus, for me, of all the gods alone,
Be aiding to my wily enterprise ! [*Knocks at the door.*

Enter GRIME *as from the house.*

Grime. How now! who knocks there? what would
you have?
From whence came you? where do you dwell?

425

Wily. I am, forsooth, a sempster's maid hard by,
That hath brought work home to your daughter.

  Grime. Nay, are you not
Some crafty quean that comes from George-a-Greene,
That rascal, with some letters to my daughter?
I will have you search'd.

  Wily. Alas, sir, it is Hebrew unto me,
To tell me of George-a-Greene or any other!
Search me, good sir, and if you find a letter
About me, let me have the punishment that's due.

  Grime. Why are you muffled? I like you the worse
    for that.

  Wily. I am not, sir, asham'd to show my face;
Yet loth I am my cheeks should take the air:
Not that I'm chary of my beauty's hue,
But that I'm troubled with the toothache sore.

                                    [*Unmuffles.*

  Grime. [*aside*]. A pretty wench, of smiling counten-
    ance!
Old men can like, although they cannot love;
Ay, and love, though not so brief as young men
    can.—
Well, go in, my wench, and speak with my daughter.

                    [*Exit* WILY *into the house.*

I wonder much at the Earl of Kendal,
Being a mighty man, as still he is,
Yet for to be a traitor to his king,
Is more than God or man will well allow.
But what a fool am I to talk of him!
My mind is more here of the pretty lass.
Had she brought some forty pounds to town,
I could be content to make her my wife:
Yet I have heard it in a proverb said,
He that is old and marries with a lass,
Lies but at home, and proves himself an ass.

Enter, from the house, BETTRIS *in* WILY'S *apparel.*

How now, my wench! how is't? what, not a word?—
Alas, poor soul, the toothache plagues her sore.—
Well, my wench,
Here is an angel for to buy thee pins,   [*Gives money.*
And I pray thee use mine house;
The oftener, the more welcome: farewell.   [*Exit.*

   Bet. O blessèd love, and blessèd fortune both!
But, Bettris, stand not here to talk of love,
But hie thee straight unto thy George-a-Greene:
Never went roebuck swifter on the downs
Than I will trip it till I see my George.   [*Exit.*

SCENE II.—*A Wood near Wakefield.*

Enter the EARL OF KENDAL, LORD BONFIELD, SIR
GILBERT ARMSTRONG, *and* JENKIN.

   Ken. Come away, Jenkin.
   Jen. Come, here is his house. [*Knocks at the door.*]
      —Where be you, ho?
   Geo. [*within*]. Who knocks there?
   Ken. Here are two or three poor men, father, would
speak with you.
   Geo. [*within*]. Pray, give your man leave to lead me
forth.
   Ken. Go, Jenkin, fetch him forth.
      [JENKIN *leads forth* GEORGE-A-GREENE *disguised.*
   Jen. Come, old man.

Ken. Father, here are three poor men come to question thee
A word in secret that concerns their lives.

Geo. Say on, my sons.

Ken. Father, I am sure you hear the news, how that
The Earl of Kendal wars against the king.
Now, father, we three are gentlemen by birth,
But younger brethren that want revenues,
And for the hope we have to be preferr'd,
If that we knew that we shall win,
We will march with him : if not,
We will not march a foot to London more.
Therefore, good father, tell us what shall happen,
Whether the king or the Earl of Kendal shall win.

Geo. The king, my son.

Ken. Art thou sure of that ?

Geo. Ay, as sure as thou art Henry Momford,
The one Lord Bonfield, the other Sir Gilbert [Armstrong].

Ken. Why, this is wondrous, being blind of sight,
His deep perceiverance should be such to know us.

Arm. Magic is mighty and foretelleth great matters.——
Indeed, father, here is the earl come to see thee,
And therefore, good father, fable not with him.

Geo. Welcome is the earl to my poor cell,
And so are you, my lords ; but let me counsel you
To leave these wars against your king, and live in quiet.

Ken. Father, we come not for advice in war,
But to know whether we shall win or leese.[1]

Geo. Lose, gentle lords, but not by good King
Edward ;
A baser man shall give you all the foil.

Ken. Ay, marry, father, what man is that ?

Geo. Poor George-a-Greene, the Pinner.

Ken. What shall he ?

---

[1] Lose.

Geo. Pull all your plumes, and sore dishonour you.

Ken. He! as how?

Geo. Nay, the end tries all; but so it will fall out.

Ken. But so it shall not, by my honour Christ.
I'll raise my camp, and fire Wakefield town,
And take that servile Pinner George-a-Greene,
And butcher him before King Edward's face.

Geo. Good my lord, be not offended,
For I speak no more than art reveals to me:
And for greater proof,
Give your man leave to fetch me my staff.

Ken. Jenkin, fetch him his walking-staff.

Jen. [*giving it.*] Here is your walking-staff.

Geo. I'll prove it good upon your carcases;
A wiser wizard never met you yet,
Nor one that better could foredoom your fall.
Now I have singled you here alone,
I care not though you be three to one.

Ken. Villain, hast thou betray'd us?

Geo. Momford, thou liest, ne'er was I traitor yet;
Only devis'd this guile to draw you on
For to be combatants.
Now conquer me, and then march on to London:
It shall go hard but I will hold you task.

Arm. Come, my lord, cheerly, I'll kill him hand to
hand.

Ken. A thousand pound to him that strikes that
stroke!

Geo. Then give it me, for I will have the first.

        [*Here they fight;* GEORGE *kills* SIR GILBERT
           ARMSTRONG, *and takes the other two
           prisoners.*

Bon. Stay, George, we do appeal.

Geo. To whom?

Bon. Why, to the king:

For rather had we bide what he appoints,
Then here be murder'd by a servile groom.

Ken. What wilt thou do with us?

Geo. Even as Lord Bonfield wish'd,
You shall unto the king : and, for that purpose,
See where the Justice is plac'd.

Enter Justice.

Jus. Now, my Lord of Kendal, where be all your
threats ?
Even as the cause, so is the combat fallen,
Else one could never have conquer'd three.

Ken. I pray thee, Woodroffe, do not twit me ;
If I have faulted, I must make amends.

Geo. Master Woodroffe, here is not a place for many
words :
I beseech ye, sir, discharge all his soldiers,
That every man may go home unto his own house.

Jus. It shall be so. What wilt thou do, George ?

Geo. Master Woodroffe, look to your charge ;
Leave me to myself.

Jus. Come, my lords.

[*Exeunt all except* GEORGE.

SCENE III.—*A Wood near Wakefield.*

GEORGE-A-GREENE *discovered.*[1]

Geo. Here sit thou, George, wearing a willow wreath,
As one despairing of thy beauteous love :
Fie, George ! no more ;

[1] Here the scene may be supposed to have changed, although
George has not left the stage. In the quarto the scene runs on
without break.

Pine not away for that which cannot be.
I cannot joy in any earthly bliss,
So long as I do want my Bettris.

Enter JENKIN.

Jen. Who see a master of mine?

Geo. How now, sirrah! whither away?

Jen. Whither away! why, who do you take me to be?

Geo. Why, Jenkin, my man.

Jen. I was so once indeed, but now the case is altered.

Geo. I pray thee, as how?

Jen. Were not you a fortune-teller to-day?

Geo. Well, what of that?

Jen. So sure am I become a juggler. What will you say if I juggle your sweetheart?

Geo. Peace, prating losel! her jealous father
Doth wait o'er her with such suspicious eyes,
That, if a man but dally by her feet,
He thinks it straight a witch to charm his daughter.

Jen. Well, what will you give me, if I bring her hither?

Geo A suit of green, and twenty crowns besides.

Jen. Well, by your leave, give me room. You must give me something that you have lately worn.

Geo. Here is a gown, will that serve you?

[*Gives gown.*

Jen Ay, this will serve me. Keep out of my circle, lest you be torn in pieces by she-devils.—Mistress Bettris, once, twice, thrice!

[JENKIN *throws the gown in, and* BETTRIS *comes out.*[1]
O, is this no cunning?

Geo. Is this my love, or is it but her shadow?

Jen. Ay, this is the shadow, but here is the substance.

[1] Through a door at the back of the stage.

Geo. Tell me, sweet love, what good fortune brought
    thee hither?
For one it was that favour'd George-a-Greene.

Bet. Both love and fortune brought me to my George,
In whose sweet sight is all my heart's content.

Geo. Tell me, sweet love, how cam'st thou from thy
    father's?

Bet. A willing mind hath many slips in love:
It was not I, but Wily, thy sweet boy.

Geo. And where is Wily now?

Bet. In my apparel, in my chamber still.

Geo. Jenkin, come hither: go to Bradford,
And listen out your fellow Wily.—
Come, Bettris, let us in,
And in my cottage we will sit and talk.

                [Exeunt.

ACT THE FOURTH

SCENE I.—*Camp of* KING EDWARD.

Enter KING EDWARD, JAMES, KING OF SCOTS,
LORD WARWICK, CUDDY, *and* Train.

 EDW. Brother of Scotland, I do
　　　 hold it hard,
　　　Seeing a league of truce was late
　　　　confirm'd
　　　'Twixt you and me, without dis-
　　　　pleasure offer'd
　　　You should make such invasion in
　　　　my land.
The vows of kings should be as oracles,
Not blemish'd with the stain of any breach;
Chiefly where fealty and homage willeth it.

　K. James. Brother of England, rub not the sore afresh;
My conscience grieves me for my deep misdeed.
I have the worst; of thirty thousand men,
There 'scap'd not full five thousand from the field.

　K. Edw. Gramercy, Musgrove, else it had gone hard:
Cuddy, I'll quite thee well ere we two part.

K. James. But had not his old father, William
    Musgrove,
Play'd twice the man, I had not now been here.
A stronger man I seldom felt before ;
But one of more resolute valiance,
Treads not, I think, upon the English ground.

  K. Edw. I wot well, Musgrove shall not lose his
    hire.

  Cud. An it please your grace, my father was
Five-score and three at midsummer last past :
Yet had King Jamy been as good as George-a-Greene,
Yet Billy Musgrove would have fought with him.

  K. Edw. As George-a-Greene !
I pray thee, Cuddy, let me question thee.
Much have I heard, since I came to my crown,
Many in manner of a proverb say,
"Were he as good as George-a-Greene, I would strike
    him sure : "
I pray thee, tell me, Cuddy, canst thou inform me,
What is that George-a-Greene ?

  Cud. Know, my lord, I never saw the man,
But mickle talk is of him in the country :
They say he is the Pinner of Wakefield town :
But for his other qualities, I let alone.

  War. May it please your grace, I know the man
    too well.

  K. Edw. Too well ! why so, Warwick ?

  War. For once he swing'd me till my bones did
    ache.

  K. Edw. Why, dares he strike an earl ?

  War. An earl, my lord ! nay, he will strike a king,
Be it not King Edward. For stature he is fram'd
Like to the picture of stout Hercules,
And for his carriage passeth Robin Hood.
The boldest earl or baron of your land,

That offereth scath unto the town of Wakefield,
George will arrest his pledge unto the pound ;
And whoso resisteth bears away the blows,
For he himself is good enough for three.

   K. Edw. Why, this is wondrous : my Lord of Warwick,
Sore do I long to see this George-a-Greene.
But leaving him, what shall we do, my lord,
For to subdue the rebels in the north ?
They are now marching up to Doncaster.—

   Enter one with the EARL OF KENDAL *prisoner.*

Soft ! who have we there ?
   Cud. Here is a traitor, the Earl of Kendal.
   K. Edw. Aspiring traitor ! how darest thou
Once cast thine eyes upon thy sovereign
That honour'd thee with kindness, and with favour?
But I will make thee buy this treason dear.
   Ken. Good my lord,—
   K. Edw. Reply not, traitor.—
Tell me, Cuddy, whose deed of honour
Won the victory against this rebel ?
   Cud. George-a-Greene, the Pinner of Wakefield.
   K. Edw. George-a-Greene ! now shall I hear news
Certain, what this Pinner is.
Discourse it briefly, Cuddy, how it befell.
   Cud. Kendal and Bonfield, with Sir Gilbert
      Armstrong,
Came to Wakefield town disguis'd,
And there spoke ill of your grace ;
Which George but hearing, fell'd them at his feet,
And, had not rescue come into the place,
George had slain them in his close of wheat.
   K. Edw. But, Cuddy,
Canst thou not tell where I might give and grant

Something that might please
And highly gratify the Pinner's thoughts ?

Cud. This at their parting George did say to me :
" If the king vouchsafe of this my service,
Then, gentle Cuddy, kneel upon thy knee,
And humbly crave a boon of him for me."

K. Edw. Cuddy, what is it ?

Cud. It is his will your grace would pardon them,
And let them live, although they have offended.

K. Edw. I think the man striveth to be glorious.
Well, George hath crav'd it, and it shall be granted,
Which none but he in England should have gotten.—
Live, Kendal, but as prisoner,
So shalt thou end thy days within the Tower.

Ken. Gracious is Edward to offending subjects.

K. James. My Lord of Kendal, you're welcome to the
    court.

K. Edw. Nay, but ill-come as it falls out now ;
Ay, ill-come indeed, were't not for George-a-Greene.
But, gentle king, for so you would aver,
And Edward's betters, I salute you both,
And here I vow by good Saint George,
You'll gain but little when your sums are counted.
I sore do long to see this George-a-Greene :
And for because I never saw the north,
I will forthwith go see it ;
And for that to none I will be known, we will
Disguise ourselves and steal down secretly,
Thou and I, King James, Cuddy, and two or three,
And make a merry journey for a month.—
Away, then, conduct him to the Tower.—
Come on, King James, my heart must needs be merry,
If fortune makes such havoc of our foes.   [*Exeunt.*

SCENE II.—Robin Hood's *Retreat.*

Enter Robin Hood, Maid Marian, Scarlet,
and Much.

Rob. Why is not lovely Marian blithe of cheer?
What ails my leman,[1] that she gins to lour?
Say, good Marian, why art thou so sad?

Mar. Nothing, my Robin, grieves me to the heart
But, whensoever I do walk abroad,
I hear no songs but all of George-a-Greene;
Bettris, his fair leman, passeth me:
And this, my Robin, galls my very soul.

Rob. Content: what recks it us though George-a-
        Greene be stout,
So long as he doth proffer us no scath?
Envy doth seldom hurt but to itself;
And therefore, Marian, smile upon thy Robin.

Mar. Never will Marian smile upon her Robin,
Nor lie with him under the greenwood shade,
Till that thou go to Wakefield on a green,
And beat the Pinner for the love of me.

Rob. Content thee, Marian, I will ease thy grief,
My merry men and I will thither stray;
And here I vow that, for the love of thee,
I will beat George-a-Greene, or he shall beat me.

Scar. As I am Scarlet, next to Little John,
One of the boldest yeomen of the crew,
So will I wend with Robin all along,
And try this Pinner what he dares do.

Much. As I am Much, the miller's son,
That left my mill to go with thee,
And nill repent that I have done,

                    [1] Love.

This pleasant life contenteth me ;
In aught I may, to do thee good,
I'll live and die with Robin Hood.

Mar. And, Robin, Marian she will go with thee,
To see fair Bettris how bright she is of blee.[1]

Rob. Marian, thou shalt go with thy Robin.—
Bend up your bows, and see your strings be tight,
The arrows keen, and everything be ready,
And each of you a good bat on his neck,
Able to lay a good man on the ground.

Scar. I will have Friar Tuck's.

Much. I will have Little John's.

Rob. I will have one made of an ashen plank,
Able to bear a bout or two.—
Then come on, Marian, let us go ;
For before the sun doth show the morning day,
I will be at Wakefield to see this Pinner, George-a-
    Greene.   [*Exeunt*

SCENE III.—*At Bradford.*

A Shoemaker *discovered at work : enter* JENKIN,
    carrying a staff.[2]

Jen. My masters, he that hath neither meat nor
money, and hath lost his credit with the alewife, for
anything I know, may go supperless to bed.—But, soft !
who is here ? here is a shoemaker ; he knows where is
the best ale.—Shoemaker, I pray thee tell me, where is
the best ale in the town ?

---

[1] Colour, complexion.
[2] The stage direction in the quarto is : Enter a Shoemaker sitting
upon the stage at work : Jenkin to him.

Shoe. Afore, afore, follow thy nose ; at the sign of the Egg-shell.

Jen. Come, shoemaker, if thou wilt, and take thy part of a pot.

Shoe. [*coming forward*]. Sirrah, down with your staff, down with your staff.

Jen. Why, how now ! is the fellow mad ? I pray thee tell me, why should I hold down my staff ?

Shoe. You will down with him, will you not, sir ?

Jen. Why, tell me wherefore ?

Shoe. My friend, this is the town of merry Bradford, and here is a custom held, that none shall pass with his staff on his shoulders but he must have a bout with me ; and so shall you, sir.

Jen. And so will I not, sir.

Shoe. That will I try. Barking dogs bite not the sorest.

Jen. [*aside*]. I would to God I were once well rid of him.

Shoe. Now, what, will you down with your staff ?

Jen. Why, you are not in earnest, are you ?

Shoe. If I am not, take that. [*Strikes him.*

Jen. You whoreson, cowardly scab, it is but the part of a clapperdudgeon [1] to strike a man in the street. But darest thou walk to the town's end with me ?

Shoe. Ay, that I dare do ; but stay till I lay in my tools, and I will go with thee to the town's end presently.

Jen. [*aside*]. I would I knew how to be rid of this fellow.

Shoe. Come, sir, will you go to the town's end now, sir ?

Jen. Ay, sir, come.—

[*Scene changes to the town's end*].

Now we are at the town's end, what say you now ?

Shoe. Marry, come, let us even have a bout.

[1] Beggar.

Jen. Ha, stay a little; hold thy hands, I pray thee.

Shoe. Why, what's the matter?

Jen. Faith, I am Under-pinner of a town, and there is an order, which if I do not keep, I shall be turned out of mine office.

Shoe. What is that, sir?

Jen. Whensoever I go to fight with anybody, I use to flourish my staff thrice about my head before I strike, and then show no favour.

Shoe. Well, sir, and till then I will not strike thee.

Jen. Well, sir, here is once, twice:—here is my hand, I will never do it the third time.

Shoe. Why, then, I see we shall not fight.

Jen. Faith, no: come, I will give thee two pots of the best ale, and be friends.

Shoe. [*aside*]. Faith, I see it is as hard to get water out of a flint as to get him to have a bout with me: therefore I will enter into him for some good cheer.—My friend, I see thou art a faint-hearted fellow, thou hast no stomach to fight, therefore let us go to the ale-house and drink.

Jen. Well, content: go thy ways, and say thy prayers, thou 'scapest my hands to-day. [*Exeunt.*

SCENE IV.—*At Wakefield.*

Enter GEORGE-A-GREENE *and* BETTRIS.

Geo. Tell me, sweet love, how is thy mind content?
What, canst thou brook to live with George-a-Greene?

Bet. O, George, how little pleasing are these words!
Came I from Bradford for the love of thee,
And left my father for so sweet a friend?
Here will I live until my life do end.

Geo. Happy am I to have so sweet a love.—
But what are these come tracing here along?
　Bet. Three men come striking through the corn, my
　　love.

Enter ROBIN HOOD, MAID MARIAN, SCARLET *and*
　　　　　　　　　　MUCH.

　Geo. Back again, you foolish travellers,
For you are wrong, and may not wend this way.
　Rob. That were great shame.　Now, by my soul, proud
　　sir,
We be three tall [1] yeomen, and thou art but one.—
Come, we will forward in despite of him.
　Geo. Leap the ditch, or I will make you skip.
What, cannot the highway serve your turn,
But you must make a path over the corn?
　Rob. Why, art thou mad? dar'st thou encounter three?
We are no babes, man, look upon our limbs.
　Geo. Sirrah, the biggest limbs have not the stoutest
　　hearts.
Were ye as good as Robin Hood and his three merry
　　men,
I'll drive you back the same way that ye came..
Be ye men, ye scorn to encounter me all at once;
But be ye cowards, set upon me all three,
And try the Pinner what he dares perform.
　Scar. Were thou as high in deeds
As thou art haughty in words,
Thou well might'st be a champion for the king:
But empty vessels have the loudest sounds,
And cowards prattle more than men of worth.
　Geo. Sirrah, darest thou try me?
　Scar. Ay, sirrah, that I dare.
　　　　　[*They fight, and* GEORGE-A-GREENE *beats him.*
　　　　　　　　[1] Bold, brave.

Much. How now! what, art thou down?——
Come, sir, I am next.

       [They fight, and GEORGE-A-GREENE *beats him.*

  Rob. Come, sirrah, now to me: spare me not,
For I'll not spare thee.

  Geo. Make no doubt I will be as liberal to thee.

           [They fight; ROBIN HOOD *stays.*

  Rob. Stay, George, for here I do protest,
Thou art the stoutest champion that ever I
Laid hands upon.

  Geo. Soft, you sir! by your leave, you lie ;
You never yet laid hands on me.

  Rob. George, wilt thou forsake Wakefield,
And go with me?
Two liveries will I give thee every year,
And forty crowns shall be thy fee.[1]

  Geo. Why, who art thou?

  Rob. Why, Robin Hood :
I am come hither with my Marian
And these my yeomen for to visit thee.

  Geo. Robin Hood!
Next to King Edward art thou lief[2] to me.
Welcome, sweet Robin; welcome, Maid Marian;
And welcome, you my friends. Will you to my poor
    house?
You shall have wafer-cakes your fill,
A piece of beef hung up since Martlemas,
Mutton and veal: if this like you not,
Take that you find, or that you bring, for me.

  Rob. Godamercies, good George,
I'll be thy guest to-day.

  Geo. Robin, therein thou honourest me.
I'll lead the way.   *[Exeunt.*

    [1] See the ballad printed in the Appendix.   [2] Dear.

ACT THE FIFTH

SCENE I.—*At Bradford.*

Enter KING EDWARD *and* KING JAMES *disguised;
each carrying a staff.*

EDW. Come on, King James; now
    we are thus disguis'd,
There's none, I know, will take us to
    be kings:
I think we are now in Bradford,
Where all the merry shoemakers
    dwell.

Enter several Shoemakers.

First Shoe. Down with your staves, my friends,
Down with them.
  K. Edw. Down with our staves! I pray thee, why so?
  First Shoe. My friend, I see thou art a stranger here,
Else wouldst thou not have question'd of the thing.
This is the town of merry Bradford,
And here hath been a custom kept of old,
That none may bear his staff upon his neck,
But trail it all along throughout the town,
Unless they mean to have a bout with me.

443

K. Edw. But hear you, sir, hath the king granted you
this custom?

First Shoe. King or kaisar, none shall pass this way,
Except King Edward;
No, not the stoutest groom that haunts his court;
Therefore down with your staves.

K. Edw. What were we best to do?

K. James. Faith, my lord, they are stout fellows;
And, because we will see some sport,
We will trail our staves.

K. Edw. Hear'st thou, my friend?
Because we are men of peace and travellers,
We are content to trail our staves.

First Shoe. The way lies before you, go along.

Enter ROBIN HOOD *and* GEORGE-A-GREENE, *disguised.*

Rob. See, George, two men are passing through the
     town,
Two lusty men, and yet they trail their staves.

Geo. Robin, they are some peasants trick'd in yeoman's
     weeds.—
Hollo, you two travellers!

K. Edw. Call you us, sir?

Geo. Ay, you. Are ye not big enough to bear
Your bats upon your necks, but you must trail them
Along the streets?

K. Edw. Yes, sir, we are big enough; but here is a
     custom kept,
That none may pass, his staff upon his neck,
Unless he trail it at the weapon's point.
Sir, we are men of peace, and love to sleep
In our whole skins, and therefore quietness is best.

Geo. Base-minded peasants, worthless to be men!
What, have you bones and limbs to strike a blow,

And be your hearts so faint you cannot fight?
Were't not for shame, I would drub your shoulders well,
And teach you manhood 'gainst another time.

   First Shoe. Well preach'd, Sir Jack! down with your
      staff!

   K. Edw. Do you hear, my friends? an you be wise,
      keep down
Your staves, for all the town will rise upon you.

   Geo. Thou speakest like an honest, quiet fellow:
But hear you me; in spite of all the swains
Of Bradford town, bear me your staves upon your necks,
Or, to begin withal, I'll baste you both so well,
You were never better basted in your lives.

   K. Edw. We will hold up our staves.

     [GEORGE-A-GREENE *fights with the* Shoemakers, *and*
       beats them all down.

   Geo. What, have you any more?
Call all your town forth, cut and longtail.[1]

     [*The* Shoemakers *recognise* GEORGE-A-GREENE.

   First Shoe. What, George-a-Greene, is it you? A
     plague found [2] you!
I think you long'd to swinge me well.
Come, George, we will crush a pot before we part.

   Geo. A pot, you slave! we will have an hundred.——
Here, Will Perkins, take my purse; fetch me
A stand of ale, and set in the market-place,
That all may drink that are athirst this day;
For this is for a fee to welcome Robin Hood
To Bradford town.

     [*The stand of ale is brought out, and they fall*
       a-drinking.

Here, Robin, sit thou here;
For thou art the best man at the board this day.

---

  [1] Derived first from the language of the chase, this phrase probably
came to mean " dogs of all kinds."   [2] Confound.

You that are strangers, place yourselves where you will.
Robin, here's a carouse to good King Edward's self;
And they that love him not, I would we had
The basting of them a little.

Enter the EARL OF WARWICK *with other* Noblemen,
bringing out the King's *garments; then* GEORGE-A-
GREENE *and the rest kneel down to the* King.

K. Edw. Come, masters, ale—fellows.—Nay, Robin,
You are the best man at the board to-day.—
Rise up, George.

Geo. Nay, good my liege, ill-nurtur'd we were, then :
Though we Yorkshire men be blunt of speech,
And little skill'd in court or such quaint fashions,
Yet nature teacheth us duty to our king ;
Therefore I humbly beseech you pardon George-a-
Greene.

Rob. And, good my lord, a pardon for poor Robin ;
And for us all a pardon, good King Edward.

First Shoe. I pray you, a pardon for the shoemakers.

K. Edw. I frankly grant a pardon to you all :
[*They rise.*

And, George-a-Greene, give me thy hand ;
There's none in England that shall do thee wrong.
Even from my court I came to see thyself ;
And now I see that fame speaks naught but truth.

Geo. I humbly thank your royal majesty.
That which I did against the Earl of Kendal,
'Twas but a subject's duty to his sovereign,
And therefore little merits such good words.

K. Edw. But ere I go, I'll grace thee with good
deeds.
Say what King Edward may perform,
And thou shalt have it, being in England's bounds.

Geo. I have a lovely leman,
As bright of blee as is the silver moon,
And old Grime her father will not let her match
With me, because I am a Pinner,
Although I love her, and she me, dearly.
K. Edw. Where is she?
Geo. At home at my poor house,
And vows never to marry unless her father
Give consent; which is my great grief, my lord.
K. Edw. If this be all, I will despatch it straight;
I'll send for Grime and force him give his grant:
He will not deny King Edward such a suit.

Enter JENKIN.

Jen. Ho, who saw a master of mine? O, he is gotten
into company, an a body should rake hell for company.
Geo. Peace, ye slave! see where King Edward is.
K. Edw. George, what is he?
Geo. I beseech your grace pardon him; he is my
man.
First Shoe. Sirrah, the king hath been drinking with
us, and did pledge us too.
Jen. Hath he so? kneel; I dub you gentlemen.
First Shoe. Beg it of the king, Jenkin.
Jen. I will.—I beseech your worship grant me one
thing.
K. Edw. What is that?
Jen. Hark in your ear.
[*Whispers* K. EDW. *in the ear.*
K. Edw. Go your ways, and do it.
Jen. Come, down on your knees, I have got it.
First Shoe. Let us hear what it is first.
Jen. Marry, because you have drunk with the king,
and the king hath so graciously pledged you, you shall

be no more called Shoemakers; but you and yours, to
the world's end, shall be called the trade of the Gentle
Craft.

First Shoe. I beseech your majesty reform this which
he hath spoken.

Jen. I beseech your worship consume this which he
hath spoken.

K. Edw. Confirm it, you would say.—
Well, he hath done it for you, it is sufficient.—
Come, George, we will go to Grime, and have thy love.

Jen. I am sure your worship will abide; for yonder is
coming old Musgrove and mad Cuddy his son.—Master,
my fellow Wily comes dressed like a woman, and Master
Grime will marry Wily. Here they come.

Enter MUSGROVE *and* CUDDY; GRIME, WILY *disguised
      as a woman,* MAID MARIAN, *and* BETTRIS.

K. Edw. Which is thy old father, Cuddy?

Cud. This, if it please your majesty.

                              [MUSGROVE *kneels.*

K. Edw. Ah, old Musgrove, stand up;
It fits not such grey hairs to kneel.

Mus. [*rising*]. Long live my sovereign!
Long and happy be his days!
Vouchsafe, my gracious lord, a simple gift
At Billy Musgrove's hand.
King James at Middleham Castle gave me this;
This won the honour, and this give I thee.

                              [*Gives sword to* K. EDW.

K. Edw. Godamercy, Musgrove, for this friendly gift;
And, for thou fell'dst a king with this same weapon,
This blade shall here dub valiant Musgrove knight.

Mus. Alas, what hath your highness done? I am
      poor.

K. Edw. To mend thy living take thou Middleham
    Castle,
And hold of me. And if thou want living, complain;
Thou shalt have more to maintain thine estate.—
George, which is thy love?

Geo. This, if please your majesty.

K. Edw. Art thou her aged father?

Grime. I am, an it like your majesty.

K. Edw. And wilt not give thy daughter unto George?

Grime. Yes, my lord, if he will let me marry with this
lovely lass.

K. Edw. What say'st thou, George?

Geo. With all my heart, my lord, I give consent.

Grime. Then do I give my daughter unto George.

Wily. Then shall the marriage soon be at an end.
Witness, my lord, if that I be a woman;

                [Throws off his disguise.
For I am Wily, boy to George-a-Greene,
Who for my master wrought this subtle shift.

K. Edw. What, is it a boy?—what say'st thou to this,
    Grime?

Grime. Marry, my lord, I think this boy hath
More knavery than all the world besides.
Yet am I content that George shall both have
My daughter and my lands.

K. Edw. Now, George, it rests I gratify thy worth:
And therefore here I do bequeath to thee,
In full possession, half that Kendal hath;
And what as Bradford holds of me in chief,
I give it frankly unto thee for ever.
Kneel down, George.

Geo. What will your majesty do?

K. Edw. Dub thee a knight, George.

Geo. I beseech your grace, grant me one thing.

K. Edw. What is that?

2 F

Geo. Then let me live and die a yeoman still:
So was my father, so must live his son.
For 'tis more credit to men of base degree,
To do great deeds, than men of dignity.

K. Edw. Well, be it so, George!

K. James. I beseech your grace despatch with me,
And set down my ransom.

K. Edw. George-a-Greene,
Set down the King of Scots his ransom.

Geo. I beseech your grace pardon me;
It passeth my skill.

K. Edw. Do it, the honour's thine.

Geo. Then let King James make good
Those towns which he hath burnt upon the borders;
Give a small pension to the fatherless,
Whose fathers he caus'd murder'd in those wars;
Put in pledge for these things to your grace,
And so return.

K. Edw. King James, are you content?

K. James. I am content, an like your majesty,
And will leave good castles in security.

K. Edw. I crave no more.—Now, George-a-Greene,
I'll to thy house; and when I have supt, I'll go
To ask and see if Jane-a-Barley be so fair
As good King James reports her for to be.
And for the ancient custom of *Vail staff,*
Keep it still, claim privilege from me:
If any ask a reason why, or how,
Say, English Edward vail'd his staff to you.

[*Exeunt omnes.*

APPENDIX

THE JOLLY PINDER OF WAKEFIELD

WITH

ROBIN HOOD, SCARLET AND JOHN,

N Wakefield there lives a jolly pindèr,
    in Wakefield all on a green,
    in Wakefield all on a green ;

There is neither knight nor squire,
    said the pindèr,
      Nor baron that is so bold,
      Nor baron that is so bold ;

Dare make a trespàss to the town of Wakefield,
    but his pledge goes to the pinfold, &c.

All this be heard three witty young men,
    'twas Robin Hood, Scarlet and John, &c.

With that they espy'd the jolly pindèr,
    as he sat under a thorn, &c.

Now turn again, turn again, said the pindèr,
    for a wrong way you have gone, &c.

For you have forsaken the king's high-way,
    and made a path over the corn, &c.

O that were great shame, said jolly Robìn,
    we being three, and thou but one, &c.

The pinder leapt back then thirty good foot,
    'twas thirty good foot and one, &c.

He leaned his back fast unto a thorn,
   and his foot against a stone, &c.

And there they fought a long summer's day,
   a summer's day so long, &c.

Till that their swords on their broad bucklèrs,
   were broke fast into their hands, &c.

Hold thy hand, hold thy hand, said bold Robin Hood,
   and my merry men everyone, &c.

For this is one of the best pindèrs,
   that ever I tryed with sword, &c.

And wilt thou forsake thy pinder's craft,
   and live in the green-wood with me? &c.

At Michaelmas next my cov'nant comes out,
   when every man gathers his fee, &c.

I'll take my blew blade all in my hand
   And plod to the green-wood with thee, &c.

Hast thou either meat or drink? said Robin Hood,
   for my merry men and me, &c.

I have both bread and beef, said the pindèr,
   and good ale of the best, &c.

And that is meat good enough, said Robin Hood,
   for such unbidden guest, &c.

O wilt thou forsake the pinder his craft,
   and go to the green-wood with me? &c.

Thou shalt have a livery twice in the year,
   the one green, the other brown, &c.

If Michaelmas day was come and gone,
   and my master had paid me my fee,
   and my master had paid me my fee,

Then would I set as little by him,
   as my master doth by me,
   as my master doth by me.

COLSTON AND CO. LTD., PRINTERS, EDINBURGH

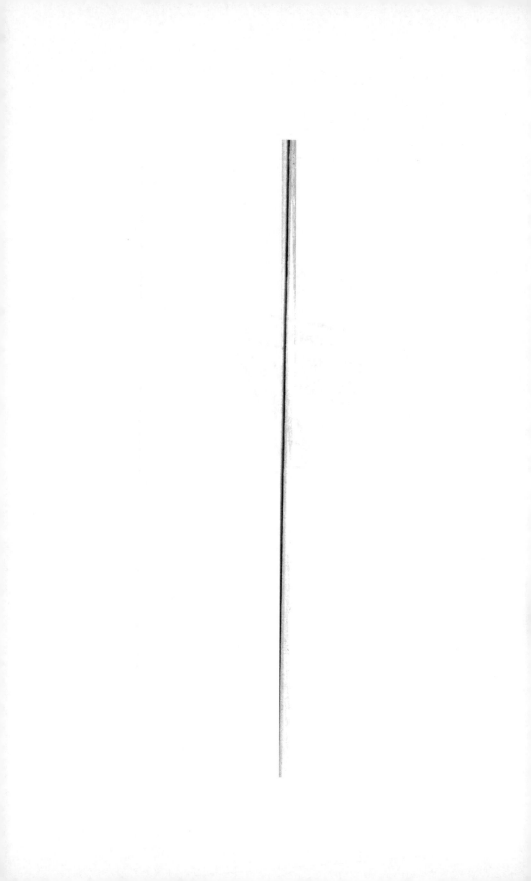

Lightning Source UK Ltd.
Milton Keynes UK
UKHW022117080223
416681UK00011B/2532

9 780342 942268